Lecture Notes in Computer Science 5806

Commenced Publication in 1973
Founding and Former Series Editors:
Gerhard Goos, Juris Hartmanis, and Jan van Leeuwen

Editorial Board

David Hutchison
  Lancaster University, UK
Takeo Kanade
  Carnegie Mellon University, Pittsburgh, PA, USA
Josef Kittler
  University of Surrey, Guildford, UK
Jon M. Kleinberg
  Cornell University, Ithaca, NY, USA
Alfred Kobsa
  University of California, Irvine, CA, USA
Friedemann Mattern
  ETH Zurich, Switzerland
John C. Mitchell
  Stanford University, CA, USA
Moni Naor
  Weizmann Institute of Science, Rehovot, Israel
Oscar Nierstrasz
  University of Bern, Switzerland
C. Pandu Rangan
  Indian Institute of Technology, Madras, India
Bernhard Steffen
  University of Dortmund, Germany
Madhu Sudan
  Microsoft Research, Cambridge, MA, USA
Demetri Terzopoulos
  University of California, Los Angeles, CA, USA
Doug Tygar
  University of California, Berkeley, CA, USA
Gerhard Weikum
  Max-Planck Institute of Computer Science, Saarbruecken, Germany

Stefan Katzenbeisser
Ahmad-Reza Sadeghi (Eds.)

Information Hiding

11th International Workshop, IH 2009
Darmstadt, Germany, June 8-10, 2009
Revised Selected Papers

 Springer

Volume Editors

Stefan Katzenbeisser
Technische Universität Darmstadt
Security Engineering Group
Darmstadt, Germany
E-mail: skatzenbeisser@acm.org

Ahmad-Reza Sadeghi
Ruhr-Universität Bochum
Horst Görtz Institute for IT Security
Bochum, Germany
E-mail: ahmad.sadeghi@trust.rub.de

Library of Congress Control Number: 2009934441

CR Subject Classification (1998): D.2.11, D.4.6, K.6.5, E.3, H.2.7, K.4.4, C.2

LNCS Sublibrary: SL 4 – Security and Cryptology

ISSN   0302-9743
ISBN-10   3-642-04430-1 Springer Berlin Heidelberg New York
ISBN-13   978-3-642-04430-4 Springer Berlin Heidelberg New York

springer.com

© Springer-Verlag Berlin Heidelberg 2009
Printed in Germany

Typesetting: Camera-ready by author, data conversion by Scientific Publishing Services, Chennai, India
Printed on acid-free paper   SPIN: 12760275   06/3180   5 4 3 2 1 0

Preface

We are glad to present in this volume the proceedings of Information Hiding 2009, which was held in Darmstadt, Germany, during June 8–10, 2009. The conference was organized by the Center for Advanced Security Research Darmstadt (CASED).

Continuing the tradition of previous editions, we tried to create a balanced program, covering different aspects of information hiding, ranging from digital watermarking to steganography and steganalysis and information forensics. Furthermore, we see new topics, such as physically unclonable functions and hardware Trojan horse detection, being addressed at the conference.

The selection of the program was a very challenging task. In total, we received 55 submissions, from which we accepted 19 papers for inclusion in the proceedings. Each submission was refereed by three reviewers. At this point we would like to thank all authors who submitted their latest work to IH 2009 – thus assuring that Information Hiding continues to be the top forum of our community. Furthermore, we thank all members of the Program Committee, the local organizers and all external reviewers for their efforts to ensure an exciting and rewarding conference.

We hope that you enjoy reading the proceedings and maybe find inspiration for your future work.

July 2009

Stefan Katzenbeisser
Ahmad-Reza Sadeghi

11th Information Hiding
June 8–10, 2009, Darmstadt (Germany)

General Chair

Stefan Katzenbeisser   Technische Universität Darmstadt, Germany

Program Chair

Ahmad-Reza Sadeghi   Ruhr-Universität Bochum, Germany

Program Committee

Ross Anderson	University of Cambridge, UK
Mauro Barni	Università di Siena, Italy
Patrick Bas	Gipsa-lab, France
Jan Camenisch	IBM Zurich Research, Switzerland
François Cayre	GIPSA-Lab/Grenoble INP, France
Ee-Chien Chang	National University of Singapore
Christian Collberg	University of Arizona, USA
Ingemar J. Cox	University College London, UK
Gwenaël Doërr	University College London, UK
Jessica Fridrich	SUNY Binghamton, USA
Teddy Furon	Thomson Security Lab, France
Neil F. Johnson	Booz Allen Hamilton and Johnson & Johnson Technology Consultants, USA
Stefan Katzenbeisser	Technische Universität Darmstadt, Germany
Darko Kirovski	Microsoft Research, USA
John McHugh	Dalhousie University, Canada
Ira S. Moskowitz	Naval Research Laboratory, USA
Andreas Pfitzmann	Technische Universität Dresden, Germany
Ahmad-Reza Sadeghi	Ruhr-Universität Bochum, Germany
Phil Sallee	Booz Allen Hamilton, USA
Kaushal Solanki	Mayachitra Inc., USA
Kenneth Sullivan	Mayachitra Inc., USA

Local Organization

Cornelia Reitz	Center of Advanced Security Research Darmstadt
Andrea Püchner	Technische Universität Darmstadt
Christian Wachsmann	Ruhr-Universität Bochum, Germany

External Reviewers

Allwein, Gerard
Armknecht, Frederik
Baras, Cleo
Bloom, Jeffrey
Böhme, Rainer
Craver, Scott
Farid, Ahmed
Franz, Elke
Gloe, Thomas
Heide, David
Kang, Myong H.
Kirchner, Matthias
Köpsell, Stefan

Liu, Yali
Memon, Nasir
Mironov, Ilya
Øverlier, Lasse
Raskin, Victor
Schönfeld, Dagmar
Schulz, Steffen
Sunar, Berk
Thomborson, Clark
Wachsmann, Christian
Westfeld, Andreas
Winkler, Antje
Wu, Xianyong

Table of Contents

Steganography

Steganalysis

Watermarking

Fingerprinting

Hiding in Unusual Content, Novel Applications

Forensics

Supraliminal Audio Steganography: Audio Files Tricking Audiophiles

Heather Crawford and John Aycock

Department of Computer Science
University of Calgary
2500 University Drive N.W.
Calgary, Alberta, T2N 1N4
{crawfoha,aycock}@ucalgary.ca

Abstract. A supraliminal channel is one in which the secret message is encoded in the semantic content of a cover object, and that is robust against an active warden. Such channels frequently have a very low embedding rate and therefore are unsuitable for more than simply exchanging steganographic public keys. This paper introduces a proof-of-concept supraliminal channel that uses WAV files to provide a high-bitrate method of embedding information in common media.

1 Introduction

Steganography is often explained using the Prisoners' Problem as was first proposed by Simmons in 1983 [1]. Alice and Bob must communicate their escape plans in the presence of Wendy the warden, who can be either active, passive, or malicious. The different types of warden vary only in how much they can change the messages passed between Alice and Bob: a passive warden can make no changes, an active warden can make small changes, and a malicious warden can make large changes, or even inject spoofed messages into the message stream. Clearly, the type of warden assumed will make a difference to whether Alice and Bob trust the messages at all. If the warden determines that Alice and Bob are exchanging anything other than innocuous messages, they are thrown into solitary confinement where they are no longer able to communicate, and thus cannot plan their escape.

While the Prisoners' Problem provides a general framework that can be used to compare steganographic algorithms, it does not (and should not) describe all types of steganography. Most steganography is *subliminal* in that the secret information being passed from Alice to Bob is hidden from Wendy, and Alice and Bob have, where necessary, exchanged stego keys prior to sending messages. If Wendy perceives that a secret communication has been exchanged, then the goal of steganography has failed. This can be summed up as "A goal of steganography is to avoid drawing suspicion to the transmission of hidden information. If suspicion is raised, then this goal is defeated"[2, p. 73]. This goal, however, does not limit us to subliminal steganography. In 1998, Craver introduced the

S. Katzenbeisser and A.-R. Sadeghi (Eds.): IH 2009, LNCS 5806, pp. 1–14, 2009.

the idea of *supraliminal* steganography. In this method, a *supraliminal channel*, that is, a channel in which information is not hidden from but also cannot be changed significantly by the warden [3], is used to transmit the secret message. The goal is to convince Wendy that the secret message is actually innocuous, such as noise in an audio recording or color degradation in a still image. Thus, supraliminal steganography is still a type of message hiding despite the fact that the message itself can be perceived by the warden.

A supraliminal channel is formally defined by Craver [3] as a channel that is:

⋆ **Robust**, meaning that in order to make changes to the message contained in the channel, the warden would have to make significant changes to the stego-object. The amount of change required to accomplish this is usually only of concern to a malicious rather than active warden.
⋆ **Blatant**, which means that the contents of the channel (i.e., the message) are available to anyone who has access to the stego-object.
⋆ **Inconspicuous**, which means that just knowing that there is a channel does not imply that there is a message.

The formal definition also assumes that Wendy is an active warden, and so may only make small changes to the stego-object. The term *small changes* is admittedly subjective, but the intent is that there is a comparatively large amount of *perceptually significant* (e.g., visible or audible) information that cannot be changed by the warden. It is in such information that a message may be passed, although it is usually assumed that the channel has a low embedding rate.

In this paper, we describe a form of supraliminal steganography that uses audio recordings as the cover objects. The premise is that adding additional sounds such as drum beats, hihats, or simple noise will not be perceived by the warden as a message, but instead as normal parts of the audio recording. It is clear that this method will work best by varying the type of audio recording to suit the sounds chosen to represent the message bits, because there are fewer restrictions on the choice of cover object than on the choice of message sounds, since the message sounds must be selected so that they can be easily distinguished from one another. It is also clear, however, that the message sounds can be customized to a particular cover object, thereby negating the problem of over-audibility, which would alert Wendy to not only the channel, which is acceptable, but also to the presence of the secret message, which is unacceptable. As an example, consider a cover object that is a piece of classical music played on a piano. If the message was encoded using, say, two different notes of an electric guitar to represent the binary bits, then the message would be clearly audible and would also be easily identified as something that has likely been added to the original classical music composition. If the cover object was changed to a piece of heavy metal music, or alternatively if the sounds representing the binary bits were changed to two different piano notes, then the message would still be clearly audible but would not seem out of place and would therefore not necessarily gain the attention of the warden.

The rest of this paper is organized as follows: Section 2 describes the work already done in this area and how the work described in this paper relates to it. In Section 3 we discuss the different types of cover objects and how they were chosen. In Section 4 we introduce our stegosystem in detail, including how to embed and extract, as well as the embedding rate. In Section 5 we discuss the results of our experimentation, and in Section 6 we summarize our work and discuss the results, and introduce some future work that may use the work described in this paper as a basis.

2   Related Work

While there is a substantial and growing body of work of steganography research in general, there is very little work that has been done in the area of supraliminal steganography. As described above, the idea of a supraliminal channel was described by Craver in 1998 [3], and was shown to be viable by Craver et al. in 2008 [4]. In the latter work, the authors show that a supraliminal channel can be embedded in Apple's iChat application by using the ability to change the background in the video portion of the iChat. The authors noted certain limitations, such as the replacement of the pseudo-random number generator used with the video application, which was modified to contain message bits rather than just pseudo random bits, as well as the limitations in convincing the public to use animated special effects when they have a choice not to do so, so that the proposed channel may be used to send a message. There are also links between supraliminal steganography work and *content-aware* steganography, which embeds the secret message into the semantics of the cover object rather than the binary representation of the object [5]. This implies that Alice and Bob must understand what the cover object *represents* rather than simply what the cover object *is*. For example, content-aware stegosystems must determine that an image cover object contains, say, a blue chair and a lamp rather than just the fact that the cover object is an image. This distinction is important since supraliminal steganography requires realistic changes to the cover object in order to limit Wendy's knowledge of the message.

The work outlined in this paper is distinct from the work described above in three key ways. First, the cover objects are all audio files rather than still or video images. Second, there can be variations in the representation of the message based on the content of the cover object. Third, this work outlines both embedding and extracting details, and presents an embedding rate for this type of stegosystem.

3   Cover Objects

The selection of cover objects for many steganographic applications is fairly straightforward because many of these applications modify specific bits in the data that make up the cover, as with Least Significant Bit (LSB) steganography [6]. Alternatively, the stegosystem can modify a particular part of a specific type of file such as embedding a message into a MIDI file by adding extra MIDI commands [7,8]. With our method, however, the selection of the cover object

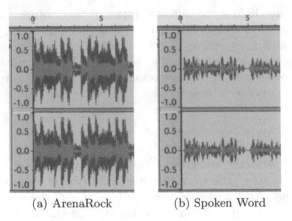

(a) ArenaRock   (b) Spoken Word

Fig. 1. Waveforms for arena rock (left) and spoken word (right) cover objects. The top waveform in each example represents the left channel and the bottom waveform represents the right channel.

is instrumental to the success of the method. To that end we chose to use four different genres of music: hip hop, arena rock, drum machine, and reggae, in addition to a spoken word audio file as an additional cover object. Note that all audio files, as seen in Figure 1, were in WAV format and were sampled at 44100 Hz. Another consideration that affected the results of our work was the choice of sounds used to represent the message bits. After some experimentation, we chose open and closed hihat sounds because they blended well with the different genres of music chosen and thus were audible but did not attract undue attention.

The purpose of the customization of cover objects and message sounds was to limit the likelihood that the message would be noticed by the warden and seen as a message. Note that the intention was not to *hide* the message; this would negate the point of this work, which is a proof-of-concept application of a *supraliminal* channel. Thus, the sounds comprising the message can be heard and are visible in the waveforms for each stego-object, as seen in Figure 3. The matching of cover object to message sound is simply to make it more difficult to distinguish the added sounds as a message, since the sounds representing ones and zeros are inserted at regular intervals to facilitate retrieval. The next section will describe the method in more detail, at which time the rationale for our choices of cover objects and message sounds will become apparent.

4   Implementation

The music tracks were selected from a website that provides free sounds and music for use in game development, movies, and new music [9], and the spoken word track used was a recording of the first author speaking. All of the tracks selected are free, widely available, and without copyright. The message used in all test cases was "Hello,world!", unless stated otherwise. Each character in the message was converted to its 7-bit ASCII equivalent, zero-padded to eight bits. In other words, the most significant bit of each byte will be zero, which becomes important during the extraction process described in Section 4.2. We do this without loss of generality because a binary message that requires the full eight bits can be Base64 encoded [10], for example. Once the binary values have been determined, they are written to a text file and used as input to the next step in the process: the embedding algorithm.

4.1   Embedding

The embedding algorithm is written in Nyquist, which is a specialized form of LISP used in the Audacity audio editor [11] to process audio files via scripts. The pseudocode can be found in Program 1, and works as follows: after the preprocessing stage described above, the binary representation of each character is read into the embed function where it is converted into an array of sounds that represent the ones and zeros. Each sound is added to an array and is separated by a 0.15 second long period of silence in order to make the sounds more distinct from each other, and to facilitate message extraction. Thus, the finished message representation of "Hello,world!" is an array of sounds and silences that is then converted into a 47.5 second long Nyquist Sound object that can be manipulated identically to other Sound objects, such as the cover object. The sounds that represent ones and zeros can be selected by the user to match a particular cover object; the sounds chosen for the work described in this paper were an open and closed hihat. The waveform for the message alone can be seen in Figure 2. The next step was to embed the encoded message in the cover object. First, if the cover object is a stereo track, as are both samples shown in Figure 1, the cover object is split into two separate channels and the message is mixed into only one of the two. If the cover object has only one channel, the single channel is duplicated before mixing in the message. Next, we create a stereo track that consists of the newly mixed channel and a copy of the original channel (note that the second channel from the original cover object can be used provided that it is identical to the first channel), creating the stego-object as shown in Figure 3.

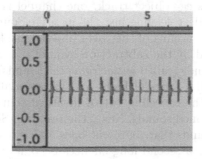

Fig. 2. Waveform of an encoded message. The thinner waves represent ones, the thicker waves represent zeros. This waveform shows the beginning of the message "Hello,world!".

Note in the figure that the message is mixed with the top channel shown; the bottom channel contains only music. Since the message is mixed only into one channel of the message, it can be heard from only one speaker rather than two, as is the case for the original cover object. For many of the music genres tested the message was not particularly noticeable, although it *can* be clearly heard. Now that the stego-object has been created, it can be sent to the recipient, who would then use the following extraction algorithm to retrieve the message.

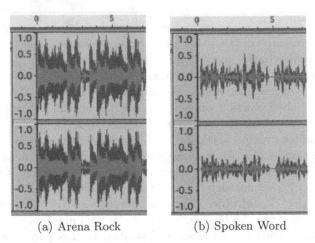

(a) Arena Rock   (b) Spoken Word

Fig. 3. Waveforms for arena rock (left) and spoken word (right) stego-objects. The message is embedded in the top track.

4.2   Extraction

The extraction algorithm as seen in Program 2 is essentially a reversal of the embedding algorithm, although the reversal is relatively complex compared to the embedding process. The first step is to isolate the Nyquist Sound object containing the message from the stego-object. Since the cover object is identical in both channels of the stereo stego-object track, one channel is inverted, which then cancels out the cover object, leaving just the message Sound. In the pseudocode for this algorithm, the canceling of the cover object (also known as a *center pan remover*), is represented by the subtraction symbol (-), and consists of adding and multiplying the sounds (called *butterflying* the sounds) and then passing the resulting sound through a series of high- and low-pass filters in sequence. The effect this produces is the canceling out of identical sounds in each track, i.e., removing the center panned sounds. Next, the resulting Sound object is broken up into the series of sounds that represent ones and zeros in the message. This is where the inserted 0.15 second long silences become very useful. We used a Silence Finder plug-in [1] for Audacity written by David R. Sky that finds silences within a given audio track and marks the starting point of each period of silence.

---

[1] This plug-in is included with the standard installation of Audacity.

Program 1. Pseudocode for the embedding algorithm

```
function embed {
    // open the cover object and split it into two channels
    array cover = open("coverobject.wav")
    left_channel = cover[left]
    right_channel = cover[right]

    // create the message sound
    Sound message = CreateMessage ("messageinput.txt")

    // mix the message into one of the two cover channels
    stego_channel = left_channel + message

    // make a new stereo track and save it
    array stego[2]
    stego[left] = stego_channel
    stego[right] = right_channel
    save "stegoobject.wav"
}


function CreateMessage (text binarymessage) {
// the argument for this function is the message in binary format

    // open the sounds that will represent the ones and zeros
    // in the message
    zero_sound = open ("hihat0.wav")
    one_sound = open ("hihat1.wav")

    // loop through the binary message and substitute chosen
    // sounds for ones and zeros
    List message_list = [ ]
    for each element in binarymessage {
        if element == 0 then
            push (0, message_list)
      else
            push(1, message_list)
    }

    // now make this list of sounds into a Nyquist Sound object
    Sound msg = nil
    for each element in message_list {
        msg = append (msg, element)
    }
    save "messageobject.wav"
}
```

This plug-in code was modified to instead add the start time of the silence, which corresponded with the end of the previous sound, to a list. The output of this was a list of times that represented the *end* of each sound that made up the original message. The length of the given sound is known, so the start of each sound can be accurately calculated, and the first sound of the message is always a zero because the maximum 7-bit ASCII value is 127 (01111111). Thus, the first sound extracted is considered a zero. We measure its peak, which is the maximum amplitude of a sound. Each sound that is subsequently extracted from the message sound is compared with the peak for zero; if the amplitude matches within ±0.005, it is considered a zero, and if there is no match the sound is considered a one. The matching for the peaks is performed within a range of possible values because the addition of noise in a cover object with very large peaks can alter the peaks of the message sounds slightly, although the sounds are still distinct enough to be retrieved. Note that the peaks for the zero and one sounds differ in amplitude by 0.028 so it is unlikely that a zero sound will be mistaken for a one sound due to the fuzzy matching during extraction, provided the matching range is less than the difference in peaks between one and zero sounds. The matching value is placed in a list, which results in a binary string that represents the message. Since each letter of the message contained eight bits, the binary string was broken into groups of eight, which were then converted back into letters via their 7-bit ASCII value, thereby reconstituting the original message.

4.3   Noise

It is well-known that transmitting digital data can cause the data to become corrupted, depending on the transmission medium. For example, data packets may become corrupted during transmission over a network [12]. At the bit level, this means that some bits can be flipped during transmission. Specifically for audio, these bit flips are often heard as a degradation in the sound quality that is often referred to as *noise*. The greater the number of bit flips, the more obvious the degradation becomes until the original audio is completely lost. If the audio file is in fact a stego-object, it is important that the message can be recovered reliably if noise is added during transmission. To this end, we created both a white noise and an ambient noise recording and added it to each of the test tracks *after* the message was embedded in order to test whether the addition of noise affected the quality of the extraction algorithm described above. The white noise was a 47.5 second long track that was generated automatically using Audacity. The ambient noise was a recording taken from the first author's laptop of the sounds in her lab environment, as well as those sounds generated by gently tapping and blowing on the microphone. The waveforms for both sounds can be seen in Figure 4. The results of these tests are discussed in the following section.

Program 2. Pseudocode for the extraction algorithm

```
function extract {
      // open the stego object and invert one of the two channels
      array stego = open (''stegoobject.wav")
      stego[right] = invert (stego[right])

      // remove the identical parts of the two channels
      message = stego[left] - stego[right]

      // use silence finder plug-in to find silences between message
      // bit sounds
      // returns list of start times for silences
      silenceList = silenceFinder (message)

      // get the first sound, which is always zero, and get its peak
      zero_peak = peak (clip (message, 0.0, pop (silenceList)))
      push (0, messagelist)

      //loop through the rest of the message
      while (! endofmessage){
          starttime = endtime (zeropeak)
          endtime = pop (silencelist)
          soundpeak = peak (clip (message, starttime, endtime))

          if ((zeropeak - 0.005) < soundpeak >= (zeropeak + 0.005))
              push (0, messagelist)
          else
              push (1, messagelist)
      }

      // decode the binary back into ASCII and save
      finalmessage = decode (messagelist)
      save ''finalmessage.wav"
}

function clip (msg_sound, start_time, end_time) {
      // this function takes the single sound that represents
      // the entire message and extracts out a sound
      // representing either one or zero from the start;
      // the start time and end time represent the length of
      // the sound to extract
}
```

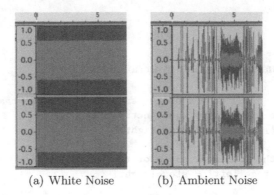

(a) White Noise   (b) Ambient Noise

Fig. 4. Waveforms representing white noise (left) and ambient noise (right)

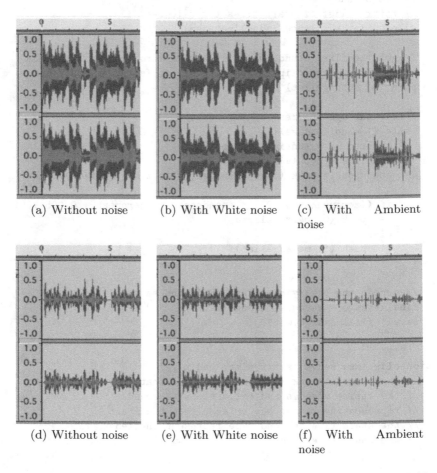

(a) Without noise   (b) With White noise   (c) With   Ambient
                                                noise

(d) Without noise   (e) With White noise   (f) With   Ambient
                                                noise

Fig. 5. Waveforms for stego-objects for Arena Rock (a - c) and Spoken Word (d - f)

5 Results

5.1 No Noise

The first results we discuss are from the group of tracks that did not contain noise. In all five cases: hip hop, arena rock, drum machine, reggae, and spoken word, the message "Hello,world!" was recovered correctly with no bit errors and no incorrect letters in the text. Several message lengths were tested next including a message containing 500 characters; the test results in this case were slightly different. There were approximately three (3) errors in characters, which corresponded to three bit flips out of 4000 bits (500 8-bit characters). This is a Bit Error Rate (BER) of approximately 0.00075, which means that approximately 0.75% of the bits were flipped. These errors do not significantly affect the readability of the message, but could be corrected using an error detection and correction algorithm[2].

5.2 Noise

Adding noise to the stego-object *after* the message had been embedded, as seen in Figure 5 meant that the noise was added equally to both the cover object track and the message-containing track, and thus affects both tracks equally. Adding white noise to the stego-object had no effect on being able to extract the "Hello,world!" message - we were still able to extract all messages with 100% accuracy, even without resorting to using techniques such as Hamming codes [13] to detect and correct single-bit errors. Note that achieving this accuracy was only possible by matching the sounds in the message object that represent one and zero to a range of possible values rather than to the exact peak of the representative sound. Matching within a range of values did not affect the results of the tests conducted on the samples that had no noise added to them. For the 500 character long message, there were more errors than seen in the tests conducted without added noise, although the text was still readable by a human. There were 47 character errors out of the 500 original characters, which corresponded to 53 bit flip errors out of 4000 bits. This is a BER of approximately 0.01325, which means that approximately 1.325% of the bits were flipped. While this error rate is higher than seen when noise was not added, it is still within an acceptable range since the recovered message could be read and understood easily.

The situation changed dramatically for the samples to which ambient noise was added. The message was not recoverable at all from any of the five genres used; the number of errors was sufficient that using Hamming codes to detect and correct errors was not feasible. In most cases, the message recovered consisted solely of ones, with the occasional zero. We also attempted to use Audacity's Noise Removal plug-in to remove the noise prior to extraction, with no success.

---

[2] Error detection and correction codes may add structure to a series of bits. Such structure would make the channel more conspicuous. However, a repeated structure (or rhythm) may actually make the hidden message less conspicuous because a certain amount of regularity is assumed in drum beats, for example.

Table 1. BER results for the tests performed. The two messages used are "Hello,world!" and a 500 character sample from a Sherlock Holmes book by Sir Arthur Conan Doyle.

	No Noise		White Noise		Ambient Noise	
	"Hello,world!"	Sherlock	"Hello,world!"	Sherlock	"Hello,world!"	Sherlock
Msg Len(bits)	96	4000	96	4000	96	4000
Char Errors	0	3	0	47	12	500
Bit Flips	0	3	0	53	96	4000
BER	0.0%	0.75%	0.0%	1.325%	100%	100%

By removing the noise we also removed many of the peaks that represented the message, which left nothing to compare the extracted message sounds to. Thus, the addition of ambient noise caused the message to be completely unrecoverable. It is likely that the ambient noise patterns highlighted a weakness in the extraction method rather than a true loss of the message sounds. Possible corrections for this, which are left as future work, are to use a matched filter, or another type of filter that is specific to the type of sounds used to represent ones and zeros. The results of all tests are summarized in Table 1.

5.3 Embedding Rate

The embedding rate for this method is comparable, and even improves upon, the typically low embedding rates seen in other supraliminal channels. While Craver considers the embedding rate of most channels to be low enough to only warrant transmission of a stego key for use with a subliminal channel, our method has the luxury of nearly unlimited length cover objects, which means that the cover object can be selected to suit the length of message created. For our test examples, the sounds representing both one and zero were 0.34 seconds long, and the silence between each message sound was 0.15 seconds long. So, 0.49 seconds of cover object are required to embed one bit of information. Thus, the total amount of time to embed the message "Hello,world!" is:

$$12 \text{ characters} * 8 \text{ bits per character} = 96 \text{ bits in the message} \tag{1}$$

$$(96 \text{ bits} * 0.34 \text{ seconds per bit}) + (95 \text{ spaces} * 0.15 \text{ seconds}) = 46.89 \text{ seconds} \tag{2}$$

Thus, our method has an overall embedding rate of approximately one message bit per second of cover object audio. This number can be increased by reducing the amount of silence between the message bits, and by selecting shorter sounds to represent the message bits. Add these changes to the fact that the length of the cover object can be as long as is desired, and the supraliminal channel described in this document becomes a viable method for transmitting information of all types rather than just message keys.

6   Discussion and Conclusions

The results of our work provide a proof-of-concept that supraliminal audio steganography is viable. We used five different genres of audio recordings and embedded the message "Hello,world!" into each. In each test case we were able to recover the message with no or very few errors, up to the test limit of 500 characters per message. The addition of noise to the stego-object added a dimension of realism to the tests and also caused some messages to be unrecoverable. We hypothesize that the messages to which ambient noise was added were unrecoverable since the non-uniform nature of the ambient noise waveform (Figure 4(b)) matched the peaks on the message waveform (Figure 2) and thus made it impossible to match the distorted message sound to the original sound, which effectively obscured the message. Our conclusion is that supraliminal audio steganography is viable, and with some work, could be come a reliable method of supraliminal steganography.

What remains is to show that our method conforms to the formal definition of a supraliminal channel, as given in Section 1. First, the method described in this paper is robust because it is not obvious either by listening to the stego-objects or looking at their waveforms which sounds are part of the cover and which are part of the message. Thus, the only viable way that a warden could obliterate the message would be to make significant changes to the cover object *and* the message object, which means the warden would have to be malicious rather than active. Furthermore, it is possible to further hide the message in plain sight by matching the sounds representing the message to the cover object, as discussed in Section 3. The method described here can also be considered a blatant channel since the mixed-in sounds are audible to all who listen to the stego-object, and with careful study of the waveform, can be distinguished from the cover-object. Also, since the channel described here is independent of the format of the audio cover object, it is possible to embed messages in any type of audio file, thereby supporting the idea that our channel is indeed publicly accessible. Lastly, our method is also inconspicuous since the message sounds themselves, although audible, only add to the overall sound of the cover object and would not necessarily be considered a message in and of themselves. In the case of a well-known or famous cover object, for instance a Top 40 song that was at Number 1 for several weeks and received much airplay on the radio, we hypothesize that the message itself would be more easily perceived by a listener than with an unfamiliar song, but that the differences would not be seen as a message, but just added sounds or even just noise. Thus, the channel described in this paper can be considered a supraliminal channel according to the formal definition.

There are several areas in this work that could be improved. The first is in making improvements to the embedding method that would have the message in both tracks of a stereo audio file so that it is heard from both speakers and thus is less obvious to the listener. The second improvement we suggest is to protect the message from the addition of noise so that the message can still be recovered if noise is added during transmission, and it would make the overall system more usable if the user could customize the cover object music to the exact message in order to make the message less perceptible but still audible.

One major focus of future work is to improve the extraction method so that ambient noise is no longer a limiting factor. Possibilities for this improvement include using a matched filter to find specific sounds, and matching the message sounds to the beat of the music in the cover object.

Acknowledgement

The second author's research is supported in part by a grant from the Natural Sciences and Engineering Research Council of Canada.

References

1. Simmons, G.J.: The Prisoners' Problem and the Subliminal Channel. In: Chaum, D. (ed.) Advances in Cryptology 1981 - 1997, pp. 51–67. Plenum Press, New York (1984)
2. Johnson, N.F., Duric, Z., Jajodia, S.: Information Hiding: Steganography and Watermarking - Attacks and Countermeasures. Kluwer Academic Publishers, Dordrecht (2001)
3. Craver, S.: On Public-Key Steganography in the Presence of an Active Warden. In: Aucsmith, D. (ed.) IH 1998. LNCS, vol. 1525, pp. 355–368. Springer, Heidelberg (1998)
4. Craver, S., Li, E., Yu, J., Atakli, I.: A Supraliminal Channel in a Videoconferencing Application. In: Solanki, K., Sullivan, K., Madhow, U. (eds.) IH 2008. LNCS, vol. 5284, pp. 283–293. Springer, Heidelberg (2008)
5. Bergmair, R., Katzenbeisser, S.: Content-Aware Steganography: About Lazy Prisoners and Narrow-Minded Wardens. In: Camenisch, J.L., Collberg, C.S., Johnson, N.F., Sallee, P. (eds.) IH 2006. LNCS, vol. 4437, pp. 109–123. Springer, Heidelberg (2007)
6. Cvejic, N., Seppanen, T.: Increasing the Capacity of LSB-based Audio Steganography. In: Proceedings of 2002 IEEE Workshop on Multimedia Signal Processing, pp. 336–338 (2002)
7. Inoue, D., Matsumoto, T.: A Scheme of Standard MIDI Files Steganography and Its Evaluation. In: Delp III, E.J., Wong, P.W. (eds.) Proceedings of SPIE Security and Watermarking of Multimedia, vol. 4675, pp. 194–205. SPIE, San Jose (2002)
8. Adli, A., Nakao, Z.: Three Steganography Algorithms for MIDI Files. In: Proceedings of the Fourth International Conference on Machine Learning and Cybernetics, vol. 4, pp. 2401–2404. IEEE, Los Alamitos (2005)
9. TeraMedia: soundsnap.com: High-quality sound effects and loops. Webpage (2008)
10. Josefsson, S.: Base16, Base32, and Base64 Encoding: Request for Comments 3548, Network Working Group (July 2003), http://www.faqs.org/rfcs/rfc3548.html (last checked January 16, 2009)
11. Mazzoni, D.: Audacity: Free Audio Editor and Recorder (January 2009), http://audacity.sourceforge.net/ (last checked January 16, 2009)
12. Lam, T.T., Karam, L.J., Bazzi, R.A., Aboudsleman, G.P.: Reduced-Delay Selective ARQ for Low Bit-Rate Image and Multimedia Data Transmission. In: Proceedings of IEEE International Conference on Acoustics, Speech, and Signal Processing (ICASSP) 2005, vol. 2, pp. 309–312. IEEE Computer Society Press, Los Alamitos (2005)
13. Bhattacharrya, D., Nandi, S.: An Efficient Class of SEC-DED-AUED Codes. In: Proceedings of the Third International Symposium on Parallel Architectures, Algorithms, and Networks (I-SPAN), pp. 410–416. IEEE Computer Society, Los Alamitos (1997)

An Epistemological Approach to Steganography

Rainer Böhme

Technische Universität Dresden
Institute of Systems Architecture
01062 Dresden, Germany
rainer.boehme@tu-dresden.de

Abstract. Steganography has been studied extensively in the light of information, complexity, probability and signal processing theory. This paper adds epistemology to the list and argues that Simmon's seminal prisoner's problem an empirical dimension, which cannot be ignored (or defined away) without simplifying the problem substantially. An introduction to the epistemological perspective on steganography is given along with a structured discussion on how the novel perspective fits into the existing body of literature.

1   Steganography and Steganalysis as Empirical Sciences

A broad definition of steganography includes all endeavours to communicate in such a way that the existence of the message cannot be detected. A more specific problem description that triggered research in modern digital steganography is given in the *prisoner's problem* formulated by Gustavus Simmons [1] in 1983: Two prisoners want to cook up an escape plan together. They may communicate with each other, but all their communication is monitored by a warden. As soon as the warden gets to know about an escape plan, or any kind of scrambled communication in which he suspects one, he would punish them severely. Therefore the inmates must hide their secret messages in inconspicuous cover text.

Adapting this metaphor to information technology, a *steganographic system* builds upon an open communication system and is defined by the set of permissible communication objects (i.e., cover and stego objects as messages to be transmitted on the underlying channel), modelled as sequences $x = (x_1, \dots, x_n)$ over a discrete alphabet $\mathcal{X}$, the set of possible secret messages $\mathcal{M}$, a pair of publicly known functions to embed and extract secret messages in/from communication objects, and a key space $\mathcal{K}$ [2]. Keys $k \in \mathcal{K}$ parametrise the embedding and extraction function to bind successful extraction to the knowledge of the correct key. The protection goal *undetectability* [3] is satisfied if stego objects $x^{(1)} \in \mathcal{X}^*$ are indistinguishable from plain covers $x^{(0)} \in \mathcal{X}^*$, i.e., when the distribution of stego objects $x^{(1)} \sim \mathcal{P}_1$ matches the distribution $\mathcal{P}_0$ of typical cover objects on the channel [4].

In other words, the goal of steganographic systems is to generate output that is equal to *something outside the steganographic system*. This implies that we cannot succeed in designing secure steganography without studying the outside

S. Katzenbeisser and A.-R. Sadeghi (Eds.): IH 2009, LNCS 5806, pp. 15–30, 2009.

of the system! So we conclude and argue that steganography, according to its common definition and in the predominant setting, should be considered as genuinely empirical discipline; unlike cryptology and related fields of information security. This may sound inconvenient from a purely mathematical or theoretical standpoint, but it makes both steganography and steganalysis particularly interesting engineering problems.

Nevertheless, it is not wise to abandon the realm of theory entirely in approaching steganography and steganalysis as mere inductive disciplines. So in this paper, we recur to basic information theory as well as statistical theory and combine them with epistemology to lay theoretical foundations on which the engineering problems can be formulated. The foundations also allow to deduct when and under which assumptions we can expect solutions in terms of security guarantees, and where rather not. Such insight helps to reappraise prior art on theoretical and practical steganography and steganalysis.

Since we focus on undetectability, this exposition is limited to passive adversaries [5] and it is further organised as follows: Section 2 proposes a classification system for approaches to secure steganography based on the assumptions behind their security analysis. This allows us to organise discoveries and results in the literature and helps to identify cases, in which our epistemological approach applies. The ideas behind our approach draw on the theory of Karl Popper [6]. They are further elaborated in Section 3. Section 4 is devoted to a reflection on the existing body of knowledge and shows ways to integrate it in our approach. Unlike typical 'related work' chapters, this discussion is intended to form an equally important part of our contribution. Section 5 concludes the paper.

2   Classification of Approaches to Secure Steganography

A cursory view on the steganography literature must leave a confusing picture. There exists a stark contrast between, on the one hand, constructions with strong security claims, embodied in titles such as "Provably" [7] or "Perfectly Secure Steganography" [8] that can be found even in conjunction with the attribute "Efficient" [9], and, on the other hand, successful steganalysis against virtually every embedding method that offers noteworthy capacity: "Attacks on Steganographic Systems" [10], "Breaking [...] Steganography with First Order Statistics" [11] or "Universal Detection" [12]. This list of examples can be continued arbitrarily.

The roots of this apparent contradiction lie in different assumptions, which are (too) often only implicit. This paper aims at making them explicit, and we have identified two dimensions along which they can be structured, namely:

1. assumptions on the limits of the adversary (short: *adversary assumptions*),
2. assumptions on the cover source (short: *cover assumptions*).

The first dimension corresponds to the classical distinction in cryptography, where *information-theoretic* security denotes security against computationally unconstrained adversaries, *complexity-theoretic* security assumes bounds on the adversary's available space and time (typically by a polynomial in the security parameter ℓ), and the residual *heuristic* class subsumes all methods for which no security proofs are known[1].

Cover assumptions on the second dimension are unique to steganography. (There is no direct counterpart to covers in cryptography.) We define:

Definition 1. *(Artificial covers). Sequences of symbols x_i drawn from a theoretically defined* probability distribution $\mathcal{P}_0$ *over a discrete alphabet $\mathcal{X}$ constitute* **artificial covers**. *There is no uncertainty about the parameters of this (joint) distribution, regardless whether a channel with this distribution actually exists in reality.*

Uniform random numbers [4], i. i. d. sequences with arbitrary marginal distribution [8], and discrete alphabet Markov chains or fields belong to this class.

Definition 2. *(Empirical covers). Digital representations of parts of reality constitute* **empirical covers**. *They have to be obtained through observation of reality and can be expressed as finite sequences of symbols x_i over a discrete alphabet $\mathcal{X}$, i. e., this corresponds to a high-dimensional measurement process. The multidimensional cover distribution $\mathcal{P}_0$ is generally unknown and can only be estimated from repeated measurements.*

All kinds of digitised media data, such as images, audio or video files, belong to this class. Typical empirical covers are characterised by high dimensionality (in the order of thousands) and non-negligible, often non-linear, interdependencies between attributes on different dimensions.

Our distinction between artificial and empirical covers resembles—but is not exactly the same—the distinction between *structured* and *unstructured* covers in [13]. A similar distinction can also be found in [14], where our notion of artificial covers is called *analytical model* as opposed to *high-dimensional models*.[2]

Combining adversary assumptions and cover assumptions in a single 3×2 table leads us to a classification scheme of approaches to secure steganography (cf. Table 1). We will go through each cell individually and discuss why and under which conditions secure steganography against passive adversaries can be expected. This classification also allows us to associate articles in the literature to individual cells and thereby resolve the ostensible contradictions.

Information-theoretic security requires that ε-undetectability or even perfect undetectability ($\varepsilon = 0$) is provable. These proofs typically show that some distance measure between cover and stego distribution ($\mathcal{P}_0$ and $\mathcal{P}_1$) decreases exponentially in a security parameter ℓ. For the proof to be valid, these measures must bound the relative entropy between two sources with distributions $\mathcal{P}_0$ and

---

[1] Other authors use the terms *unconditional* and *conditional* for *information-theoretic* and *complexity-theoretic*, respectively.

[2] We do not follow this terminology because it confounds the number of dimensions with the nature of cover generating processes. We believe that although both aspects are often confounded in practice, they should be separated conceptually.

Table 1. Classification of approaches to secure steganography

adversary assumption (capacity bound)	cover assumption	
	artificial	**empirical**
information-theoretic (infimum of joint entropy of random variables and key)	**possible** but finding a secure embedding function can be NP-hard [4,15]	**impossible**
complexity-theoretic ($\frac{\text{cover size } n}{\text{min. sampling unit}}$)	**possible** but embedding is not always efficient [7,16]	**possible** if sampling oracle exists (observability) [7]
heuristic (0 as cover size $n \to \infty$, asymptotically square root of n [17,18,19])	**likely insecure** since steganalyst knows the cover distribution [20]	**possible** security depends on the relative accuracy of steganographer's and steganalyst's cover model

(The capacity bounds are discussed in Section 4.4 below)

$\mathcal{P}_1$. This is only possible for artificial covers as distances from unknown high-dimensional distributions functions cannot be computed. Even with $\mathcal{P}_0$ known, finding secure embedding (and extraction) functions can be very difficult. Cachin [15] shows that the general solution corresponds to solving the NP-hard partition problem. Nevertheless, easy instances of the partition problem can be found for simple example channels like i. i. d. random numbers, public keys, etc. [4,5]. When combined with information-theoretically secure authentication codes, even security against active adversaries is achievable [21,8] (though not further detailed here). The blind spot of all security proofs for artificial covers is a mismatch between the specification of $\mathcal{P}_0$ an the actual channel distribution. Theoretically tractable distributions tend to appear barely in practice.

Interestingly, complexity-theoretically secure steganography is possible in both artificial and empirical covers. The trick is to allow access to an oracle which can sample from the cover distribution [22, Def. 3.2]. For artificial covers, such an oracle can always be constructed (but may be computationally expensive, as pointed out in [16]), whereas finding good oracles for empirical covers is more difficult. The main obstacle is also the comparatively low capacity of these constructions, as detailed below in Section 4.4.

If no security proofs are known for a given embedding method (heuristic class), and this method is applied to artificial covers, then we have to assume that the adversary knows the specification of $\mathcal{P}_0$ [20]. Given enough stego objects, the adversary can identify deviations of $\mathcal{P}_1$ from the theoretical distribution. Since it is very unlikely that a method which is not designed to be provably secure, accidentally preserves $\mathcal{P}_0$, we label this cell as 'likely insecure'. The conclusion for the remaining and most relevant cell in practice[3] is more differentiated. If $\mathcal{P}_0$ is generally unknown (empirical covers), then this limits both the ability of the steganographer as well as the steganalyst. Their respective success depends on their knowledge about reality, reflected in cover models. Since knowledge about reality is so decisive, it is necessary to study the process how knowledge about reality can be obtained. This creates the link between steganography and epistemology, the study of knowledge and justified belief.

3 Models for Empirical Cover Sources

In this section we develop a theoretical framework to describe the role of knowledge about empirical covers in the construction of secure steganographic systems and respective counter-technologies. The notion of *cover model* will be used as a tool to express knowledge about reality, more specifically about $\mathcal{P}_0$. Before we do that, we have to reflect on a common hidden assumption in the interpretation of Simmon's anecdote and define what constitutes a general empirical cover source.

In Simmon's model [1], messages exchanged between the communication partners must be inconspicuous, that is indistinguishable from 'plausible' covers. However, *plausibility* is an informal and imprecise criterion. A common approach is to define plausibility in a probabilistic sense, i.e., likely messages are plausible *by definition*. We call this tweak *plausibility heuristic* and note that this goes along with an extreme simplification of the original problem statement. Without going into further details, this includes the assumption of a universal as opposed to fragmented and context-specific notion of plausibility, the simplification of reasoning and cognition to probability functions (breathing a mechanistic view of the world), and the ignorance of strategic interaction by anticipation of other parties' likely notion of plausibility. In this paper, we join all steganography theorists and accept these simplifications to build a tractable framework.

Now let $\mathcal{S}$ (mnemonic 'scene') be an infinite set of possible natural phenomena, of which digital representations are conceivable. Digital representation are created either by digitisation of real natural phenomena, or they are generated representations to imitate arbitrary imaginary natural phenomena.[4] Alphabet $\mathcal{X}$ is a finite set of, possibly ordered, discrete symbols which form the support for digital representations of elements of $\mathcal{S}$ in n-ary sequences $\boldsymbol{x} \in \mathcal{X}^n$. Without loss of generality, we assume n to be finite and, to simplify our notation, constant. Applying the plausibility heuristic, we imagine a universal stochastic *cover generating process* Generate : $\mathcal{S} \rightarrow \mathcal{X}^n$ to define a probability space $(\Omega, \mathcal{P}_0)$ with $\Omega = \mathcal{X}^n$ and $\mathcal{P}_0 : \mathfrak{P}(\mathcal{X}^n) \rightarrow [0, 1]$. ($\mathfrak{P}$ is the power set operator.) $\mathcal{P}_0$ fulfils the probability axioms, hence

---

[3] Almost all practical steganographic algorithms belong to this cell. A strict interpretation of Simmon's anecdote suggest that only empirical covers define a steganography problem.

[4] Note that this definition avoids to make a distinction on the philosophical question as to whether a (one) cognisable reality exists (denied in constructivism), as any element of $\mathcal{S}$ can either be based on observation of reality or result from human creativity (produced with the assistance of computers).

$$P_0\left(\{\boldsymbol{x}\}\right) \geq 0, \ \forall \boldsymbol{x} \in \varOmega, \tag{1}$$

$$P_0\left(\varOmega\right) = 1, \ \text{and} \tag{2}$$

$$P_0\left(\cup_i\{\boldsymbol{x}_i\}\right) = \sum_i P_0\left(\{\boldsymbol{x}_i\}\right). \tag{3}$$

To simplify the notation, let $P\left(\boldsymbol{x}\right)$ be equivalent to $P\left(\{\boldsymbol{x}\}\right)$.

All covers $\boldsymbol{x}^{(0)}$ and stego objects $\boldsymbol{x}^{(1)}$ are elements of $\mathcal{X}^n$, so that the assignment between covers and stego objects is given by function $\mathsf{Embed} : \mathcal{M} \times \mathcal{X}^n \times \mathcal{K} \to \mathcal{X}^n$, depending on message $\boldsymbol{m} \in \mathcal{M}$ and key $\boldsymbol{k} \in \mathcal{K}$.

As stego and cover objects share the same domain, a passive steganalyst's problem is to find a binary partition of $\mathcal{X}^n$ to classify cover and stego objects $\mathsf{Detect} : \mathcal{X}^n \to \{\mathsf{cover}, \mathsf{stego}\}$ based on the probability that a suspect object $\boldsymbol{x}^{(i)}$ appears as a realisation of clean covers, $\mathrm{Prob}(i = 0|\boldsymbol{x}^{(i)})$, or stego objects, $\mathrm{Prob}(i = 1|\boldsymbol{x}^{(i)}) = 1 - \mathrm{Prob}(i = 0|\boldsymbol{x}^{(i)})$.

The Neyman-Pearson lemma suggests the likelihood ratio test (LRT) as *most powerful* discriminator between plain covers and stego objects for a given threshold τ [23]:

$$\varLambda(\boldsymbol{x}^{(i)}) = \frac{P_0(\boldsymbol{x}^{(i)})}{P_1(\boldsymbol{x}^{(i)})} \tag{4}$$

$$\mathsf{Detect}(\boldsymbol{x}^{(i)}) = \begin{cases} \{\mathsf{cover}\} & \text{for} \quad \varLambda(\boldsymbol{x}^{(i)}) > \tau \\ \{\mathsf{stego}\} & \text{otherwise.} \end{cases} \tag{5}$$

'Most powerful' means, for any given false positive probability α, a threshold τ exists so that the resulting missing probability β is minimal over all possible detection functions [24]. Note that this theorem only holds for tests between two point hypotheses. While it is easy to write down these formal relations, for practical systems, the equations are of limited use for epistemological (and computational) reasons. More precisely, although $\varOmega$ is finite, $P_0(\boldsymbol{x}^{(i)})$ is incognisable in practice. The probability of each element in $\varOmega$ appearing as cover depends on a probability distribution over $\mathcal{S}$, which must be assumed to have infinite support, and as knowledge about it is limited to experience with finite observations, it can never be complete. Consequently, because P_1 depends on P_0 via function Embed, for non-pathologic functions Embed,[5] P_1 is not cognisable, either. This restricts both computationally unbounded and bounded adversaries. The latter may face additional difficulties because computing values of P_1 is inefficient in general. (It involves exhaustive iteration over the key and message spaces.)[6]

---

[5] P_1 could be known if the output of Embed is independent of the cover input, for example, if Embed overwrites the whole cover signal with the message, or generates an entirely artificial cover.

[6] Computationally unbounded adversaries have an advantage if the secrecy of the message $\boldsymbol{m}$, protected by key $\boldsymbol{k}$, is only conditionally secure and the message $\boldsymbol{m}$ contains structure (or is known), so that an exhaustive search over key space $\mathcal{K}$, with $|\mathcal{K}| < |\mathcal{M}|$, allows inference on the existence of a secret message. This, however, is a cryptographic problem (that can be solved by using information-theoretically secure encryption) and not a steganographic one.

3.1   Defining Cover Models

The impossibility to find ground truth on the cover distribution does not prevent practitioners from developing embedding functions and detectors. They thereby rely – explicitly or implicitly – on *models* of the 'true' cover generating process. If the models are good enough, that means their mismatch with reality is not substantial, then this approach is viable. We think of models as formalisable probabilistic rules, which are assumed to govern a not fully known or understood data generation process. In the area of steganography, this process is the above-introduced cover generating process.

Steganographic methods based on imperfect cover models can be secure *unless* the steganalyst uses a more accurate cover model. So the cat-and-mouse race between steganographers and steganalysts actually takes place in the realm of models. Early literature has already reflected on the need for cover models (without naming them so) and presented options to express them formally:

> "What does the steganalyst know about the cover [...] a priori? He might know it entirely, or a probability space that it is chosen from, or a family of probability spaces indexed by external events (e. g., that a letter 'it is raining' is less likely in good weather), or some predicate about it. This knowledge will often be quite fuzzy." [2, p. 349]

We believe that imposing any functional form for cover models unduly restricts their design space, so we propose a rather broad definition which can be linked to epistemological theory.

Definition 3. *(Cover model). Cover models are hypotheses on $\mathcal{P}_0$.*

If we adhere to the notion of hypotheses in the sense of Popper's [6] critical rationalism, a school of philosophical epistemology inspired by discovery in sciences, then cover models can only be falsified, but it is impossible to validate them completely. Cover models that are falsifiable, and thus empirical, but not (yet) falsified are retained until they will actually be falsified. This sequence of trial and error resembles pretty well the chronology of research in practical digital steganography and steganalysis.[7] A hypothesis is said to be falsified if empirical facts (e. g., a set of observed covers) are unlikely in the light of the hypothesis, more formally, if $\mathrm{Prob}(x_1, \ldots, x_N \mid \text{Hypothesis})$ is very small.[8]

A frequently quoted analogy to illustrate Popper's epistemologic theory is Newton's theory of universal gravitation, which allows predictions that are sufficiently accurate for many practical purposes. This is so despite Einstein showed

---

[7] Cryptography was a similarly inexact science before Shannon [25] came up with the information-theoretic underpinnings in 1949. It is questionable whether such a breakthrough can be expected for steganography as well, since secrecy in terms of relative entropy can be formalised and applied to finite domains, whereas plausibility for general covers cannot.

[8] A common fallacy is to misunderstand this classical frequentist approach as test of the hypothesis conditional to the data, i. e., $\mathrm{Prob}(\text{Hypothesis} \mid x_1, \ldots, x_N)$. Evaluating this expression would require a prior on the hypothesis, which is hardly available for cover models (and enter the realm of Bayesian inference).

that Newton's theory is merely an approximation in his more general theory of relativity, which itself leaves unexplained phenomena and therefore is just a better approximation of the incognisable ultimate truth.

3.2   Options for Formulating Cover Models

We have defined $\mathcal{P}_0$ as function that maps arbitrary subsets of $\Omega = \mathcal{X}^n$ to a probability measure between 0 and 1 while fulfilling the probability axioms. Since there exist various possibilities to state hypotheses on a function such as $\mathcal{P}_0$, we can distinguish several ways to formulate cover models.

- **Direct cover models.** Obviously, hypotheses can be formulated by direct assignment of probabilities to individual elements $x_1^{(0)}, x_2^{(0)}, \cdots \in \Omega$, for example $x_1^{(0)} \mapsto 0.1, x_2^{(0)} \mapsto 0.05$, asf. Hypotheses for cover models need not assign a probability to *all* elements of Ω. Also incomplete mappings are valid cover models (as long as they remain falsifiable in theory, i.e., a probability must be assigned to at least one non-trivial subset of Ω).
  Direct formulations of cover models are impractical due to complexity and observability constraints. That means it is tedious to assign a value to every possible cover (complexity) and impossible to empirically determine the 'right' value for each cover (observability).
- **Indirect cover models.** One difficulty in specifying direct cover models is the large size of Ω which results from the n dimensions in $\mathcal{X}^n = \Omega$. Indirect cover models reduce the dimensionality by defining projections $\mathsf{Project} : \mathcal{X}^n \to \mathcal{Z}^k$ with $k \ll n$. Note that the support $\mathcal{Z}$ of the co-domain can differ from alphabet $\mathcal{X}$. Now probabilities $\pi_1, \pi_2, \ldots$ can be assigned to individual elements $z_1, z_2, \cdots \in \mathcal{Z}^k$, which indirectly specifies the values of $\mathcal{P}_0$ for disjoint subsets of Ω as follows:

$$z \mapsto \pi \quad \Leftrightarrow \quad \{x^{(0)} | x^{(0)} \in \Omega \wedge \mathsf{Project}(x^{(0)}) = z\} \mapsto \pi . \qquad (6)$$

  As outlined in [14], feature sets of universal (aka 'blind') detectors can be seen as projection function and trained classifiers constitute indirect cover models with (implied) probabilities induced from the training set.
- **Conditional cover models.** Conditional cover models are generalisations of indirect cover models and deal with the combination of the remaining k dimensions of $z \in \mathcal{Z}^k$ after the projection. In practice, there are cases where the marginal distribution of a subspace of $\mathcal{Z}^k$ is not known (or incognisable), but hypotheses can be formulated on the conditional distribution with respect to *side information* available to the steganographer or steganalyst. Conditional cover model, or their generalisation as *mixture models*, are convenient to deal with heterogeneity in empirical cover sources. For example, distinct image acquisition processes or pre-processing histories result in covers of the same format, but with utmost different statistical properties (e.g., never-compressed vs. JPEG pre-compressed images, scanned vs. camera images, asf.). And it is known that steganographic security may be sensitive to these differences in practice [26,27,28].

– **Stego models.** Finally, stego models can be seen as special cases of indirect cover models, in which Embed serves as projection rule. Since they depend on a specific embedding function, stego models are most useful in (targeted) steganalysis (and least useful for security analysis). They are in fact hypotheses on $\mathcal{P}_1$, which are sometimes easier to formulate intuitively from an analysis of the embedding function. For example, the proof that embedding algorithm F5 [29] is not vulnerable to the specific chi-squared detector in [10] is based on what we would call a stego model.

The implications of this empirical perspective are manifold and range from the strength of security claims down to the selection of test data. In this context, one insight is most pertinent: if we express our knowledge about empirical covers in cover models, then those can be tested against reality independent of specific steganographic systems or detectors. Cover models which (temporarily) withstand their falsification attempts can be used to derive new embedding function. This procedure is not only more efficient, but also avoids misconceptions about the security of practical steganographic systems for which intuition lacks to conceive a corresponding targeted detector immediately. (Recent examples [30,31,32] have shown that the convenient conjecture in [33], claiming that universal steganalysis would offer a reliable first assessment on the security of novel embedding methods, is pre-mature, at least so for current universal detectors.)

4 Relations to Prior Art

With more than two decades of active research, steganography can be considered a fairly mature area (by the standards of computer science). For the sake of systematics, proposals of fundamental nature should strive to integrate themselves into existing work. Many ideas and concepts touched in this paper are already out there, but they reside in disperse publications, each with a different focus, and sometimes hidden behind unexpected terminology. The short survey in this section recalls important concepts in the literature and links them to our work.

4.1 Information-Theoretic Bounds

Cachin's information-theoretic definition [4,15] of steganographic security based on the Kullback-Leibler divergence (KLD) [34] and the deterministic processing theorem, which bound the error rates in steganalysis, is widely accepted in the literature. Since KLD is the expectation of the log-likelihood ratio of the Neyman-Pearson lemma, it is the most accurate measure of undistinguishability and thus undetectability. It is useful for security proofs in artificial covers, along with other measures of statistical [7], variational [35], or Bhattacharyya [36] distance that all bound KLD asymptotically from above. More recently, attempts to estimate (with compromises) KLD and related metrics apply to empirical covers and serve as theoretically-founded yet practical security metrics [23,18].

4.2 Indeterminism and Cover Composition

Early literature on digital steganography already concluded that a necessary requirement for secure steganographic communication is the existence of a public channel, on which sending indeterministic[9] covers is 'plausible' [5,37,38]. This led to a *cover composition theory*, according to which covers can be regarded as being composed of an indeterministic and a deterministic part. While the former is necessary for steganographic security, the latter is indispensable to ensure plausibility: completely indeterministic covers are indistinguishable from random numbers. If these were plausible, then steganography could be reduced to cryptography. (In that sense, random numbers act as 'covers' in cryptography.)

To show that the separation of covers into indeterministic and deterministic parts is fully compatible with our proposed theory, we can distinguish between two possible sources of indeterminism along the dimension of cover assumptions.

- **Artificial indeterminism** is introduced by the definition of the channel in *artificial covers*. In this case, the process generating the indeterministic output is fully known to both steganographer and steganalyst. Merely the internal state (i.e., the realisations) are hidden from the steganalyst. The entropy of the indeterminism can be exploited for secure steganographic communication.
- **Empirical indeterminism** exists because the true relation is too complex to make predictions. So unknown or not well understood mechanisms are replaced by random variables. This applies to all *empirical covers*, the cover generating process of which we believe is incognisable and thus can never be fully understood.

The cover composition theory allows us to combine artificial and empirical covers in a single steganographic system. For example, a typical cover *pre-processing operation* can be thought of being indeterministic *by definition*, similar to artificial covers. It contributes the indeterministic part of the cover. The empirical cover can safely be used as deterministic part. It is important to note that the secure capacity of this construction is bounded by the entropy of the artificial part. All modifications to the empirical (i.e., deterministic) part risk detection by a steganalyst with a superior cover model.

4.3 "Paradigms"

Early theoretical work also distinguished different "paradigms" for the construction of steganographic systems [39,40,41]. We briefly revisit them from the point of view of our framework.

The *cover modification* paradigm closely corresponds to the standard setting: a steganographic semantic is embedded by a sequence of mutually independent modifications of a cover given as input to the embedding function. These covers have to be regarded as empirical covers, and the common heuristic is that insecurity grows monotonically with the embedding distortion (ceteris paribus, i.e., fixed embedding function). As a result, secure steganography according to this paradigm strives to minimise the impact of (unavoidable) distortion.

---

[9] Unless otherwise stated, *indeterminism* is used with respect to the uninvolved observer (warden). The output of indeterministic functions may be deterministic for those who know a (secret) internal state.

Contrary, the *cover construction* paradigm follows the idea that distortion minimisation is only a second-best solution. What really matters is not the distance of the stego object from the concrete cover given as input, but the plausibility of the output of the embedding function. A strict interpretation even omits the cover input and assumes that plausible covers can be generated by the embedding function (e. g., computer-generated art [42]). This corresponds to our notion of artificial covers, with all their disadvantages. Their plausibility is highly questionable—in particular when constructed on cryptographically secure random number generators to introduce artificial indeterminism. A weaker form of this paradigm assumes an indeterministic, but plausible cover transformation process [39], such as JPEG double compression [43] or stochastic dithering [44]. These constructions gain some plausibility from the real covers used as input, while at the same time achieving security by the indeterminism of the transformation process (see also Section 4.2 above).

Finally, the *cover selection* paradigm achieves (provable) security by requiring a large corpus of possible covers as input to the embedding function. The embedding function selects and transmits an object which already contains the steganographic semantic. If the semantic is independent[10] from all other properties of the cover, then this corresponds directly to most approaches in our class of complexity-theoretic security. Note that this independence condition is violated in approaches that first select the most difficult-to-steganalyse cover and then embed as in the modification paradigm (e. g., [45]). Here, the resulting stego distribution is dissimilar to the original channel (difficult-to-steganalyse objects are over-represented), which conflicts with Cachin's security condition and thus renders the approach asymptotically insecure.

4.4 Capacity Theorems

Capacity theorems express the achievable steganographic security as a function of the payload size p (usually scaled to $0 \leq p \leq 1$ as proportion of the maximum available bits with steganographic semantic). While constant (positive) capacity is achievable for artificial covers [8], every embedding function that modifies empirical covers, to remain ε-secure against general adversaries, can only embed at a decreasing rate as the cover size (or the number of covers in a sequential setting) increases [17,18]. This is so because every steganographic change violates the true distribution $\mathcal{P}_0$, and every additional change accumulates evidence that ultimately allows to distinguish a sequence of samples of $\mathcal{P}_1$ from the adversary's model of $\mathcal{P}_0$ with a fixed probability of error.

It is possible to state the order of magnitude of the achievable secure capacity along the dimension of adversary assumptions (as indicated in the left-most column of Table 1). Since information-theoretic steganography implies information-theoretic cryptography (hiding the existence of a message also conceals its content), Shannon's [25] upper bounds apply equally in steganography: the size of

---

[10] In fact, it is sufficient if finding dependencies is sufficiently hard, e. g., as hard as breaking a one-way function.

the message cannot grow securely above the logarithm of the size of the key space $(\log |\mathcal{K}|)$ [46, Sect. II.C].

For oracle-based constructions in the class of complexity-theoretic security, the *minimum sampling unit* (measured in the number of symbols) determines the capacity of the resulting steganographic system. While it is not too difficult to draw independent samples from an unordered set of digital photographs (i. e., the minimum sampling unit is the size of an entire image), it is *very* difficult to draw the intensity of the pixel at position (u, v) conditional to all pixels $(i, j), 1 \leq i < u, 1 \leq j < v$ (minimum sampling unit 1 if $\mathcal{X}$ is the range of intensity values). Obviously it makes a difference if the capacity is about 1 bit *per image* in the former case or *per pixel* in the latter. Within certain limits, capacity can be traded off against embedding complexity through coding or algorithmic improvements of the oracle query strategy [9,47].

Steganography in the heuristic class can only be temporarily secure, and thus capacity for finite cover sequences is governed by the aforementioned sub-linear relationship, which has been shown theoretically [17,19] and experimentally [18] to be actually a "square root law" [11].

4.5   Kerckhoffs' Principle

Kerckhoffs' design principle for cryptographic systems [12] essentially states that the security of a system must not rely on the secrecy of its algorithms [20]. This has been framed as a principle of prudence, which is also embodied in the (stricter) chosen plaintext threat model and its extension to the Dolev-Yao threat model for public key cryptography and protocol analysis [48]. Ker [49,19] already pointed out difficulties in the right interpretation of Kerckhoffs' principle for steganography. However, his critique was mainly focused on the complete knowledge of payload distribution (in batch steganalysis scenarios), while he argued that the adversary should be allowed to have complete knowledge of the cover source. This, however, appears unrealistic against the backdrop of empirical covers and the incognisability of $\mathcal{P}_0$. It would leave us with the option to either grant the adversary super-natural capabilities (out of prudence, as in [19]), or abandon Kerckhoffs' principle for steganography. So a rigourous and smart interpretation of Kerckhoffs' principle for empirical covers remains an open research question.

5   Summary, Conclusions and Outlook

This paper contributes a proposal to structure approaches to (provably) secure steganography by their implied assumptions (1) on the limits of the adversary

---

[11] The square root law is supported with evidence for fixed cover models of the adversary (either artificial in [17,19] or by practical steganalysers in [18]). However, so far it does not anticipate adversaries who refine their cover models adaptively.

[12] Although steganography is actually mentioned in Kerckhoffs' 1883 article, his design principle is not specified for information hiding applications [20, p. 7].

and (2) on the nature of covers. For the latter in particular, it is suggested that a distinction should be made between artificial and empirical covers.

We have further argued that security analyses for empirical covers touch the realm of epistemology. Based on Karl Popper's theory, our approach suggests: claims of secure steganography can only hold conditional to assumptions on the cover source, or temporarily retained until they will be falsified by observations of reality. The paper is complemented by a comprehensive literature survey that integrates formerly rather independent prior art into our conceptual framework.

5.1   Open Research Questions

The exposition in this paper has contributed a novel perspective, touched many existing concepts, and identified a couple of unsolved problems. One of them is the need of complexity metrics for cover models. If cover models shall be specified more explicitly and compared against empirical evidence, then Occam's razor has to be born in mind: superior models should exhibit *higher explanatory power* at the *same number of assumptions or parameters*. So we need ways to quantify the complexity of cover models to enable a fair comparison. Another aspect disregarded so far is a deeper reflection on the minimum sampling unit and its relation to capacity. As mentioned in Section 4.4, capacity laws exist for information-theoretically secure steganography in empirical covers (called "perfect steganography" [19]), and for heuristic steganography in empirical covers ("imperfect steganography"). The remaining non-trivial cells of Table 1 are open to future investigation. Finally, and related to this, the security in empirical covers depends on the steganalyst's knowledge of the cover source ($\mathcal{P}_0$) and the amount of evidence available to distinguish any abnormality in a concrete communication relation. This means that a complexity-theoretic adversary is bound by the number of possible stego objects observable on the channel, or, in other words, that computing cycles (and memory) cannot always compensate for missing observations. It appears relevant and interesting to study these *observability bounds* with refined complexity-theoretic analyses that distinguish between the cost of different oracle calls.

5.2   Conclusion on the Notion of Steganography

One may argue about the view that it is just the uncertainty about the cover distribution that distinguishes steganography from other security techniques, like cryptography. So every attempt to work around it simplifies the problem to a mere coding and crypto exercise. (Which certainly are of academic value, too, but solve a different problem.) As the term "steganography" is commonly used to subsume constructions with and without the empirical dimension, it is unlikely that a more precise terminology can be established and will be adopted by the community. So our hope is that this paper has clarified the distinction and we would be glad to see at least more explicit references to the class of steganography problem studied—i. e., empirical versus artificial covers—in future publications.

5.3   Outlook on the Empirical Perspective in Related Domains

We expect that this empirical perspective is equally applicable and relevant to other domains in information security where protection goals involve *system outputs to be indistinguishable from something outside the system*. This applies, for instance, to certain application in multimedia forensics and tamper hiding [50] and to some systems that try to ensure *unlinkability* [3] for privacy protection.

Acknowledgements

The author wants to thank Andrew Ker and Matthias Kirchner for their useful comments on earlier versions of this work. This work has been supported in part by the EU Network of Excellence "Future of the Identity in the Information Society" (FIDIS, http://fidis.net). The views and conclusions contained herein should not be interpreted as necessarily representing official policies of the funding organisation.

References

1. Simmons, G.J.: The prisoners' problem and the subliminal channel. In: Chaum, D. (ed.) Proceedings of CRYPTO, Santa Barbara, CA, pp. 51–67 (1983)
2. Pfitzmann, B.: Information hiding terminology. In: Anderson, R.J. (ed.) IH 1996. LNCS, vol. 1174, pp. 347–350. Springer, Heidelberg (1996)
3. Pfitzmann, A., Hansen, M.: Anonymity, unlinkability, undetectability, unobservability, pseudonymity, and identity management – A consolidated proposal for terminology (2008), http://dud.inf.tu-dresden.de/Anon_Terminology.shtml (Version 0.31)
4. Cachin, C.: An information-theoretic model for steganography. In: Aucsmith, D. (ed.) IH 1998. LNCS, vol. 1525, pp. 306–318. Springer, Heidelberg (1998)
5. Anderson, R.J.: Stretching the limits of steganography. In: Anderson, R.J. (ed.) IH 1996. LNCS, vol. 1174, pp. 39–48. Springer, Heidelberg (1996)
6. Popper, K.R.: Logik der Forschung (The Logic of Scientific Discovery), Wien. Springer, Heidelberg (1935) (Translation to English 1959)
7. Hopper, N.J., Langford, J., Ahn, L.v.: Provable secure steganography. In: Yung, M. (ed.) CRYPTO 2002. LNCS, vol. 2442, pp. 77–92. Springer, Heidelberg (2002)
8. Wang, Y., Moulin, P.: Perfectly secure steganography: Capacity, error exponents, and code constructions. IEEE Trans. on Information Theory 54, 2706–2722 (2008)
9. Kiayias, A., Raekow, Y., Russell, A.: Efficient steganography with provable security guarantees. In: Barni, M., Herrera-Joancomartí, J., Katzenbeisser, S., Pérez-González, F. (eds.) IH 2005. LNCS, vol. 3727, pp. 118–130. Springer, Heidelberg (2005)
10. Westfeld, A., Pfitzmann, A.: Attacks on steganographic systems. In: Pfitzmann, A. (ed.) IH 1999. LNCS, vol. 1768, pp. 61–76. Springer, Heidelberg (2000)
11. Böhme, R., Westfeld, A.: Breaking Cauchy model-based JPEG steganography with first order statistics. In: Samarati, P., Ryan, P.Y.A., Gollmann, D., Molva, R. (eds.) ESORICS 2004. LNCS, vol. 3193, pp. 125–140. Springer, Heidelberg (2004)
12. Barbier, J., Filiol, É., Mayoura, K.: Universal detection of JPEG steganography. Journal of Multimedia 2, 1–9 (2007)

13. Fisk, G., Fisk, M., Papadopoulos, C., Neil, J.: Eliminating steganography in Internet traffic with active wardens. In: Petitcolas, F.A.P. (ed.) IH 2002. LNCS, vol. 2578, pp. 18–35. Springer, Heidelberg (2003)
14. Pevný, T., Fridrich, J.: Benchmarking for steganography. In: Solanki, K., Sullivan, K., Madhow, U. (eds.) IH 2008. LNCS, vol. 5284, pp. 251–267. Springer, Heidelberg (2008)
15. Cachin, C.: An information-theoretic model for steganography. Information and Computation 192, 41–56 (2004)
16. Hundt, C., Liskiewicz, M., Wölfel, U.: Provably secure steganography and the complexity of sampling. In: Madria, S.K., et al. (eds.) ISAAC 2006. LNCS, vol. 4317, pp. 754–763. Springer, Heidelberg (2006)
17. Ker, A.D.: A capacity result for batch steganography. IEEE Signal Processing Letters 14, 525–528 (2007)
18. Ker, A.D., Pevný, T., Kodovský, J., Fridrich, J.: The square root law of steganographic capacity. In: Proc. of ACM Multimedia and Security Workshop (MMSEC), Oxford, UK, pp. 107–116 (2008)
19. Filler, T., Ker, A.D., Fridrich, J.: The square root law of steganographic capacity for Markov covers. In: Delp, E.J., Wong, P.W., Dittmann, J., Memon, N.D. (eds.) Media Forensics and Security XI (Proc. of SPIE), San Jose, CA, vol. 7254 (2009)
20. Kerckhoffs, A.: La cryptographie militaire. Journal des sciences militaires IX, 5–38, 161–191 (1883),
http://www.petitcolas.net/fabien/kerckhoffs/crypto_militaire_1.pdf
21. Shikata, J., Matsumoto, T.: Unconditionally secure steganography against active attacks. IEEE Trans. on Information Theory 54, 2690–2705 (2008)
22. Katzenbeisser, S., Petitcolas, F.A.P.: Defining security in steganographic systems. In: Delp, E.J., Wong, P.W. (eds.) Security, Steganography and Watermarking of Multimedia Contents IV (Proc. of SPIE), San Jose, CA, vol. 4675, pp. 50–56 (2002)
23. Ker, A.D.: The ultimate steganalysis benchmark. In: Proc. of ACM Multimedia and Security Workshop (MMSEC), Dallas, Texas, USA, pp. 141–147 (2007)
24. Neyman, J., Pearson, E.: On the problem of the most efficient tests of statistical hypotheses. Philosophical Transactions of the Royal Society of London. Series A (Mathematical or Physical Character) 231, 289–337 (1933)
25. Shannon, C.: Communication theory of secrecy systems. Bell System Technical Journal 28, 656–715 (1949)
26. Ker, A.D.: Resampling and the detection of LSB matching in colour bitmaps. In: Delp, E.J., Wong, P.W. (eds.) Security, Steganography and Watermarking of Multimedia Contents VII (Proc. of SPIE), San Jose, CA, vol. 5681, pp. 1–15 (2005)
27. Ker, A.D., Böhme, R.: Revisiting weighted stego-image steganalysis. In: Delp, E.J., Wong, P.W., Dittmann, J., Memon, N.D. (eds.) Security, Forensics, Steganography and Watermarking of Multimedia Contents X (Proc. of SPIE), San Jose, CA, vol. 6819 (2008)
28. Böhme, R.: Weighted stego-image steganalysis for JPEG covers. In: Solanki, K., Sullivan, K., Madhow, U. (eds.) IH 2008. LNCS, vol. 5284, pp. 178–194. Springer, Heidelberg (2008)
29. Westfeld, A.: F5 – A steganographic algorithm. In: Moskowitz, I.S. (ed.) IH 2001. LNCS, vol. 2137, pp. 289–302. Springer, Heidelberg (2001)
30. Solanki, K., Sarkar, A., Manjunath, B.S.: YASS: Yet another steganographic scheme that resists blind steganalysis. In: Furon, T., Cayre, F., Doërr, G., Bas, P. (eds.) IH 2007. LNCS, vol. 4567, pp. 16–31. Springer, Heidelberg (2008)
31. Cancelli, G., Barni, M.: MPSteg-color: A new steganographic technique for color images. In: Furon, T., Cayre, F., Doërr, G., Bas, P. (eds.) IH 2007. LNCS, vol. 4567, pp. 1–15. Springer, Heidelberg (2008)

32. Pevný, T., Fridrich, J.: Novelty detection in blind steganalysis. In: Proc. of ACM Multimedia and Security Workshop (MMSEC), Oxford, UK, pp. 167–176 (2008)
33. Fridrich, J.: Feature-based steganalysis for JPEG images and its implications for future design of steganographic schemes. In: Fridrich, J. (ed.) IH 2004. LNCS, vol. 3200, pp. 67–81. Springer, Heidelberg (2004)
34. Kullback, S.: Information Theory and Statistics. Dover, New York (1968)
35. Zhang, W., Li, S.: Security measurements of steganographic systems. In: Jakobsson, M., Yung, M., Zhou, J. (eds.) ACNS 2004. LNCS, vol. 3089, pp. 194–204. Springer, Heidelberg (2004)
36. Korzhik, V.I., Imai, H., Shikata, J., Morales-Luna, G., Gerling, E.: On the use of Bhattacharyya distance as a measure of the detectability of steganographic systems. LNCS Trans. on Data Hiding and Multimedia Security 3, 23–32 (2008)
37. Franz, E., Jerichow, A., Möller, S., Pfitzmann, A., Stierand, I.: Computer based steganography: How it works and why therefore any restrictions on cryptography are nonsense, at best. In: Anderson, R. (ed.) IH 1996. LNCS, vol. 1174, pp. 7–21. Springer, Heidelberg (1996)
38. Zöllner, J., Federrath, H., Klimant, H., Pfitzmann, A., Piotraschke, R., Westfeld, A., Wicke, G., Wolf, G.: Modeling the security of steganographic systems. In: Aucsmith, D. (ed.) IH 1998. LNCS, vol. 1525, pp. 306–318. Springer, Heidelberg (1998)
39. Franz, E., Pfitzmann, A.: Einführung in die Steganographie und Ableitung eines neuen Stegoparadigmas (Introduction to steganography and derivation of a new stego-paradigm). Informatik Spektrum 21, 183–193 (1998)
40. Franz, E., Pfitzmann, A.: Steganography secure against cover-stego-attacks. In: Pfitzmann, A. (ed.) IH 1999. LNCS, vol. 1768, pp. 29–46. Springer, Heidelberg (2000)
41. Dittmann, J.: Digitale Wasserzeichen (Digital watermarking). Springer, Heidelberg (2000)
42. Craver, S., Li, E., Yu, J., Atalki, I.: A supraliminal channel in a videoconferencing application. In: Solanki, K., Sullivan, K., Madhow, U. (eds.) IH 2008. LNCS, vol. 5284, pp. 283–293. Springer, Heidelberg (2008)
43. Fridrich, J., Goljan, M., Soukal, D.: Perturbed quantization steganography with wet paper codes. In: Proc. of ACM Multimedia and Security Workshop (MMSEC), pp. 4–15. ACM Press, New York (2004)
44. Franz, E., Schneidewind, A.: Adaptive steganography based on dithering. In: Proc. of ACM Multimedia and Security Workshop (MMSEC), pp. 56–62. ACM Press, New York (2004)
45. Kharrazi, M., Sencar, H., Memon, N.: Cover selection for steganographic embedding. In: Proc. of IEEE ICIP, pp. 117–120 (2006)
46. Cayre, F., Fontaine, C., Furon, T.: Watermarking security: Theory and practice. IEEE Trans. on Signal Processing 53, 3976–3987 (2005)
47. Le, T.v., Kurosawa, K.: Efficient Public Key Steganography Secure Against Adaptively Chosen Stegotext Attacks. Report 2003/244. Cryptology ePrint Archive (2003), http://eprint.iacr.org/2003/244
48. Dolev, D., Yao, A.: On the security of public key protocols. IEEE Trans. on Information Theory 29, 198–208 (1983)
49. Ker, A.D.: Perturbation hiding and the batch steganography problem. In: Solanki, K., Sullivan, K., Madhow, U. (eds.) IH 2008. LNCS, vol. 5284, pp. 45–59. Springer, Heidelberg (2008)
50. Kirchner, M., Böhme, R.: Tamper hiding: Defeating image forensics. In: Furon, T., Cayre, F., Doërr, G., Bas, P. (eds.) IH 2007. LNCS, vol. 4567, pp. 326–341. Springer, Heidelberg (2008)

Fisher Information Determines Capacity of ε-Secure Steganography

Tomáš Filler and Jessica Fridrich

Department of ECE, SUNY Binghamton, NY, USA
{tomas.filler,fridrich}@binghamton.edu

Abstract. Most practical stegosystems for digital media work by applying a mutually independent embedding operation to each element of the cover. For such stegosystems, the Fisher information w.r.t. the change rate is a perfect security descriptor equivalent to KL divergence between cover and stego images. Under the assumption of Markov covers, we derive a closed-form expression for the Fisher information and show how it can be used for comparing stegosystems and optimizing their performance. In particular, using an analytic cover model fit to experimental data obtained from a large number of natural images, we prove that the ±1 embedding operation is asymptotically optimal among all mutually independent embedding operations that modify cover elements by at most 1.

1 Introduction

The key concept in essentially all communication schemes is the channel capacity defined as the amount of information, or largest payload, that can be safely transmitted over the channel. So far, the capacity of steganographic channels was studied mainly for the case of perfectly secure stegosystems, for which the number of bits that can be safely transmitted in an n-element cover (the *steganographic capacity*) scales linearly w.r.t. n. In this sense, the communication rate (payload per cover element)[1] is *non-vanishing* [1,2,3]. A crucial assumption in these works is the full knowledge of the cover source or the detector. In practice, when dealing with empirical cover sources, such as digital media files, it is unlikely that the communicating parties (Alice and Bob) will have the same knowledge as the Warden. In fact, history teaches us that no matter how sophisticated Alice and Bob are in creating their steganographic scheme that embeds in empirical covers, it is relatively easy for the Warden to identify statistics violated by the embedding and thus mount an attack. Consequently, practical stegosystems are likely to exhibit positive KL divergence between cover and stego objects in some appropriate cover model. We call such systems *imperfect*.

For imperfect stegosystems, the communication rate is not a good descriptor of the channel because it approaches zero with increasing n. Alice, however, still

---

[1] In this paper, we measure "capacity" as the total number of bits and instead use the term "communication rate" for capacity expressed per cover element.

S. Katzenbeisser and A.-R. Sadeghi (Eds.): IH 2009, LNCS 5806, pp. 31–47, 2009.
© Springer-Verlag Berlin Heidelberg 2009

needs to know what level of risk she is exposing herself to when sending a message to Bob. It is critical for her to know how much information she can send using her stegosystem in an n-element cover while keeping the KL divergence between cover and stego objects below some chosen ε. It was recently shown that under fairly general assumptions, the amount of information that she can hide scales as $r\sqrt{n}$ [4], with r constant. This *Square Root Law of imperfect steganography* (SRL) was experimentally verified for various embedding algorithms in both spatial and DCT domains [5]. The SRL was also proved by Ker [6] for the case of batch steganography.

In this paper, we propose to use the proportionality constant r from the SRL as a more refined measure of steganographic capacity of imperfect stegosystems. By the form of the law, the constant r, for which we coin the term *the root rate*, essentially expresses the capacity per square root of cover size. We derive a closed form expression for the root rate under the assumption that covers form a Markov chain and embedding is realized by applying a sequence of independent embedding operations to individual cover elements. The root rate depends on the Fisher information rate w.r.t. the the change rate, which was shown to be a perfect security descriptor equivalent to the KL divergence between distributions of cover and stego objects [7]. Expressing the Fisher information rate analytically as a quadratic form allows us to evaluate, compare, and optimize security of stegosystems. To this end, we derive an analytic cover model from a large database of natural images represented in the spatial domain and show that the ± 1 embedding operation is asymptotically optimal among all mutually independent embedding operations that modify cover elements by at most 1. Finally, using the Fisher information rate, we compare security of several practical stegosystems, including LSB embedding and ± 1 embedding. Our findings appear to be consistent with results previously obtained experimentally using steganalyzers and are in good agreement with the recent experimental study reported in [8].

This paper is structured as follows. In the next section, we introduce notation and formulate our assumptions. In Section 3, we introduce the concept of the root rate as a measure of steganographic capacity of imperfect stegosystems. At the same time, we derive a closed form expression for the Fisher information rate on which the root rate depends. Section 4 contains the theoretical foundation for comparing stegosystems and for maximizing the root rate with respect to the embedding operation for a fixed cover source. In Section 5, we present comparison of several known embedding operations for three spatial domain analytic cover models derived from databases of raw, JPEG, and scanned images. Also, we prove that ternary ± 1 embedding has the highest root rate among all stegosystems that modify cover elements by at most 1. The paper is concluded in Section 6.

2   Assumptions

The results reached in this paper will be derived from three basic assumptions. The first assumption concerns the impact of embedding. We postulate that the stego object is obtained by applying a mutually independent embedding operation to each cover element. This type of embedding can be found in majority of practical embedding methods (see, e.g., [9] and the references therein). The second assumption is our model of covers. We require the individual cover elements to form a first-order stationary Markov chain because this model is analytically tractable while allowing study of more realistic cover sources with memory. Finally, the third assumption essentially states that the resulting stegosystem is imperfect.

Throughout the paper, we use $\mathbb{A} = (a_{ij})$ to denote a matrix with elements a_{ij}, calligraphic font $(\mathcal{X})$ to denote sets, and capital letters (X, Y) to denote random variables, both vector and scalar. If y is a vector with components $y = (y_1, \ldots, y_n)$, y_k^l denotes the subsequence $y_k^l = (y_k, \ldots, y_l)$. If $Y = (Y_1, \ldots, Y_n)$ is a random vector with underlying probability distribution P, then $P(Y_k^l = y_k^l)$ or simply $P(y_k^l)$ denotes the marginal probability $P(Y_k = y_k, Y_{k+1} = y_{k+1}, \ldots, Y_l = y_l)$.

An n-element cover source will be represented using a random variable $X_1^n \triangleq (X_1, \ldots, X_n)$ distributed according to some general distribution $P^{(n)}$ over $\mathcal{X}^n$, $\mathcal{X} \triangleq \{1, \ldots, N\}$. A specific cover object is a realization of X_1^n and will be denoted with the corresponding lower case letter $x_1^n \triangleq (x_1, \ldots, x_n) \in \mathcal{X}^n$. A stegosystem is a triple $S_n = (X_1^n, Emb^{(n)}, Ext^{(n)})$ consisting of the random variable describing the cover source, embedding mapping $Emb^{(n)}$, and extraction mapping $Ext^{(n)}$. The embedding mapping $Emb^{(n)}$ applied to X_1^n induces another random variable $Y_1^n \triangleq (Y_1, \ldots, Y_n)$ with probability distribution $Q_\beta^{(n)}$ over $\mathcal{X}^n$. Specific realizations of Y_1^n are called stego objects and will be denoted $y_1^n \triangleq (y_1, \ldots, y_n)$. Here, $\beta \geq 0$ is a scalar parameter of embedding whose meaning will be explained shortly.

The specific details of the embedding (and extraction) mappings are immaterial for our study. We only need to postulate the *probabilistic impact* of embedding.

Assumption 1. [Mutually independent embedding] *The embedding algorithm modifies every cover element X_k independently to a corresponding element of the stego object Y_k with probability*

$$Q_\beta(Y_k = j | X_k = i) \triangleq b_{ij}(\beta) = \begin{cases} 1 + \beta c_{ii} & \text{if } i = j \\ \beta c_{ij} & \text{otherwise,} \end{cases} \tag{1}$$

for some constants $c_{ij} \geq 0$ for $i \neq j$. Note that because $\sum_{j=1}^{N} b_{ij} = 1$, we must have $c_{ii} = -\sum_{j \neq i} c_{ij}$ for each $i \in \mathcal{X}$. Also note that we can find sufficiently small β_0 such that $b_{ii}(\beta) > 0$ for $\beta \in [0, \beta_0]$ and all $i \in \mathcal{X}$. The embedding and extraction mappings also impose a bound on the range of β, $\beta \in [0, \beta_{MAX}]$.

The matrix $\mathbb{C} \triangleq (c_{ij})$ reflects the inner workings of the embedding algorithm, while the parameter β captures the *extent* of embedding changes. Due to the fact that $Pr(Y_k \neq X_k) = -\beta c_{ii}$, we can think of β as a parameter controlling the relative number of changes or the change rate. Because the matrix $\mathbb{B}_\beta \triangleq (b_{ij}(\beta))$ does not depend on $k \in \{1, \ldots, n\}$ or the history of embedding changes, one can say that the stego object is obtained from the cover by applying to

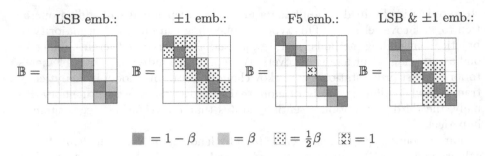

Fig. 1. Examples of several embedding methods in the form of a functional matrix $\mathbb{B}$. The last matrix represents an embedding method that uses LSB embedding to embed in the first two cover values and ternary ± 1 embedding in the last four values.

each cover element a Mutually Independent embedding operation (we speak of *MI embedding*). The independence of embedding modifications implies that the conditional probability of the stego object given the cover object can be factorized, i.e., $Q_\beta^{(n)}(Y_1^n|X_1^n) = \prod_{i=1}^n Q_\beta(Y_i|X_i)$. For simplicity, we omit the index β from the functional matrix $\mathbb{B}_\beta$.

Many embedding algorithms across different domains use MI embedding. Representative examples are LSB embedding, ± 1 embedding, stochastic modulation, Jsteg, MMx, and various versions of the F5 algorithm [9]. Examples of matrix $\mathbb{B}$ for four selected embedding methods are shown in Figure 1. The last matrix $\mathbb{B}$ in this figure represents a practical method that merges ternary ± 1 embedding with LSB embedding.

Next, we formulate our assumption about the cover source.

Assumption 2. [Markov cover source]. *We assume that the cover source X_1^n is a first-order stationary Markov Chain (MC) over $\mathcal{X}$, to which we will often refer as just Markov chain for brevity. This source is completely described by its stochastic transition probability matrix $\mathbb{A} \triangleq (a_{ij}) \in \mathbb{R}^{N \times N}$, $a_{ij} = Pr(X_k = j|X_{k-1} = i)$, and by the initial distribution $Pr(X_1)$. The probability distribution induced by the MC source generating n-element cover objects satisfies $P^{(n)}(X_1^n = x_1^n) = P^{(n-1)}(X_1^{n-1} = x_1^{n-1})a_{x_{n-1}x_n}$, where $P^{(1)}(X_1)$ is the initial distribution. We further assume that the transition probability matrix of the cover source satisfies $a_{ij} \geq \delta > 0$, for some δ and thus the MC is irreducible. The stationary distribution of the MC source is a vector $\pi \triangleq (\pi_1, \ldots, \pi_N)$ satisfying $\pi\mathbb{A} = \pi$. In this paper, we will always assume that the initial distribution $P^{(1)}(X_1) = \pi$, which implies $P^{(n)}(X_k) = \pi$ for every n and k. This assumption simplifies the analysis without loss of generality because the marginal probabilities $P^{(n)}(X_k)$ converge to π with exponential rate w.r.t. k (see Doob [10], equation (2.2) on page 173). In other words, MCs "forget" their initial distribution with exponential rate.*

Under the above assumption and the class of MI embedding, the source of stego images no longer exhibits the Markov property and forms a Hidden Markov Chain[2] (HMC) instead [12]. The HMC model is described by its hidden states (cover elements) and output transition probabilities (MI embedding). Hidden states are described by the cover MC, while the output probability transition matrix $\mathbb{B}$ is taken from the definition of MI embedding.

Unless stated otherwise, in the rest of this paper $Q_\beta^{(n)}$ denotes the probability measure induced by the HMC source embedded with parameter β into n-element MC cover objects. By the stationarity of the MC source, the marginal probabilities $P^{(n)}(X_k^{k+1}) = P^{(2)}(X_1^2)$ and $Q_\beta^{(n)}(Y_k^{k+1}) = Q_\beta^{(n)}(Y_1^2)$ for all k. Sometimes, we will omit the number of elements, n, and denote as P and Q_β the probability distributions over cover and stego images, respectively.

The third assumption we formulate concerns the entire stegosystem S_n. In this work, we only deal with imperfect stegosystems.

Assumption 3. [FI condition]. *We assume the stegosystem $S_n = (X_1^n, Emb^{(n)},$ $Ext^{(n)})$ to be imperfect, meaning that it is not perfectly secure in the sense of Cachin [13], i.e., the KL divergence $D_{KL}(P^{(n)}\|Q_\beta^{(n)}) > 0$ for $\beta > 0$. For our special case of Markov cover sources X_1^n and MI embedding $Emb^{(n)}$, this assumption can be equivalently stated in two different forms:*

1. *The pair $(P^{(2)}, Q_\beta^{(2)})$ does not satisfy the so called* Fisher Information *condition,*

$$\forall y_1^2 \in \mathcal{X}^2 \quad \left(P^{(2)}(X_1^2 = y_1^2) > 0\right) \;\Rightarrow\; \left(\frac{d}{d\beta}Q_\beta^{(2)}(y_1^2)|_{\beta=0} = 0\right). \quad (2)$$

2. *There exists a pair of states (i,j) such that*

$$P(X_1^2 = (i,j)) \neq Q_\beta(Y_1^2 = (i,j)) \text{ for all } \beta > 0. \quad (3)$$

For proof of these statements, see [7, Cor. 7].

Finally, we would like to stress that Assumptions 1–3 are not overly restrictive and will likely be satisfied for all practical steganographic schemes in some appropriate representation of the cover. For example, a stegosystem that preserves the Markov model is likely to be detectable by computing higher-order dependencies among pixels. Thus, the stegosystem will become imperfect when representing the cover as pairs or groups of pixels/coefficients or some other quantities computed from the cover.

3   Capacity of Imperfect Stegosystems

In this section, we introduce the concept of root rate as a measure of capacity of imperfect stegosystems. We start by explaining the relationship between

---

[2] In contrast to [11], we opted not to approximate stego objects by Markov chain as it is not entirely clear what consequences this simplifying step has.

steganographic capacity of stegosystems satisfying Assumptions 1–3 and the Fisher information w.r.t. the parameter β

$$I_n(0) = E_P \left[\left(\frac{d}{d\beta} \ln Q_\beta^{(n)}(y_1^n) \Big|_{\beta=0} \right)^2 \right]. \tag{4}$$

Then in Section 3.2, we derive its closed form expression and write it in terms of the expected relative payload α instead of parameter β as this form is more informative for the steganographer.

3.1   Fisher Information in Steganography

Fisher information is a fundamental quantity that frequently appears in theoretical steganography and in general in signal detection and estimation. For example, the Cramer-Rao lower bound states that the reciprocal of Fisher information, $1/I_n(\beta)$, is the lower bound on the variance of unbiased estimators of β (quantitative steganalyzers). Fisher information also appears in the leading term of Taylor expansion of the KL divergence $d_n(\beta) \triangleq D_{KL}(P^{(n)}||Q_\beta^{(n)}) = \beta^2 I_n(0)/(2\ln 2) + O(\beta^3)$, where

$$D_{KL}\left(P^{(n)}||Q_\beta^{(n)}\right) \triangleq \sum_{x_1^n \in \mathcal{X}^n} P^{(n)}(x_1^n) \log_2 \frac{P^{(n)}(x_1^n)}{Q_\beta^{(n)}(x_1^n)}.$$

From here, we see that zero KL divergence implies zero Fisher information. Although the opposite is not true in general, it holds for all stegosystems with MI embedding and arbitrary cover model [7]. For such stegosystems, Fisher information $I_n(0)$ represents a perfect security descriptor equivalent to the KL divergence. Fisher information was also proposed for benchmarking steganalyzers [14].

The relationship between the Fisher information rate and steganographic capacity of stegosystems satisfying Assumptions 1–3 was established in [4]. It was essentially shown that such stegosystems are subject to the Square Root Law, which means that payloads that grow faster than $\sqrt{n}$, i.e., $\lim_{n\to\infty} \beta(n)n/\sqrt{n} = \infty$, can be detected arbitrarily accurately, whereas payloads that grow slower than $\sqrt{n}$, i.e., $\beta(n)n/\sqrt{n} \leq K < \infty$, lead to ε-secure stegosystems, $d_n(\beta) < \varepsilon$.[3] This result tells us that the payload that can be securely transmitted over the steganographic channel scales as $r\sqrt{n}$. Consequently, the sequence of embedding parameters $\beta(n)$ must approach zero for ε-secure systems and thus the communication rate tends to zero. Due to this fact, it makes sense to evaluate steganographic capacity in the limit of $\beta(n) \to 0$.

---

[3] Here, we assumed that there exists a linear relationship between $\beta(n)$ and the relative payload $\alpha(n)$ (e.g., the stegosystem does not employ matrix embedding). Indeed, application of matrix embedding does not invalidate our arguments as $\alpha(n)$ differs from $\beta(n)$ only by a multiplicative factor bounded by $\log n$.

3.2   Root Rate

The problem of steganalysis can be formulated as the following hypothesis testing problem

$$H_0 : \beta = 0$$
$$H_1 : \beta > 0. \tag{5}$$

We show that for small (and known) β and large n, the likelihood ratio test with test statistic

$$\frac{1}{\sqrt{n}}T_{\beta_0}^{(n)}(X) = \frac{1}{\sqrt{n}}\ln\left(Q_{\beta_0}^{(n)}(X)/P^{(n)}(X)\right), \tag{6}$$

is a mean-shifted Gauss-Gauss problem.[4] This property, usually called the Local Asymptotic Normality (LAN) of the detector, allows us to quantify and correctly compare security of embedding algorithms operating on the same MC cover model for small values of β.

In this case, the detector performance can be completely described by the deflection coefficient d^2, which parametrizes the ROC curve as it binds the probability of detection, P_D, as a function of the false alarm probability, P_{FA},

$$P_D = Q\left(Q^{-1}(P_{FA}) - \sqrt{d^2}\right).$$

Here, $Q(x) = 1 - \Phi(x)$ and $\Phi(x)$ is the cdf of a standard normal variable $N(0,1)$. Large value of the deflection coefficient implies better detection or weaker steganography.

First, we state the LAN property for the HMC model w.r.t. the embedding parameter β and then extend this result with respect to the relative payload α.

Theorem 1. [LAN of the LLRT]. *Under Assumptions 1–3, the likelihood ratio (6) satisfies the local asymptotic normality (LAN), i.e., under both hypotheses and for values of β up to order β^2*

$$\sqrt{n}\left(T_{\beta}^{(n)}/n + \beta^2 I/2\right) \xrightarrow{d} N(0, \beta^2 I) \ under \ H_0 \tag{7}$$

$$\sqrt{n}\left(T_{\beta}^{(n)}/n - \beta^2 I/2\right) \xrightarrow{d} N(0, \beta^2 I) \ under \ H_1, \tag{8}$$

where I is the Fisher information rate, $I = \lim_{n\to\infty}\frac{1}{n}I_n(0)$, and $\xrightarrow{d}$ is the convergence in distribution. The detection performance is thus completely described by the deflection coefficient

$$d^2 = \frac{(\sqrt{n}\beta^2 I/2 + \sqrt{n}\beta^2 I/2)^2}{\beta^2 I} = n\beta^2 I.$$

---

[4] In hypothesis testing, the problem of testing $N(\mu_0, \sigma^2)$ vs. $N(\mu_1, \sigma^2)$ is called the mean-shifted Gauss-Gauss problem and its detection performance is completely described by the deflection coefficient $d^2 = (\mu_0 - \mu_1)^2/\sigma^2$ [15, Chapter 3].

Proof. Due to limited space, we only provide a brief outline of the proof. The Gaussianity of the test statistic follows from the Central Limit Theorem (CLT) due to the fact that the test statistic is close to being i.i.d. Formal proof of this uses exponential forgetting of the prediction filter [16, Lemma 9] and follows similar steps as the proof of the CLT for Markov chains [10]. The mean and variance of the likelihood ratio (6) is obtained by expanding (6) in Taylor series w.r.t. β and realizing that the leading term is the quadratic term containing the Fisher information rate.

We now reformulate the conclusion of the theorem in terms of the payload rather than the parameter β. Matrix embedding (syndrome coding) employed by the stegosystem may introduce a non-linear relationship $\beta = f(\alpha)$ between both quantities. In general, the payload embedded at each cover element may depend on its state $i \in \mathcal{X}$ (e.g., see the last two matrices in Figure 1). Thus, the expected value of the relative payload that can be embedded in each cover is $\alpha(\beta) = \sum_{i \in \mathcal{X}} \pi_i \alpha_i(\beta)$, where $\alpha_i(\beta)$ stands for the number of bits that can be embedded into state $i \in \mathcal{X}$ and π_i is the stationary distribution of the MC. The value of β for which α is maximal will be denoted as β_{MAX}

$$\beta_{MAX} = \arg\max_{\beta} \alpha(\beta).$$

For example, for ternary ± 1 embedding $\beta_{MAX} = 2/3$ and $\alpha_i(\beta_{MAX}) = \log_2 3$, while for binary ± 1 embedding $\beta_{MAX} = 1/2$ and $\alpha_i(\beta_{MAX}) = 1$ (see Figure 1 for the corresponding matrices). Notice that the matrix $\mathbb{C}$ is the same for both embedding methods. The only formal difference is the range of the parameter β. We also remark that unless all α_i are the same, the maximal payload will depend on the distribution of individual states π_i.

To simplify our arguments, we assume a linear relationship between β and α (e.g., we do not consider in this paper the effects of matrix embedding). Therefore, we can write

$$\beta = f(\alpha) = \frac{\beta_{MAX}}{\alpha_{MAX}} \alpha, \tag{9}$$

where $\alpha \in [0, \alpha_{MAX}]$ and $\alpha_{MAX} = \alpha(\beta_{MAX})$ denotes the average number of bits that can be embedded into cover element while embedding with $\beta = \beta_{MAX}$ (maximum change rate).

From (9), the deflection coefficient can be expressed in terms of the relative payload α by substituting $\beta = f(\alpha)$ from (9) into Q_β

$$d^2 = n\alpha^2 \left(\frac{\beta_{MAX}}{\alpha_{MAX}} \right)^2 I. \tag{10}$$

In practice, Alice can control statistical detectability by bounding $d^2 < \varepsilon$ for some fixed ε, obtaining thus an upper bound on the total number of bits (payload) αn that can be safely embedded (this requires rearranging the terms in (10))

$$\alpha n \leq \frac{\alpha_{MAX}}{\beta_{MAX}} \sqrt{\frac{\varepsilon}{I}} n. \tag{11}$$

In analogy to the communication rate, it is natural to define *the root rate*

$$r \triangleq \frac{\alpha_{MAX}}{\sqrt{I}\beta_{MAX}} \tag{12}$$

as the quantity that measures steganographic security of imperfect stegosystems in bits per square root of cover size per square root of KL divergence. We use the root rate for comparing stegosystems with a MC cover model.

In the next theorem, proved in the appendix, we establish the existence of the main component of the root rate, the Fisher information rate I, and express it in a closed form.

Theorem 2. [Fisher information rate]. *Let* $\mathbb{A} = (a_{ij})$ *define the MC cover model and* $\mathbb{B}$, *defined by matrix* $\mathbb{C} = (c_{ij})$, *capture the embedding algorithm. Then, the normalized Fisher information* $I_n(0)/n$ *approaches a finite limit* I *as* $n \to \infty$. *This limit can be written as* $I = \mathbf{c}^T \mathbb{F} \mathbf{c}$, *where* $\mathbf{c}$ *is obtained by arranging* $\mathbb{C}$ *into a column vector of size* N^2 *with elements* c_{ij}.[5] *The matrix* $\mathbb{F}$ *of size* $N^2 \times N^2$ *is defined only in terms of matrix* $\mathbb{A}$ *and does not depend on the embedding algorithm. The elements of matrix* $\mathbb{F}$ *are*

$$f_{(i,j),(k,l)} = [j = l]V(i,j,k) - U(i,j,k,l), \tag{13}$$

where by the Iverson notation $[j = l]$ *is one if* $j = l$ *and zero otherwise and*

$$V(i,j,k) = \left(\sum_{z \in \mathcal{X}} \pi_z a_{zi} \frac{a_{zk}}{a_{zj}} \right) \left(\sum_{z \in \mathcal{X}} a_{iz} \frac{a_{kz}}{a_{jz}} \right)$$

$$U(i,j,k,l) = \pi_i \left(a_{ik} - a_{il} \frac{a_{jk}}{a_{jl}} \right) + \pi_k \left(a_{ki} - a_{kj} \frac{a_{li}}{a_{lj}} \right).$$

Moreover, $|I_n(0)/n - I| \leq C/n$ *for some constant* C. *This constant depends only on the elements of matrix* $\mathbb{A}$ *and not on the embedding algorithm. The quadratic form* $I(\mathbf{c}) = \mathbf{c}^T \mathbb{F} \mathbf{c}$ *is semidefinite, in general.*

By inspecting the proof of the theorem, the matrix $\mathbb{F}$ can be seen as the Fisher information rate matrix w.r.t. the parameters $\{b_{ij} | 1 \leq i, j \leq N\}$. It describes the natural sensitivity of the cover source to MI embedding. The quadratic form then combines these sensitivities with coefficients given by the specific embedding method and allows us to decompose the intrinsic detectability caused by the cover source from the detectability caused by the embedding algorithm.

Corollary 1. *For the special case when the MC degenerates to an i.i.d. cover source with distribution* $P = \pi$, *the Fisher information rate simplifies to*

$$I = \sum_{i,j,k \in \mathcal{X}} c_{ij} \frac{\pi_i \pi_k}{\pi_j} c_{kj}.$$

---

[5] The order of elements in $\mathbb{C}$ is immaterial as far as the same ordering is used for pairs (i, j) and (k, l) in matrix $\mathbb{F}$.

4   Maximizing the Root Rate

In the previous section, we established that the steganographic capacity of imperfect stegosystems should be measured as the root rate (12) defined as the payload per square root of the cover size and per square root of KL divergence. The most important component of the root rate is the stegosystem's Fisher information rate, for which an analytic form was derived in Theorem 2. The steganographer is interested in designing stegosystems (finding $\mathbb{C}$) with the highest possible root rate. This can be achieved by minimizing the Fisher information rate or by embedding symbols from a larger alphabet, i.e., increasing the ratio α_{MAX}/β_{MAX}. In this section, we describe two general strategies for maximizing the root rate that are applicable to practical stegosystems. In Section 5, we draw conclusions from experiments when these strategies are applied to real cover sources formed by digital images.

Before proceedings with further arguments, we point out that the highest root rate is obviously obtained when the Fisher information rate is zero, $I = 0$. This can happen for non-trivial embedding ($\mathbb{C} \neq 0$) in certain sources because the Fisher information rate is a semidefinite quadratic form. Such stegosystems, however, would be perfectly secure and thus by Assumption 3 are excluded from our consideration.[6]

The number of bits, α_i, that can be embedded at each state $i \in \mathcal{X}$ is bounded by the entropy of the ith row of $\mathbb{B} = \mathbb{I} + \beta\mathbb{C}$, $H(\mathbb{B}_{i\bullet})$. Thus, in the most general setting, we wish to maximize the root rate

$$\frac{\sum \pi_i H\left(\mathbb{B}_{i\bullet}(\beta_{MAX})\right)}{\beta_{MAX}} \frac{1}{\sqrt{I}}$$

w.r.t. matrix $\mathbb{C}$. The nonlinear objective function makes the analysis rather complicated and the result may depend on the distribution of individual states π. Moreover, even if we knew the optimal solution, care needs to be taken in interpreting such results, because a practical algorithm allowing us to communicate the entropy of the additive noise may not be available. We are only aware of a few practical embedding algorithms that communicate the maximal amount of information (LSB embedding with binary symbols and ± 1 embedding with ternary symbols). In practice, stochastic modulation [17] can be used in some cases to embed information by adding noise with a specific pmf (matrix $\mathbb{C}$), but the specific algorithms described in [17] are suboptimal.

In the rest of this section, we present two different approaches how to optimize the embedding algorithm under different settings that are practically realizable.

4.1   Optimization by Convex Combination of Known Methods

One simple and practical approach to optimize the embedding method is obtained by combining existing stegosystems $S^{(1)}$ and $S^{(2)}$. Suppose Alice and

---

[6] An example of such a stegosystem is LSB embedding in i.i.d. covers with $\pi_{2i} = \pi_{2i+1}$ for all i.

Bob embed a portion of the message into λn elements, $0 < \lambda < 1$, using $S^{(1)}$ and use the remaining $(1 - \lambda)n$ elements to embed the rest of the message using $S^{(2)}$. If both parties select the elements pseudo-randomly based on a stego key, the impact on a single cover element follows a distribution obtained as a convex combination of the noise pmfs of both methods. Note that the methods are allowed to embed a different number of bits per cover element since Bob knows which symbol to extract from each part of the stego object. Let $S^{(i)}$ represent the ith embedding method with matrix $\mathbb{C}^{(i)}$, or its vector representation $\mathbf{c}^{(i)}$, with ratio $\rho^{(i)} = \alpha_{MAX}^{(i)}/\beta_{MAX}^{(i)}$ for $i \in \{1,2\}$. The root rate $r(\lambda)$ of the method obtained by the above approach (convex embedding) with parameter λ can be written as

$$
\begin{aligned}
r(\lambda) &= \frac{\lambda\rho^{(1)} + (1 - \lambda)\rho^{(2)}}{\sqrt{(\lambda\mathbf{c}^{(1)} + (1 - \lambda)\mathbf{c}^{(2)})^T \mathbb{F}(\lambda\mathbf{c}^{(1)} + (1 - \lambda)\mathbf{c}^{(2)})}} \\
&= \frac{\lambda\rho^{(1)} + (1 - \lambda)\rho^{(2)}}{\sqrt{\lambda^2 I^{(1)} + (1 - \lambda)^2 I^{(2)} + 2\lambda(1 - \lambda)I^{(1,2)}}},
\end{aligned}
\tag{14}
$$

where $I^{(i)}$ is the Fisher information rate of $S^{(i)}$ and $I^{(1,2)} = \left(\mathbf{c}^{(1)}\right)^T \mathbb{F}\mathbf{c}^{(2)}$. Here, we used the symmetry of $\mathbb{F}$ to write $I^{(1,2)} = I^{(2,1)}$.

4.2   Minimizing the Fisher Information Rate

In an alternative setup, we deal with the problem of optimizing the shape of the additive noise pmf under the assumption that the number of bits, α_i, embedded at each state $i \in \mathcal{X}$ is constant. For example, we may wish to determine the optimal pmf that would allow us to communicate 1 bit per element ($\alpha_i = 1$, $\forall i \in \mathcal{X}$) by changing each cover element by at most 1. In this problem, the ratio α_{MAX}/β_{MAX}, as well as the cover model (matrix $\mathbb{A}$), are fixed and known. The task is to minimize the Fisher information rate I.

We formulate our optimization problem by restricting the form of the matrix $\mathbb{C} = (c_{ij})$, or its vector representation $\mathbf{c} = (c_{ij}) \in R^{N^2 \times 1}$, to the following linear parametric form

$$
\mathbf{c} = \mathbb{D}v + e,
\tag{15}
$$

where $\mathbb{D} = (d_{ij})$ is a full-rank real matrix of size $N^2 \times k$, e is a real column vector of size N^2, and $v = (v_1, \ldots, v_k)^T$ is a k-dimensional column vector. We assume $v \in \mathcal{V}$, where $\mathcal{V}$ is bounded by a set of linear inequalities[7] and the constraint $\sum_j c_{ij} = 0$ for all $i \in \{1, \ldots, N\}$. In other words, we decompose the matrix $\mathbb{C}$ into k real parameters v_i, $i \in \{1, \ldots, k\}$. The following example shows one such representation for a stegosystem whose embedding changes are at most 1.

Example 1. [Tridiagonal embedding]. We set $c_{ii} = -1$, $c_{i,i-1} = v_{i-1}$, and $c_{i,i+1} = 1 - v_{i-1}$ for $i \in \{2, \ldots, N - 1\}$ (and suitably defined at the boundaries). This allows us to model ± 1 embedding, LSB embedding, and all possible MI embedding methods that modify every element by at most 1. By setting $c_{ii} = -1$ for

---

[7] E.g., we must have $\mathbb{B} \geq 0$.

all i, we constrain ourselves to stegosystems that embed the same payload into every state $i \in \mathcal{X}$ for all $\beta \geq 0$. This model has $k = N - 2$ parameters and the set $\mathcal{V}$ is formed by $v_j \in [0, 1]$, $j \in \{1, \ldots, k\}$.

Our task is to minimize the Fisher information rate for embedding methods given by (15). The function $I(v) = (\mathbb{D}v + e)^T \mathbb{F}(\mathbb{D}v + e)$ can attain its minimum either at a point with a zero gradient[8] (a critical point) or on the boundary of $\mathcal{V}$. We now derive a set of linear equations for the set of all possible critical points. This approach will be used in Section 5 to prove that ternary ± 1 embedding is asymptotically optimal within the class of tridiagonal embedding in spatial domain.

For our parametrization, the gradient w.r.t. every parameter v_j can be expressed as

$$\frac{\partial}{\partial v_j} I(v) = \frac{\partial}{\partial v_j}(\mathbb{D}v + e)^T \mathbb{F}(\mathbb{D}v + e) = 2(\mathbb{D}_{\bullet j})^T \mathbb{F}(\mathbb{D}v + e),$$

where $\mathbb{D}_{\bullet j}$ is the jth column of matrix $\mathbb{D}$. Because every possible candidate v_0 for the optimal parameters must satisfy $(\partial/\partial v_j)I(v)|_{v=v_0} = 0$ for every $j \in \{1, \ldots, k\}$, all critical points are solutions of the following linear system

$$\mathbb{D}^T \mathbb{F} \mathbb{D} v = -\mathbb{D}^T \mathbb{F} e. \tag{16}$$

If this system has a unique solution $v_0 \in \mathcal{V}$, then v_0 corresponds to matrix $\mathbb{C}$ achieving the global minimum of the Fisher information rate, which corresponds to the best MI embedding method w.r.t. $\mathcal{V}$ and a given MC cover source.

5   Experiments

In the previous section, we outlined two strategies for maximizing the root rate for practical stegosystems. This section presents specific results when these strategies are applied to stegosystems operating on 8-bit gray-scale images represented in the spatial domain. Although images are two dimensional objects with spatial dependencies in both directions, we represent them in a row-wise fashion as a first-order Markov Chain over $\mathcal{X} = \{0, \ldots, 255\}$. The MC model represents the first and simplest step of capturing pixel dependencies while still retaining the important advantage of being analytically tractable. Then, we adopt a parametric model for the transition probability matrix of this Markov cover source and show that it is a good fit for the empirical transition probability matrix $\mathbb{A}$ estimated from a large number of natural images. We use the analytic model to evaluate the root rate (12) of several stegosystems obtained by a convex combinations of known methods. Finally, we show that the optimal embedding algorithm that modifies cover elements by at most 1 is very close to ± 1 embedding.

In principle, in practice we could calculate the Fisher information rate using equation (13) with an empirical matrix $\mathbb{A}$ estimated from a large number of

---

[8] Note that the semidefiniteness of $\mathbb{F}$ guarantees that the extremum must be a minimum.

images. However, this approach may give misleading results because (13) is quite sensitive to small perturbations of a_{ij} with a small value (observe that $I = +\infty$ if $a_{ij} = 0$). We do not expect this to be an issue in practice since rare transitions between distant states are probable but content dependent, which makes them difficult to be utilized for steganalysis. Because small values of a_{ij} can not be accurately estimated in practice, we represent the matrix $\mathbb{A}$ with the following parametric model

$$a_{ij} = \frac{1}{Z_i} e^{-(|i-j|/\tau)^\gamma}, \qquad (17)$$

where $Z_i = \sum_{j=1}^{256} e^{-(|i-j|/\tau)^\gamma}$ is the normalization constant. The parameter γ controls the shape of the distribution, whereas τ controls its "width." The model parameters were found in the logarithmic domain using the least square fit between (17) and its empirical estimate. To validate this model, we carried out the least square fit separately for three image databases: never compressed images taken by several digital cameras[9] (CAMRAW), digital scans[10] (NRCS), and decompressed JPEG images[11] (NRCS-JPEG). Figure 2 shows the comparison between the empirical matrix $\mathbb{A}$ estimated from the CAMRAW database and the corresponding fit. Although this model cannot capture some important macroscopic properties of natural images, such as pixel saturations, it remains analytically tractable and is valid for many natural images.

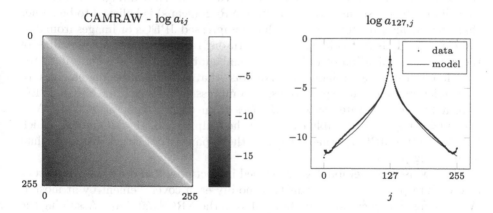

Fig. 2. Left: plot of the empirical matrix $\mathbb{A}$ estimated from CAMRAW database in log domain. Right: comparison of the 128th row of matrix $\mathbb{A}$ estimated from the same database with the analytic model (17).

The left part of Figure 3 shows the root rate (14), $r(\lambda)$, for a convex combination of LSB and ± 1 embedding, $\lambda \in [0, 1]$, for different image sources. The higher

---

[9] Expanded version of CAMERA_RAW database from [18] with 4547 8-bit images.

[10] Contains 2375 raw scans of negatives coming from the USDA Natural Resources Conservation Service (http://photogallery.nrcs.usda.gov).

[11] Images from NRCS database compressed with JPEG quality factor 70.

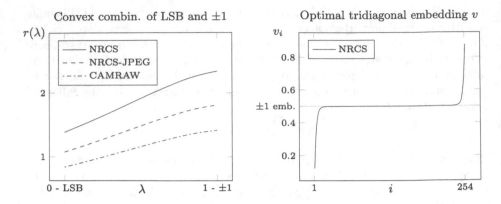

Fig. 3. Left: the root rate $r(\lambda) = \alpha_{MAX}/(\beta_{MAX}\sqrt{I})$ of a convex combination of LSB and ± 1 embedding for different image sources. Right: optimal parameters $v = (v_1, \ldots, v_{254})$ of MI embedding (15) minimizing the Fisher information rate while modifying cover elements by at most 1. The difference between ± 1 embedding and optimal MI embedding is due to boundary effects that vanish as $N \to \infty$.

the root rate $r(\lambda)$, the better the stegosystem. The results are consistent with the thesis that ± 1 embedding is less detectable than LSB embedding. Similarly, the capacity of stegosystems with covers from NRCS (scans) is believed to be higher than the capacity of stegosystem with decompressed JPEGs or images from digital cameras. This fact is in agreement with our result obtained for all values of the convex combination of LSB and ± 1 embedding and we attribute it to the fact that scans contain a higher level of noise that masks embedding changes. In contradiction with our expectations, decompressed JPEGs from NRCS-JPEG have a higher root rate than raw images from digital cameras (CAMRAW). This phenomenon is probably caused by the simplicity of the MC model, which fails to capture JPEG artifacts because they span across larger distances than neighboring pixels.

We now use the methodology described in Section 4.2 and maximize the root rate with respect to stegosystems that modify each cover element by at most 1. We do so for the cover model fit obtained from the NRCS database. Assuming the embedding operation is binary, it can embed one bit per cover element. Thus, it is sufficient to find the MI embedding that attains the minimum Fisher information rate. We use the parametrization from Example 1 and solve the system of equations (16). This system has only one solution $v = (v_1, \ldots, v_{254}) \in \mathcal{V} = [0, 1]^{254}$ and thus it represents MI embedding with minimum Fisher information rate. This solution is shown in the right part of Figure 3 along with the representation of the ± 1 embedding operation. The optimal MI embedding differs from ± 1 embedding only at the boundary of the dynamic range. This is due to the finite number of states in the MC model. We experimentally verified that the relative number of states with $|v_i - 0.5| \geq \delta$ tends to zero for a range of $\delta > 0$ as $N \to \infty$ for fixed parameters of the analytic model.[12] Thus, the boundary effect is negligible for large N. This suggests that the loss in capacity when using ± 1 embedding algorithm is negligible for large N or, in other words, ± 1 embedding is asymptotically optimal.

6   Conclusion

In sharp contrast with the well established fact that the steganographic capacity of perfectly secure stegosystems increases linearly with the number of cover elements, n, a recently derived result states that steganographic capacity of a quite wide class of imperfect stegosystems is only proportional to $\sqrt{n}$. The communication rate of imperfect stegosystems is thus non-informative because it tends to zero with n. Instead, an appropriate measure of capacity is the constant of proportionality in front of $\sqrt{n}$, for which we coin the term the *root rate* whose unit is bit per square root of cover size per square root of KL divergence. The root rate is shown to be inversely proportional to the square root of the Fisher information rate of the stegosystem. Adopting a Markov model for the cover source, we derive an analytic formula for the root rate with Fisher information rate expressible as a quadratic form defined by the cover transition probability matrix evaluated at a vector fully determined by the embedding operation. This analytic form is important as it enables us to compare the capacity of imperfect stegosystems as well as optimize their embedding operation (maximize the root rate). We fit a parametric model through the empirical transition probability matrix for neighboring pixels of real images and use this model to compute and compare the root rate of known steganographic schemes and their convex combinations. In agreement with results previously established experimentally using blind steganalyzers, our analysis indicates that ternary ± 1 embedding is more secure than LSB embedding and it is also optimal among all embedding methods that modify pixels by at most 1. Furthermore, by analyzing image databases of raw images from different sources, we established that the root rate is larger for images with higher noise level as is to be expected. Among the surprising results of our effort, we point out the fact that the root rate for ± 1 embedding is only about twice larger than for LSB embedding, which contrasts with the fact that current best steganalyzers for LSB embedding are markedly more accurate than the best steganalyzers of ± 1 embedding. This hints at the existence of significantly more accurate detectors of ± 1 embedding that are yet to be found.

The results presented here offer several interesting research directions worth pursuing in the future. In particular, we may attempt to determine the embedding operation that maximizes the root rate for a given Markov cover source for a wider class of matrices $\mathbb{C}$. Additionally, we intend to extend our results to JPEG images represented in the DCT domain using appropriate analytic models.

---

[12] We believe the same to be true for all $\delta > 0$.

Acknowledgements

The work on this paper was supported by Air Force Office of Scientific Research under the research grant number FA9550-08-1-0084. The U.S. Government is authorized to reproduce and distribute reprints for Governmental purposes notwithstanding any copyright notation there on. The views and conclusions contained herein are those of the authors and should not be interpreted as necessarily representing the official policies, either expressed or implied of AFOSR or the U.S. Government.

References

1. Wang, Y., Moulin, P.: Perfectly secure steganography: Capacity, error exponents, and code constructions. IEEE Transactions on Information Theory, Special Issue on Security (June 2008)
2. Comesana, P., Pérez-Gonzáles, F.: On the capacity of stegosystems. In: Dittmann, J., Fridrich, J. (eds.) Proceedings of the 9th ACM Multimedia & Security Workshop, Dallas, TX, September 20-21, pp. 3–14 (2007)
3. Harmsen, J.J., Pearlman, W.A.: Capacity of steganographic channels. Submitted to IEEE Transactions on Information Theory (2008), http://arxiv.org/abs/0810.4171
4. Filler, T., Fridrich, J., Ker, A.D.: The square root law of steganographic capacity for Markov covers. In: Delp, E.J., Wong, P.W., Memon, N., Dittmann, J. (eds.) Proceedings SPIE, Electronic Imaging, Security and Forensics of Multimedia XI, San Jose, CA, January 18-21 (2009)
5. Ker, A.D., Pevný, T., Kodovský, J., Fridrich, J.: The square root law of steganographic capacity. In: Ker, A., Dittmann, J., Fridrich, J. (eds.) Proceedings of the 10th ACM Multimedia & Security Workshop, Oxford, UK, September 22-23, pp. 107–116 (2008)
6. Ker, A.D.: A capacity result for batch steganography. IEEE Signal Processing Letters 14(8), 525–528 (2007)
7. Filler, T., Fridrich, J.: Complete characterization of perfectly secure stego-systems with mutually independent embedding operation. In: Proceedings IEEE, International Conference on Acoustics, Speech, and Signal Processing, Taipei, Taiwan, April 19-24 (2009)
8. Ker, A.D.: Estimating steganographic Fisher information in real images. In: Katzenbeisser, S., Sadeghi, A.-R. (eds.) IH 2009. LNCS, vol. 5806, pp. 73–88. Springer, Heidelberg (2009)
9. Kodovský, J., Fridrich, J., Pevný, T.: Statistically undetectable JPEG steganography: Dead ends, challenges, and opportunities. In: Dittmann, J., Fridrich, J. (eds.) Proceedings of the 9th ACM Multimedia & Security Workshop, Dallas, TX, September 20-21, pp. 3–14 (2007)
10. Doob, J.L.: Stochastic processes, 1st edn. Wiley, New York (1953)
11. Sullivan, K., Madhow, U., Manjunath, B., Chandrasekaran, S.: Steganalysis for Markov cover data with applications to images. IEEE Transactions on Information Forensics and Security 1(2), 275–287 (2006)
12. Sidorov, M.: Hidden Markov models and steganalysis. In: Dittmann, J., Fridrich, J. (eds.) Proceedings of the 6th ACM Multimedia & Security Workshop, Magdeburg, Germany, September 20-21, pp. 63–67 (2004)

13. Cachin, C.: An information-theoretic model for steganography. In: Aucsmith, D. (ed.) IH 1998. LNCS, vol. 1525, pp. 306–318. Springer, Heidelberg (1998)
14. Ker, A.D.: The ultimate steganalysis benchmark? In: Dittmann, J., Fridrich, J. (eds.) Proceedings of the 9th ACM Multimedia & Security Workshop, Dallas, TX, September 20-21, pp. 141–148 (2007)
15. Kay, S.M.: Fundamentals of Statistical Signal Processing, Detection Theory, vol. II. Prentice-Hall, Englewood Cliffs (1998)
16. Filler, T.: Important properties of normalized KL-divergence under HMC model. Technical report, DDE Lab, SUNY Binghamton (2008), http://dde.binghamton.edu/filler/kl-divergence-hmc.pdf
17. Fridrich, J., Goljan, M.: Digital image steganography using stochastic modulation. In: Delp, E.J., Wong, P.W. (eds.) Proceedings SPIE, Electronic Imaging, Security, Steganography, and Watermarking of Multimedia Contents V, Santa Clara, CA, January 21-24, vol. 5020, pp. 191–202 (2003)
18. Goljan, M., Fridrich, J., Holotyak, T.: New blind steganalysis and its implications. In: Delp, E.J., Wong, P.W. (eds.) Proceedings SPIE, Electronic Imaging, Security, Steganography, and Watermarking of Multimedia Contents VIII, San Jose, CA, January 16-19, vol. 6072, pp. 1–13 (2006)
19. Filler, T.: Fisher information determines capacity of ε-secure steganography - proofs. Technical report, SUNY Binghamton (2009), http://dde.binghamton.edu/filler/pdf/Fill09ihwproofs.pdf

Appendix

Proof of Theorem 2: Here, we only present the main idea of the proof, leaving all technical details to the report [19]. The decomposition of the sequence $I_n(0)/n$ to a quadratic form and its properties can be obtained directly from the definition of Fisher information

$$
\frac{1}{n}I_n(0) = \frac{\ln 2}{n}\frac{\partial^2}{\partial\beta^2}d_n(\beta)\Big|_{\beta=0} =
$$

$$
= -\sum_{(i,j)}\sum_{(k,l)}\frac{\ln 2}{n\ln 2}E_P\Big[\underbrace{\Big(\frac{\partial^2}{\partial b_{ij}b_{kl}}\ln Q_\beta(Y_1^n)\Big|_{\mathbb{B}=\mathbb{I}}\Big)}_{\triangleq g(Y_1^n,i,j,k,l)}\Big]\underbrace{\Big(\frac{\partial b_{ij}}{\partial\beta}\Big|_{\beta=0}\Big)}_{=c_{ij}}\underbrace{\Big(\frac{\partial b_{kl}}{\partial\beta}\Big|_{\beta=0}\Big)}_{=c_{kl}}.
$$

The derivatives of the log-likelihood are evaluated at $\mathbb{B} = \mathbb{I}$ because $\mathbb{B}(\beta) = \mathbb{I} + \beta\mathbb{C}$ and $\beta = 0$. By using $Q_\beta(y_1^n) = \sum_{x_1^n\in\mathcal{X}^n}P(x_1^n)Q_\beta(y_1^n|x_1^n)$, the random variable $g(Y_1^n,i,j,k,l)$ does not depend on the embedding method. This is because the derivatives are evaluated at $\mathbb{B} = \mathbb{I}$ and thus only contain the elements of the cover source transition matrix $\mathbb{A}$. The proof of the convergence of $-\frac{1}{n}E_P[g(Y_1^n,i,j,k,l)]$ to $f_{(i,j),(k,l)}$ and its closed form is more involved and is presented in the report [19]. The semidefinitness of the quadratic form follows from semidefiniteness of the Fisher information matrix $\mathbb{F}$. It is not positively definite because for an i.i.d. cover source all rows of matrix $\mathbb{F}$ coincide and are thus linearly dependent.

Fast BCH Syndrome Coding for Steganography

Rongyue Zhang, Vasiliy Sachnev, and Hyoung Joong Kim

CIST
Graduate School of Information Management and Security
Korea University
Seoul, 136-701, Korea
ryue.zh@gmail.com, bassvasys@hotmail.com, khj-@korea.ac.kr

Abstract. This paper presents an improved data hiding technique based on BCH (n, k, t) syndrome coding. The proposed data hiding method embeds data to a block of input data (for example, image pixels, wavelet or DCT coefficients, etc.) by modifying some coefficients in a block in order to null the syndrome of the BCH coding. The proposed data hiding method can hide the same amount of data with less computational time compared to the existed methods. Contributions of this paper include the reduction of both time complexity and storage complexity as well. Storage complexity is linear while that of other methods are exponential. Time complexity of our method is almost negligible and constant for any n. On the other hand, time complexity of the existing methods is exponential. Since the time complexity is constant and storage complexity is linear, it is easy to extend this method to a large n which allows us to hide data with small embedding capacity. Note that small capacities are highly recommended for steganography to survive steganalysis. The proposed scheme shows that BCH syndrome coding for data hiding is now practical ascribed to the reduced complexity.

Keywords: BCH coding, data hiding, error correction code, steganography, syndrome coding.

1 Introduction

The dramatic advance in communication and information techniques requires keeping more attention on the information security. Important information such as secret message, corporate data, and private details have to be protected from any illegal manipulation or malicious attacks. Data hiding technology can protect such valuable information from monitoring or filtering all packets over insecure networks. Steganography can enable the development of a covert channel for undetectable communication. Among many purposes, the most important issue of steganography is keeping the presence of hidden message from stego media (i.e., images in this paper). Good steganographic methods make it hard for the adversaries to tell stego images from ordinary images. Only suspicious images need to be intercepted and analyzed; otherwise, due to limited computing resources, analyzing all images is impractical and intractable for timely detection.

S. Katzenbeisser and A.-R. Sadeghi (Eds.): IH 2009, LNCS 5806, pp. 48–58, 2009.

Steganalysis techniques are as smart as steganography techniques. Thus, passing the steganalysis is getting more difficult since many powerful techniques have been developed. One possible solution is to modify cover image as little as possible. Crandall [2] introduced the matrix encoding idea to improve the embedding efficiency for steganography. F5 proposed by Westfeld [8] is the first implementation of the matrix encoding concept to reduce modification of the quantized DCT coefficients. Since F5, steganographers take the reduction of embedding capacity sincerely and coding theory into consideration. Basically the matrix encoding technique in F5 modifies at most 1 coefficient among n nonzero coefficients to hide k bits. For example, the matrix encoding method modifies at most one coefficients among seven coefficients to hide three bits like a $(7, 3)$ Hamming code. Thus, distortion of image is reduced at the cost of sacrificing the embedding capacity. Now, not all coefficients have to be modified by using $(n, k, 1)$ code where $n = 2^k - 1$. Modified matrix encoding (MME) [5] uses $(n, k, 2)$ code where one more coefficients may be changed in each group compared with the matrix encoding. Main concept of the matrix encoding technique is "the less number of modification to the DCT coefficients, the less amount of distortion in the image."

Later, Schönfeld and Winkler [6] find a way to hide data using more powerful error correction code. They use the structured BCH codes with syndrome coding for data embedding. Schönfeld and Winkler introduce two ways for computing syndrome. Embedding based on the classic approach by finding a coset leader using a parity check matrix H as needed for matrix encoding, is complex and time consuming. Second approach uses a generator polynomial $g(x)$ to find a balanced solution between low embedding complexity and high embedding efficiency. Schönfeld and Winkler [6] show that the second approach is way less complex than the the first approach based on H. They reduce the embedding complexity further by syndrome coding based on H combined with look-up tables. Look-up table approaches reduce time complexity considerably compared to the classic approach based on exhaustive search. Even with their dramatic reduction of complexity, the BCH coding approach is still too slow to be used for real-time applications when n is large. Larger n is desirable from the steganographic point of view because embedding efficiency is better.

To reduce the time complexity further, an advanced way to find roots for embedding to syndrome code over Galois field is presented in this paper. The proposed method can easily find coset leaders of the BCH code using roots of quadratic and cubic polynomials in the Galois field. The roots are calculated before embedding and stored in the look-up tables. Thus, this method does not require exhaustive search to find the roots. Note that the look-up table size for (n, k, t) BCH codes of Schönfeld and Winkler is 2^k [6,7] while our size is just n where $2^k \gg n$. It is obvious that our approach has significant advantage in terms of storage complexity over their methods. In addition, time complexity of their methods depends on the magnitude of n and grows exponentially. Thus, their method is feasible only for small n. However, in our scheme, the time complexity is independent of n. Thus, our method can hide data much faster than the techniques proposed by Schönfeld and Winkler [6,7].

The paper is organized as follows. Section 2 presents the computation on the Galois field for quadratic and cubic polynomial and preprocessing steps. Section 3 presents the data hiding procedure using syndrome code based on the computation in the Galois field. The experimental results are presented in Section 4. Section 5 concludes this paper.

2   BCH Syndrome Coding for Embedding

Binary BCH (n, k, t) codes can correct up to t errors, where n is the codeword length and k is the code dimension. The BCH code(n, k, t) with parity check matrix H is described as follows:

$$H = \begin{bmatrix} 1 & \alpha & \alpha^2 & \alpha^3 & \cdots & \alpha^{n-1} \\ 1 & (\alpha^3) & (\alpha^3)^2 & (\alpha^3)^3 & \cdots & (\alpha^3)^{n-1} \\ & & & \vdots & & \\ 1 & (\alpha^{2t-1}) & (\alpha^{2t-1})^2 & (\alpha^{2t-1})^3 & \cdots & (\alpha^{2t-1})^{n-1} \end{bmatrix}, \quad (1)$$

where α is a primitive element in $GF(2^m)$. A block of binary data, e.g., LSB values of cover data, $\{v_0, v_1, \cdots, v_{n-1}\}$ over GF(2) can be represented by a polynomial of X over GF(2^m) such as $\mathbf{v}(X) = v_0 + v_1 X + v_2 X^2 + \cdots + v_{n-1} X^{n-1}$. Embedding message $\mathbf{m}$ into the cover data $\mathbf{v}$ produces the stego data $\mathbf{r}$ which is represented as $\mathbf{r}(X) = r_0 + r_1 X + r_2 X^2 + \cdots + r_{n-1} X^{n-1}$. The relation between $\mathbf{m}$ and $\mathbf{r}$ can be expressed as a matrix form as follows:

$$\mathbf{m} = \mathbf{r} \cdot H^T. \quad (2)$$

Decoder also use Equation (2) to extract message from the stego data. By hiding message, some of the cover data bits are flipped from 0 to 1 and vice versa. Let $\mathbf{e}(X)$ be the flip pattern that represents which bit positions are flipped. As a result, stego data is modified according to the flip pattern as follows:

$$\mathbf{r}(X) = \mathbf{v}(X) + \mathbf{e}(X). \quad (3)$$

From Equations (2) and (3), we have

$$\mathbf{m} - \mathbf{v} \cdot H^T = \mathbf{e} \cdot H^T. \quad (4)$$

The left-hand side of Equation (4) is called syndrome $\mathbf{S}$. In other words, the syndrome is expressed as follows:

$$\mathbf{S} = \mathbf{m} - \mathbf{v} \cdot H^T \quad (5)$$

or, equivalently

$$\mathbf{S} = \mathbf{e} \cdot H^T. \quad (6)$$

From the steganographic point of view, our objective is to find a minimal number of flips of $\mathbf{e}(X)$ satisfying Equation (6) in order to decrease distortion. This is the syndrome coding. Data hiding by BCH coding solves Equation (6) based on the vector $\mathbf{e}$. The solution shows the proper positions of the elements in vector $\mathbf{v}(X)$ to be modified in order to hide message $\mathbf{m}$ to vector $\mathbf{v}(X)$. The stego vector $\mathbf{r}(X)$ is calculated according to Equation (3). The hidden message can be recovered from stego vector $\mathbf{r}(X)$ using Equation (2).

2.1 Framework of Our BCH Syndrome Coding

Flip pattern contains the location information where bits are flipped by data hiding. Assume that the flip pattern $\mathbf{e}(X)$ has ν flips in locations $(j_1, j_2, \cdots, j_\nu)$ which are the indexes of the coefficients to be modified for hiding message $\mathbf{m}$. Based on this location information, the flip pattern can be expressed as follows:

$$\mathbf{e}(X) = X^{j_1} + X^{j_2} + \cdots + X^{j_\nu}, \tag{7}$$

where $0 \le j_1 < j_2 < \cdots < j_\nu < n$. From Equations (1), (6) and (7), obtain the following set of equations:

$$\begin{aligned} S_1 &= \alpha^{j_1} + \alpha^{j_2} + \cdots + \alpha^{j_\nu} \\ S_2 &= (\alpha^{j_1})^3 + (\alpha^{j_2})^3 + \cdots + (\alpha^{j_\nu})^3 \\ &\vdots \\ S_t &= (\alpha^{j_1})^{2t-1} + (\alpha^{j_2})^{2t-1} + \cdots + (\alpha^{j_\nu})^{2t-1} \end{aligned} \tag{8}$$

where $\alpha^{j_1}, \alpha^{j_2}, \cdots, \alpha^{j_\nu}$ are unknown values.

Solution of the steganographic problem is getting $\alpha_1^j, \alpha^{j_2}, \cdots, \alpha^{j_\nu}$. The powers $j_1, j_2, \cdots, j_\nu$ refer to the indexes of the coefficients to be modified in vector $\mathbf{e}(X)$ (see Equation (7)). In general, the set of Equations (8) has 2^k possible solutions which form a coset. Each solution may have a different flip pattern. The solution which has the flip pattern with the smallest number of flips is called coset leader.

Determine α^{j_l} for $l = 1, 2, \cdots, \nu$ from the syndrome components S_i. For convenience' sake, assume that

$$\beta_l = \alpha^{j_l} \tag{9}$$

where $1 \le l \le \nu$, and j_l is a lth flip location number. For example, assume that there are three flips like $[1\ 1\ 0\ 0\ 0\ 0\ 1]$ in a flip pattern, j_1 is 0, j_2 is 1, and j_3 is 6.

Express a set of equations as follows:

$$\begin{aligned} S_1 &= \beta_1 + \beta_2 + \cdots + \beta_\nu \\ S_2 &= \beta_1{}^3 + \beta_2{}^3 + \cdots + \beta_\nu{}^3 \\ &\vdots \\ S_t &= \beta_1{}^{2t-1} + \beta_2{}^{2t-1} + \cdots + \beta_\nu{}^{2t-1} \end{aligned} \tag{10}$$

Note that Equations (8) and (6) are the same except the variables. Define a new polynomial as follows:

$$\sigma(X) = (X + \beta_1)(X + \beta_2) \cdots (X + \beta_\nu) = X^\nu + \sigma_1 X^{\nu-1} + \cdots + \sigma_\nu \tag{11}$$

The roots of $\sigma(X)$ are $\beta = \{\beta_1, \beta_2, ..., \beta_\nu\}$. Here, $\sigma(X)$ is called flip location polynomial. In order to find roots β, the coefficients of the $\sigma(X)$ must be determined. The relationship between coefficients of $\sigma(X)$ and β_ls is represented as follows:

$$\sigma_1 = \beta_1 + \beta_2 + \cdots + \beta_\nu$$
$$\sigma_2 = \beta_1\beta_2 + \beta_2\beta_3 + \cdots + \beta_{\nu-1}\beta_\nu$$
$$\vdots \tag{12}$$
$$\sigma_\nu = \beta_1\beta_2 \cdots \beta_\nu$$

The *Newton's identities* for β and syndrome S are derived as follows:

$$S_1 + \sigma_1 = 0$$
$$S_2 + \sigma_1 S_1^2 + \sigma_2 S_1 + \sigma_3 = 0$$
$$S_3 + \sigma_1 S_1^4 + \sigma_2 S_2 + \sigma_3 S_1^2 + \sigma_4 S_1 + \sigma_5 = 0 \tag{13}$$
$$\vdots$$

Again, a set of equations in Equation (13) may have many solutions because they are under-determined. However, objective of steganography is to find the solution for $\sigma(X)$ with minimal degree. This $\sigma(X)$ will produce the flip pattern with minimal number of flips.

Once the $\sigma(X)$ is determined, the next step is to find the roots β. The roots of $\sigma(X)$ can be easily found by using Chien's search method [1] based on substituting $1, \alpha, \alpha^2, \cdots, \alpha^{n-1}$, where $n = 2^m - 1$ from $\sigma(X)$. But, when m is getting large, the search area rapidly scales up by 2^m, and, as a result, the time to find the roots of $\sigma(X)$ is exponentially increased.

In this paper, we use BCH scheme with $t = 2$. According to Gorenstein et al [4] the maximal degree of polynomial $\sigma(X)$ can not be larger than 3 for $t = 2$. Zhao et al. [9] present an algorithm based on fast look-up tables for finding roots of the quadric or cubic polynomial $\sigma(X)$. For the integrity of article, Section 2.2 presents a brief introduction of construction the fast look-up tables and solving the quadratic and cubic polynomials.

2.2 Lookup Tables in GF(2^m)

For a pair of quadratic polynomials in GF(2^m), $f(x) = x^2 + \sigma_1 x + \sigma_2$ and $f(y) = y^2 + y + \frac{\sigma_2}{\sigma_1^2}$, where $\sigma_1 \neq 0$, if y_0 is a root of $f(y)$, then $y_0 + 1$ is another root of $f(y)$ and $x_0 = \sigma_1 y_0$ and $x_1 = \sigma_1 y_0 + \sigma_1$ are the two roots of $f(x)$. Proof can be found in appendix A. Lookup table $\mathbf{q}$ with size $n \times 1$ keeps the roots of any y_0 of the family of quadratic polynomials $f_i(y) = y^2 + y + i$, where $i = 1, 2, \cdots, 2^m - 1$ in GF(2^m). If there is no roots for some $f_i(y)$, corresponding position in the table is marked as -1. The roots of the $f(x) = x^2 + \sigma_1 x + \sigma_2$ can be easily found in the look-up table $\mathbf{q}$ in position $\frac{\sigma_2}{\sigma_1^2}$.

In case of cubic polynomials $f(x) = x^3 + \sigma_1 x^2 + \sigma_2 x + \sigma_3$ in GF(2^m), we introduce two parameters, a and b, such as $a = \sigma_1^2 + \sigma_2$ and $b = \sigma_1 \sigma_2 + \sigma_3$. We can find another cubic polynomials $f(y) = y^3 + y + \frac{b}{a^{\frac{3}{2}}}$ which is a pair of $f(x) =$

$x^3 + \sigma_1 x^2 + \sigma_2 x + \sigma_3$. If y_j $(j = 1, 2, 3)$ is a root of $f(y)$, then $x_j = a^{\frac{1}{2}} y_j + \sigma_1$ is a root of $f(x)$. Proof can be found in appendix A. Similar to the quadratic polynomial, a look-up table $\mathbf{c}$ with size $n \times 3$ keeps roots y_j $(j = 1, 2, 3)$ of the family of cubic polynomials $f_i(y) = y^3 + y + i$. If there are not three roots for some $f_i(y)$, the ith row of the table are marked as -1. The roots of the $f(x) = x^3 + \sigma_1 x^2 + \sigma_2 x + \sigma_3$ can be found in the look-up table $\mathbf{c}$ in position $\frac{b}{a^{\frac{3}{2}}}$, where $a = \sigma_1^2 + \sigma_2$ and $b = \sigma_1 \sigma_2 + \sigma_3$. In order to simplify the embedding process by flipping three coefficients, the indexes of the rows whose entries are not marked as -1 (i.e., entries having three roots) are recorded in another look-up table $\boldsymbol{\kappa}$. The size of $\boldsymbol{\kappa}$ is denoted as D, where $D = \lceil \frac{C_n^3}{2^{2k}} \rceil$. Table 1 shows relations between n and D for some small values m.

Table 1. Relations among m, n, and D with small values m

m	5	6	7	8	9
n	31	63	127	255	512
D	5	10	21	42	85

The look-up tables $\mathbf{q}$ and $\mathbf{c}$ are used for proposed embedding method. The roots in the table $\mathbf{q}$ and $\mathbf{c}$ are called basic roots.

2.3   Data Hiding Using Syndrome Coding

The proposed data hiding method is based on BCH syndrome coding (n, k, t), where the size of each block is $n = 2^m - 1$, $m = 3, 4, 5, ...$, and the embedding capacity for each block is $M_b = m \cdot t$. The proposed method uses $t = 2$ in this paper. For $t = 2$, since the BCH code (n, k, t) is quasi-orthogonal, its cover radius is 3 [4]. Thus, the Hamming weight of each coset leader is not more than 3. The maximum number of flips in $\mathbf{e}(X)$ is 3 for any possible syndrome.

For a syndrome $S = \{S_1 S_2\}$ computed by Equation (5), do the following steps (see Appendix B to know why this method works):

1) If $S = 0$, no need to change any coefficients because $\mathbf{e} = 0$ is satisfying Equation (6). Otherwise go to Step 2.
2) If $S_2 + S_1^3 = 0$, there is a vector $\mathbf{e}(X)$ which requires just one flip in order to satisfy Equation(6). The root is $\beta_1 = S_1$, the flip location is $j_1 = \log(\beta_1)$, and the flip pattern is $\mathbf{e}(X) = X^{j_1}$. Otherwise go to Step 3.
3) Check for two-flip case. Let $o = \frac{S_2 + S_1^3}{S_1^3}$ be the index in the look-up table $\mathbf{q}$. The basic root $y_1 = \mathbf{q}(o)$ can be obtained from the look-up table $\mathbf{q}$ in row o. If $y_1 \neq -1$, there is $\mathbf{e}(X)$ that requires two flips in order to satisfy Equation (6). The roots of the flip location polynomials are $\beta_1 = S_1 y_1$ and $\beta_2 = S_1 y_1 + S_1$, the flip locations are $j_1 = \log(\beta_1)$ and $j_2 = \log(\beta_2)$, and the flip pattern is $\mathbf{e}(X) = X^{j_1} + X^{j_2}$. If $y_1 = -1$, go to Step 4.
4) In case of 3 flips, there are at most D flip patterns $\mathbf{e}(X)$. For each $d = 1, 2, \cdots, D$, find $o = \boldsymbol{\kappa}(d)$. The o is the index of the look-up table $\mathbf{c}$. Get three

basic roots: $y_1 = \mathbf{c}(o,1)$, $y_2 = \mathbf{c}(o,2)$, and $y_3 = \mathbf{c}(o,3)$. Let $p = (\frac{S_1^3+S_2}{o})^{\frac{1}{3}}$, then the roots of $\mathbf{e}(X)$ are $\beta_1 = py_1 + S_1$, $\beta_2 = py_2 + S_1$ and $\beta_3 = py_3 + S_1$. Three flip locations are $j_i = \log(\beta_i)$, where $i = 1,2,3$. The flip pattern is $\mathbf{e}(X) = X^{j_1} + X^{j_2} + X^{j_3}$. After processing all d, we can get all three flip patterns $\mathbf{e}$. If only one $\mathbf{e}$ is needed, use any o from $\boldsymbol{\kappa}$, and process Step 4 for this o.

3   Comparison

The proposed scheme for data hiding method based on BCH syndrome coding is compared with that proposed by Schönfeld and Winkler [6,7]. The basic contribution of their methods are the relaxation of the classical exhaustive search methods. They achieve significant improvement over existing classical methods. However, their schemes have two significant drawbacks. These methods still require exhaustive search (i.e., 2^k rather than 2^n where $n > k$ but slightly smaller in magnitude) and time complexity grows exponentially. The numbers of necessary XOR operations for parity check matrix search and for polynomial search are shown in Table 1. For more details refer to the article [7].

Table 2. Time complexity of embedding of Schönfeld and Winkler [7] and ours

BCH scheme	Polynomial $g(x)$	Parity check matrix	Our method
(15,7,2)	2,066	1,920	
(31,21,2)	53,933	65,011,712	Three comparisons,
(63,51,2)	895,776	$\approx 10^{15}$	two table look-ups,
(127,113,2)	11,009,491	$\approx 10^{34}$	and three simple computations

The proposed method does not require exhaustive search. Lookup table size is also manageable. One look-up table for quadratic polynomial is $n \times 1$ in size, and the other look-up table for cubic polynomial is $n \times 3$. In order to hide data to one block the proposed method has to access look-up table three times and makes simple mathematical operations. These operations include computing $S_2 + S_1^3$, $o = \frac{S_2+S_1^3}{S_1^3}$, and $p = (\frac{S_2+S_1^3}{o})^{\frac{1}{3}}$ (see Section 2.3). These procedure allows up to three-bit flipping. All roots of cubic polynomials are used for flipping three bits. Similarly, all roots of quadratic polynomials are used for flipping two bits. Coset leader is used to flip bits. In case of flipping three bits, the proposed method always can find all possible positions to be modified. The proposed method has flexibility to choose the best candidates for embedding. The methods proposed by Schönfeld and Winkler [7] can not guarantee the best solution and also can not find all of them. As a result, the proposed method significantly outperforms previous BCH based data hiding method proposed by them.

4   Conclusions

Data hiding using BCH codes has been proposed by Schönfeld and Winkler [6,7]. Our paper presents an advanced method based on BCH syndrome coding and using look-up tables. Contributions of this paper include the reduction of both time complexity and storage complexity as well. Storage complexity is $O(n)$ while that of other methods are exponential such as $O(2^k)$ where $2^k \gg n$. Time complexity of our method is almost negligible and constant for any n with $t = 2$. On the other hand, time complexity of the existing methods is exponential. Since the time complexity is constant and storage complexity is linear, it is easy to extend this method to large n which allows us to hide data with small embedding capacity. Note that small capacities are highly recommended for steganography to survive steganalysis. The proposed scheme shows that BCH syndrome coding for data hiding is now practical ascribed to the reduced complexity.

Acknowledgment

This work was in part supported by ITRC and BK21 Project, Korea University and IT R&D program (Development of anonymity-based u-knowledge security technology, 2007-S001-01).

References

1. Chien, R.T.: Cyclic decoding produce for the Bose-Chaudhuri-Hocquenghem codes. IEEE Transactions on Information Theory 11, 549–557 (1965)
2. Crandall, R.: Some notes on steganography, Posted on Steganography Mailing List (1998), http://os.inf.tu-dresden.de/~westfeld/crandall.pdf
3. Fridrich, J., Goljan, M., Lisoněk, P., Soukal, D.: Writing on wet paper. IEEE Transactions on Signal Processing 53(10), part 2, 3923–3935 (2005)
4. Gorenstein, D., Peterson, W.W., Zierler, N.: Two-error correcting Bose-Chaudhuri codes are quasi-perfect. Information and Control 3, 291–294 (1960)
5. Kim, Y., Duric, Z., Richards, D.: Modified matrix encoding technique for minimal distortion steganography. In: Camenisch, J.L., Collberg, C.S., Johnson, N.F., Sallee, P. (eds.) IH 2006. LNCS, vol. 4437, pp. 314–327. Springer, Heidelberg (2007)
6. Schönfeld, D., Winkler, A.: Embedding with syndrome coding based on BCH codes. In: Proceedings of the 8th ACM Workshop on Multimedia and Security, pp. 214–223 (2006)
7. Schönfeld, D., Winkler, A.: Reducing the complexity of syndrome coding for embedding. In: Furon, T., Cayre, F., Doërr, G., Bas, P. (eds.) IH 2007. LNCS, vol. 4567, pp. 145–158. Springer, Heidelberg (2008)
8. Westfeld, A.: F5: A steganographic algorithm: High capacity despite better steganalysis. In: Moskowitz, I.S. (ed.) IH 2001. LNCS, vol. 2137, pp. 289–302. Springer, Heidelberg (2001)
9. Zhao, Z., Wu, F., Yu, S., Zhou, J.: A lookup table based fast algorithm for finding roots of quadric or cubic polynomials in the GF(2^m). Journal of Huazhong University of Science and Technology (Nature Science Edition) 33(2), 70–72 (2005)

Appendix A

Roots of quadratic polynomials in $GF(2^m)$

For a pair of quadratic polynomials in $GF(2^m)$, consider $f(x) = x^2 + \sigma_1 x + \sigma_2$ and $g(y) = y^2 + y + \frac{\sigma_2}{\sigma_1^2}$, where $\sigma_1 \neq 0$.

Proposition 1: If y_0 is a root of $g(y)$, then $y_0 + 1$ is another root of the $g(y)$.

Proof:

$$g(y_0 + 1) = (y_0 + 1)^2 + (y_0 + 1) + \frac{\sigma_2}{\sigma_1^2}$$
$$= y_0^2 + 2y_0 + 1 + y_0 + 1 + \frac{\sigma_2}{\sigma_1^2}$$
$$= y_0^2 + y_0 + \frac{\sigma_2}{\sigma_1^2}$$
$$= g(y_0).$$

Proposition 2: If y_0 is a root of $g(y)$, then $x_0 = \sigma_1 y_0$ and $x_1 = \sigma_1 y_0 + \sigma_1$ are the two roots of the $f(x)$.

Proof:

$$f(x_0) = (x_0)^2 + \sigma_1 x_0 + \sigma_2$$
$$= (\sigma_1 y_0)^2 + \sigma_1(\sigma_1 y_0) + \sigma_2$$
$$= \sigma_1^2 y_0^2 + \sigma_1^2 y_0 + \sigma_2$$
$$= \sigma_1^2 (y_0^2 + y_0 + \frac{\sigma_2}{\sigma_1^2})$$
$$= \sigma_1^2 g(y_0).$$

Roots of Cubic Polynomials in the $GF(2^m)$

For the cubic polynomials $f(x) = x^3 + \sigma_1 x^2 + \sigma_2 x + \sigma_3$ in the $GF(2^m)$, where $a = \sigma_1^2 + \sigma_2$ and $b = \sigma_1 \sigma_2 + \sigma_3$, we can find other two pair cubic polynomials $g(y) = y^3 + ay + b$ and $h(z) = z^3 + z + \frac{b}{a^{\frac{3}{2}}}$.

Proposition 3: If y_0 is a root of $g(y)$, then $x_0 = y_0 + \sigma_1$ is a root of $f(x)$.

Proof:

$$f(x_0) = (y_0 + \sigma_1)^3 + \sigma_1(y_0 + \sigma_1)^2 + \sigma_2(y_0 + \sigma_1) + \sigma_3$$
$$= y_0^3 + 4\sigma_1 y_0^2 + (5\sigma_1^2 + \sigma_2)y_0 + 2\sigma_1^3 + \sigma_1\sigma_2 + \sigma_3$$
$$= y_0^3 + (\sigma_1^2 + \sigma_2)y_0 + \sigma_1\sigma_2 + \sigma_3$$
$$= y_0^3 + ay_0 + b$$
$$= g(y_0).$$

Proposition 4: If z_0 is a root of $h(z)$, then $y_0 = a^{\frac{1}{2}} z_0$ is a root of $g(y)$.

Proof:

$$
\begin{aligned}
g(y_0) &= (a^{\frac{1}{2}} z_0)^3 + a(a^{\frac{1}{2}} z_0) + b \\
&= a^{\frac{3}{2}} z_0^3 + a^{\frac{3}{2}} z_0 + b \\
&= a^{\frac{3}{2}} (z_0^3 + z_0 + \frac{b}{a^{\frac{3}{2}}}) \\
&= a^{\frac{3}{2}} h(z_0).
\end{aligned}
$$

Proposition 3 and **Proposition 4** state that if any of z_i $(i = 1, 2, 3)$ is a root of $h(z)$, then $x_i = a^{\frac{1}{2}} z_i + \sigma_1$ is a root of $f(x)$.

Appendix B

The *Newton's identities* for $t = 2$ is described as follow:

$$
\begin{aligned}
S_1 + \sigma_1 &= 0, \\
S_2 + \sigma_1 S_1^2 + \sigma_2 S_1 + \sigma_3 &= 0.
\end{aligned} \tag{14}
$$

Data hiding by flipping one coefficient: For flipping one coefficient, the value of ν should be 1. The flip location polynomials in Equation (11) becomes $\sigma(X) = X + \sigma_1$. This implies $\sigma_2 = \sigma_3 = 0$ in Equation (14). Then, Equation (14) becomes

$$
\begin{aligned}
S_1 + \sigma_1 &= 0, \\
S_2 + S_1^3 &= 0.
\end{aligned} \tag{15}
$$

Thus, if $S_2 + S_1^3 = 0$, the vector $\mathbf{e}(X)$ has only one flip that satisfies Equation (6) (see Equation (15)). The corresponding root of $\sigma(X)$ is $\beta_1 = S_1$. The flip location is $j_1 = \log(\beta_1)$. The flip pattern is $\mathbf{e}(X) = X^{j_1}$.

Data hiding by flipping 2 coefficients: In this case, $\nu = 2$. The flip location polynomials in Equation (11) is denoted as:

$$
\sigma(X) = X^2 + \sigma_1 X + \sigma_2. \tag{16}
$$

Then, Equation (14) becomes

$$
\begin{aligned}
S_1 + \sigma_1 &= 0, \\
S_2 + \sigma_1 S_1^2 + \sigma_2 S_1 &= 0.
\end{aligned} \tag{17}
$$

According to Equation (17) the index o is computed as follows: $o = \frac{\sigma_2}{\sigma_1^2} = \frac{S_2 + S_1^3}{S_1^3}$

The basic roots $y_1 = \mathbf{q}(o)$ are obtained from the quadratic table $\mathbf{q}$ by using index o. Roots of (16) are $\beta_1 = S_1 y_1$ and $\beta_2 = S_1 y_1 + S_1$. The flip locations are $j_i = \log(\beta_i)$, where $i = 1, 2$, and the flip pattern is $\mathbf{e}(X) = X^{j_1} + X^{j_2}$.

Data hiding by flipping 3 coefficients: $\nu = 3$. The flip location polynomials in Equation (11) becomes

$$\sigma(X) = X^3 + \sigma_1 X^2 + \sigma_2 X + \sigma_3. \tag{18}$$

Equation (14) have three unknown variables with two equations that provides one dimensional degree of freedom, so there are more than one solution.

In order to get solutions, calculate the index o of the cubic roots table as follows:

$$o = \frac{b}{a^{\frac{3}{2}}}, \tag{19}$$

where $a = \sigma_1^2 + \sigma_2$ and $b = \sigma_1\sigma_2 + \sigma_3$, The three basic roots are obtained from the lookup table $\mathbf{c}$, $y_i = \mathbf{c}(o, i)$, where $i = 1, 2, 3$. From Equation (19), get $a^{\frac{1}{2}} = (\frac{b}{o})^{\frac{1}{3}}$, denote $p = a^{\frac{1}{2}}$. From Equation (14), get $b = S_1^3 + S_2$. Thus, the roots of Equation (18) are $\beta_i = py_i + S_1$, where $i = 1, 2, 3$.

Embedding Ratio Estimating for Each Bit Plane of Image

Chunfang Yang, Xiangyang Luo, and Fenlin Liu

Zhengzhou Information Science and Technology Institute,
Zhengzhou 450002, China
chunfangyang@126.com, liufenlin@vip.sina.com, xiangyangluo@126.com

Abstract. MSLB replacement steganography has attracted researchers' attentions. However, existing steganalysis methods for MLSB replacement steganography have been just designed under the assumption that the embedding ratios in all stego bit planes are equal. Therefore, when the messages are embedded into different bit planes with different lengths independently, a new, principled method is introduced to estimate the embedding ratio in each stego bit plane based on a sample pair model. The new method estimates the embedding ratio in each bit plane in sequence according to the priority of each bit plane's significance. A series of experiments show that the presented steganalysis method has significantly smaller bias than applying SPA method, a typical steganalysis for LSB steganography, to estimate the embedding ratio in each bit plane directly.

1 Introduction

Research on hiding data into digital multimedia objects, such as images, audios, and videos, has advanced considerably over the past decade. Much of this work has been focused on steganography and steganalysis. Steganography refers to the science of covert communication, and steganalysis is the opposite of steganography. Nowadays, a large number of steganography tools have been developed based on replacement of the least significant bit (LSB) plane with secret message because of its extreme simplicity. The widespread availability of these tools has led to increased interests in steganalysis techniques for LSB replacement. Therefore, there have existed many detection methods to judge the presence of LSB replacement and estimate the embedding ratio, such as RS (regular and singular groups) method [1], DIH (difference image histogram) method [2], SPA (sample pair analysis) method [3], and some improved variant [4, 5] of these representative steganalysis methods. However, when the hidden message in stego images is very short (e.g. embedding ratio is less than 2%), these methods are not very effective. Additionally, their estimation errors can be further reduced to improve the accuracy of payload locations estimation [6].

Therefore, Ker [7] put all of above to a general framework called structural steganalysis, which has been applied to the case of pixel groups of size three [7] and four [8]. The obtained detectors outperform previous known detectors when

S. Katzenbeisser and A.-R. Sadeghi (Eds.): IH 2009, LNCS 5806, pp. 59–72, 2009.

applying them to images with short hidden message, but are inferior to others for larger message and substantially more complicated than the previous generations of structural detectors. S. Dumitrescu et al. [9] exploited the similar principle to propose a framework which can estimate the embedding ratio robustly for a class of digital media contents, and this framework has been applied to the case of pixel groups of size three. In addition, Fridrich et al. [10] defined a weighted stego image to design a different detector which outperforms structural steganalysis for large message and is known as "WS (weighted steganalysis)". Ker and Böhme [11] improved the WS estimator by upgrading its three components: cover pixel prediction, least-squares weighting, and bias correction, and derived the specialized WS estimator for sequentially-placed payload.

But all of above were just designed for LSB steganography specifically, it can not be expected that they can give correct answers for the size of payload in LSB plane when embedding is also carried out in other-LSB planes ([12] has given the reason for 2LSB embedding). Some relevant works have reported that secret message can not only be embedded in LSBs, but also be embedded in multiple least-significant bits (MLSBs) in [13, 14]. This educes an apparent question—how to estimate the embedding ratio in MLSBs. Especially when the secret messages embedded into different bit planes have different lengths, how to estimate the embedding ratio for each bit plane?

There have been some steganalysis methods proposed for embedding equal ratio of message into MLSB planes [12, 15-19]. And they were mainly designed for two distinct MLSB steganography paradigms: (1) randomly select fixed number of bits from the l LSB planes of an image and replace them with the message bits (IMLSB steganography, "I" means the messages are embedded into each bit plane independently.); (2) randomly select fixed number of pixels and replace their l LSBs with the message fragments with size of l (TMLSB steganography, "T" means this embedding paradigm is typical.). X. Yu et al. [15] extended the WS steganalysis method, obtaining "l-WS" method, to detect MLSB steganography for fixed l, where l denotes the number of least-significant bit planes. In [12], Ker considered two distinct embedding paradigms to embed data into the 2LSB planes, and extended the method of "structural steganalysis" for them. The extended methods were called as "I2Couples" and "2Couples" respectively. In [16, 17], the authors were enlightened by SPA method to derive a quartic equation to estimate the ratio of message embedded by I2LSB steganography. In [18], X. Yu et al. fitted the deviation of a statistic after embedding from it of cover as a quadratic equation to estimate the embedding ratio of above two distinct MLSB steganography paradigms. The Ref. [19] modeled the MLSB replacement operation, and then two novel steganalysis frameworks were designed for above two steganography paradigms. Surely, the other steganalysis methods, such as RS, DIH, SPA and universal blind steganalysis [20], also can detect the MLSB steganography, but can not estimate the embedding ratio in each bit plane when the secret messages embedded into different bit planes have different lengths. In this paper, we denote this steganography paradigm as "ID-MLSB steganography", where "I" means the independence of the effects on different bit planes, and "D" denotes that the message lengths in different bit planes are different.

In this paper, succeeding to [19], the model will be utilized to estimate the embedding ratio for each bit plane of image. The effect of ID-MLSB steganography on each possible sample pair form will be analyzed by adopting the relationships among trace subsets. Based on the assumption that the messages embedded in lower bit planes will not influence the estimation of embedding ratios in higher bit planes, this paper will estimate the embedding ratios in higher bit planes, and then regard obtained embedding ratios as known parameters to estimate the embedding ratios in lower ones. Experimental results indicate that the new steganalysis method is more powerful than applying the SPA method in each bit plane directly.

This paper is constructed as follows. In Section 2, we will briefly introduce the sample pair models for LSB and MLSB replacement steganography. In Section 3, the steganalysis method for ID-MLSB steganography will be described. Finally, a series of experimental results with a test set of 3075 natural images are given in Section 4. And the paper is closed in Section 5 with the conclusion.

2   Sample Pair Models of LSB and MLSB Replacement

Throughout this paper, the digital signal is represented by the succession of samples $s_1, s_2, \cdots, s_N$, where the index represents the location of a sample in a digital signal, N denotes the total number of samples in a digital signal and b denotes the total number of bits in a sample. A two-tuple $\langle i, j \rangle$ is named as a sample pair, where i and j are the indexes of samples and $1 \leq i, j \leq N$. Let $\Re$ be the set of all adjacent sample pairs $\langle i, j \rangle$, $i \neq j$. Actually, the model in [19] can be built not only for pixel pairs, but also for other sample pairs such as audio sample pairs.

2.1   Sample Pair Model of LSB Replacement

In [3], for each integer m, $0 \leq m \leq 2^{b-1} - 1$, C_m denoted the trace set of $\Re$(in [3], $\Re$ was the set of all sample pairs initially) that consisted of the sample pairs whose values differed by m in the first $(b - 1)$ bits. Then the trace set C_m, $0 < m \leq 2^{b-1} - 1$, was partitioned into four trace subsets X_{2m-1}, X_{2m}, Y_{2m}, Y_{2m+1}, and the trace set C_0 was partitioned into two trace subsets X_0 and Y_1. Suppose that a random message is embedded using LSB replacement randomly with embedding ratio $2p$. Then for each sample pair, the probability that neither sample is altered is $(1 - p)^2$, the probability that either sample is altered is $p(1 - p)$, and the probability that both are altered is p^2. The alteration of either sample in a sample pair will move the sample pair into another trace subset of the same trace set. All the trace subsets and the transition relationships make up of a sample pair model of LSB replacement.

Then the equations were derived to estimate the embedding ratio of LSB replacement steganography based on above sample pair model and the hypotheses:

for the sample pair in natural images whose samples differ by $2m + 1$, the even component has approximately equivalent probability to be larger as the odd component, viz.

$$|X_{2m+1}| \approx |Y_{2m+1}|. \tag{1}$$

where $0 \leq m \leq 2^{b-1} - 2$, $|\bullet|$ denotes the cardinality of set $\bullet$.

2.2   Sample Pair Model of MLSB Replacement

It is clear that MLSB steganography only modifies the l least-significant bit planes. So [19] defined an extended trace set C_m of $\Re$ to contain the sample pairs whose values differ by m in the first $(b - l)$ bits, viz.

$$C_m = \{\langle i, j \rangle \mid |\lfloor s_i/L \rfloor - \lfloor s_j/L \rfloor| = m, i \neq j\} \tag{2}$$

where $L = 2^l$, $0 \leq m \leq \tilde{L} - 1$ and $\tilde{L} = 2^{b-l}$. And each trace set C_m can be partitioned into L^2 different trace subsets labeled by the MLSBs of sample values in the contained sample pairs as follows:

$$Q_{0,\pi_1,\pi_2} = \{\langle i, j \rangle | s_i = Lk + \pi_1, s_j = Lk + \pi_2, 0 \leq k \leq \tilde{L} - 1, 1 \leq i \neq j \leq N\}, \tag{3}$$

$$\begin{aligned} Q_{m,\pi_1,\pi_2} = \{\langle i, j \rangle | s_i = L(k - m) + \pi_1 \text{ and } s_j = Lk + \pi_2, \\ \text{or } s_i = Lk + L - 1 - \pi_1 \text{ and } s_j = L(k - m) + L - 1 - \pi_2, \\ m \leq k \leq \tilde{L} - 1, 1 \leq i \neq j \leq N\} \end{aligned} \tag{4}$$

where $1 \leq m \leq \tilde{L} - 1$, $0 \leq \pi_1, \pi_2 \leq L - 1$.

Because MLSB steganography only modifies the l least-significant bit planes, each sample pair will be modified by L^2 possible patterns which are defined as L^2 so-called modification patterns: $[0, 0]$, $[0, 1]$, ..., $[0, L\text{-}1]$, $[1, 0]$, $[1, 1]$, ..., $[1, L\text{-}1]$, ..., $[L\text{-}1, L\text{-}1]$, where the bit 1 in the i-th LSB of the first (or second) element denotes that the i-th LSB of the first (or second) sample in the sample pair is reversed, and the bit 0 denotes the unrevised case. Then, after being modified by pattern $[\pi_1, \pi_2]$, the MLSBs of a sample pair's two samples can be obtained by carrying out exclusive OR between the elements in modification pattern and the samples' MLSBs of cover sample pair. In other words, if a sample pair $\langle i, j \rangle$ belongs to the trace subset Q_{m,π_1,π_2} and is modified by pattern $[\tau_1, \tau_2]$ during MLSB embedding, the stego sample pair will belong to trace subset $Q'_{m,\pi_1 \oplus \tau_1, \pi_2 \oplus \tau_2}$. In this paper, each sample is denoted by s_i or s'_i according to that the sample is obtained from the natural or stego digital signal after MLSB steganography. The same convention is also applied to set such that Z and Z' are the sets before and after MLSB steganography.

However, given a stego signal, one can access only to the stego signal and not to the cover signal. Thus, [19] introduced another partition of $\Re$:

$$X_{Lm+u} = \{\langle i, j \rangle | |s_i - s_j| = Lm + u, \text{and } \max(s_i, s_j) \bmod L < u, 1 \leq i \neq j \leq N\}, \tag{5}$$

$$Y_{Lm+u} = \{\langle i,j \rangle || s_i - s_j | = Lm + u, \text{and} \max(s_i, s_j) \bmod L \geq u, 1 \leq i \neq j \leq N\}, \tag{6}$$

and validated the following statistical properties of digital images by empirical evidences: for any integer $m(0 \leq m \leq \tilde{L} - 2)$,

$$(L - u)|X_{Lm+u}| \approx u|Y_{Lm+u}|, \tag{7}$$

where $0 \leq u \leq L - 1$. Then the relationships between X_{Lm+u}, Y_{Lm+u} and Q_{m,π_1,π_2} were given in [19] as follows: for $0 \leq u \leq L - 1$,

$$X_{Lm+u} = \bigcup_{v=0}^{u-1} Q_{m+1,L+v-u,v}, \text{ for } 0 \leq m \leq \tilde{L} - 2; \tag{8}$$

$$Y_{Lm+u} = \bigcup_{v=u}^{L-1} Q_{m,v-u,v}, \text{ for } 1 \leq m \leq \tilde{L} - 1; \tag{9}$$

$$Y_u = \bigcup_{v=u}^{L-1} \left(Q_{0,v-u,v} \cup Q_{0,v,v-u} \right). \tag{10}$$

3 Steganalysis of Embedding in MLSBs with Different Ratios

3.1 Estimating Embedding Ratio in Each Bit Plane

When ID-MLSB steganography is carried out on a digital image, the secret message bits are embedded into the l least-significant bit planes with different embedding ratios, and in each bit plane the message bits are embedded randomly. $2p_k$ is used to denote the proportion of message length to the maximum payload of MLSB steganography in the k-th least-significant bit plane. It reflects that the size of the secret message in the k-th LSB plane equals in $2p_k N$ bits. And the message is a random sequence of bits. Then each bit in the i-th LSB plane will be modified with the probability p_k. From the definition of modification pattern, the modification pattern $[\pi_1, \pi_2]$ will occur in the l LSBs of a sample pair with probability

$$\rho_{2l}(\pi_1, \pi_2) = \rho_{2l}(\pi_1 L + \pi_2) = \prod_{k=1}^{l} q_k^{2-bit(\pi_1,k)-bit(\pi_2,k)} p_k^{bit(\pi_1,k)+bit(\pi_2,k)} \tag{11}$$

where $q_k = 1 - p_k$, $bit(\pi,k) = \lfloor \pi/2^{k-1} \rfloor \bmod 2$ denotes the k-th LSB of π.

Then the following theorem will depict the probability that a sample pair transfers from one trace subset to another under ID-MLSB steganography.

Theorem 1. *When the message is embedded into the l least-significant bit planes via ID-MLSB steganography, for $0 \le m \le \tilde{L} - 1$,*

$$Q'_{m,l} = A_l^{\otimes 2} Q_{m,l} \tag{12}$$

where $A_l = \begin{pmatrix} q_l & p_l \\ p_l & q_l \end{pmatrix} \otimes \begin{pmatrix} q_{l-1} & p_{l-1} \\ p_{l-1} & q_{l-1} \end{pmatrix} \otimes \cdots \otimes \begin{pmatrix} q_1 & p_1 \\ p_1 & q_1 \end{pmatrix}$, $A_l^{\otimes 2l}$ is the 2-th Kronecker power of matrix A_l and $Q_{m,l} = (|Q_{m,0,0}|, |Q_{m,0,1}|, \cdots, |Q_{m,L-1,L-1}|)^T$.

Proof. For $0 \le m \le \tilde{L} - 1$, let $i = \pi_1 L + \pi_2$, $j = \tau_1 L + \tau_2$. From the definition of Kronecker product and A_l,

$$A_l(\pi_1, \tau_1) = \prod_{k=1}^{l} q_k^{1-bit(\pi_1,k) \oplus bit(\tau_1,k)} p_k^{bit(\pi_1,k) \oplus bit(\tau_1,k)}$$

and

$$A_l(\pi_2, \tau_2) = \prod_{k=1}^{l} q_k^{1-bit(\pi_2,k) \oplus bit(\tau_2,k)} p_k^{bit(\pi_2,k) \oplus bit(\tau_2,k)}.$$

So

$$\begin{aligned} \mathbf{A}_l^{\otimes 2}(i,j) &= \mathbf{A}_l(\pi_1, \tau_1) \mathbf{A}_l(\pi_2, \tau_2) \\ &= \prod_{k=1}^{l} q_k^{2-bit(\pi_1 \oplus \tau_1,k) - bit(\pi_2 \oplus \tau_2,k)} p_k^{bit(\pi_1 \oplus \tau_1,k) + bit(\pi_2 \oplus \tau_2,k)} \end{aligned} \tag{13}$$

When a sample pair transfers from Q_{m,π_1,π_2} to Q'_{m,π_1,π_2} under ID-MLSB steganography, the modification pattern $[\pi_1 \oplus \tau_1, \pi_2 \oplus \tau_2]$ must occur. From (11), the probability of the occurrence of this modification pattern is

$$\rho_{2l}(\pi_1 \oplus \tau_1, \pi_2 \oplus \tau_2) = \prod_{k=1}^{l} q_k^{1-bit(\pi_1 \oplus \tau_1,k) - bit(\pi_2 \oplus \tau_2,k)} p_k^{bit(\pi_1 \oplus \tau_1,k) + bit(\pi_2 \oplus \tau_2,k)} \tag{14}$$

The equations (13) and (14) are accordant with each other. So (12) is given.

It can be seen that the matrix $\mathbf{A}_l$ is not singular except that anyone of p_k, $1 \le k \le l$, is 1/2. So the following equation can be derived from (12):

$$\mathbf{Q}_{m,l} = (\mathbf{A}_l^{-1})^{\otimes 2} \mathbf{Q}'_{m,l} \tag{15}$$

where $\mathbf{A}_l^{-1} = \dfrac{1}{\prod\limits_{k=1}^{l} (1-2p_k)} \begin{pmatrix} q_l & -p_l \\ -p_l & q_l \end{pmatrix} \otimes \begin{pmatrix} q_{l-1} & -p_{l-1} \\ -p_{l-1} & q_{l-1} \end{pmatrix} \otimes \cdots \otimes \begin{pmatrix} q_1 & -p_1 \\ -p_1 & q_1 \end{pmatrix}$. For $i = \pi_1 L + \pi_2$ and $j = \tau_1 L + \tau_2$, it follows that

$$(\mathbf{A}_l^{-1})^{\otimes 2}(i,j) = \prod_{k=1}^{l} \frac{P_k(p_k, \pi_1, \tau_1, \pi_2, \tau_2)}{(1-2p_k)^2}. \tag{16}$$

where $P_k(p_k, \pi_1, \tau_1, \pi_2, \tau_2)$
$= (1-p_k)^{2-bit(\pi_1 \oplus \tau_1,k) - bit(\pi_2 \oplus \tau_2,k)} (-p_k)^{bit(\pi_1 \oplus \tau_1,k) + bit(\pi_2 \oplus \tau_2,k)}.$

Hereafter, $\mathbf{A}(i,:)$ and $\mathbf{A}(:,j)$ denote the i-th row vector and j-th column vector of matrix $\mathbf{A}$ respectively. And the following equation can be derived from (15):

$$|Q_{m,\pi_1,\pi_2}| = (\mathbf{A}_l^{-1})^{\otimes 2}(\pi_1 L + \pi_2, :)\mathbf{Q}'_{m,l}. \tag{17}$$

Applying (17) in (8) - (10) respectively, one can obtain

$$\prod_{k=1}^{l}(1-2p_k)^2|X_{Lm+u}| = \sum_{v=0}^{u-1}(\mathbf{A}_l^{-1})^{\otimes 2}(L(L+v-u)+v,:)\mathbf{Q}'_{m+1,l}, 0 \le m \le \tilde{L}-2, \tag{18}$$

$$\prod_{k=1}^{l}(1-2p_k)^2|Y_{Lm+u}| = \sum_{v=u}^{L-1}(\mathbf{A}_l^{-1})^{\otimes 2}((v-u)L+v,:)\mathbf{Q}'_{m,l}, 1 \le m \le \tilde{L}-1, \tag{19}$$

$$\prod_{k=1}^{l}(1-2p_k)^2|Y_u| = \sum_{v=u}^{L-1}((\mathbf{A}_l^{-1})^{\otimes 2}((v-u)L+v,:)+(\mathbf{A}_l^{-1})^{\otimes 2}(vL+v-u,:))\mathbf{Q}'_{m,l}, \tag{20}$$

Applying (16) to (18)-(20) and making them simple yield the following three equations:

$$\prod_{k=1}^{l}(1-2p_k)^2|X_{Lm+u}| =$$
$$\sum_{\tau_1=0}^{L-1}\sum_{\tau_2=0}^{L-1}\sum_{v=0}^{u-1}(\prod_{k=1}^{l}P_k(p_k, L+v-u, \tau_1, v, \tau_2)|Q'_{m+1,\tau_1,\tau_2}|), 0 \le m \le \tilde{L}-2; \tag{21}$$

$$\prod_{k=1}^{l}(1-2p_k)^2|Y_{Lm+u}| =$$
$$\sum_{\tau_1=0}^{L-1}\sum_{\tau_2=0}^{L-1}\sum_{v=u}^{L-1}(\prod_{k=1}^{l}P_k(p_k, v-u, \tau_1, v, \tau_2)|Q'_{m,\tau_1,\tau_2}|), 1 \le m \le \tilde{L}-1; \tag{22}$$

$$\prod_{k=1}^{l}(1-2p_k)^2|Y_u| =$$
$$\sum_{\tau_1=0}^{L-1}\sum_{\tau_2=0}^{L-1}\sum_{v=u}^{L-1}((\prod_{k=1}^{l}P_k(p_k, v-u, \tau_1, v, \tau_2) + \prod_{k=1}^{l}P_k(p_k, v, \tau_1, v-u, \tau_2))|Q'_{m,\tau_1,\tau_2}|). \tag{23}$$

When $u = 0$, two sides of (7) is always equal to 0, so (7) is not useful for discrimination between cover and stego objects at this time. Therefore, from (21) - (23) together with (7), the following equations can be obtained to estimate the value of p_k, $1 \le k \le l$:

$$(L-u)\sum_{\tau_1=0}^{L-1}\sum_{\tau_2=0}^{L-1}\sum_{v=0}^{u-1}(\prod_{k=1}^{l}P_k(p_k, L+v-u, \tau_1, v, \tau_2)|Q'_{m+1,\tau_1,\tau_2}|)$$
$$-u\sum_{\tau_1=0}^{L-1}\sum_{\tau_2=0}^{L-1}\sum_{v=u}^{L-1}(\prod_{k=1}^{l}P_k(p_k, v-u, \tau_1, v, \tau_2)|Q'_{m,\tau_1,\tau_2}|) = 0, \tag{24}$$

and

$$(L-u)\sum_{\tau_1=0}^{L-1}\sum_{\tau_2=0}^{L-1}\sum_{v=0}^{u-1}(\prod_{k=1}^{l}P_k(p_k,L+v-u,\tau_1,v,\tau_2)|Q'_{1,\tau_1,\tau_2}|)-u\sum_{\tau_1=0}^{L-1}\sum_{\tau_2=0}^{L-1}\sum_{v=u}^{L-1}$$

$$((\prod_{k=1}^{l}P_k(p_k,v-u,\tau_1,v,\tau_2)+\prod_{k=1}^{l}P_k(p_k,v,\tau_1,v-u,\tau_2))|Q'_{0,\tau_1,\tau_2}|)=0,$$

$$(25)$$

where $1\le m\le\tilde{L}-2$, $1\le u\le L-1$.

It can be seen that the l different embedding ratios of l least significant bit planes are l unknown parameters of equation (24) and (25). In this paper, the rightmost bit of a pixel value is the least significant bit. When one right-shifts all the pixels of an image r bits, the assumption (7) will still hold for enough small r. Therefore, one can right-shift all the pixels $k-1$ bits, then adopt equation (24) or (25) with $l-k+1$ instead of l to obtain $p_k,p_{k+1},\ldots,p_l$. It can be seen that the equations could lead to up to 2 roots for each p_k, $1\le k\le l$. Although the estimated value has estimation error, the error can not be too large. Therefore, we will discard implausible roots outside (-0.05, 0.55) to view them as meaningless values, and select the root whose absolute value is least as the estimation of p_k. When $2p_k$ is close to 1, the matrix $\mathbf{A}_l$ becomes ill-conditioned (it is not invertible when $2p_k=1$), then the equations are likely to have no real root. Thus, when the equations have no real root, the embedding ratio will be viewed as 1.

3.2   Improving the Accuracy of Estimation

In [21], Böhme and Ker observed that the error of steganalysis estimator should be decomposed into two components: between-image error which is entirely due to the assumption about cover images, and within-image error which is due to the correlations between the secret message and cover. Ker has shown in [22] that the magnitude of within-image error is generally much smaller than that of between-image error, unless that the embedded payload is very large. Thus, the obvious improvement way is to reduce the between-image error by selecting the m and u for which the assumption holds best. However, the best m and u differ in different images. And if one selects certain m and u, the number of the pixel pairs utilized will be too few to respond to the embedding enough sensitively, especially for large m and small images. In order to make the most of the possible information of steganography, for $0\le i\le j\le\tilde{L}-2$, $\bigcup_{m=i}^{j}C_m$ and $\bigcup_{m=i}^{j}Q_{m,\pi_1,\pi_2}$ are used instead of C_m and Q_{m,π_1,π_2}, $0\le\pi_1,\pi_2\le L-1$. Then, the following assumption can be made:

$$(L-u)\left|\bigcup_{m=i}^{j}X_{Lm+u}\right|\approx u\left|\bigcup_{m=i}^{j}Y_{Lm+u}\right|.\qquad(26)$$

To combine the assumption (26) for $u=1,2,\ldots,L-1$, the following assumption is presented: for natural images,

$$\sum_{u=1}^{L-1}(L-u)\left|\bigcup_{m=i}^{j}X_{Lm+u}\right|\approx\sum_{u=1}^{L-1}u\left|\bigcup_{m=i}^{j}Y_{Lm+u}\right|.\qquad(27)$$

Based on this assumption, the new equations can be obtained to estimate the value of p_k, $1 \le k \le l$: for $1 \le i \le j \le \tilde{L} - 2$,

$$
\begin{aligned}
&\sum_{u=1}^{L-1} \sum_{m=i}^{j} ((L-u) \sum_{\tau_1=0}^{L-1} \sum_{\tau_2=0}^{L-1} \sum_{v=0}^{u-1} (\prod_{k=1}^{l} P_k(p_k, L+v-u, \tau_1, v, \tau_2) |Q'_{m+1,\tau_1,\tau_2}|)) \\
&- \sum_{u=1}^{L-1} \sum_{m=i}^{j} (u \sum_{\tau_1=0}^{L-1} \sum_{\tau_2=0}^{L-1} \sum_{v=u}^{L-1} (\prod_{k=1}^{l} P_k(p_k, v-u, \tau_1, v, \tau_2) |Q'_{m,\tau_1,\tau_2}|)) = 0,
\end{aligned}
\tag{28}
$$

and for $0 \le j \le \tilde{L} - 2$,

$$
\begin{aligned}
&\sum_{u=1}^{L-1} \sum_{m=0}^{j} ((L-u) \sum_{\tau_1=0}^{L-1} \sum_{\tau_2=0}^{L-1} \sum_{v=0}^{u-1} (\prod_{k=1}^{l} P_k(p_k, L+v-u, \tau_1, v, \tau_2) |Q'_{m+1,\tau_1,\tau_2}|)) \\
&- \sum_{u=1}^{L-1} \sum_{m=0}^{j} (u \sum_{\tau_1=0}^{L-1} \sum_{\tau_2=0}^{L-1} \sum_{v=u}^{L-1} (\prod_{k=1}^{l} P_k(p_k, v-u, \tau_1, v, \tau_2) |Q'_{m,\tau_1,\tau_2}|)) \\
&- \sum_{u=1}^{L-1} (u \sum_{\tau_1=0}^{L-1} \sum_{\tau_2=0}^{L-1} \sum_{v=u}^{L-1} (\prod_{k=1}^{l} P_k(p_k, v, \tau_1, v-u, \tau_2) |Q'_{0,\tau_1,\tau_2}|)) = 0.
\end{aligned}
\tag{29}
$$

4   Experimental Results

The steganalysis detector derived above would be evaluated in the following experimental setup: downloaded 3075 images from http://photogallery.nrcs.usda.gov, originally very high resolution color images in format 'tiff'; then converted them to grayscale images in format 'bmp'; scaled them down to about 256×183, 512×366 and 768×549 to obtain 3 groups of cover images which were called as Gresize1, Gresize2 and Gresize3; cropped them to leave about 256×256, 512×512 and 768×768 in the center to obtain another 3 groups of cover images which were called as Gcrop1, Gcrop2 and Gcrop3. (The tool used was Advanced Batch Converter 3.8.20, and the interpolation filter was bilinear.) Then messages were embedded into these images with the embedding ratios $2p_k \in \{0, 0.1, 0.2, 0.3, 0.4\}$ via ID-3LSB embedding. The new detector for ID-3LSB embedding was called as ID3SPA where SPA indicated that the new detector was designed based on the sample pair analysis.

The horizontal and vertical adjacent pixel pairs would be utilized to steganalyze. This is a representative option in existing literatures. In order to make the presented method maintain steady for different images, $(i, j) = (0, 7)$ will be adopted in equation (29) for $l = 3$ because the trace sets would contain the most pixels in an image for this selection. For evaluating the performance, the new method was compared with the method - right-shifting all the pixels $k - 1$ bits, and then applying SPA method to estimate $2p_k$ directly. From [23], the distribution of the compound error is heavy-tailed. So the median and IQR (interquartile range) are more representative than the mean and standard deviation to evaluate the performances of the two methods.

4.1   Experimental Results for Resized Images

Table 1 compared ID3SPA with SPA on the errors of estimated embedding ratio in 2nd-LSB plane of resized image when the embedding ratio in 3rd-LSB plane was $2p_3 \in \{0, 0.1, 0.2, 0.3, 0.4\}$. From the experimental results, it could be seen that the new method had smaller bias than SPA method. As shown by the table, although the new method didn't not have significant better performance when the higher bit planes did not contain embedded message, viz. when estimating $2p_2$ for $2p_3 = 0$, the new method performed significant better than SPA when there existed embedded message in the higher bit planes. Especially, when the embedding ratios in the higher bit planes were large, the new method achieved markedly lower bias of estimation errors than SPA method (seeing Fig. 1(a)). And in all the groups of resized images, the spreads of estimation errors of two methods were very close (seeing "IQR$\times 10^2$" columns in Table 1 and Fig. 1(b)).

Table 1. Comparing the new method and SPA on the accuracy when estimating $2p_2$ for $2p_3 \in \{0, 0.1, 0.2, 0.3, 0.4\}$ and images in Gresize1-3

		Gresize1				Gresize2				Gresize3			
		median$\times 10^2$		IQR$\times 10^2$		median$\times 10^2$		IQR$\times 10^2$		median$\times 10^2$		IQR$\times 10^2$	
$2p_3$	$2p_2$	new	SPA	new	SPA	new	SPA	new	SPA	new	SPA	new	SPA
	0	-0.05	-0.00	3.41	3.42	0.00	0.04	2.37	2.36	0.01	0.04	1.90	1.89
	0.1	-0.07	-0.04	3.24	3.24	-0.00	0.02	2.31	2.29	0.01	0.04	1.83	1.80
0	0.2	-0.03	-0.00	3.12	3.12	0.01	0.03	2.08	2.10	0.01	0.03	1.70	1.68
	0.3	-0.07	-0.04	3.10	3.11	-0.03	-0.01	1.96	1.95	-0.01	0.01	1.58	1.57
	0.4	-0.03	-0.01	3.11	3.07	-0.00	0.01	1.93	1.92	0.02	0.05	1.44	1.43
	0	-0.04	0.06	3.57	3.51	-0.00	0.12	2.42	2.39	0.02	0.16	1.91	1.91
	0.1	-0.03	0.08	3.34	3.37	-0.04	0.08	2.28	2.24	0.01	0.13	1.82	1.75
0.1	0.2	0.04	0.12	3.37	3.38	-0.02	0.09	2.14	2.14	-0.02	0.12	1.75	1.66
	0.3	-0.02	0.06	3.30	3.29	-0.01	0.14	2.02	1.97	-0.02	0.07	1.61	1.59
	0.4	0.00	0.09	3.14	3.13	-0.02	0.08	1.94	1.92	-0.03	0.06	1.51	1.46
	0	-0.01	0.41	3.72	3.61	0.02	0.48	2.45	2.41	0.02	0.50	1.94	1.92
	0.1	0.05	0.38	3.53	3.43	0.04	0.49	2.41	2.32	-0.01	0.45	1.90	1.78
0.2	0.2	-0.03	0.35	3.45	3.38	0.02	0.39	2.22	2.19	-0.02	0.39	1.77	1.68
	0.3	0.04	0.33	3.45	3.40	-0.01	0.32	2.22	2.08	0.01	0.37	1.68	1.59
	0.4	-0.03	0.19	3.35	3.29	0.03	0.34	2.07	2.02	0.00	0.33	1.59	1.49
	0	-0.05	0.94	4.03	3.81	-0.02	1.09	2.54	2.52	0.00	1.16	2.08	2.04
	0.1	-0.05	0.75	3.83	3.64	0.02	0.96	2.54	2.45	0.04	1.06	1.94	1.92
0.3	0.2	-0.02	0.74	3.61	3.56	-0.04	0.84	2.31	2.34	-0.02	0.88	1.84	1.78
	0.3	-0.05	0.66	3.80	3.52	0.01	0.79	2.31	2.24	-0.01	0.79	1.83	1.70
	0.4	-0.01	0.58	3.65	3.48	0.05	0.66	2.20	2.07	0.02	0.69	1.64	1.54
	0	-0.02	1.73	4.28	3.94	-0.03	2.01	2.78	2.77	-0.01	2.09	2.19	2.29
	0.1	0.05	1.57	4.21	3.83	-0.02	1.80	2.73	2.58	-0.01	1.88	2.06	2.08
0.4	0.2	-0.15	1.31	4.08	3.76	0.02	1.62	2.61	2.50	-0.00	1.68	1.96	1.92
	0.3	-0.03	1.19	3.97	3.55	0.00	1.44	2.45	2.32	0.00	1.45	1.89	1.82
	0.4	0.04	1.07	4.11	3.54	0.03	1.22	2.48	2.21	-0.00	1.27	1.81	1.71

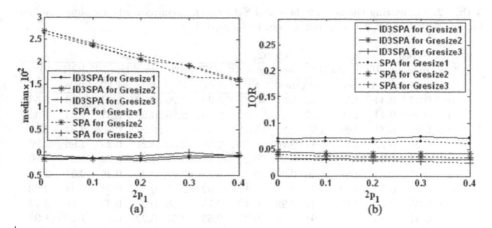

Fig. 1. Performances of ID3SPA and SPA for estimating $2p_1$ when $2p_3 = 0.3$, $2p_2 = 0.4$ and the cover image groups were Gresize1-3

Furthermore, with the sizes of images becoming larger, the bias of estimation errors didn't vary very much, but the spreads of estimation errors of two methods all were reduced a lot. This improvement may not only be ascribed to the increase of sample pairs utilized, but also owed to that spreading the same texture to larger images would increase the degree of smooth.

4.2   Experimental Results for Cropped Images

For the images cropped, the same processes were done. Then Table 2 and Fig. 2 gave the experimental results. In contrast with section 4.1, the estimation errors were larger because of larger departure of assumptions (1) and (7) from reality for cropped images. However, the new method still owned significant smaller bias than SPA when there existed embedded message in the higher bit planes, especially when the embedding ratios in the higher bit planes were large (seeing Fig. 2(a)). And the spreads of estimation errors of two methods were still very close (seeing "IQR$\times 10^2$" columns in Table 2 and Fig. 2(b)).

It was a pity that when the embedding ratio in LSB became larger, the bias would grow so much that they were larger than it of SPA by any possibility (seeing Fig. 2(a)). This may be the combined effect of larger departure of assumption (7) from reality for cropped images and more serious ill-condition of matrix $\mathbf{A}_l$.

The experiments indicate that the new methods have attractive results in the case of ID-MLSB steganography. This may be ascribed to that the new method considers the effect of embedding message into higher bit planes on estimating the embedding ratios in lower bit planes.

Table 2. Comparing the new method and SPA on the accuracy when estimating $2p_2$ for $2p_3 \in \{0, 0.1, 0.2, 0.3, 0.4\}$ and images in Gcrop1-3

$2p_3$	$2p_2$	Gcrop1 median×10²		Gcrop1 IQR×10²		Gcrop2 median×10²		Gcrop2 IQR×10²		Gcrop3 median×10²		Gcrop3 IQR×10²	
		new	SPA	new	SPA	new	SPA	new	SPA	new	SPA	new	SPA
0	0	0.37	0.44	4.54	4.53	0.31	0.35	3.22	3.20	0.30	0.34	2.54	2.54
	0.1	0.36	0.44	4.30	4.27	0.26	0.32	2.89	2.89	0.28	0.31	2.34	2.35
	0.2	0.26	0.31	4.05	4.05	0.27	0.31	2.75	2.74	0.27	0.30	2.14	2.11
	0.3	0.24	0.29	3.84	3.84	0.16	0.19	2.59	2.55	0.21	0.23	1.96	1.96
	0.4	0.24	0.29	3.81	3.78	0.24	0.27	2.27	2.26	0.19	0.22	1.81	1.80
0.1	0	0.37	0.53	4.67	4.56	0.30	0.47	3.23	3.25	0.28	0.45	2.61	2.53
	0.1	0.36	0.53	4.39	4.31	0.27	0.44	2.92	2.97	0.26	0.41	2.41	2.42
	0.2	0.35	0.52	4.17	4.11	0.29	0.42	2.75	2.68	0.22	0.37	2.16	2.14
	0.3	0.31	0.45	3.96	3.91	0.26	0.36	2.53	2.57	0.23	0.35	1.99	1.98
	0.4	0.24	0.40	3.90	3.75	0.22	0.35	2.34	2.31	0.17	0.28	1.77	1.74
0.2	0	0.38	0.95	4.85	4.76	0.33	0.90	3.30	3.31	0.28	0.79	2.65	2.66
	0.1	0.24	0.83	4.57	4.40	0.29	0.81	3.06	3.08	0.28	0.74	2.36	2.41
	0.2	0.32	0.75	4.46	4.27	0.25	0.69	2.79	2.76	0.26	0.66	2.23	2.25
	0.3	0.39	0.74	4.26	4.08	0.25	0.66	2.59	2.64	0.24	0.59	1.98	2.03
	0.4	0.26	0.59	4.12	3.91	0.31	0.63	2.47	2.42	0.16	0.47	1.87	1.83
0.3	0	0.50	1.54	5.16	4.93	0.30	1.47	3.44	3.56	0.31	1.42	2.70	2.85
	0.1	0.33	1.37	4.73	4.68	0.31	1.31	3.22	3.32	0.30	1.32	2.52	2.61
	0.2	0.28	1.14	4.59	4.42	0.32	1.21	2.92	2.99	0.24	1.14	2.33	2.39
	0.3	0.22	1.10	4.37	4.24	0.32	1.10	2.73	2.76	0.25	1.04	2.15	2.16
	0.4	0.33	0.99	4.29	3.98	0.43	1.04	2.56	2.51	0.19	0.89	2.00	1.95
0.4	0	0.31	2.31	5.65	5.41	0.34	2.38	3.48	3.76	0.30	2.30	2.72	3.15
	0.1	0.36	2.17	5.27	4.90	0.25	2.07	3.27	3.55	0.30	2.09	2.61	2.86
	0.2	0.36	1.97	5.00	4.59	0.38	1.95	3.07	3.15	0.28	1.92	2.44	2.57
	0.3	0.31	1.66	4.84	4.39	0.41	1.73	2.95	2.88	0.23	1.67	2.22	2.33
	0.4	0.29	1.50	4.87	4.28	0.54	1.58	2.87	2.69	0.21	1.42	2.14	2.07

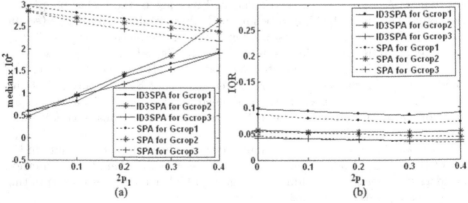

Fig. 2. Performances of ID3SPA and SPA for estimating $2p_1$ when $2p_3 = 0.3$, $2p_2 = 0.4$ and the cover image groups were Gcrop1-3

5   Conclusion

In this paper, based on the sample pair model of MLSB replacement, a new paradigm of MLSB steganography, ID-MLSB steganography, was considered, and then a new steganalysis method for ID-MLSB steganography was proposed. The new method estimated the embedding ratio of image's each bit plane in sequence according to the priority of each bit plane's significance. A series of experiments show that the presented steganalysis method owns significantly better performance than applying the existing typical steganalysis method, SPA method, to estimate the embedding ratio in each bit plane directly. In next step, we will research how to use the framework to analyze other spatial steganography based on the image bit planes.

Acknowledgments. This work is supported by the "863" Program of China (Grant No. 2006AA10Z409), the Basic and Frontier Technology Research Program of Henan Province (Grant No. 082300410150), the Science and Technology Program of Zhengzhou City (Grant No. 083SGYG21125), and the Excellent Doctoral Dissertation Innovation Found of Information Science and Technology Institute (Grant No. BSLWCX200804).

References

1. Fridrich, J., Goljan, M., Du, R.: Reliable Detection of LSB Steganography in Color and Grayscale Images. In: Proc. ACM Workshop Multimedia Security, on Ottawa, Canada, October 2001, pp. 27–30 (2001)
2. Zhang, T., Ping, X.: A New Approach to Reliable Detection of LSB Steganography in Natural Images. Signal Processing 83(8), 2085–2093 (2003)
3. Dumitrescu, S., Wu, X., Wang, Z.: Detection of LSB Steganography via Sample Pair Analysis. IEEE Transactions on Signal Processing 51(7), 1995–2007 (2003)
4. Ker, A.: Improved Detection of LSB Steganography in Grayscale Images. In: Fridrich, J. (ed.) IH 2004. LNCS, vol. 3200, pp. 97–115. Springer, Heidelberg (2004)
5. Lu, P., Luo, X., Tang, Q., Shen, L.: An Improved Sample Pairs Method for Detection of LSB Embedding. In: Fridrich, J. (ed.) IH 2004. LNCS, vol. 3200, pp. 116–127. Springer, Heidelberg (2004)
6. Ker, A., Lubenko, I.: Feature Reduction and Payload Location with WAM Steganalysis. In: Delp III, E.J., Wong, J. (eds.) Proc. SPIE, Security, Forensics, Steganography and Watermarking of Multimedia Contents XI, vol. 7254, 0A (2009)
7. Ker, A.: A General Framework for the Structural Steganalysis of LSB Replacement. In: Barni, M., Herrera-Joancomartí, J., Katzenbeisser, S., Pérez-González, F. (eds.) IH 2005. LNCS, vol. 3727, pp. 296–311. Springer, Heidelberg (2005)
8. Ker, A.: Fourth-Order Structural Steganalysis and Analysis of Cover Assumptions. In: Delp III, E.J., Wong, P.W. (eds.) Proc. SPIE, Security, Steganography, and Watermarking of Multimedia Contents VIII, vol. 6072, pp. 25–38 (2006)
9. Dumitrescu, S., Wu, X.: A New Framework of LSB Steganalysis of Digital Media. IEEE Transactions on Signal Processing 53(10), 3936–3947 (2005)
10. Fridrich, J., Goljan, M.: On Estimation of Secret Message Length in LSB Steganography in Spatial Domain. In: Delp III, E.J., Wong, P.W. (eds.) Proc. SPIE, Security, Steganography, and Watermarking of Multimedia Contents VI, vol. 5306, pp. 23–34 (2004)

11. Ker, A., BÖhme, R.: Revisiting Weighted Stego-Image Steganalysis. In: Delp III, E.J., Wong, P.W., et al. (eds.) Proc. SPIE, Security, Forensics, Steganography and Watermarking of Multimedia Contents X, vol. 6819, p. 681905 (2008)
12. Ker, A.: Steganalysis of Embedding in Two Least-Significant Bits. IEEE Transactions on Information Forensics and Security 2(1), 46–54 (2007)
13. Wu, N., Hwang, M.: Data Hiding: Current Status and Key Issues. International Journal of Network Security 4(1), 1–9 (2007)
14. Nguyen, B., Yoon, S., Lee, H.: Multi Bit Plane Image Steganography. In: Shi, Y.Q., Jeon, B. (eds.) IWDW 2006. LNCS, vol. 4283, pp. 61–70. Springer, Heidelberg (2006)
15. Yu, X., Tan, T., Wang, Y.: Extended Optimization Method of LSB Steganalysis. In: Proc. IEEE International Conference on Image Processing, vol. 2, pp. 1102–1105 (2005)
16. Luo, X., Wang, Q., Yang, C., Liu, F.: Detection of LTSB Steganography Based on Quartic Equation. In: Proc. 8th International Conference on Advanced Communication Technology, on Phoenix Park, Korea, February 2006, pp. 20–22 (2006)
17. Luo, X., Yang, C., Wang, D., Liu, F.: LTSB Steganalysis Based on Quartic Equation. In: Shi, Y.Q. (ed.) Transactions on Data Hiding and Multimedia Security II. LNCS, vol. 4499, pp. 68–90. Springer, Heidelberg (2007)
18. Yu, X., Babaguchi, N.: A Fast and Effective Method to Detect Multiple Least Significant Bits Steganography. In: Proc. ACM Symposium on Applied Computing, Fortaleza, Cear, Brazil, March 2008, pp. 1443–1447 (2008)
19. Yang, C., Lin, F., Luo, X., Liu, B.: Steganalysis Frameworks of Embedding in Multiple Least-Significant Bits. IEEE Transactions on Information Forensics and Security 3(4), 662–672 (2008)
20. Luo, X., Wang, D., Wang, P., Liu, F.: A Review on Blind Detection for Image Steganography. Signal Process. 88(9), 2138–2157 (2008)
21. Böhme, R., Ker, A.: A Two-Factor Error Model for Quantitative Steganalysis. In: Delp III, E.J., Wong, P.W. (eds.) Proc. SPIE, Security, Steganography and Watermarking of Multimedia Contents VIII, vol. 6072, pp. 59–74 (2006)
22. Ker, A.: Derivation of Error Distribution in Least Squares Steganalysis. IEEE Transactions on Information Forensics and Security 2(2), 140–148 (2007)
23. Böhme, R.: Assessment of Steganalytic Methods Using Multiple Regression Models. In: Barni, M., Herrera-Joancomartí, J., Katzenbeisser, S., Pérez-González, F. (eds.) IH 2005. LNCS, vol. 3727, pp. 278–295. Springer, Heidelberg (2005)

Estimating Steganographic Fisher Information in Real Images

Andrew D. Ker

Oxford University Computing Laboratory,
Parks Road, Oxford OX1 3QD, England
adk@comlab.ox.ac.uk

Abstract. This paper is concerned with the estimation of steganographic capacity in digital images, using information theoretic bounds and very large-scale experiments to approximate the distributions of genuine covers. The complete distribution cannot be estimated, but with carefully-chosen algorithms and a large corpus we can make local approximations by considering groups of pixels. A simple estimator for the local quadratic term of Kullback-Leibler divergence (*Steganographic Fisher Information*) is presented, validated on some synthetic images, and computed for a corpus of covers. The results are interesting not so much for their concrete capacity estimates but for the comparisons they provide between different embedding operations, between the information found in differently-sized and -shaped pixel groups, and the results of DC normalization within pixel groups. This work suggests lessons for the future design of spatial-domain steganalysis, and also the optimization of embedding functions.

1 Introduction

Arguably the most vital question for steganographers is to estimate, given a particular cover and embedding method, the amount of information that can securely be embedded: this is the *capacity* of the cover, relative to a specific level of detection risk. Information theoretic quantities, particularly the *Kullback-Leibler (KL) divergence* between cover and stego distributions, can bound the secure embedding capacity [1,2] but, naturally, they require knowledge of these distributions and this seems infeasible for digital media. Whilst information theory has produced interesting results about the rate of capacity growth [3,4], these do not specify concrete payload sizes for particular, real-world, covers.

In this work, we aim to estimate enough of the distribution of digital images in order to draw conclusions about embedding capacity in real pictures (although it will turn out that the more interesting conclusions are not the concrete capacities derived, but the comparisons between embedding methods and the amounts of evidence found in pixel groups of different types). Our information theoretic starting point is the classic connection between hypothesis testing and KL divergence, promoted in steganography by Cachin [1]. Estimating the KL divergence empirically appears, at first sight, an impossible task: such estimators, e.g. [5], are notoriously unstable, subject to either bias or large dispersion, and typically

S. Katzenbeisser and A.-R. Sadeghi (Eds.): IH 2009, LNCS 5806, pp. 73–88, 2009.

require very large samples even for variables of low dimension. In the case of entire images the dimensionality is potentially millions, and even a huge corpus of cover images only samples the distribution with extreme sparsity. These problems do seem to prohibit direct estimation of KL divergence in images.

However, we can make some progress with two adjustments. First, rather than aiming directly for the KL divergence, we estimate its asymptotic behaviour as payload size tends to zero, which (under reasonable conditions) is determined by *Fisher's Information*; we propose an estimator which seems to exhibit more stability than those for KL divergence. Second, we consider small groups of pixels instead of complete images, modelling an image as an independent collection of pixel groups. This is certainly a significant move away from the original problem, because images are *not* constructed in this way, but it is a fact that most steganalysis methods treat images exactly as if they *were* made up of independent collections of small pixel groups (often groups as small as size 1 or 2), so the information theoretic bounds on capacity at least apply to such detectors.

This paper contains: (Sect. 2) definition of *Steganographic Fisher Information*, refined into two quantities, I_c and I_p, which have different steganographic significance; (Sect. 3) a description of a simple estimator for I_c; (Sect. 4) a series of experiments estimating I_c and I_p for different types of pixel groups, and discussion of the significance of these results; (Sect. 5) a conclusion.

Some notation conventions are used throughout: random variables and distributions will be denoted by upper-case letters, and realizations of random variables the corresponding lower case. Vectors of either random variables or realizations will be set boldface $\boldsymbol{x} = (x_1, \ldots . x_n)$, with n implicit. All logs will be to natural base.

2   KL Divergence and Steganographic Fisher Information

Steganalysis is an example of hypothesis testing, and capacity can be measured using the connection between KL divergence and accuracy of hypothesis tests. Let us model stego objects as random variables with distribution $P(\lambda)$, where λ indicates the payload size. We assume that each stego object consists of a number of *locations*, whose interdependence may be arbitrary. Since detectors do not detect payload directly – they can only detect changes caused by the payload embedding – and since most embedding methods make embedding changes of approximately constant magnitude, we will measure payload *size* by the *rate* of embedding changes introduced (i.e. λ indicates changes per cover location).

A detector must decide whether an object or sequence of objects is a realisation from $P(0)$ or $P(\lambda)$ for $\lambda > 0$. By the data processing theorem [1], any detector must have false positive and negative probabilities (α, β) satisfying

$$\alpha \log \tfrac{\alpha}{1-\beta} + (1 - \alpha) \log \tfrac{1-\alpha}{\beta} \leq D_{\mathrm{KL}}(P(0) \,\|\, P(\lambda)), \qquad (1)$$

where D_{KL} represents the Kullback-Leibler (KL) divergence

$$D_{\mathrm{KL}}(P \,\|\, Q) = \int \log\left(\tfrac{\mathrm{d}P}{\mathrm{d}Q}\right) \mathrm{d}P.$$

If the steganographer sets a maximum *risk* – a minimum on α and β, see [3] – the normal effect of (1) is to set a maximum on λ, the secure capacity relative to the maximum risk and chosen embedding method.

In general, (1) cannot be inverted to find the bound on λ. However, in [6] it is argued that the most important feature of embedding is its *asymptotic* capacity, as the relative payload tends to zero. This is because repeated communication must reduce the embedding rate, or face eventual certain detection. In which case, it is sufficient to consider the asymptotic behaviour of $D_{\mathrm{KL}}(P(0) \| P(\lambda))$ as $\lambda \to 0$, and given regularity conditions (see [7]), we have a simple expansion

$$D_{\mathrm{KL}}(P(0) \| P(\lambda)) \sim \tfrac{1}{2}I\lambda^2 + O(\lambda^3)$$

where I is *Fisher's Information* for the distribution $P(\lambda)$ at zero, i.e. KL divergence is locally quadratic. In [6] the quadratic coefficient $\tfrac{1}{2}I$ was called the *Q-factor*, but we revert to the standard terminology and measure I.

Fisher Information can be scaled in at least two different ways, so for avoidance of doubt we will write it I_c, which we call *Steganographic Fisher Information (SFI) with respect to change rate*, when λ, as above, measures the embedding change rate. If the logs are to natural base, KL divergence is measured in "nats", and I_c is measured in *nats per change rate squared*.

However the quantity I_c is not appropriate to compare the security of embedding methods which store different payloads per embedding change, nor is it appropriate to compare across different cover sizes. We therefore introduce another type of SFI, which we call I_p, taking these factors into account. Well-established terminology (see e.g. [8]) is to describe the average number of payload bits conveyed per embedding change as the *embedding efficiency e*: for simple LSB replacement $e = 2$, but for alternative embedding methods e can be significantly higher. Then a measure of risk per information transmitted is I_c/e^2 (nats per payload rate squared). To compare differently-sized covers, we swap KL divergence for KL divergence *rate*: the limit as $n \to \infty$ of $1/n$ times the KL divergence of cover/stego objects of size n. KL divergence rate is well-defined for well-behaved sources, so it makes sense to divide SFI by the cover size n to obtain a size-independent measure of evidence. Therefore we define *Steganographic Fisher Information with respect to payload rate*

$$I_p = \frac{I_c}{ne^2}. \tag{2}$$

I_p is measured in *symbol nats per bit squared* and it has the following interpretation: if one embeds a (small) payload of p bits in a cover with n locations, using an embedding method with I_p symbol nats per bit squared, one expects to produce a KL divergence of approximately $I_p(p^2/n)$ nats. This reflects the square root law of steganographic capacity [9]. I_p can be used to compare the security of different embedding methods in covers of arbitrary size.

The constant r in the asymptotic capacity $r\sqrt{n}$ of covers of size n is called the *root rate*, and it can now be determined (it is inversely proportional to $\sqrt{I_p}$) but for our purposes this is not necessary. We merely need to know that higher SFI corresponds to less secure embedding and consequently lower capacity.

2.1 Embedding Domain and Embedding Operations

Although the theory in this paper is applicable to any finite-size, finite-valued cover, we will consider only single-channel, byte-valued, digital images. The embedding methods we investigate will include the classic least significant bit (LSB) replacement (abbreviated LSB-R), replacement of 2 LSBs of each pixel with payload (2LSB-R), and the modified LSB method known as *LSB matching* (LSB-M) where the decision to increment or decrement a byte with non-matching LSB is taken at random unless forced at the extreme of the range. LSM matching is also known as ± 1 *embedding* but we eschew this terminology: although "± 1" accurately describes the effect of embedding in LSB matching, it also describes the embedding operation of *ternary embedding* (Ter-M), where each cover pixel conveys $\log_2 3$ bits of information in its remainder (mod 3). Note that these embedding methods have the following embedding efficiencies: for LSB-R and LSB-M $e = 2$, for 2LSB-R $e = 8/3$, and for Ter-M $e = (3/2) \log_2 3$.

2.2 On Groups of Pixels

It is not tractable to estimate the SFI for entire images. Instead, we will imagine that they are made up of many independent pixel *groups*, where the groups are of fixed size such as 1×2 pixels, 2×2, 3×3, etc. In effect, we reduce each image to its histogram of groups: in the case of 1×1 groups this is the standard histogram, in the case of 1×2 groups it is the *adjacency histogram* or *co-occurrence matrix*.

In reducing an image to its higher-order histogram, we are destroying information. Therefore the information theoretic bound (1) does not apply universally: there might be detectors which beat this bound, if they do not make the same reduction of information. However, it is a fact that most leading steganalysis methods use only a histogram of pixel groups of fixed size. It is obvious that histogram-based detectors such as the venerable Chi-Square detector [10] use only the histogram, but also consider that LSB replacement detectors such as SPA [11] and Couples/ML [12] use only the adjacency histogram, the Triples method [13] uses only the frequencies of triplets of pixels, and even the WS detector [14,15] uses a local filtering operation to determine prediction residuals and sums weighted residuals, so it can be expressed as a function of the histogram of groups of 3×3, or 5×5 pixels. The same is true for many detectors of LSB matching: [16] is based on the histogram, and the calibrated version in [17] can be computed from the histogram of 2×2 groups in the original. Many detectors for steganography in JPEG images consider the 8×8 DCT blocks separately, and total histograms based on those blocks (the same is not necessarily true for so-called calibrated methods, but most of their features are expressible in terms of 16×16 blocks). None of this is very surprising when one considers that image models, and therefore steganalysis methods, tend to work locally.

So there is much useful information to be found in bounds on detection accuracy, even when only small groups of pixels are considered. Indeed, comparing the amount of information found in pixel groups of different size may give interesting pointers to groups from which better steganalysis could be developed.

Furthermore, most of the LSB replacement detectors do not even consider the full adjacency histogram, preserving only the pixel difference and parity: later, we will be able to measure the amount of information thus destroyed.

3   Estimating Steganographic Fisher Information

We begin with a calculation of I_c, and then give a simple estimator for it. We can convert to I_p later. Let us suppose that the cover is made up of a fixed-length sequence of symbols $(X_1, \ldots, X_n)$ draw from finite alphabet $\mathcal{X}$: these could represent the pixels of a cover image, quantized DCT coefficients, or some more complicated 1-1 transformation of the cover. The corresponding stego object is $(Y_1, \ldots, Y_n)$. For simplicity of calculations, in this work we will restrict our attention to certain classes of embedding:

1. We suppose that the embedding operation affects each cover symbol independently and equiprobably; when a cover symbol is altered by embedding, $Y_i \neq X_i$, we say that location i has undergone an *embedding change*. The probability that each location receives an embedding change, the *change rate*, will be denoted α. The embedding operation is therefore completely described by α and the embedding transition probabilities $P(Y = y \mid X = x \wedge Y \neq X)$.

2. We suppose that if a cover symbol changes, it changes to one of a fixed number of alternatives equiprobably. The number of alternatives for each cover symbol is known as the embedding *valency* v. That is, for each $x \in \mathcal{X}$ there exists a set $A(x)$ with cardinality v such that

$$P(Y = y \mid X = x \wedge Y \neq X) = \begin{cases} \frac{1}{v}, & \text{for } y \in A(x) \\ 0, & \text{otherwise.} \end{cases}$$

3. We assume that the distribution of cover sequences $P(\boldsymbol{X} = \boldsymbol{x})$ is such that $P(\boldsymbol{X} = \boldsymbol{x}) = 0 \iff P(\boldsymbol{Y} = \boldsymbol{x}) = 0$; a simple sufficient condition is $P(\boldsymbol{X} = \boldsymbol{x}) > 0$ for all $\boldsymbol{x} \in \mathcal{X}^n$.

The first seems necessary to form a tractable probabilistic model of embedding. The second condition is included only because it simplifies the algebra; the last is necessary for SFI to be well-defined.

Examples of such embedding operations include simple LSB replacement: $v = 1$, and for each x, $A(x) = \{\bar{x}\}$ where $\bar{x}$ indicates the integer x with the LSB flipped. In 2LSB replacement, $v = 3$ and $A(x) = \{\bar{x}, \hat{x}, \hat{\bar{x}}\}$, where $\hat{x}$ indicates x with the 2nd LSB flipped. LSB matching does not, strictly speaking, fit these conditions because the valency is not constant (0 and 255 can only change to one alternative, all others to two alternatives). However, if the cover does not contain any extreme-valued symbols then this issue never occurs, and if the embedding were modified to allow 0 and 255 to interchange under embedding then LSB matching has $v = 2$ and $A(x) = \{x - 1, x + 1\}$ (addition modulo 256). Since changing 0 to 255, or vice versa, would be a rare occurrence, we may loosely model LSB matching under this framework and postpone to future work the extension to more general embedding operations [18].

Now we may compute I_p for finite (fixed-length) sequences of cover symbols, by computing the KL divergence and extracting the leading term in α, as follows. Fix n, then $P((Y_1, \ldots, Y_n) = (x_1, \ldots, x_n))$ can be expressed as

$$
P(\boldsymbol{X} = \boldsymbol{x}) + \alpha \left[-nP(\boldsymbol{X} = \boldsymbol{x}) + \tfrac{1}{v} \sum_{|\boldsymbol{x}-\boldsymbol{y}|=1} P(\boldsymbol{X} = \boldsymbol{y}) \right]
$$

$$
+ \alpha^2 \left[\tfrac{n(n-1)}{2} P(\boldsymbol{X} = \boldsymbol{x}) - \tfrac{n-1}{v} \sum_{|\boldsymbol{x}-\boldsymbol{y}|=1} P(\boldsymbol{X} = \boldsymbol{y}) + \tfrac{1}{v^2} \sum_{|\boldsymbol{x}-\boldsymbol{y}|=2} P(\boldsymbol{X} = \boldsymbol{y}) \right] + O(\alpha^3)
$$

where $|\boldsymbol{x} - \boldsymbol{y}| = 1$ is shorthand to indicate that all but 1 of x_i and y_i are equal, and for the remaining index $y_i \in A(x_i)$, $|\boldsymbol{x} - \boldsymbol{y}| = 2$ analogously. Then, using $\log(1 + z) \sim z - \frac{z^2}{2} + O(z^3)$,

$$
-P(\boldsymbol{X} = \boldsymbol{x}) \log \left(\frac{P(\boldsymbol{Y} = \boldsymbol{x})}{P(\boldsymbol{X} = \boldsymbol{x})} \right) \sim \alpha \left[nP(\boldsymbol{X} = \boldsymbol{x}) - \tfrac{1}{v} \sum_{|\boldsymbol{x}-\boldsymbol{y}|=1} P(\boldsymbol{X} = \boldsymbol{y}) \right]
$$

$$
+ \frac{\alpha^2}{2} \left[nP(\boldsymbol{X} = \boldsymbol{x}) - \tfrac{2}{v} \sum_{|\boldsymbol{x}-\boldsymbol{y}|=1} P(\boldsymbol{X} = \boldsymbol{y}) - \tfrac{2}{v^2} \sum_{|\boldsymbol{x}-\boldsymbol{y}|=2} P(\boldsymbol{X} = \boldsymbol{y}) + \frac{\left(\sum_{|\boldsymbol{x}-\boldsymbol{y}|=1} P(\boldsymbol{X}=\boldsymbol{y}) \right)^2}{v^2 P(\boldsymbol{X} = \boldsymbol{x})} \right]
$$

$$
+ O(\alpha^3).
$$

Now observe that $\sum_{\boldsymbol{x} \in \mathcal{X}^n} P(\boldsymbol{X} = \boldsymbol{x}) = 1$, $\sum_{\boldsymbol{x}} \sum_{|\boldsymbol{x}-\boldsymbol{y}|=1} P(\boldsymbol{X} = \boldsymbol{y}) = nv$, and $\sum_{\boldsymbol{x}} \sum_{|\boldsymbol{x}-\boldsymbol{y}|=2} P(\boldsymbol{X} = \boldsymbol{y}) = \frac{n(n-1)v^2}{2}$. Thus, discarding terms $O(\alpha^3)$ and above,

$$
D_{\mathrm{KL}}(\boldsymbol{X} \| \boldsymbol{Y}) = \sum_{\boldsymbol{x} \in \mathcal{X}^n} -P(\boldsymbol{X} = \boldsymbol{x}) \log \left(\frac{P(\boldsymbol{Y} = \boldsymbol{x})}{P(\boldsymbol{X} = \boldsymbol{x})} \right) \sim \frac{\alpha^2}{2} \left[\frac{\left(\sum_{|\boldsymbol{x}-\boldsymbol{y}|=1} P(\boldsymbol{X}=\boldsymbol{y}) \right)^2}{v^2 P(\boldsymbol{X} = \boldsymbol{x})} - n^2 \right]
$$

and we have computed the SFI I_c (nats per change rate squared) as a relatively simple function of the distribution of cover sequences.

But how to estimate the SFI empirically? We propose a simple and naive solution. Suppose a large corpus of cover sequences (of fixed size) from which one extracts the empirical distribution, which we will write

$$
p(\boldsymbol{x}) = \#\text{occurrences of } \boldsymbol{x}/\text{size of corpus}.
$$

For a particular embedding method, we can write $q(\boldsymbol{x}) = \sum_{|\boldsymbol{x}-\boldsymbol{y}|=1} p(\boldsymbol{y})$ and then estimate the SFI by

$$
\widehat{I}_c = \frac{1}{v^2} \sum_{\boldsymbol{x}} q(\boldsymbol{x})^2 / p(\boldsymbol{x}) - n^2. \tag{3}
$$

The sum must be taken over nonzero $p(\boldsymbol{x})$.

Theorem 1. *Under our assumptions, $\widehat{I}_c$ is a consistent estimator: for all $\epsilon > 0$, $P(|\widehat{I}_c - I_c| > \epsilon) \to 0$ as the corpus size tends to ∞.*

The proof is omitted for lack of space, as was much of the preceding detail. Neither will we attempt to develop confidence intervals for the estimate (perhaps bootstraps can be applied). One could hope for much more accurate estimators inspired by those for KL divergence, but methods such as nearest-neighbours [5] seem primarily for continuous random variables. Our focus is on applying this simple estimator to get some indicative results about steganographic security.

3.1   Implementation Challenges

We do need a sufficiently large corpus: too few samples will lead not only to inaccuracies in $p(\boldsymbol{x})$, but also many cases of $p(\boldsymbol{x}) = 0$ and hence terms missing from the sum in (3)[1]. And, despite the simple form of the estimator, very large data sets present computational challenges.

When estimating the SFI for pixel groups of size n, there are potentially 256^n different values: while it is easy to store the histogram of such values for $n = 1, 2, 3$, current computer memories are unlikely to be large enough for $n = 4$, and certainly not for $n \geq 5$ (our experiments will involve n as large as 9). The histogram may be somewhat sparse (with adjacent pixels more likely to take similar values) but even an efficient data structure cannot contain the entire histogram in memory at once. For example, in experiments on genuine images with $n = 8$ the histogram requires 47GB to store, and the data structures which make the counting process efficient more than double the memory requirement.

We must trade space for time, and therefore adopt the following procedure:

1. Each image in the corpus is considered in turn, divided into pixel groups (including, if required, DC normalization – see Subsect. 4.3), and a running total of the frequency of each group is kept. For this purpose a red-black tree is used, with the pixel value sequences as keys (sorted lexicographically) and frequency of occurrence as values. This allows logarithmic-time update and insertion, and also rapid access to the data, sorted by key, via a tree traversal. When all memory is exhausted, the (key, value) pairs are written out to disk in key order (the tree structure can be discarded) and a new histogram begins. At the end of this process, we have a number of histograms with overlapping keys, each sorted by key.
2. The histograms are merged by shuffle-sorting. The result is written to disk in chunks no larger than half the available memory; these chunks concatenate to the complete histogram of pixel groups $(\boldsymbol{x}, p(\boldsymbol{x}))$, sorted by $\boldsymbol{x}$.
3. We adjoin the value of $q(\boldsymbol{x})$ to each entry for $p(\boldsymbol{x})$:
   For each $i = 1, \ldots, n$,
       for each $y \in A(x_i)$,
           $q(\boldsymbol{x}) \mathrel{+}= p(x_1, \ldots, x_{i-1}, y, x_{i+1}, \ldots, x_n)$.
   Note that the value of $p(x_1, \ldots, x_{i-1}, y, x_{i+1}, \ldots, x_n)$ may be stored in a different histogram chunk than $p(\boldsymbol{x})$, so we must be prepared to load two chunks

---

[1] One warning is found in the observed value of $\sum_{p(\boldsymbol{x})>0} q(\boldsymbol{x})$: if the SFI is finite, this should total nv and lower values indicate missing terms due to insufficiently-sampled data.

at a time. Because the chunks are sorted, $p(x_1, \ldots, x_{i-1}, y, x_{i+1}, \ldots, x_n)$ can be located using binary search and, in practice, is always found in one of the three or five nearest chunks to $p(\boldsymbol{x})$.

4. Finally, the entries $(\boldsymbol{x}, p(\boldsymbol{x}), q(\boldsymbol{x}))$ are scanned through, and $\widehat{I_c}$ computed via (3). At the same time, $\sum_{p(\boldsymbol{x}) > 0} q(\boldsymbol{x})$ can be computed for an indication as to whether the histograms are under-sampled.

Overall, the algorithm has time complexity $O(N \log N)$, where N is the number of pixel groups in the corpus (though this ignores the effect of the available memory size: more memory means that the histograms are split into fewer chunks, making everything more efficient). Similar performance could be achieved by storing more data on disk and using B-trees to cache as much in memory as possible, but the implementation would be more complicated.

In the interests of making the most of our corpus, we allow pixel groups to overlap at the counting stage. Additionally, we may expect that the statistical properties of natural images are invariant under rotation, so we re-use each image in four orientations (except for groups of size 1×1, for which nothing is gained). Although this might introduce minor discrepancies into the calculations, since the groups are not truly independent, we expect any such effect to be negligible, though we recognise that some image acquisition operations (e.g. colour filter arrays) are not necessarily rotationally symmetric.

4   Results

We now perform some experiments, first to validate the accuracy of the SFI estimator on synthetic images, then to examine properties of genuine images under various embedding methods.

One thousand synthetic images, sized 2000×1500, were generated by taking each pixel independently at random with distribution $P(X = x) = \frac{1}{3} 2^{-|128-x|}$ (we may ignore the negligible probability that this value falls outside the range 0–255). As well as providing simple calculations for exact KL divergence, this distribution produced joint histograms with a sparsity somewhat similar to the genuine images tested later (nonetheless, further validation experiments should be carried out). Depending on pixel group size, just under 3×10^9 pixel groups are available from which to construct the empirical histograms.

For real images, we used a library of 3200 never-compressed grayscale images taken from a digital camera in RAW format, approximately 4.5 Mpixels each. As part of the conversion process from RAW to grayscale, some denoising was applied. We initially performed experiments on all 3200 images, but those results were skewed by areas of saturation in the pictures. Although saturation is an arguably natural, and certainly common, artifact we preferred to avoid it and selected 2118 of the images under the crude criterion that no more than 5000 pixels per image fall outside the range [5, 250]. It may be valuable to return to the study of saturated images in future work. The genuine image corpus is therefore 10 Gpixels in size; including the extra data obtained by rotating the images, just over 4×10^{10} pixel groups are available to construct empirical histograms.

Table 1. Synthetic images: comparison of estimates for I_c with the true values; 4 sig. fig. displayed

Group shape	Number of bins	Embed function	$\widehat{I_c}$	True I_c
1×1	61	LSB-R	0.5000	0.5000
1×2	1719	LSB-R	1.000	1.000
1×3	28385	LSB-R	1.500	1.500
1×4	315408	LSB-R	2.002	2.000
1×5	2480380	LSB-R	2.515	2.500
1×6	14307151	LSB-R	3.062	3.000
1×7	61866127	LSB-R	3.533	3.500
1×8	203899284	LSB-R	2.804	4.000

Experimental base: approx. 3×10^9 pixel groups

The SFI for pixel groups of two or three can be estimated in matter of minutes, but for groups as large as eight or nine it takes many days, and the work was distributed amongst a small cluster of 12 machines. The total CPU time required for our experiments was approximately 6 weeks and the joint histogram rows $(x, p(x), q(x))$ required 630GB of storage (intermediate calculations required over 2TB of storage). We also studied three smaller cover image sets, and report their results very briefly in the Subsect. 4.5.

4.1 Series 1: Synthetic Images

If $P(X = x) = \frac{1}{3}2^{-|128-x|}$ then it is simply to verify that, after LSB flipping,

$$P(Y = y) = \begin{cases} \frac{1}{6}2^{-|128-y|}, & y \text{ even and } y \geq 128 \text{ or } y \text{ odd and } y < 128, \\ \frac{2}{3}2^{-|128-y|}, & y \text{ odd and } y > 128 \text{ or } y \text{ even and } y < 128. \end{cases}$$

For single pixels, therefore, the true value of I_c for LSB replacement evaluates to $\frac{1}{2}$. Since pixels are independent in these synthetic images, the KL divergence of a group of pixels is additive, so for a group of n pixels $I_c = \frac{n}{2}$.

We computed the empirical histograms for groups of $1, 2, \ldots, 8$ pixels, from the 1000 synthetic images, and hence estimated I_c using (3). Tab. 1 demonstrates how we will display the results: the number of nonempty histogram bins can be used for an indication of how dispersed were the observed groups. The estimator shows close accordance with the true value up to $n = 7$, but the histograms are under-sampled when $n = 8$ and the estimate is far off. As an indication of under-sampling, the value of $\sum_{p(x)>0} q(x)$ was only 7.67 when it should have been 8: this indicates that approximately 4% of the true terms of (3) are missing from the estimate. We also tested estimators for I_c under 2LSB-R and LSB-M embedding, with similar results. These experiments validate the accuracy of the estimator, but we must beware of under-sampled histograms.

Table 2. Real images: comparison of different embedding methods; 3 sig. fig. displayed

Group shape	Number of bins	Embed function	$\widehat{I_c}$	$\widehat{I_p}$
1×1	256	LSB-R	0.000826	0.000207
		2LSB-R	0.00236	0.000332
		LSB-M	0.000110	0.0000275
		Ter-M	0.000110	0.0000195
1×2	56603	LSB-R	0.775	0.0968
		2LSB-R	2.26	0.159
		LSB-M	0.247	0.0309
		Ter-M	0.247	0.0219
1×3	4430576	LSB-R	3.96	0.330
		2LSB-R	26.4	1.24
		LSB-M	1.86	0.155
		Ter-M	1.86	0.110
1×4	116786674	LSB-R	15.6	0.973
		2LSB-R	355	12.5
		LSB-M	9.00	0.563
		Ter-M	9.00	0.398
1×5	897195813	LSB-R	40.5	2.02
		2LSB-R	5440	153
		LSB-M	24.3	1.21
		Ter-M	24.3	0.859
1×6	2822410982	LSB-R	75.2	3.13
		2LSB-R	8940	209
		LSB-M	44.7	1.86
		Ter-M	44.7	1.32

Experimental base: approx. 4×10^{10} *pixel groups*

4.2   Series 2: Comparison of Spatial-Domain Embedding Functions

Next, we fix on groups of size 1-6 pixels, and turn to our library of genuine images. We will compare the SFI of the embedding methods LSB-R, 2LSB-R, LSB-M, and Ter-M. As previously mentioned, a fair comparison must take into account the greater payload carried by 2LSB-R and Ter-M, so we convert estimates of I_c into I_p via (2). The results are displayed in Tab. 2 with estimated SFI displayed to 3 sig. fig., but we stress that the estimator accuracy, for large pixel groups, is probably not as high as this.

The most obvious feature is that more evidence about the presence of steganography (higher SFI) is found in larger pixel groups: this will be examined separately in a later series of experiments. We expected to see that LSB matching is more secure than LSB replacement, and this is well-supported by the larger SFI of the latter. Rather surprising, to the author, is the observation that the difference between I_p estimate for LSB replacement and LSB matching reduces for larger pixel groups, appearing to settle on a ratio of only roughly 1.7, which means that a payload approximately 1.3 times the size can be embedded by LSB-M at equivalent risk (but when restricted to pixel pairs, the ratio is higher). Thus LSB-M is "approximately 1.3 times more secure" than LSB-R in a fundamental sense. This ratio is smaller than one might expect from experimental performance of the current best detectors for LSB-R and LSB-M.

The relationship between ternary embedding and LSB matching is not very interesting, merely a result of the increased embedding efficiency of the former. The comparison between LSB replacement and 2LSB replacement was a surprise: in [19] it was conjectured that 2LSB replacement might be slightly more secure on a per-payload basis, but our results here are quite the opposite. Closer examination of the sum (3) showed that pixel groups such as $(4x, 4x, 4x + 3, 4x)$ were dominant, occurring almost never in cover images but often in stego images (because of cover groups of flat pixels). This might be an artifact of the denoising process undergone by the covers and we stress that these results, comparing security of embedding methods, are only applicable to this set of covers.

4.3   Series 3: The Effect of DC Normalization

We might believe that the DC level of pixel groups is immaterial to their frequency, e.g. that for fixed y the pairs $(x, x + y)$ should occur approximately equally often, regardless of the value of x. This amounts to normalizing the overall DC level of each group: we could exploit this to get a better estimate of the pooled histograms. And even if we do not believe that DC level is irrelevant, we know that many steganalysis methods – particularly those for LSB replacement – discard some of the DC information. For example the Triples [13] uses the frequencies of the *trace subsets* $(2x, 2x + y, 2x + z)$, $(2x + 1, 2x + 1 + y, 2x + 1 + z)$, where y and z are fixed but x may vary: effectively, this removes the DC information except for preserving the parity of the leading pixel. Intuitively, parity is important for exploiting the "pairs of values" effects inherent in LSB replacement, so one would expect that it should be preserved. As another example, the detectors for 2LSB replacement in [19] preserve the value of the leading pixel up to (mod 4), again reflecting the structure of the embedding process.

We implemented options to subtract a constant from each pixel group so that the value of a "key pixel" in the group (selected to be as close as possible to the centre) is reduced either to zero (effectively only pixel *differences* are preserved), or to its remainder (mod 2) or (mod 4). Table 3 displays the resulting estimates of I_p for two different group sizes and with LSB-M, LSB-R, and 2LSB-R embedding. From left to right, more information is discarded: first all DC information is preserved, then only the value (mod 4) of the key pixel is kept, then the value (mod 2), and finally the key pixel is zeroed and only the differences are retained. As expected, the evidence (SFI) decreases as the information is removed. But the decrease is uneven: most information about LSB replacement is preserved under normalization (mod 2) or (mod 4), but not complete normalization; this

Table 3. Real images: the effect of pixel group DC normalization; 3 sig. fig. displayed

Group shape	Embed function	$\widehat{I}_p$, with DC-normalization			
		none	(mod 4)	(mod 2)	complete
1×2	LSB-R	0.0968	0.0831	0.0831	0.0233
	2LSB-R	0.159	0.129	0.0689	0.0585
	LSB-M	0.0309	0.0233	0.0233	0.0233
1×4	LSB-R	0.973	0.813	0.813	0.460
	2LSB-R	12.5	9.50	3.61	2.79
	LSB-M	0.563	0.460	0.460	0.460

Experimental base: approx. 4×10^{10} pixel groups

is exactly what was expected. Most information about 2LSB replacement is preserved if the normalization preserves DC (mod 4), but not (mod 2). And the security of LSB matching and LSB replacement are almost exactly equal if no DC information is preserved. We can interpret this to mean that the *only* additional weakness of LSB replacement, over LSB matching, is the pairs of values effect.

This suggests that LSB replacement detectors are right to consider pixel groups (usually pairs) only up to (mod 2) and pixel difference: little could be gained by retaining all DC information, and their cover models would be less widely-applicable if no normalization were performed.

4.4   Series 4: The Effect of Pixel Group Size and Shape

Our final series of SFI estimates is to compare the information found in pixel groups of different size and shape. We tested groups ranging from 1 to 9 pixels, including groups of different shape (2×2 versus 1×4, 1×5 versus five pixels arranged in a "plus" shape, etc). The experiments are confined to LSB replacement, and were repeated with and without DC normalization up to (mod 2) of the key pixel. For large groups of pixels, only the normalized groups are reported, because the raw pixel groups are grossly under-sampled.

Estimates of I_c and I_p are displayed in Tab. 4. There are many comparisons to draw. As we saw before, DC normalization does not destroy very much information if parity is preserved, typically 10–20%. There is almost no information in the individual pixel histograms but, as one would expect, more and more information is found in groups of larger size. Comparing the values of I_p, we see that this is true even on a per-pixel basis. We had hoped to observe the per-pixel information levelling off as the group size was increased, and there is some suggestion that it might approach a limit on the order of $I_p = 3$–4, but experiments on even larger group sizes would be necessary to validate this.

An initially-surprising result was that pixel groups $2 \times n$ contained substantially less information than $1 \times 2n$ (and a cross of 5 pixels less than a group of 1×5). This is counterintuitive since one expects that pixels spatially-closer

Table 4. Real images: the effect of pixel group size and shape; 3 sig. fig. displayed

Group shape	Raw groups			DC normalized (mod 2)		
	No. bins	$\widehat{I_c}$	$\widehat{I_p}$	No. bins	$\widehat{I_c}$	$\widehat{I_p}$
1×1	256	0.000826	0.000207	—		
1×2	56603	0.775	0.0968	512	0.665	0.0831
1×3	4430576	3.96	0.330	108456	3.36	0.280
1×4	116786674	15.6	0.973	6025600	13.0	0.815
2×2	123249057	7.52	0.470	5628177	6.77	0.423
1×5	897195813	40.5	2.02	105345419	31.9	1.59
"plus"	1190184977	9.94	0.497	129473835	8.15	0.408
1×6	2822410982	75.2	3.13	662797209	57.5	2.40
2×3	2771668936	32.8	1.37	631647082	26.7	1.11
1×8	—			4107782343	111	3.48
2×4	—			3594071886	68.2	2.13
3×3	—			5624145091	71.1	1.98

Experimental base: approx. 4×10^{10} *pixel groups*

should be more tightly coupled, but recall that the question is whether embedding creates unusual groups: a row of four pixels $(x, x, x+1, x)$ is less common in covers, relative to its frequency in stego images, than the same pixels arranged in a square because of smooth gradients. Much more could be said on this issue, particularly in regard to image pre-processing, but lack of space precludes it.

4.5 A Brief Robustness Check

The experimental results above are for just one set of covers, and the images were particularly well-behaved: they had been denoised in the conversion to bitmap format, and saturated images were excluded. In order to test the robustness of our conclusions, we repeated the experiments (only for small pixel groups) in three other cover sets: one of never-compressed pictures from a mixture of digital cameras (1.5 Gpixels), one of JPEG compressed images (5 Gpixels), and one set of resampled JPEG images (4 Gpixels). That more evidence is found in 1×4 than 2×2 groups was confirmed in all sets, as was that LSB-M is more secure than LSB-R, though their I_p ratio varied widely. In our main set, 2LSB-R appeared more detectable than LSB-R, and this also held for the alternative set of digital camera images, but not in the JPEG images: this probably reflects that quantization noise masks the larger stego-signal of 2LSB-R.

Finally, the preservation of almost all evidence of LSB-R under DC normalization (mod 2) was confirmed in two of the three case, but not the digital camera images. Further inspection showed that this was due to saturation in the covers: DC normalization deletes such evidence. The effect of saturation seems important: if not excluded from the corpus, it is the contribution of almost-saturated groups of pixels which dominate the sum in (3). This suggests that saturation might be exploited by steganalysis to substantial effect. Although it is easy to dismiss such detectors as trivial and dependent on flawed covers, they might be a valuable addition in practice, since saturation seems to be a common occurrence.

5   Conclusions

The beauty of empirical Steganographic Fisher Information estimation is that it enables us to quantify, in a properly information-theoretic way, how much evidence of payload exists in various types of pixel groups. Since almost all steganalysis methods can be described in terms of a high-order histogram, it also tells us about the fundamental security of different embedding functions[2].

Some results were as expected: larger groups contain more evidence, LSB-M is more secure than LSB-R, and pixel difference preserves most of the information about LSB-R if, and only if, the parity information is maintained. Some of the results were a surprise: more information exists in $1 \times 2n$ than $2 \times n$ groups, LSB-M is not orders of magnitude more secure than LSB-R, and 2LSB-R is particularly poor, though this last may not hold in noisier covers.

Natural directions for further research include the estimation of SFI in JPEG images, where perhaps the results can be used for feature selection as well as evaluation of embedding methods. Our experimental results required a lot of computation; they call for a better estimator for SFI than the simple plug-in histogram used here, otherwise larger pixel groups will require a heroic effort and a massive corpus. Some sort of confidence interval for the estimate can be found by bootstrapping, but this cannot take into account terms missing from (3). We believe that such effects, and more generally the problem that KL divergence is infinite if there is even the tiniest (and therefore insignificant) chance that a stego object takes a value never taken by a cover, are worthy of more study, and perhaps KL divergence can be replaced by something else. Also, we had to assume (implicitly) that the steganalyst has complete knowledge of the cover source. By Kerckhoffs' principle we should certainly be cautious about assuming less, but this is imposed anyway when we use KL divergence to measure security.

In principle, SFI estimation allows optimization of embedding: it is possible to extend this work to arbitrary independent embedding (beyond the constant-valency model in Sect. 3) and then to balance embedding efficiency against I_c to derive the optimal embedding function [18]. It should be stressed that such optimality holds only for the cover sets on which the experiments are performed. Still, wide experimentation may help clarify the best shape for stego noise and the best embedding strategies amongst LSB, 2LSB, and (mod k)-matching.

It is instructive to compare the performance of contemporary detectors with the KL divergence predictions given, for small payloads, by $D_{\mathrm{KL}}(P(0) \parallel P(\lambda)) \sim \frac{1}{2}I_c\lambda^2$. Such results are postponed to future work, but initial experiments showed

---

[2] Some steganalysis methods may, however, make use of heterogeneity of the groups of pixels within individual images, even if they are described solely in terms of a joint histogram. It is difficult to understand how this affects the information theoretic bounds provided by SFI.

that structural detectors based on pairs of pixels DC normalized (mod 2), such as SPA [11], come very close to the bound. This may explain why, despite much literature using the same techniques, only small increments in performance have been achieved. On the other hand, the Triples detector [13], based on pixel triplets, is a long way from the bound. This suggests that the *symmetries* cover model is not using all the possible information in larger pixel groups, and perhaps structural steganalysis should look there for performance improvements.

References

1. Cachin, C.: An information-theoretic model for steganography. Information and Computation 192(1), 41–56 (2004)
2. Wang, Y., Moulin, P.: Perfectly secure steganography: Capacity, error exponents, and code constructions. IEEE Transactions on Information Theory 54(6), 2706–2722 (2008)
3. Ker, A.: A capacity result for batch steganography. IEEE Signal Processing Letters 14(8), 525–528 (2007)
4. Filler, T., Ker, A., Fridrich, J.: The square root law of steganographic capacity for Markov covers. In: Proc. SPIE, Media Forensics and Security XI, vol. 7254, pp. 0801–0811 (2009)
5. Pronzato, L., Leonenko, N., Savani, V.: A class of Renyi information estimators for multidimensional densities. Annals of Statistics 36(5), 2153–2182 (2008)
6. Ker, A.: The ultimate steganalysis benchmark? In: Proc. 9th ACM Workshop on Multimedia and Security, pp. 141–148 (2007)
7. Kullback, S.: Information Theory and Statistics. Dover, New York (1968)
8. Fridrich, J., Soukal, D.: Matrix embedding for large payloads. IEEE Transactions on Information Forensics and Security 1(3), 390–394 (2006)
9. Ker, A., Pevný, T., Kodovský, J., Fridrich, J.: The square root law of steganographic capacity. In: Proc. 10th ACM Workshop on Multimedia and Security, pp. 107–116 (2008)
10. Westfeld, A., Pfitzmann, A.: Attacks on steganographic systems. In: Pfitzmann, A. (ed.) IH 1999. LNCS, vol. 1768, pp. 61–76. Springer, Heidelberg (2000)
11. Dumitrescu, S., Wu, X., Wang, Z.: Detection of LSB steganography via sample pair analysis. IEEE Transactions on Signal Processing 51(7), 1995–2007 (2003)
12. Ker, A.: A fusion of maximum likelihood and structural steganalysis. In: Furon, T., Cayre, F., Doërr, G., Bas, P. (eds.) IH 2007. LNCS, vol. 4567, pp. 204–219. Springer, Heidelberg (2008)
13. Ker, A.: A general framework for the structural steganalysis of LSB replacement. In: Barni, M., Herrera-Joancomartí, J., Katzenbeisser, S., Pérez-González, F. (eds.) IH 2005. LNCS, vol. 3727, pp. 296–311. Springer, Heidelberg (2005)
14. Fridrich, J., Goljan, M.: On estimation of secret message length in LSB steganography in spatial domain. In: Proc. SPIE, Security, Steganography, and Watermarking of Multimedia Contents VI, vol. 5306, pp. 23–34 (2004)
15. Ker, A., Böhme, R.: Revisiting WS steganalysis. In: Proc. SPIE, Security, Forensics, Steganography and Watermarking of Multimedia Contents X, vol. 6819, pp. 0501–0517 (2008)

16. Harmsen, J., Pearlman, W.: Higher-order statistical steganalysis of palette images. In: Proc. SPIE, Security and Watermarking of Multimedia Contents V, vol. 5020, pp. 131–142 (2003)
17. Ker, A.: Steganalysis of LSB matching in grayscale images. IEEE Signal Processing Letters 12(6), 441–444 (2005)
18. Ker, A.: Estimating the Information Theoretic Optimal Stego Noise. In: Proc. 8th International Workshop on Digital Watermarking (to appear, 2009)
19. Ker, A.: Steganalysis of embedding in two least significant bits. IEEE Transactions on Information Forensics and Security 2(1), 46–54 (2007)

Fast Determination of Sensitivity in the Presence of Countermeasures in BOWS-2

Andreas Westfeld

HTW Dresden
Faculty of Computer Science and Mathematics
PF 120701
01008 Dresden, Germany
andreas.westfeld@htw-dresden.de

Abstract. The second Break Our Watermarking System (BOWS-2) contest exposed a watermarking algorithm named Broken Arrows (BA) to worldwide attacks. In its second episode, the previously existing daily limit of 30 oracle calls per IP address was lifted to allow for sensitivity analysis. Often disrespected because of their extensive oracle use, sensitivity attacks can reveal up to one bit of information about the watermark in each experiment. In this paper we describe how we circumvented BA's countermeasures against sensitivity attacks.

1 Introduction

Broken Arrows (BA) is a watermarking technique by Teddy Furon and Patrick Bas [1], which was especially designed for the second edition of the Break Our Watermarking System contest (BOWS-2) [2]. BOWS-2 came in three sequential episodes to study the robustness and security of watermarking in three different contexts. The goal in each episode was the same: Render the watermark unreadable to the online detector in three given images (cf. Figure 1) while preserving the best possible quality (in terms of averaged PSNR). The conditions during the episodes were different: The first scenario (Episode 1) was about the robustness against common image processing tools (compression, denoising, filtering, etc.) with the following restrictions:

- only 30 calls to the online-detector were allowed per day and participant,
- an attempt is considered successful only if the watermark is unreadable and the PSNR is at least 20 dB, and
- no information about the watermarking algorithm will be provided.

During Episode 2, which was dedicated to oracle attacks, the daily limit of oracle requests was dropped. If the participant signed an agreement [3] in which the contender forswears reverse engineering in order to disclose the algorithm and/or secret key, an offline detector (executable binary) was provided to reduce the load of the online detector. Note that this binary did not contain the secret key for the official three pictures of the contest. The offline kit came with another three images marked with a different key.

S. Katzenbeisser and A.-R. Sadeghi (Eds.): IH 2009, LNCS 5806, pp. 89–101, 2009.

Fig. 1. Images from the second episode of the contest: FALL, LOUVRE, and CASIMIR

Episode 3 covered all threats that occur if a large set of images watermarked with the same secret key is released. During this last episode, a daily limit of 10 trials per participant was re-introduced. However, the participants had access to a database with 10,000 images that have been marked with the same key.

This paper focuses on the second episode of the contest from mid October 2007 to mid January 2008. Despite several countermeasures in BA, the results of our best sensitivity attack are close to 50 dB PSNR and took about 200,000 oracle requests per 512×512 greyscale image. In Section 2 we describe the design of our method including the response to BA's countermeasures. Section 3 presents the experimental results of the proposed sensitivity method in the second episode of BOWS-2 and concludes the paper.

2   Methods

2.1   Sensitivity Attack

The sensitivity attack was introduced by Cox and Linnartz in 1997 [4]. It estimates the watermark of correlation based systems with linear complexity. Note that in the case of BA, the watermark is only one out of 30 patterns generated from the key—the one that is closest to the host and consequently causes the least distortion when embedded. The watermark can be used to find the closest unmarked image. However, since it is only $\frac{1}{30}$ of all potential pseudorandom patterns, it is not equivalent to the key. In theory the key can be found as the seed that is necessary to generate the watermark. However, this is computationally infeasible. Comesaña et al. [5] generalised the sensitivity attack to find the closest unmarked image for watermarking schemes that are not correlation based. However, since BA *is* correlation based, we adapt the method described in [4] to our specific needs.

A sensitivity attack studies the effect of single host elements, whether they contribute to the strength or removal of the watermark, in order to generate a sweeping success in a combined attack in which all host elements are slightly changed in accordance with their sensitivity.

The sensitivity attack usually operates in the spatial domain and does not require any prior knowledge of the watermarking system. BA applies the watermark in the first three levels of a DWT decomposition. This is what we already knew from experiments in Episode 1. It was confirmed in the algorithm description of BA, which was disclosed afterwards in Episode 3. The sensitivity attack is not bound to a particular domain. Applied to DWT coefficients, the sensitivity analysis can be skipped more easily for parts of the host that BA leaves unused. In addition, the analysis works best in the domain that was used for embedding, because we can analyse the elements of the watermark independently there. This is advantageous to the attacker especially in the presence of specific countermeasures. Even if the watermark resided in the DCT or spatial domain, there is no fundamental restriction when the sensitivity is analysed in the DWT domain: It might just take a bit longer.

2.2 Randomised Detection Boundary

One countermeasure, a randomised detection boundary [6], ensures that manipulation of a single host element alone can not clearly cross the randomised zone of the boundary. Because of the limited image dynamics an attacker cannot change a single host element with arbitrary strength. The randomisation introduces a grey decision range in which the detector randomly decides between "Watermark is still there" and "Watermark has been removed" (cf. Figure 2). In the figure this range appears rather small and easy to get over. Nevertheless

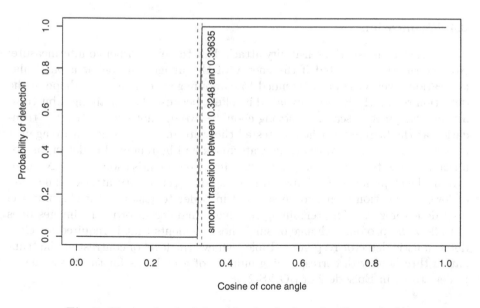

Fig. 2. The randomised detection border impedes the analysis

we needed a change in brightness by about $\pm 5{,}000$ to jump over it. The dynamics in brightness, however, is limited to the usual range $0\ldots 255$ (black $\ldots$ white in the greyscale images used in BOWS-2).

The goal of the randomisation is to force an attacker to submit the same image over and over again (e.g., ten times) in order to notice a growing or decreasing tendency of the watermarking strength by majority decision and to deduce the sensitivity of one single element of the host that was changed. Randomisation will not change the linear time complexity of the attack, but the running time would increase tenfold in our example. This is worth avoiding if the attack already takes a week per image without any countermeasure.

2.3   Normalisation

There is hope for the attacker (surprisingly) due to a countermeasure against another attack that is called *valuemetric scaling*: It protects the watermark against a simple change in contrast by which all brightness values in the image are multiplied with the same factor. A normalisation of the feature vector that is extracted from the image makes the detection score (cosine of cone angle, abscissa in Figure 2) virtually independent of valuemetric scaling.

Because of this normalisation the watermark is still detectable in images reduced to about one percent of contrast, resulting in only a few levels of grey [7]. With the reduction of contrast, the dynamics of the image is relatively extended. If the contrast is reduced to $\frac{1}{20}$, a single host element can be changed 20 times stronger. Thus the grey detection zone can be skipped.

2.4   Truncation

Normalisation assists the sensitivity attack. But there's another countermeasure: No watermark is detected if the energy of the image falls below a particular truncation level. Originally intended to camouflage the hypercone shape of the detection region [1], it certainly failed its effect because the remaining robustness against valuemetric scaling is strong enough—we did not even notice the truncation at the beginning, when we tested the watermark's lasting nature against reduction in contrast. Anyway, the watermark will be rendered undetectable for a scaling close to zero when it is overwhelmed by quantisation noise.[1] Normalisation develops its useful impact rather against sensitivity attacks. The level of lower truncation seems to be selected in order to just prevent skipping the grey detector zone. The remaining relative dynamics in ordinary images does not allow the profound change of single host elements that is required for clear deterministic detector responses. Table 1 shows the level of contrast at the truncation threshold with corresponding number of grey-levels for the three images under attack in Episode 2 of BOWS-2.

---

[1] Initially we considered this a random side effect of quantisation or a measure that reduces the share of false positives.

Table 1. Contrast level at the truncation threshold of the BA detector

Image	Contrast level	Levels of grey
FALL	0.01367	4
LOUVRE	0.02523	7
CASIMIR	0.02492	7

2.5 A Customised Boundary Image

The starting point for a sensitivity attack is usually a random image close to the detection boundary in which the watermark is still detected. Some minor modifications to this *boundary image* cause the detector to respond "removed" while the watermark is still detected after other modifications. If there is a blurred detection range instead of a clear boundary, the boundary image may also be *on* the boundary in the middle of the randomised range. This way, the distance to a deterministic decision is only half the range: A positive change of a single host element will shift the image in one deterministic area, while a negative change will shift it to the other.

Table 2. Range of DWT coefficients before and after blunting

Image	Marked original	Blunted image
FALL	$-573.0\ldots+420.7$	$-60.1\ldots+60.1$
LOUVRE	$-508.3\ldots+581.2$	$-29.3\ldots+29.3$
CASIMIR	$-389.4\ldots+488.6$	$-11.3\ldots+11.3$

One possible remedy against truncation is the selection of a custom-made image. In Section 2.4 we talked about *ordinary* images. However, for a sensitivity attack, the image does not have to look nice. We use the following trick: To reduce the dynamics range of the image without substantial change in contrast, we partially equalise the proportions in the distribution of values. In a first step we sort the DWT coefficients of the image by magnitude. The coefficients in the strongest five percent quantile[2] are nullified. This step removes the most significant contours in the image that are likely to saturate when the sensitivity of the corresponding coefficients is tested (cf. Table 2 and Figure 3). In a second step we reduce the contrast of the image to a level that is safely above the truncation threshold.

To preserve the level of contrast and the distribution of coefficients, but still shift the image close to the detection boundary, we have mixed the marked original with a de-watermarked version of the image prior to the two steps that we

---

[2] This value was chosen by gut feeling after looking at the distribution of DWT coefficients in the given images.

Fig. 3. Strong contours blunted (left) and contrast reduced in the boundary image with a single saturated coefficient in the image centre (right)

just described (blunting and reduction). We gained the de-watermarked version using a regression-based technique that was developed in Episode 1 of BOWS-2 [8]. The mixing ratio p is determined in an iteration that involves the online detector (interval bisection):

$$\text{mixed image} = p \cdot \text{de-watermarked image} + (1 - p) \cdot \text{marked original}$$

Figure 4 summarises the procedure that finds a rough estimate of p. The change that is applied to single host elements will influence the estimate. Therefore we run the procedure in Fig. 4 twice. The two runs are only different in the saturation after contrast reduction. One time the DWT coefficient is saturated in positive direction (with the final result p^+), another time in negative direction (with the final result p^-). The results of the two runs are averaged to determine a mean value $p = \frac{1}{2}(p^+ + p^-)$ that is used to start the sensitivity analysis.

2.6 Sensitivity Analysis

Despite the random influence of the boundary the estimate p is remarkably stable. However, because the quality of our sensitivity analysis relies on the precision of p, we add a run of 400 self-adjusting double sensitivity tests (one oracle call for positive change, one for negative). If p is set correctly, we will get opposing detector results. If we get identical answers (two times "removed" or two times "still there") p has to be adjusted (decreased resp. increased) prior to subsequent tests.[3]

---

[3] We used the stepsize $\frac{1}{32}|p^+ - p^-|$ for fine-tuning p. Coefficients close to the image border might suffer from clipping effects. So we disregarded a three elements wide margin around the DWT subband and used only coefficients that were nullified in the blunting step.

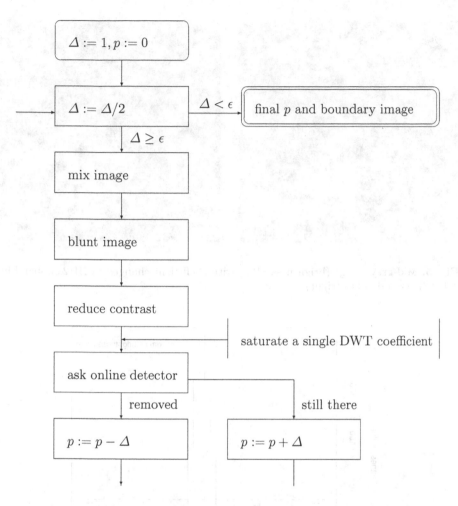

Fig. 4. Construction of the boundary image

We assume that almost all further coefficients lead to opposing detector results. Hence each of them is tested only in one direction (the positive direction, without restricting generality). Once all desired coefficients have been tested, the sensitivities are scaled and added to the corresponding coefficients. This is a bit tricky, because the detection region has a double hypercone shape in BA (i.e., negative watermarks are detected as well). The process of finding the correct scale is again supported by a countermeasure: This time the truncation threshold increases the gap between the two cones and makes it easier to find. This is necessary because we need an anchor point in the region where the watermark is not detected, before we can iteratively find the tangent to the detection boundary. For example, the range of the tangent scalefactor in which the watermark

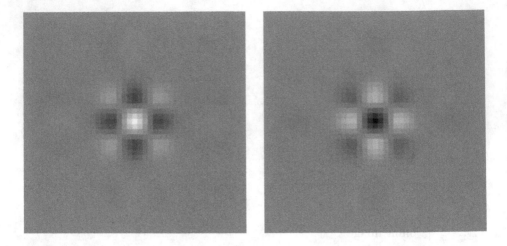

Fig. 5. Mid-grey image (brightness=128) with coefficient changed in HH2 subband by +444 (left) and −444 (right)

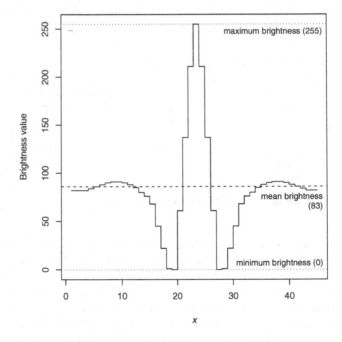

Fig. 6. Lateral cut through the wavelet in Fig. 7 (left)

is not detected in the image FALL is 1.194...1.25. Below 1.194 we are in one truncated cone shaped detection region, above 1.25 we are in the other. Thus the stepsize for the anchor search must be smaller than 5 percent.

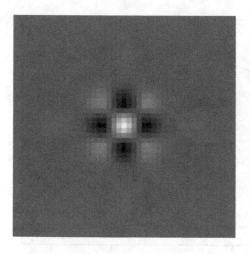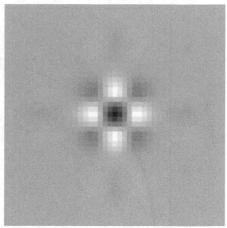

Fig. 7. Grey image with coefficient changed in HH2 subband by +601 (left, brightness=83) and −601 (right, brightness=172)

Neighbouring DWT coefficients of the same subband overlap in the spatial domain. As already mentioned in Section 2.1 the attack works best if the sensitivity can be analysed independently for each watermarked element. Therefore we try to keep the crosstalk small between neighbouring coefficients. We determined the level at which coefficients start saturating (cf. Figure 5). In the HH2 subband of a neutral, mid-grey image (brightness=128), the saturation starts at ±444. This value dependends on both, the kind of decomposition (for HH2 it is ±444 but for HL2 and LH2 it is ±561) and the level (HH1 ±257, HH0 ±175). In addition we notice that for a positive change (cf. Figure 5, left) white will saturate before the black level is even reached, while a negative change can create deep black without saturated white (cf. Figure 5, right).

We can enhance the saturation limit by 35 percent if the mean brightness of the image coincides with the average of the saturated wavelet. Figure 6 shows a lateral cut through the optimised wavelet. The mean brightness is only 83 here (cf. Figure 7, left), which exhausts the whole range completely. For negative saturation of the coefficient (−601) the mean brightness has to be $255 - 83 = 172$ (cf. Figure 7, right).

3   Results and Conclusion

We determined the sensitivity of three subbands (HH0, LH0, HL0) in all three images. During Christmas holidays 2007 we left the remaining subbands from decomposition levels 1 and 2 in an unsupervised run of the analysis. Unfortunately our parameter choice was not general enough to fit all three images. Apart from the tests in the subband HH1 of the image FALL, which the parameters were tailored for, hardly any result was different from "removed".

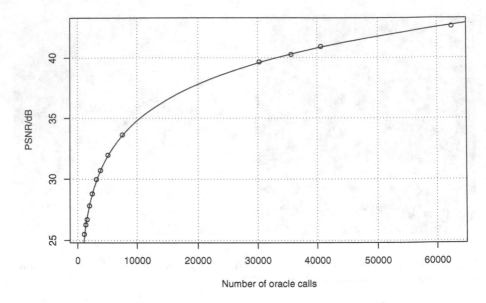

Fig. 8. Learning curve for the proposed sensitivity analysis (image FALL, HH0 subband only)

Figure 8 shows the learning curve of the image FALL for the proposed attack. The diagram shows the curve for the first 64k tests only (subband HH0). After 10,000 tests the PSNR is 35 dB, and 42.8 dB when the complete subband is done. 150,000 further tests are necessary to increase the result by another 5 dB.

Table 3. Final results of Episode 2 (average PSNR=49.49 dB)

Image	PSNR	Subbands	p	Contrast	Tangent scalefactor
FALL	47.35 dB	3	0.308	0.03	1.194
	47.80 dB	4	0.308	0.03	1.00[a]
LOUVRE	52.25 dB	3	0.186	0.10	0.624
CASIMIR	49.51 dB	3	0.834	0.10	0.905

[a] 1.00 for HH0, 1.08 for HL0/LH0, and 1.45 for HH1

The final results are shown in Table 3. The average of our best three images is 49.49 dB, which is the second best PSNR in Episode 2. Due to its high energy in high frequencies, the image FALL can be most weakened in contrast before the detector truncates. The density of DWT coefficients seems to be very different between LOUVRE and CASIMIR. Obviously the 5 percent strong coefficients that are nullified contribute more to the watermark in CASIMIR than in LOUVRE. This turns up when the mixed image requires a de-watermarked share of 83 % in CASIMIR vs. 19 % in LOUVRE.

The end of this Episode was similar to eBay: After a phase of unimportant, rather entertaining bids, where the PSNR was obviously tailored, just exceeding the top, to kid (or "call") the fellows, a longer quiet phase followed in the Hall of Fame. Finally, when the ultimate bids were posted, we had no chance to re-run the analysis of the remaining subbands before Episode 2 ended.[4] Maybe it is worth to study this psychological aspect in a subsequent challenge. Another interesting sideline is how the stories told by the two persiflaged main characters of the action movie *Broken Arrow*[5], Maj. Deakins and Capt. Hale, who lead through the challenge, influenced the fortunes of BOWS-2. Would calculated misleading information complicate the work of an attacker?

For instance, we tried to find out if the perceptual hashing technique used to increase the diversity of the key was ever there or just a story to distract attackers from the real target. Deakins and Hale told the technique was disabled after the first week of the contest because it was not mature enough. Indeed, the detector spotted the watermark again in some images that have been successfully attacked before. Just a plain bugfix or destruction of an important foundation by the contestants? If a perceptual hash diversifies the key, how can three images still be detected by the same detector after the perceptual hash was disabled, regardless which image is submitted under which name? The only solution is to use a series of three detectors with three "pre-diversified" keys. This means the watermark detected by the first key will result in a shorter latency of the request. Although the different times can be hidden by an artificial delay, we were able to measure the different latency. If the watermark is detected, the minimum latency for CASIMIR is 1.2 seconds, followed by LOUVRE with 1.6 seconds and finally FALL 2.0 seconds. The latency is also 2.0 seconds for an image if no watermark is detected. Note that FALL was also among the three images that was given in Episode 1. Another image from the first episode, SHEEP, was not detected in Episode 2. The third image from the first episode, SOUVENIR, was detected with CASIMIR's minimum latency. Consequently, SOUVENIR and FALL have different keys. Thus we had three different keys during the first episode as well.

Figure 9 shows the latency of the detector responses. The ticks on the abscissa of the diagrams mark the beginning of a day at 0h CET. In the diagram to the left we see the behaviour of the detector in an early phase of Episode 2, when the server, which is a multicore machine, is almost idle. The timing of the detector reveals two cleanups during night, at 0h and 4h CET, when the answer times suddenly reset to their minimum, growing afterwards continuously. The reason of this increasing latency is unclear. Maybe each request generates a ticket, which is matched against a database that is emptied twice a night. The responses are dark coloured if the watermark is still detected and light if the watermark has

---

[4] Note that the difference between our result and the top (0.75 dB) might look small at first sight. However, since the learning curve (cf. Fig. 8) flattens out, the difference is substatial at this level (about 50 dB). We congratulate The Merry Bowmen of UVIGO to this impressive victory.

[5] With John Travolta and Christian Slater, 1996.

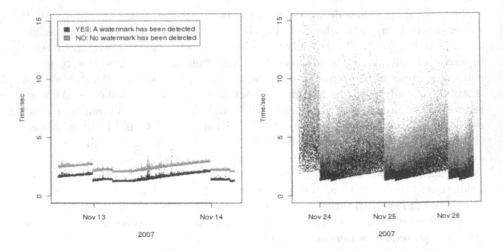

Fig. 9. Latency of oracle calls for subbands HL0 (left) and LH0 (right) of CASIMIR with 65,536 coefficients each

been removed. In the left diagram we clearly see two traces of different colours. Consequently the latency depends on this detector decision. To the right the server is under a higher load level. Instead of the two clear traces we rather have two overlapping bands. The overall time for the analysis of a subband of similar size took one day longer on the heavy loaded server (i.e., an increase of about 70 %). However, the detector latency still depends on the decision. Hardly any light coloured latency is below 2 seconds. Note that the same plot for the image FALL would not show any dependency between latency and decision. For LOUVRE the two traces would be closer to each other (about half the distance).

In summary we have developed a sensitivity analysis against BA, which does not suffer much from particular countermeasures. In our further work we will analyse to what extent a different choice of parameters in the watermarking algorithm can spoil the attacker's approach. It is probably easy to change the parameters in order to affect the current setting of the proposed attack. The attacker's response to this is hard to estimate. Would a stronger randomisation be more effective against oracle attacks?

Acknowledgements

The author thanks Pedro Comesaña for an interesting e-mail discussion on sensitivity, the key, and the detection region. The author also thanks Patrick Bas and Teddy Furon, who organised this motivating contest in a very entertaining way. BOWS-2 was a very pleasant research adventure.

References

1. Furon, T., Bas, P.: Broken arrows. EURASIP Journal on Information Security 2008, Article ID 597040 (2008)
2. ECRYPT: BOWS-2, Break our watermarking system, 2nd edn. (2007), http://bows2.gipsa-lab.inpg.fr
3. Furon, T., Bas, P.: License agreement (2007), http://bows2.gipsa-lab.inpg.fr/Bo-blog/Images/BOWS2-agreement.pdf
4. Cox, I.J., Linnartz, J.P.M.G.: Public watermarks and resistance to tampering. In: IEEE International Conference on Image Processing ICIP 1997, Santa Barbara, California, USA, vol. 3, pp. 3–6 (1997)
5. Comesaña, P., Pérez-Freire, L., Pérez-González, F.: The blind Newton sensitivity attack. In: Delp III, E.J., Wong, P.W. (eds.) Security, Steganography and Watermarking of Multimedia Contents VIII (Proc. of SPIE), San Jose, CA (2006)
6. El Choubassi, M., Moulin, P.: On the fundamental tradeoff between watermark detection performance and robustness against sensitivity analysis attack. In: Delp III, E.J., Wong, P.W. (eds.) Security, Steganography and Watermarking of Multimedia Contents VIII (Proc. of SPIE), San Jose, CA, pp. 1–12 (2006)
7. Miller, M.L., Doërr, G.J., Cox, I.: Applying informed coding and embedding to design a robust high-capacity watermark. IEEE Trans. on Image Processing 13, 792–807 (2004)
8. Westfeld, A.: A regression-based restoration technique for automated watermark removal. In: Proc. of ACM Multimedia and Security Workshop 2008, MM&Sec08, pp. 215–219. ACM Press, New York (2008)

A Phase Modulation Audio Watermarking Technique

Michael Arnold, Peter G. Baum, and Walter Voeßing

Thomson, Corporate Research Hannover
{michael.arnold,peter.baum}@thomson.net

Abstract. Audio watermarking is a technique, which can be used to embed information into the digital representation of audio signals. The main challenge is to hide data representing some information without compromising the quality of the watermarked track and at the same time ensure that the embedded watermark is robust against removal attacks. Especially providing perfect audio quality combined with high robustness against a wide variety of attacks is not adequately addressed and evaluated in current watermarking systems. In this paper, we present a new phase modulation audio watermarking technique, which among other features provides evidence for high audio quality. The system combines the alteration of the phase with the spread spectrum concept and is referred to as Adaptive Spread Phase Modulation (ASPM). Extensive benchmarking provide the evidence for the inaudibility of the embedded watermark and the good robustness.

1 Introduction

Copy prevention and copyright protection applications have been the main motivations of the audio watermarking research field to fight piracy especially in the music sector. Nevertheless, there is a range of application scenarios beyond that of content protection for which digital watermarks are also very much suitable. One example is the use for audience rating. This *active* monitoring scenario (see [1]) embeds different time varying information like a channel identification and a time code at the broadcaster site. The watermark detection is performed at a number of panelists households equipped with a detector. The information can be analyzed in order to gather statistics about the audience listening and watching habits. This scenario makes high demands on the watermarking system. The broadcaster require perfect audio quality at the embedding site, whereas the conditions under which the detector site at the panelists households operates cannot be fully controlled. There may be uncontrollable environmental noise, clock deviations between playback and recording of the watermarked tracks and an acoustic path transmission.

Several approaches have been developed to embed information into audio data. From the existing algorithms, a few categories of methods can be identified according to certain aspects built into the different schemes. A variety of watermarking algorithms [2,3,4,5,6] are based on so-called *echo hiding* methods.

S. Katzenbeisser and A.-R. Sadeghi (Eds.): IH 2009, LNCS 5806, pp. 102–116, 2009.

Echo hiding algorithms embed watermarks into a signal $c_o(t)$ by adding echos $c_o(t - \Delta t)$ to produce a marked signal $c_w(t)$. A disadvantage is the complexity of this method due to the number of transformations which have to be computed for detection, which is performed in the Cepstrum domain. The probably most widely used watermarking techniques are based on the spread spectrum concept. Several of these methods modify the magnitudes of the transform domain [7,8]. The algorithm presented by Kirovski et al. [9] uses the modulated complex lapped transform (MCLT) and modifies the magnitude of the MCLT coefficients in the dB scale rather in linear scale. They use a psychoacoustic model, which quantifies the audibility of the MCLT magnitude coefficient. The so-called patchwork technique first presented by Bender et al. [10] is equivalent to the spread spectrum method. This method was also applied to the magnitudes in the Fourier domain [11,12].

Due to the fact that information when the signal occurs in time is contained in the phase of the spectrum, use of magnitudes for embedding the watermark may require a time consuming synchronization process in the detection step to achieve the right alignment between embedding and detection.

These practical considerations were the movtivation to develop an alternative audio watermarking technique referred to as Adaptive Spread Phase Modulation (ASPM). There already exist some approaches to embed the watermark into the phase of the original signal. In the first phase coding approach developed by Bender et al. [10] the whole watermark is embedded into the phase spectrum of the first block. In turn this method has a low payload and is not suitable for embedding varying watermarks into the audio stream. Another form of embedding the watermark into the phase is by performing independent multiband phase modulation [13]. Both algorithms are *non-blind watermarking* methods, since they require the original signal during the watermark retrieval, which of course limits their applicability.

In the ASPM algorithm the watermark is spread over the phases of several consecutive blocks in the audio stream. Combining the embedding in the phase with the spread spectrum concept has inherently the advantage of retaining the time information for fast synchronization and the high robustness of the spread spectrum techniques. A fair comparison of the ASPM algorithm with the existing techniques mentioned above is impossible, since it depends on various factors. Even if the data rate would be fixed and the quality of the watermarked tracks would be adapted for the different watermarking systems the benchmarking results heavily depend on the CPU requirements and the content used for testing.

The paper is structured as follows. Section 2 describes the basic watermark embedding and detection algorithm. Section 3 contains a detailed description of the underlying psychoacoustic model to ensure the high audio quality of the watermarked tracks. The presented algorithm is extensively evaluated in Sect. 4. This includes a detailed evaluation of the audio quality by conducting listening tests in Sect. 4.1. Furthermore the robustness is extensively evaluated with a lot of audio material in Sect. 4.2. The results of performance tests is presented in Sect. 4.3. Section 5 summarizes the paper with some final remarks.

2   The Audio Watermarking Algorithm

In this paper the original signal is denoted by c_o. $c_o[i]$, $i = 1, \ldots, l_{c_o}$[1] are the samples of the original signal in the time domain. An additional index of the carrier elements c_{oj} denotes a subset of the audio signal.

The algorithm splits the audio track into N_B blocks c_o^B of length l_B for embedding a symbol of the watermark. A block is partitioned into N_{SB} overlapping sub-blocks c_o^{SB} of length $l_{SB} = 1024$ samples with an overlap of $\frac{l_{SB}}{2}$ (driven by the psychoacoustic model see Sect. 3).

2.1   Generation of Reference Signals

The message $\mathbf{m}$ will be represented by a sequence of l_m separate symbols, drawn from an alphabet $\mathcal{A}$ of size $|\mathcal{A}|$. Each symbol is represented by a reference signal with the length of one symbol block, which is partitioned in sub-blocks.

Generate Random Signal for a Block in Time Domain. For all symbols, drawn from an alphabet $\mathcal{A}$ of size $|\mathcal{A}|$:

1. For each sub-block map the secret key K to the seed of a random number generator, and generate a pseudorandom sequence $\mathbf{pn}$ consisting of equiprobable elements in the range $[-\pi, +\pi]$, defining the phases in the Fourier domain.
2. Perform inverse Fourier transformation of the sub-block to derive random time signal and concatenate the signals of the sub-blocks.

Generate Sub-Blocks Reference Phases for Embedding. The partitioning of the reference signal in blocks consisting of sub-blocks shifted by $l_{SB}/2$ is done in compliance with the partitioning of the audio signal:

1. The portion of the time signal to the corresponding sub-block is windowed with a window function (1). The window function used is

$$\text{win}[n] = \begin{cases} \sin\left(\frac{\pi(n+1)}{l_{SB}+2}\right), & 0 \leq n \leq l_{SB}/2 - 1 \\ \text{win}[l_{SB} - 1 - n], & l_{SB}/2 \leq n \leq l_{SB} - 1 \ . \end{cases} \tag{1}$$

2. Each windowed sub-block of the random signal $\mathbf{r}$ is transformed into the Fourier domain $\mathbf{R}_j^{SB} = \text{DFT}(\mathbf{r}_j)$, $j = 1, \ldots, N_{SB}$ to yield the reference phases $\phi_{rj}[\omega_k]$:

$$\mathbf{W}_j^{SB}[\omega_k] = e^{i\phi_{rj}[\omega_k]} \quad \forall j \text{ with } k \in [0, \ldots, l_{SB}/2 - 1] \tag{2}$$

The reference angles are used during the embedding step. Embedding the watermark requires the application of a synthesis window prior to the final overlap-add to fade out errors due to nonlinear spectral modifications at the block boundaries, thereby suppressing audible discontinuities.

---

[1] l_{c_o} denotes the number of samples of track c_o.

Generate Reference Signal for a Block for Detection

1. The sub-blocks reference phases are generated according to Sect. 2.1.
2. Inverse transformation of the individual sub-blocks $\mathbf{w_j^{SB}} = \mathrm{IDFT}\left(\mathbf{W_j^{SB}}\right)\ \forall j$.
3. Multiplication of all sub-blocks time domain with the window function according to (1) and overlap-adding to create the reference signal $\mathbf{w^B}$.

The final reference signal is normalized to 1. The embedding process employs the $|\mathcal{A}|$ reference signals. The time domain reference signal is used during detection for correlation purposes.

2.2 Embedding a Watermark Symbol

The partitioning of the audio signal in blocks consisting of sub-blocks has to be taken into account during embedding of the watermark signal $\mathbf{w^B}$.

1. According to the symbol to be embedded the reference signal $\mathbf{w^B}$ is selected.
2. Each sub-block $\mathbf{c_o^{SB}}$ from the original signal is windowed with the window function (1) and transformed in the Fourier domain $\mathbf{C_{oj}^{SB}} = \mathrm{DFT}\left(\mathbf{c_{oj}^{SB}}\right)\ \forall j$.
3. The masking threshold is calculated from the psycho-acoustic model (see Sect. 3). It implicitly defines the maximum allowed phase changes which can be applied to the Fourier coefficient of the carrier signal without introducing audible distortions (see Fig. 1). The allowed phase change $|\Delta\phi_{oj}[\omega_k]|$ is calculated from (3) for each sub-block j and frequency ω_k (see Fig. 2).

$$|\Delta\phi_{oj}[\omega_k]| = 2\arcsin\frac{|\Delta A_{oj}[\omega_k]|/2}{|A_{oj}[\omega_k]|},\ k \in [0,\dots,l_{\mathrm{SB}}/2-1]\ . \tag{3}$$

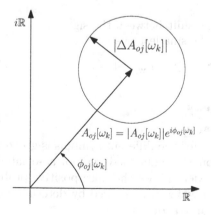

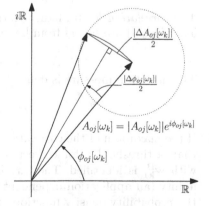

Fig. 1. Masking circle   **Fig. 2.** Perceptual phase change

4. The phases of the original signal are changed into the direction of the phases of $\mathbf{w^{SB}}$ to minimize the phase difference between reference angle and the angle of the watermarked Fourier coefficient

$$\Delta\phi_{oj}[\omega_k] = \text{sign}\left(\phi_{rj}[\omega_k] - \phi_{oj}[\omega_k]\right)|\Delta\phi_{oj}[\omega_k]|, \; k \in [0, \ldots, l_{\text{SB}}/2] \;. \quad (4)$$

The reference phases $\phi_{rj}[\omega_k]$ for a sub-block is determined by the symbol r to be embedded and the sub-block number j within the block (see Sect. 2.1). In case of noise components the allowed phase change is $\pm\pi$ (see Sect. 3.2). Therefore for noisy components the new phase will be the same as the phase of the reference pattern. Using the new phases the Fourier coefficients of the watermarked signal are

$$\mathbf{C^{SB}_{wj}}[\omega_k] = \mathbf{A_{oj}}[\omega_k] \times e^{i(\phi_{oj}[\omega_k] + \Delta\phi_{oj}[\omega_k])}, \; k \in [0, \ldots, l_{\text{SB}}/2 - 1] \;. \quad (5)$$

5. The marked block is computed by inverse transformation of the modified Fourier coefficients of the individual sub-blocks $\mathbf{c^{SB}_{wj}} = \text{IDFT}\left(\mathbf{C^{SB}_{wj}}\right) \forall j$.
6. All sub-blocks are windowed in time domain with the window function (1) and overlap-added to create the watermarked signal block $\mathbf{c^B_w}$.

2.3   Detecting a Watermark Symbol

For detecting watermarks the audio signal is partitioned in the same way as during the embedding. Since the same pseudo random generator is used, the same reference signals will be produced. In a first step all reference signals $\mathbf{w^B_k}$, $k = 1, \ldots, |\mathcal{A}|$ are generated in the time domain (see Sect. 2.1).

To detect the individual symbols loop over all audio samples:

1. Load block of audio samples $\mathbf{c^B}$ with size l_B.
2. Loop over all reference signals $\mathbf{w^B_k}$, $k = 1, \ldots, |\mathcal{A}|$: The similarity between the two length-l_B signals $\mathbf{w^B}$ and $\mathbf{c^B}$ is calculated from the *cross-correlation*

$$\hat{r}_{\mathbf{c^B w^B}}[m] = \frac{1}{l_B - |m|} \sum_{n=0}^{l_B - 1 - m} \mathbf{c^B}[n]\mathbf{w^B}[n + m], \; -l_B + 1 \le m \le l_B - 1 \quad (6)$$

The *correlation lag* m, indicates the time-shift between the signals.
3. The $|\hat{r}_{\mathbf{c^B w^B_k}}|$ are sorted from largest to the smallest one

$$|\hat{r}_{\mathbf{c^B w^B_{k1}}}| \ge |\hat{r}_{\mathbf{c^B w^B_{k2}}}| \ge \ldots \ge |\hat{r}_{\mathbf{c^B w^B_{k|\mathcal{A}|}}}| \;. \quad (7)$$

4. The detection measure is defined as

$$D_{\mathbf{c^B}} = \frac{|\hat{r}_{\mathbf{c^B w^B_{k1}}}|}{|\hat{r}_{\mathbf{c^B w^B_{k2}}}|} \;. \quad (8)$$

5. If the maximum of the correlation values for the different symbols is greater than a threshold τ for correct detection the embedded symbol associated with $\mathbf{w^B_{k1}}$ is identified. The threshold τ determines the false positive probability (an application dependent value) which was derived by determining the probability density function of unmarked content.
6. If a symbol is identified, load next block of l_B samples. Otherwise shift block of audio samples by $\frac{l_B}{2}$ samples and load next $\frac{l_B}{2}$ samples from input.

3   Psychoacoustic Phase Shaping

As in audio coding a psychoacoustic model is necessary in audio watermarking to control the audibility of signal modification. The psychoacoustic model 1 of ISO-MPEG [14] with a number of alterations and improvements is used in this system. In order to iteratively allocate the necessary bits the MPEG standard calculates the signal-to-mask ratios (SMR) of all the subbands. This is not necessary in the case of a watermarking application, since only the masking threshold for each frequency bin in a sub-block is of interest for the embedding step (see Sect. 2.2). Consequently the sound pressure level in bands, the minimum masking threshold per band and the SMR are not calculated. In addition the threshold in quiet is not taken into account. This prevents uncovering the structure of the watermark in silent fragments of the audio stream.

One of the additions added includes an attack module which prevents pre-echoes described in Sect. 3.1. Further enhancements include a peaks and noise component detection function in Sect. 3.2. These modules are especially tailored to the calculation of the phase masking threshold described in Sect. 3.3.

3.1   Attack Detection

Audibiliy issues can happen if a quiet portion of the audio block is followed by a sudden increase in audio energy, because of the spread of the phase-based watermark signal in the time domain into the quiet section of the sub-block (see the center plot in Fig. 3). To circumvent this problem the sudden increase of the audio energy is detected by an attack module based on a power constraint between consecutive sub-blocks. In case of an *attack* the phase masking threshold is set to zero and nothing is embedded in this sub-block. An attack decreases

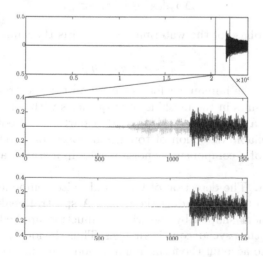

Fig. 3. Preventing pre-echoes by detecting attacks

the watermark strength not seriously, since only one sub-block of a block (used for embedding one symbol) are affected and the sub-blocks do overlap by 50 %:

1. Calculate the mean power $\hat{P}_m$ in dB in the frequency range $[f_l, f_u]$ of interest for the two overlapped sub-blocks by

$$\hat{P}_m = \sum_{k=f_l}^{f_u} P_k, \ m = j - 1, j \ . \tag{9}$$

2. If the increase in the mean power $\Delta\hat{P}$ of the current block is above a predefined attack threshold (currently $T_P = 5$ dB) the current block is marked as an attack block.

$$\Delta\hat{P} = \hat{P}_j - \hat{P}_{j-1} > T_P \tag{10}$$

The effect of the attack detection is demonstrated in the lowest of Fig. 3 which contains no watermark signal. The parameter T_P was determined experimentally.

3.2   Detecting Peaks and Noise

Preliminary Considerations. In general the spectrum $X(\omega)$ of a signal $x(n)$ is determined by its magnitude $|X(\omega)|$ – measured in dB – and its phase $\angle X(\omega)$. The information when the signal occurs in time is contained in the phase of the spectrum. By definition stationary noise signals cannot be characterized by special events at certain times due to their random fluctuations. In turn the spectral phase obeys a random behaviour carrying no audible information.

As a result of these considerations the phase of noisy components of the original signal can be arbitrarily altered without having an effect on the audibility. The allowed phase change $\Delta\phi_{oj}[\omega_k]$ for the noise component k in sub-block j is

$$\Delta\phi_{oj}[\omega_k] \in [-\pi, +\pi] \tag{11}$$

and the resulting phase of the watermarked signal is the same as the reference signal.

$$\phi_{wj}[\omega_k] = \phi_{rj}[\omega_k] \tag{12}$$

On the other hand the human ear focuses itself on the spectral peaks of sound. An effect which results in the masking of frequencies with a lower energy in the neighbourhood of a strong spectral peak at a particular frequency. Therefore (12) requires a reliable detection of tonal and noise components, because the misinterpretation of a component as noise results in a strong audible effect.

Tonal Detection. The detection of tonal and noise components is performed in the frequency domain by finding the peaks. A spectral peak is modeled as a sinusoidal component shaped by the window function applied in the time domain before doing the psychoacoustic analysis. Thus the identification of spectral peaks will take into account the form (a main lobe) with monotonically decreasing magnitudes at both sides:

- To distinguish a local peak from variations contained in a noise floor the left and right bins are checked to ensure that the magnitude of actual bin is above two thresholds T_1 and T_2 which are determined experimentally (see Fig. 4).
- All the frequencies are identified as belonging to the tonal component if they have a decreasing magnitudes on both sides (see frequency range in Fig. 4).

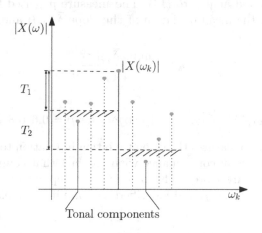

Fig. 4. Detection of tonal components

The sound pressure level $X_{tm}(k)$ of the tonal masker[2] at index k is computed by adding the identified neighbouring spectral lines belonging to the tonal group (see (18) in Sect. 3.3).

Identification of Noise Components. The noise components are characterized by random variations. During short time intervals between successive sub-blocks tonal signals are assumed to be stationary, i.e. the magnitudes $|X_j(k)|$ – in linear scale – at frequency bin k of sub-block j varies slowly over few sub-blocks. Therefore the slope of the magnitude curve is relatively constant. On the other hand, noisy components have due to their random nature a high degree of variations over sub-blocks. Thus a heuristic approach is implemented which measures the relative degree of slope variation in each frequency bin over successive sub-blocks.

The slope Δ_{kj} in sub-block j at frequency bin k is defined via

$$\Delta_{kj} = P_{kj} - \overline{P}_{kj-1} \text{ with } P_{kj} = 20 \log_{10} |X_j(\omega_k)| \tag{13}$$

and

$$\overline{P}_{kj-1} = \alpha \overline{P}_{kj-2} + (1 - \alpha) P_{kj-1} \text{ with } \alpha = 0.5 . \tag{14}$$

---

[2] Identified by the sub-script tm.

This expression – known as the *Exponentially Weighted Moving Average Filter* – calculates the average power over a series of sub-blocks by attenuating the fluctuating components and placing more emphasis on the most recent data. The deviation of the slope from the mean value is calculated from

$$\delta_{kj} = (\Delta_{kj} - \overline{\Delta}_{kj-1})^2 \tag{15}$$

with $\overline{\Delta}_{kj-1}$ calculated analog to (14). The measure p_{kj} used for noise identification is based on the mean deviation of the slope $\overline{\delta}_{kj}(\beta)$ and the mean power $\overline{P}_{kj}$ defined as

$$p_{kj} = \frac{\min_\beta \overline{\delta}_{kj}(\beta)}{\overline{P}_{kj}} \tag{16}$$

with

$$\overline{\delta}_{kj}(\beta) = \beta\overline{\delta}_{kj-1} + (1 - \beta)\delta_{kj} \text{ for } \beta = 0.6, 0.8 \ . \tag{17}$$

The definition of p_{kj} measures the slope variation in relation to the power of the average signal. This is in conformance with the fact that components having a small average power are more likely to be noisy components. The resulting p_{kj} are limited $p_{kj} = \min(1, p_{kj})$ and identified as noise if $p_{kj} > 0.5$.

3.3   Masking Threshold Computation

For the masking threshold computation a distinction has to be made between tonal and non-tonal components. The sound pressure level – measured in dB – of the tonal component for the spectral line k is denoted by $X_{tm}(k)$. The identified tonal group (see Sect. 3.2) is summed up to calculate the power of the tonal component

$$X_{tm}(k) = 10\log_{10}\left(10^{\sum_{j=k-m}^{k+n} \frac{X(j)}{10}}\right) \tag{18}$$

with m, n lower and upper distance of the tonal group of bin k. After the tonal components have been zeroed the remaining spectral lines within each critical band are summed to form the sound pressure level of the new non-tonal component $X_{nm}(k)$ corresponding to that critical band. The sound pressure levels $X_{tm}(k)$ for the tonal and $X_{nm}(k)$ are used to calculate the individual masking thresholds for tonal and non-tonal masker:

$$LT_{tm}[z(j), z(i)] = X_{tm}[z(j)] + \text{av}_{tm}[z(j)] + \text{vf}[z(j), z(i)] \tag{19}$$
$$LT_{nm}[z(j), z(i)] = X_{nm}[z(j)] + \text{av}_{nm}[z(j)] + \text{vf}[z(j), z(i)] \tag{20}$$

The masking threshold is calculated at the frequency index i. j is the frequency index of the masker. $X_{tm}(z(j))$ is the power density of the masker with index j. The term $\text{av}_{t|nm}[z(j)]$ is the so-called masking and $\text{vf}[z(j), z(i)]$ the masking function as described in [14,15]. The global masking threshold LT_g is computed by adding LT_{tm} and LT_{nm}, and finally setting $LT_g(i) = \pi, \forall i \in$ noise.

4 Evaluation

This section evaluates the performance of the audio watermarking algorithm in terms of the quality of the watermarked items and false negative errors. The false negative errors will be evaluated with respect to the robustness of the embedded watermarks. It will be not evaluated regarding the security of the system where the false negative errors are due an attack by hostile adversaries. Section 4.1 presents the quality evaluation of the developed system. For the fixed quality setting the robustness is assessed in the second Sect. 4.2.

4.1 Audio Quality Evaluation

Currently no objective metric to quantify the quality of a audio track carrying a watermark is available. Performing subjective listening tests are still the ultimate evaluation procedures to judge the quality of processed audio tracks (see [16]).

Since not only the transparency of the watermarked audio tracks is of interest, but also the relative quality the ITU-R BS.1116 standard has been selected for evaluating the quality. The recommodation BS.1116 [17][3] has been designed to assess the degree of annoyance any degradation of the audio quality causes to the listener. A continuous grading scale with the fixed points derived from the ITU-R Subjective Difference Grade (SDG) scale (Recommodation ITU-R BS.1284) [18] listed in table 1 is used.

Table 1. ITU-R five-grade impairment scale

Impairment	Grade	SDG
Imperceptible	5.0	0.0
Perceptible, but not annoying	4.0	-1.0
Slightly annoying	3.0	-2.0
Annoying	2.0	-3.0
Very annoying	1.0	-4.0

The test procedure is a so-called *double-blind A-B-C triple-stimulus* hidden reference comparison test. Stimuli A contains always the reference signal, whereas B and C are pseudorandomly selected from the coded and the reference signal. After listening to all three items, the subject has to grade either B or C according to the above mentioned grading scale. The SDG value is derived from the rating results by subtracting the scores of the actual hidden reference signal from the score of the actual coded signal:

$$SDG = Score_{Signal\ Under\ Test} - Score_{Reference\ Signal} \qquad (21)$$

A SDG value of 0 corresponds to an inaudible watermark whereas a value of -4.0 indicates an audible very annoying watermark.

---

[3] Published in 1994 and updated in 1997.

Design of the Test. The standard [17] specifies 20 subjects as an adequate size for the listening panel. Since expert listeners from the Thomson Audio Research Lab in Hannover, Germany particpted in the test, the number of listeners has been reduced to the size of eigth for an informal test. Per grading session 10 trials were conducted. Three test signals in multichannel format (5.1) – selected by our customers – with a length of 3 minutes have been presented to the listeners. The testing of multichannel watermarked audio tracks were performed in a special dedicated listening room of the Thomson Audio Research Lab.

Analysis and Interpretation of Results. The SDG values represent the data which should be used for the statistical analysis. In a graphical representation the mean SDG value and the 95% confidence interval are plotted as a function of the different audio tracks to clearly reveal the distance to transparency (SDG = 0). The results (see Fig. 5) show that the watermarked items are not distinguishable from the original tracks. The same settings used to achieve these results will be used throughout the robustness tests.

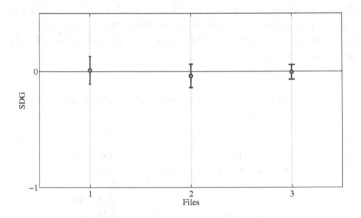

Fig. 5. Listening results for the BS.1116 test

4.2 Robustness Tests

In this paper *digital attacks* are defined as audio processing, which are typically computed on a PC or a DSP. These attacks are defined by only a few parameters and are easily reproducible (see Sect. 4.2) in contrast to the acoustic path test, which has a multitude of complex parameters. In all robustness tests 150 different sound files with a total play length of more than 12 hours were used. The sound library contained 100 pop items, 15 items containing classical music, 15 items with mostly speech signals, 10 items with jazz and experimental music, 5 radio recordings and 5 extracts from movies.

Signal Processing Attacks

Lossy Compression. Robustness against lossy compression was tested using a variety of audio codecs (see Tab. 2). Only bitrates lower or equal to 64 kBits/sec are evaluated. The algorithm shows good robustness down to 64 or 48 kBits/sec. The results demonstrate clearly the dependency not only on the bitrate, but on the codec used.

Table 2. BER (%) for lossy compression

Bitrate (kBits/sec)	MPEG 1/2 Layer II	MP3	MP3Pro	AAC	AAC+	AC3
64	13	12	9	2	2	0
48	27	13	33	5	14	–
32	60	54	54	38	53	–

Mixing Signals. The robustness against the mixing or overdubbing with varying signals for different SNR db(A) has been tested to simulate the influence of environmental noise. The results show good robustness for signals other than white or pink noise even if the disturbing signal has the same energy as the watermarked one.

Table 3. BER (%) for mixing signals

	SNR (dB(A))			
Mixed file	-10	0	10	20
whiteNoise	84	67	11	1
pinkNoise	85	63	9	1
babyCry	17	2	0	0
laughter	29	4	1	0
speechFemEngl	4	1	0	0
speechMaleGer	7	2	0	0

Addition of Echo. For the addition of an echo signal with a delay of 0 - 100 ms, a feedback of 0.5 and a Factor of 0.9 BER of 0 % was achieved.

Time Scaling. To measure the BER for time scaled signals correctly the time slices of the scaled audio tracks carrying the symbols have to be aligned with the BER symbols which are used for comparison. Otherwise a desynchronization in the two symbol strings to be compared result in a wrong BER. The ASPM algorithm includes an efficient time-scale search to cope with the problem of a manipulated time axis. The percentage of correct detection instead of the BER has been measured which includes the testing of the implemented resynchronization mechanism and the error correction.

Table 4. Detection rate (false positives = 0 %) for pitch-invariant and pitch-variable time-scaling

| | Percentage of change | | | | | |
Attack	+5	+3	+1	-1	-3	-5
Time-Stretching	92	95	99	99	96	92
Speed Decrease	97	97	100	98	94	92

In general an additional distinction has to be made between pitch-invariant time scaling[4] (see Tab. 4) and changing the playback speed which results in the modification of the pitch of the audio track.

From the results shown in these tables it can be seen that the algorithm is robust against time-stretching and changing the playback speed up to 1 % with slight decrease in the detection rate for 3 and 5 %.

Acoustic Path Tests. The recordings were done simultaneously with three microphones located at 2, 4 and 6 m distance with respect to the loudspeaker in a meeting room of Thomson's Corporate Research Center Hannover. Three cheap Labtech microphones attached to low cost pre-amplifiers were used. A RME Multiface II sound card handled the DA and AD conversion. The embedded watermark shows good robustness up to 4 m.

Table 5. BER (%) for acoustic path

Description recording	Distance (m)	BER (%)
loopback	0	0
AKG	0	1
LabTec	2	3
LabTec	4	11
LabTec	6	22

4.3   Performance Tests

Real-time watermarking systems are required in broadcast or audio-on-demand applications. The embedder has to embed a watermark in real-time or a multiple thereof if multiple channels have to be watermarked in parallel. Especially for an active monitoring like in the audience measurement scenario – mentioned in the introduction (see Sect. 1) – a fast detection mechanism is needed in order to be able to use cheap hardware on the detector site at the panelists households. The tests conducted with audio tracks in CD format verify the high performance and fast synchronization mechanisms of the implemented system (see Tab. 6).

---

[4] Also known as time-stretching.

Table 6. Performance of embedding and detection algorithm

Hardware	Embedding $\frac{t_{real-time}}{t_{embedding}}$	Detection $\frac{t_{real-time}}{t_{detection}}$
Intel Core 2 Duo 3 GHz	≈ 10	≈ 166

5 Conclusions

In this article, a new audio watermarking technique combining the altering of the phase of the original signal with spread spectrum techniques is presented. The audio quality of the original signal is preserved by applying a psychoacoustic model based on the MPEG model, which is tailored to the modification of the phases. The presented algorithm is evaluated in detail with first informal listening tests and extensive robustness tests.

The principal benefits that can be expected from the presented system are the following: a) presentation of a new type of audio watermarking algorithm that can easily be tailored to the application needs; b) presentation of a psychoacoustic model which can be used for other phase based audio watermarking algorithms; c) an extensive robustness evaluation providing evidence of the developed technique; d) an evaluation of the robustness against acoustic path transmission, an often neglected robustness test which is important in certain audio watermarking applications.

References

1. Cox, I.J., Miller, M.L., Bloom, J.A., Fridrich, J., Kalker, T.: Digital Watermarking and Steganography, 2nd edn. The Morgan Kaufmann Series in Multimedia Information and Systems. Morgan Kaufmann Publishers, Burlington (2008)
2. Gruhl, D., Lu, A., Bender, W.: Echo Hiding. In: Anderson, R.J. (ed.) IH 1996. LNCS, vol. 1174, pp. 295–315. Springer, Heidelberg (1996)
3. Oh, H., Seok, J., Hong, J., Youn, D.: New Echo Embedding Technique for Robust and Imperceptible Audio Watermarking. In: International Conference on Acoustics, Speech and Signal Processing (ICASSP), Orlando, FL, USA, pp. 1341–1344. IEEE Press, Los Alamitos (2001)
4. Ko, B.S., Nishimura, R., Suzuki, Y.: Time-Spread Echo Method for Digital Audio Watermarking using PN Sequences. In: International Conference on Acoustics, Speech and Signal Processing (ICASSP), Orlando, FL, USA, pp. 2001–2004. IEEE Press, Los Alamitos (2002)
5. Craver, S.A., Wu, M., Liu, B., Stubblefield, A., Swartzlander, B., Wallach, D.S., Dean, D., Felten, E.W.: Reading Between the Lines: Lessons from the SDMI Challenge. In: Proceedings of the 10th USENIX Security Symposium, Washington D.C., USA (August 2001)
6. Winograd, R.P.J., Jemili, K., Metois, E.: Data Hiding within Audio Signals. In: 4th International Conference on Telecommunications in Modern Satellite, Cable and Broadcasting Service, Nis, Yugoslavia, October 1999, pp. 88–95 (1999)

7. Boney, L., Tewfik, A.H., Hamdy, K.N.: Digital Watermarks for Audio Signals. In: IEEE International Conference on Multimedia Computing and Systems, Hiroshima, Japan, pp. 473–480. IEEE Press, Los Alamitos (1996)
8. Haitsma, J., van der Veen, M., Kalker, T., Bruekers, F.: Audio Watermarking for Monitoring and Copy Protection. In: Proceedings of the ACM Multimedia 2000 Workshop, Los Angeles, CA, USA, pp. 119–122. ACM Press, New York (2000)
9. Kirovski, D., Malvar, H.: Robust Covert Communication over a Public Audio Channel Using Spread Spectrum. In: Moskowitz, I.S. (ed.) IH 2001. LNCS, vol. 2137, pp. 354–368. Springer, Heidelberg (2001)
10. Bender, W., Gruhl, D., Morimoto, N., Lu, A.: Techniques for Data Hiding. IBM Systems Journal 35(3&4), 313–336 (1996)
11. Arnold, M.: Audio Watermarking: Features, Applications and Algorithms. In: Proceedings of the IEEE International Conference on Multimedia and Expo (ICME 2000), New York, USA, pp. 1013–1016. IEEE Press, Los Alamitos (2000)
12. Yeo, I.K., Kim, H.J.: Modified Patchwork Algorithm: A Novel Audio Watermarking Scheme. In: International Conference on Information Technology: Coding and Computing, Las Vegas, NV, USA, pp. 237–242. IEEE Press, Los Alamitos (2000)
13. Kuo, S.S., Johnston, J., Turin, W., Quackenbush, S.R.: Covert Audio Watermarking using Perceptually Tuned Signal Independent Multiband Phase Modulation. In: IEEE International Conference on Acoustics, Speech, and Signal Processing (ICASSP), vol. 2, pp. 1753–1756. IEEE Press, Los Alamitos (2002)
14. ISO/IEC Joint Technical Committee 1 Subcommittee 29 Working Group 11: Information technology - Coding of moving pictures and associated audio for digital storage media at up to about 1.5Mbit/s Part 3: Audio. ISO/IEC 11172-3 (1993)
15. Arnold, M., Schmucker, M., Wolthusen, S.: Techniques and Applications of Digital Watermarking and Content Protection. Artech House, Boston, USA (2003)
16. Arnold, M., Baum, P.G., Voeßing, W.: Subjective and Objective Quality Evaluation of Watermarked Audio. In: Cvejic, N., Seppänen, T. (eds.) Digital Audio Watermarking Techniques and Technologies. IGI Global, Hershey PA, USA, pp. 260–277 (2007)
17. ITU-R: Recommendation BS.1116-1, Methods for Subjective Assessement of Small Impairments in Audio Systems including Multichannel Sound Systems (1997)
18. ITU-R: Recommendation BS.1284-1, General Methods for the Subjective Assessement of Audio Quality (1997)

Forensic Tracking Watermarking against In-theater Piracy

Min-Jeong Lee, Kyung-Su Kim, and Heung-Kyu Lee

Department of Electrical Engineering and Computer Science,
Korea Advanced Institute of Science and Technology (KAIST)
Guseong-dong, Yuseong-gu, Daejeon, Republic of Korea
{mjlee,kskim,hklee}@mmc.kaist.ac.kr

Abstract. Many illegal copies of digital movies by camcorder capture
are found on the Internet or on the black market before their official
release. Due to the angle of the camcorder relative to the screen, the
copied movies are captured with perspective distortion. In this paper,
we present a watermarking scheme for tracking the pirate using local
auto-correlation function (LACF) to estimate geometric distortion. The
goals of watermarking are to find the suspected position of the camcorder
in the theater and to extract the embedded forensic marking data which
specifies theater information and time stamp. Therefore, our watermarking system provides conclusive evidence to take the pirate to the court.
Experimental results demonstrate robustness of the LACF and accuracy
of the proposed modeling.

Keywords: forensic tracking watermarking, in-theater piracy, local
auto-correlation function (LACF).

1 Introduction

Many illegal copies of digital movies are found on the Internet or on the black
market before their official release. These copies were made by recording the
projected movie with a camcorder at various angles, according to the location of
the pirate. Therefore, they are translated, rotated, scaled, and projected during
camcording so that it is easy to visually detect such recordings but hard for
watermark to survive. When an illegal copy is found on the Internet, it should
be need to find the pirate. However, the identification of the captured movie is
hard to configure by only comparing with the original movie. According to the
requirements for protecting digital cinema [1], the information about the theater
and the time is necessary and also the position of the pirate in the theater is
needed.

The watermarking technique for digital cinema provides the way to identify
when and where the movie was playing by embedding the related information
into the movie in real-time. Several papers addressed watermarking for digital
cinema. Leest et al. [2] proposed a video watermarking scheme which exploited
the temporal axis to embed watermark by changing the luminance value of each

S. Katzenbeisser and A.-R. Sadeghi (Eds.): IH 2009, LNCS 5806, pp. 117–131, 2009.

frame and hence achieved robustness against geometrical distortions. Since the luminance change between frames may occur a flickering effect, the luminance modulation has to be performed slowly and smoothly. Delannay *et al.* [3] investigated the restoration of geometrically distorted images occurred by the camera acquisition angles. The compensation of the distortion required both unmodified content and modified content. Lubin *et al.* [4] embedded watermark into low spatial-temporal frequency domain for invisible, robust, and secure watermarking. To determine spatial-temporal regions of video sequences in the embedding procedure, a vision model-based masking computation was employed. These papers neither considered the projective distortions by camcorder capture nor told us the position of the pirate. Lee *et al.* [5] presented a blind watermarking scheme for digital cinema using local auto-correlation function (LACF) to resist to projective transform and embedded watermark in real-time. But they did not use the estimated geometric distortion to find out where the pirate was in the theater.

Chupeau *et al.* [6] proposed a forensic tracking system without embedding watermark. Their scheme determined the camcorder viewing angle to the screen and derived the approximate position of the pirate in the theater using feature points. The estimation of the eight-parameter homographic model required both temporally synchronized source videos and captured videos.

In this paper, we propose a watermarking scheme for tracking the pirate using local auto-correlation function to estimate geometric distortion. The estimation process is used for both recovering watermark to extract the embedded forensic marking data and finding the approximate position of the camcorder in the theater. the forensic marking data payload contains location (serial number of the theater) information and time stamp. Therefore, our watermarking system provides conclusive evidence to take the pirate to the court. The paper is organized as follows. Sec. 2 introduces our watermarking scheme including watermark embedding and detection. Forensic tracking using LACF is suggested in Sec. 3. Experimental results are presented in Sec. 4 and Sec. 5 concludes.

2   Watermarking Scheme

2.1   Watermark Embedding

This section describes how the watermark is embedded in the host video. Figure 1 shows the embedding procedure, which is designed to satisfy the requirements for digital cinema [1]. The watermark pattern is generated and then inserted into the video frames based on spread spectrum way with considering HVS.

In the presented scheme, the watermark pattern is used in two ways: one is to carry forensic marking data and extract it robustly, the other is to find illegally camcording position. In order to accomplish both roles, the watermark pattern should have periodicity for LACF to calculate geometric distortions. The periodicity is obtained by tiling the basic pattern [7]. First of all, the basic pattern, that follows a Gaussian distribution with zero mean and unit variance, is generated using a secret key and consists of 2-D random sequence of size $(M/m \times N/n)$. M and N denote the width and the height of the host video and m and n denote the

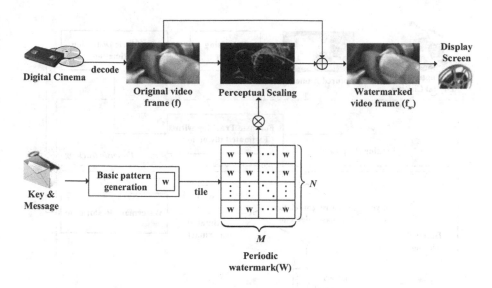

Fig. 1. Watermark embedding procedure

number of repetitions in horizontal and vertical direction, respectively. The 2-D basic pattern is then modulated to contain the bit payload (*e.g.*, serial number of the theater, time stamp, etc.). The modulated basic pattern w is repeated $m \times n$ times to get the periodicity. After a periodic watermark pattern of size $M \times N$ has been obtained, the pattern is embedded in an additive spread-spectrum way with perceptual scaling.

2.2   Watermark Detection

The entire detection process goes similar as [5]. It performs as follows: 1) find geometric distortions using the LACF on the estimated watermark pattern and 2) recover the watermark from the distortions and extract the embedded message. Figure 2 describes the process of watermark detection.

1) Estimating Geometric Distortion. Due to the fact that a blind detector is used, the embedded watermark is estimated by employing Wiener filtering as a denoising filter. Subtracting the denoised frame from the captured frame, we obtain an approximate version of the embedded watermark pattern. Both estimating geometric distortion and extracting watermark are proceeded using this extracted pattern.

As a result of camcorder capture, cinematic footage undergoes perspective-projective distortion when the position and/or viewing angle of the camcorder is changed. Let $\mathbf{x} = (x_1, x_2, x_3)^{\mathrm{T}}$ be the homogeneous vector that represents of a point in the original frame and $\mathbf{x}' = (x_1', x_2', x_3')^{\mathrm{T}}$ be the homogeneous vector that represents a point in the geometrically distorted frame. The projective

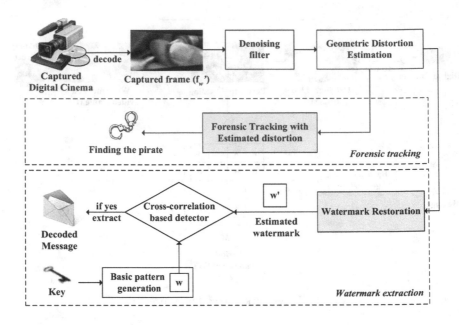

Fig. 2. Watermark detection procedure

transformation is a linear transformation on homogeneous 3-vectors represented by a non-singular 3×3 matrix [8]:

$$\mathbf{x}' = \mathbf{H}\mathbf{x}, \quad \text{where} \quad \mathbf{H} = \begin{pmatrix} h_{00} & h_{01} & h_{02} \\ h_{10} & h_{11} & h_{12} \\ h_{20} & h_{21} & h_{22} \end{pmatrix} \tag{1}$$

Note that H is a homogeneous matrix, since as in the homogeneous representation of a point, only the ratio of the matrix elements is significant. There are eight independent ratios among the nine elements of H, and it follows that a projective transformation has eight degrees of freedom (DOF). Thus, four pairs of point-to-point correspondence in the original and distorted frames are required to determine eight DOF. In this paper, four corner points of the original video frame are selected as the original points and four corner points of the distorted video frame are chosen as the corresponding distorted points. Since both the embedder and the detector know the coordinates of four original points, it only needs to know those of four distorted points.

Local auto-correlation function (LACF) is employed for estimating projective transform. It computed the auto-correlation function of two local areas of the image that are parallel to each other instead of computing auto-correlation of the whole image. As shown in Fig. 3, two horizontally parallel local areas are needed for vertical projection, while two vertically parallel local areas are needed for horizontal projection. The two parallel local areas are denoted by R_A and R_B,

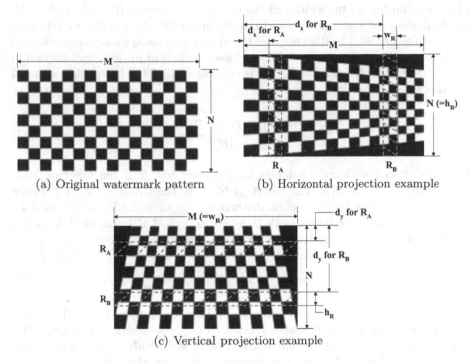

(a) Original watermark pattern   (b) Horizontal projection example

(c) Vertical projection example

Fig. 3. Examples of projection attacks

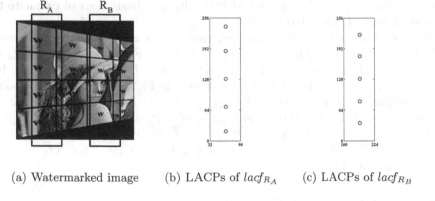

(a) Watermarked image   (b) LACPs of $lacf_{R_A}$ (c) LACPs of $lacf_{R_B}$

Fig. 4. Watermarked image and LACPs: horizontal projection $20°$ with $fp = 10^{-6}$

respectively. The application of the LACF to (x, y) of region R on the estimated watermark pattern W' is modeled as

$$lacf_R(x, y) = \sum_{i=-w_R+1}^{w_R-1} \sum_{j=-h_R+1}^{h_R-1} W'(x+d_x(R)+\frac{i}{2}, y+d_y(R)+\frac{j}{2})^2 \qquad (2)$$

where w_R and h_R are the width and the height of the region R, $d_x(R)$ and $d_y(R)$ are the distance of x-axis and y-axis from the upper-left corner point for selecting region R for LACF. The distance and the size of regions are adaptively selected by the size of the used basic pattern and lower bounds of projective distortion in a practical point of view. The LACF is calculated by FFT-based fast equation as follows:

$$lacf_R = \frac{\text{IFFT}(\text{FFT}(R) \cdot \text{FFT}(R)^*)}{|R|^2}, \tag{3}$$

where "$*$"-*operator* denotes complex conjugation and R is the selecting local parallel region R_A or R_B. The result yielded by the LACF shows a periodic peak pattern. Then the geometric distortions are estimated and reversed by using a local auto-correlation peak (LACP). The LACP is detected from the results of the LACF by applying an adaptive threshold as follows:

$$lacp > \mu_{lacf} + \alpha_{lacf}\sigma_{lacf}, \tag{4}$$

where μ_{lacf} and σ_{lacf} denote the average and standard deviation of the LACF respectively. α_{lacf} is a value that is related to the false positive error rate. Presetting the maximum false positive error rate, we calculate α_{lacf} and obtain the threshold. Figure 4 shows the results of applying the LACF results to a watermarked image that has been subjected to projective distortion. In Fig. 4(b) and Fig. 4(c), two LACF results show the different intervals between each auto-correlation peak. Using the LACF results as a basis, we can calculate the coordinates of the distorted frame.

Now, it needs to construct a mathematical model using the intervals between LACP as parameters. The application of the LACF yields LACPs of R_A on the line $x = d_x(R_A) + w_R/2$ with interval δ_A and LACPs of R_B on the line $x = d_x(R_B) + w_R/2$ with interval δ_B as shown in Fig. 5. Let four corner points of the original watermark pattern be P_1, P_2, P_3, and P_4, respectively. C_{14} is the center point of $\overline{P_1 P_4}$, C_{23} is the center point of $\overline{P_2 P_3}$, and P_v is a vanishing point which intersects the extensions of $\overline{P_1 P_2'}$ and $\overline{P_4 P_3'}$. We denote C_A as a center point of LACPs of R_A and C_B as a center point of LACPs of R_B. The length of $\overline{C_A C_B}$ is obtained by

$$\overline{C_A C_B} = d_x(R_B) + \frac{w_R}{2} - (d_x(R_A) + \frac{w_R}{2}) = d_x(R_B) - d_x(R_A) \tag{5}$$

Our goal is to obtain the coordinates of projective-distorted points P_1, P_2', P_3', P_4. In this geometry, only the coordinates of P_2' and P_3' need to be computed because the positions of P_1 and P_4 do not change. Therefore, it is necessary to know the length of $\overline{P_2' C_{23}}(= \overline{C_{23} P_3'})$. First, we define P_A which is located at intervals of $n\delta_A/2$ from C_A and P_B which is located at intervals of $n\delta_B/2$ from C_B, where n is the vertical repetition times of basic watermark pattern (n can

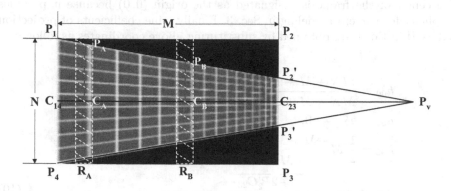

Fig. 5. A geometry of horizontally projected image

be replaced by m in case of vertical projection). Next, the similarity of triangle $\triangle P_A C_A P_v$ and $\triangle P_B C_B P_v$ is employed to obtain the length of $\overline{C_B P_v}$.

$$\overline{P_A C_A} : \overline{P_B C_B} = (\overline{C_A C_B} + \overline{C_B P_v}) : \overline{C_B P_v} \implies \overline{C_B P_v} = \frac{\overline{C_A C_B} \cdot \overline{P_B C_B}}{\overline{P_A C_A} - \overline{P_B C_B}} \quad (6)$$

The length of $\overline{C_{14} C_A}$ is obtained using $\overline{C_A P_v}$, $\overline{P_A C_A}$ and the similarity of triangle $\triangle P_A C_A P_v$ and $\triangle P_1 C_{14} P_v$.

$$\overline{P_1 C_{14}} : \overline{P_A C_A} = (\overline{C_{14} C_A} + \overline{C_A P_v}) : \overline{C_A P_v} \implies$$
$$\overline{C_{14} C_A} = \overline{C_A P_v} \left(\frac{\overline{P_1 C_{14}}}{\overline{P_A C_A}} - 1 \right) \quad (7)$$

where $\overline{P_1 C_{14}} = N/2$. Using Eq. (5) - (7), $\overline{P_2' C_{23}} (= \overline{C_{23} P_3'})$ is defined as follows:

$$\overline{P_2' C_{23}} = \frac{N(\overline{P_{14} P_v} - M)}{2 \overline{P_{14} P_v}} \quad (8)$$

Four pairs of points in Fig. 5 are transformed as follows:

$$\begin{aligned}
A(-M/2+1, N/2) &\Rightarrow A(-M/2+1, N/2) \\
B(M/2, N/2) &\Rightarrow B'(M/2, \overline{P_2' C_{23}}) \\
C(M/2, -N/2+1) &\Rightarrow C'(M/2, -\overline{P_2' C_{23}}) \\
D(-M/2+1, -N/2+1) &\Rightarrow D(-M/2+1, -N/2+1)
\end{aligned} \quad (9)$$

The center of the frame is designated as the origin $(0,0)$ because it provides simplicity for camera modeling in Sec. 3. Finally, nine coefficients of projection matrix H in Eq. 1 are obtained by substituting above coordinates as follows:

$$h_{00} = \frac{MN - M + 2\overline{P_2'C_{23}}M - 4\overline{P_2'C_{23}}}{MN - M + 2\overline{P_2'C_{23}}M - 2N + 2},$$

$$h_{01} = h_{21} = 0,$$

$$h_{02} = \frac{1}{2}M \frac{-M + MN - 2\overline{P_2'C_{23}}M - 2N + 2 + 4\overline{P_2'C_{23}}}{MN - M + 2\overline{P_2'C_{23}}M - 2N + 2},$$

$$h_{10} = \frac{-2\overline{P_2'C_{23}}}{MN - M + 2\overline{P_2'C_{23}}M - 2N + 2}, \tag{10}$$

$$h_{11} = \frac{4\overline{P_2'C_{23}}(M-1)}{MN - M + 2\overline{P_2'C_{23}}M - 2N + 2},$$

$$h_{12} = \frac{-\overline{P_2'C_{23}}(M-2)}{MN - M + 2\overline{P_2'C_{23}}M - 2N + 2},$$

$$h_{20} = \frac{2(-1 + N - 2\overline{P_2'C_{23}})}{MN - M + 2\overline{P_2'C_{23}}M - 2N + 2},$$

$$h_{22} = 1$$

2) Watermark Extraction. The basic pattern of size $(M/m \times N/n)$ is generated using a secret key as a reference watermark. The watermark pattern is recovered from the geometric distortion using the inverse matrix H^{-1} with Eq. 10. Normalized cross-correlation between the estimated watermark w' and the reference watermark pattern w can be calculated so that it can be performed in less time with FFT by

$$C = \frac{\text{IFFT}(\text{FFT}(w') \cdot \text{FFT}(w)^*)}{|w'| \cdot |w|} \tag{11}$$

If the normalized cross-correlation C exceeds a pre-defined threshold T, the hidden message is extracted successfully. The decision D to verity the existence of the watermark is made by

$$D = \max_{x,y}(C(x,y)) > T \tag{12}$$

where T is the detection threshold defined by

$$T = \mu_c + \alpha_c \sigma_c, \tag{13}$$

where μ_c is the average and σ_c is the standard deviation of $C(x,y)$. α_c is a pre-defined value that is related to false positive error rate.

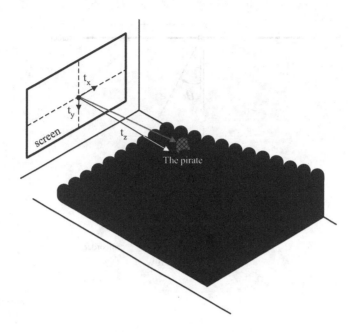

Fig. 6. Screen and camcorder geometry : 3D view

3   Forensic Tracking: Where a Camcorder Captures

3.1   Projective Geometry

For simplification purpose, we assume that the screen is planar and consider the camera models in [8]. The overall movie projection and camcorder capture consists of a screen and a camcorder. A geometrical representation is given in Fig. 6 and Fig. 7. Let now introduce the notation $\mathbf{X}$ for the world point of the screen represented by the homogeneous 4-vector $(X, Y, Z, 1)^{\mathsf{T}}$ and $\mathbf{x}$ for the captured image point by the camcorder represented by a homogenous 3-vector as defined in Eq. 1. Then the central projection mapping from world to image coordinates is given by:

$$\mathbf{x} = P\mathbf{X}, \text{ where } P = \lambda K[R \mid \mathbf{t}] \text{ with } \mathbf{t} = -R[t_x, t_y, t_z]^{\mathsf{T}} \qquad (14)$$

where P denotes a 3×4 homogeneous camera projection matrix, λ is a scale factor, and K is the camera calibration matrix. R is the rotation matrix representing the orientation of the camera coordinate frame and $[t_x, t_y, t_z]^{\mathsf{T}}$ is the coordinates of the camcorder center. The general form of the 3×3 camera calibration matrix K of a CCD camera is

$$K = \begin{bmatrix} \alpha f & 0 & 0 \\ 0 & f & 0 \\ 0 & 0 & 1 \end{bmatrix} \qquad (15)$$

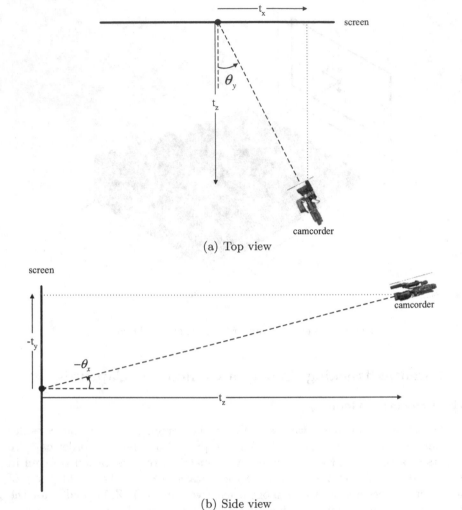

(a) Top view

(b) Side view

Fig. 7. Screen and camcorder geometry : 2D view

where f is the focal length of the camcorder, α is non-square pixel aspect ratios in case of CCD cameras. Note that the principal point is at the center of the scene. The 3×3 rotation matrix R takes the form:

$$R = R_z R_y R_x \tag{16}$$

In $\mathbb{R}^3$, coordinate system rotations of the x-, y-, and z-axis in a counter clockwise direction when looking towards the origin give the matrices

$$R_x = \begin{bmatrix} 1 & 0 & 0 \\ 0 & \cos\theta_x & \sin\theta_x \\ 0 & -\sin\theta_x & \cos\theta_x \end{bmatrix}, R_y = \begin{bmatrix} \cos\theta_y & 0 & -\sin\theta_y \\ 0 & 1 & 0 \\ \sin\theta_y & 0 & \cos\theta_y \end{bmatrix}, R_z = \begin{bmatrix} \cos\theta_z & \sin\theta_z & 0 \\ -\sin\theta_z & \cos\theta_z & 0 \\ 0 & 0 & 1 \end{bmatrix} \quad (17)$$

Then Eq. 16 is rewritten as

$$R = \begin{bmatrix} \cos\theta_z\cos\theta_y & \sin\theta_z\cos\theta_x + \cos\theta_z\sin\theta_y\sin\theta_x & \sin\theta_z\sin\theta_x - \cos\theta_z\sin\theta_y\cos\theta_x \\ -\sin\theta_z\cos\theta_y & \cos\theta_z\cos\theta_x - \sin\theta_z\sin\theta_y\sin\theta_x & \cos\theta_z\sin\theta_x + \sin\theta_z\sin\theta_y\cos\theta_x \\ \sin\theta_y & -\cos\theta_y\sin\theta_x & \cos\theta_y\cos\theta_x \end{bmatrix} \quad (18)$$

Since it assumes that the screen is planar, we can set $Z = 0$ and redefine $\mathbf{X}$ as $(X, Y, 0, 1)^{\mathsf{T}}$. Then Eq. 14 is concisely expressed as

$$\mathbf{x} = \lambda K[\mathbf{r_1}\ \mathbf{r_2}\ \mathbf{t}] \begin{pmatrix} X \\ Y \\ 1 \end{pmatrix} \quad (19)$$

where $\mathbf{r_1}$ and $\mathbf{r_2}$ are the first and second column of the matrix R. Since Eq. 19 has the same form as Eq. 1, we decompose the matrix H in Eq. 1 as follows:

$$H = \lambda K[\mathbf{r_1}\ \mathbf{r_2}\ \mathbf{t}] \quad (20)$$

As shown in Fig. 6 and Fig. 7, $\mathbf{t}$ should be estimated to determine the position of the camcorder in the theater.

3.2 Modeling the Distortion

Let the inhomogeneous coordinates of $\mathbf{x}$ be (x, y). The projective transformation of Eq. 1 can be written in inhomogeneous form as

$$\begin{cases} x = \dfrac{h_{00}X + h_{01}Y + h_{02}}{h_{20}X + h_{21}Y + h_{22}} \\ y = \dfrac{h_{10}X + h_{11}Y + h_{12}}{h_{20}X + h_{21}Y + h_{22}} \end{cases} \quad (21)$$

with:

$$\begin{cases} h_{00} = & \lambda\alpha f\cos\theta_z\cos\theta_y \\ h_{01} = & \lambda\alpha f(\sin\theta_z\cos\theta_x + \cos\theta_z\sin\theta_y\sin\theta_x) \\ h_{02} = & -\lambda\alpha f(\cos\theta_z\cos\theta_y t_x + (\sin\theta_z\cos\theta_x + \cos\theta_z\sin\theta_y\sin\theta_x)t_y + \\ & + (\sin\theta_z\sin\theta_x - \cos\theta_z\sin\theta_y\cos\theta_x)t_z) \\ h_{10} = & -\lambda f\sin\theta_z\cos\theta_y \\ h_{11} = & \lambda f(\cos\theta_z\cos\theta_x - \sin\theta_z\sin\theta_y\sin\theta_x) \\ h_{12} = & -\lambda f(-\sin\theta_z\cos\theta_y t_x + (\cos\theta_z\cos\theta_x - \sin\theta_z\sin\theta_y\sin\theta_x)t_y + \\ & + (\cos\theta_z\sin\theta_x + \sin\theta_z\sin\theta_y\cos\theta_x)t_z) \\ h_{20} = & \lambda\sin\theta_y \\ h_{21} = & -\lambda\cos\theta_y\sin\theta_x \\ h_{22} = & -\lambda(\sin\theta_y t_x - \cos\theta_y\sin\theta_x t_y + \cos\theta_y\cos\theta_x t_z) \end{cases} \quad (22)$$

Such a distortion model is actually a so-called homographic model, exactly describing the deformation of a flat scene photographed by a CCD camera, the optical axis of which is not perpendicular to the scene. Then solving the equations in Eq. 22 using the obtained projection matrix H in Eq. 10, we can identify the position of the camcorder $[t_x, t_y, t_z]^\mathrm{T}$.

4   Experimental Results

On HD-resolution clips of digital cinema, the fidelity, robustness, and accuracy of detecting the position are measured against camcorder capture attack. A 40-bit payload was embedded into each five-minutes clip to adhere to digital cinema initiatives [1]. A 2-D basic pattern whose size is 120×120 is generated and modulated to contain 2 bits of payload. Then the modulated pattern is tiled sixteen times ($m = 16$) to horizontal axis and nine times ($n = 9$) to vertical axis. Thus, the watermark pattern is formed 1920×1080 dimensions and embedded in the entire frame. To insert 40-bit payload into the five-minutes clip, a set of 20 differently modulated patterns is required. The watermark patterns in the set are repeated seven times during five minutes. For the LACF, the parameters in Eq. 2 are set for both horizontal and vertical projection. For horizontal projection, w_R is set to 120 ($= M/m$) and h_R is set to 1080 ($= N$). The $d_x(A)$ for region R_A is set to 180 and the $dx(B)$ for region R_B is set to 1500. Both $d_y(A)$ and $d_y(B)$ are set to zero. For vertical projection, w_R is set to 1920 ($= M$) and h_R is set to 120 ($= N/n$). The $d_y(A)$ is set to 180 and the $d_y(B)$ is set to 660. Both $d_x(A)$ and $d_x(B)$ are set to zero. After embedding, the average PSNR value was 46.0 dB for the test videos. Fidelity testing was performed as described in [4]. Clips were displayed using an EPSON EMP-TW1000 projector onto a wide screen. Projected clips were about 2.20m and 1.24m in horizontal and vertical directions, respectively.

Four expert observers participated in a two-alternative, forced-choice experiment in which each trial consisted of two presentations of the same clip, once with and once without the watermark present. Observers viewed the screen from two picture heights and were asked to indicate which clips contained the watermark. Each source clip was played in four times in each trial. Each trial lasted five minutes. No observer could determine the identity of the watermarked clip with certainty in any case.

4.1   Robustness Test

Against camcorder capture attack in practice, the robustness was tested, which included projective and affine transform as well as signal processing distortions at the same time. Watermarked clips were projected on a screen with the same environment for fidelity test and captured with a SONY HDR-FX1 camcorder tripod-mounted. In all cases, the 40 bits payload were extracted with the 100% reliability where average correlation values were larger than the threshold satisfying false positive probability 10^{-6}.

Table 1. Accuracy test result for synthetically projective distorted videos

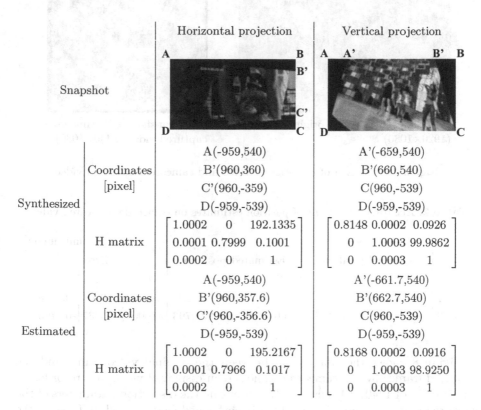

		Horizontal projection	Vertical projection
Snapshot			
Synthesized	Coordinates [pixel]	A(-959,540) B'(960,360) C'(960,-359) D(-959,-539)	A'(-659,540) B'(660,540) C(960,-539) D(-959,-539)
	H matrix	$\begin{bmatrix} 1.0002 & 0 & 192.1335 \\ 0.0001 & 0.7999 & 0.1001 \\ 0.0002 & 0 & 1 \end{bmatrix}$	$\begin{bmatrix} 0.8148 & 0.0002 & 0.0926 \\ 0 & 1.0003 & 99.9862 \\ 0 & 0.0003 & 1 \end{bmatrix}$
Estimated	Coordinates [pixel]	A(-959,540) B'(960,357.6) C'(960,-356.6) D(-959,-539)	A'(-661.7,540) B'(662.7,540) C(960,-539) D(-959,-539)
	H matrix	$\begin{bmatrix} 1.0002 & 0 & 195.2167 \\ 0.0001 & 0.7966 & 0.1017 \\ 0.0002 & 0 & 1 \end{bmatrix}$	$\begin{bmatrix} 0.8168 & 0.0002 & 0.0916 \\ 0 & 1.0003 & 98.9250 \\ 0 & 0.0003 & 1 \end{bmatrix}$

4.2 Accuracy Test

For testing accuracy of the proposed modeling, we perform two kinds of experiments on videos. One is to measure the accuracy against synthetic distortions, the other is to demonstrate the accuracy against real camcorder capture attack. Since camcorder capture attack in practice occurs not only geometric distortions but also various signal processing attacks, we primarily prove the performance of our scheme on the situation of geometric distortions only. Table 1 shows the experimental results for synthetically distorted videos. In case of synthetic distortion, the geometry of each video frame is manipulated by given geometric distortion parameters without practical shooting so the real world coordinates cannot be determined. Instead, the estimated pixel coordinates and P matrices are compared with original ones when the videos are synthesized. Four original pixel coordinates are corner points of the video frame denoting A, B, C, and D depicted in Fig. 5. In case of horizontal projection, for example, the corresponding points B' and C' are calculated but A and D are fixed. As shown in Table 1, our scheme estimate the approximate P matrix using given geometric distorted videos.

(a) Snapshot of original video (1920×1080)

(b) Snapshot of camcorder captured video (1440×1080)

Fig. 8. Comparison of the original video and camcorder captured video

Table 2. Accuracy test result of position estimates on camcorder captured videos

[unit: meter]

	Original position			Estimated position			Error		
	t_x	t_y	t_z	t'_x	t'_y	t'_z	e_x	e_y	e_z
Case 1	-1.617	0	2.3	-1.7013	0.0003	2.4226	-0.0843	-0.0003	-0.1226
Case 2	0	0.108	2.5	0.0003	0.1417	3.2793	-0.0003	-0.0337	-0.7793

Figure 8 shows the comparison between the original video frame and the captured frames by the camcorder. The screen-displayed videos are recorded at a resolution of 1440×1080 pixels. By computing the distortion parameters of the captured videos, a numerical analysis is performed as described in Table 2. We compared the original position $[t_x, t_y, t_z]^T$ of the camcorder and the estimated one $[t'_x, t'_y, t'_z]^T$ and then measured the error $[e_x, e_y, e_z]^T$. In addition to projective distortion, the captured videos suffered affine distortion and signal processing including aspect ratio change, contrast enhancement, and gamma correction. Although the error of the estimates is bigger than the cases of synthesized videos, its value does not exceed 1 meter in average. That is, when it assumes that a volume of a seat per one persion in the theater is bigger than 1.0 m^3, the errors in Table 2 are acceptable. The more the pirate wants to get visually qualified movies, the more the result of proposed modeling is exact. At worst case scenario, only one person next to the pirate would be a suspect. With an assumption that the pirate are picked out among more than one suspect, our scheme is still a strong evidence to prove his or her crime.

5 Conclusion

Many illegal copies of digital movies by camcorder capture are found on the Internet or in black market before their official release. It needs to provide conclusive evidence to take the pirate to the court for eradicating illegal camcorder capturers in the theater. To do so, we present a watermarking scheme for tracing the pirate using local auto-correlation function (LACF) to estimate geometric distortion. The message in the embedded watermark contains the information of time and location about showing a movie. The estimated geometric distortion tells about the approximate position of the pirate in the theater. Using LACF, our experiments proved the robustness against projective distortions and the accuracy of detecting the position of the pirate. Moreover, the proposed scheme was designed to embed the watermark in real-time to be applicable for digital cinema. In the future, our work can be extended to focus on the situation with combined projections.

Acknowledgments. This research is supported by Ministry of Culture, Sports and Tourism(MCST) and Korea Culture Content Agency(KOCCA) in the Culture Technology(CT) Research & Developement Program 2009, and by the IT R&D program of MKE/IITA. [2007-S017-01, Development of user-centric contents protection and distribution technology].

References

1. Digital Cinema Initiatives, LLC: Digital cinema system specification version 1.2 (2008), http://www.dcimovies.com/DCIDigitalCinemaSystemSpecv1_2.pdf
2. Leest, A., Haitsma, J., Kalker, T.: On digital cinema and watermarking. In: Proc. SPIE, vol. 5020, pp. 526–535 (2001)
3. Delannay, D., Delaigle, J., Macq, B., Barlaud, M.: Compensation of geometrical deformations for watermark extraction in the digital cinema application. In: Proc. SPIE, vol. 4314, pp. 149–157 (2003)
4. Lubin, J., Bloom, J., Cheng, H.: Robust, content-dependent, high-fidelity watermark for tracking in digital cinema. In: Proc. SPIE, vol. 5020, pp. 536–545 (2003)
5. Lee, M.J., Kim, K.S., Lee, H.Y., Oh, T.W., Suh, Y.H., Lee, H.K.: Robust watermark detection against D-A/A-D conversion for digital cinema using local auto-correlation function. In: Proc. ICIP, pp. 425–428 (2008)
6. Chupeau, B., Massoudi, A., Lefèbvre, F.: In-theater piracy: finding where the pirate was. In: Proc. SPIE, vol. 6819, pp. 68190T–1–68190T–10 (2008)
7. Maes, M., Kalker, T., Linnartz, J.P., Talstra, J., Depovere, G., Haitsma, J.: Digital watermarking for dvd video copy protection. IEEE Sig. Process. Magazine 17, 47–57 (2000)
8. Hartley, R.I., Zisserman, A.: Multiple view geometry in computer vision. Cambridge University Press, Cambridge (2004)

Self-recovery Fragile Watermarking Using Block-Neighborhood Tampering Characterization

Hong-Jie He[1], Jia-Shu Zhang[1], and Heng-Ming Tai[2]

[1] Sichuan Key Lab of Signal and Information Processing, Southwest Jiaotong University, Chengdu 610031, China
[2] Department of Electrical Engineering, University of Tulsa, Tulsa, OK 74104, USA

Abstract. In this paper, a self-recovery fragile watermarking scheme for image authentication is proposed to improve the performance of tamper detection and tamper recovery. The proposed scheme embeds the encrypted feature comprising 6-bit recovery data and 2-bit key-based data of the image block into the least significant bits (LBS) of its mapping block. The validity of a test block is determined by comparing the number of inconsistent blocks in the 3×3 block-neighborhood of the test block with that of its mapping block. Moreover, to improve the quality of the recovered image, the 3×3 block-neighborhood is also used to recover the tampered blocks whose feature hidden in another block is corrupted. Experimental result demonstrates that the proposed method outperforms conventional self-recovery fragile watermarking algorithms in tamper detection and tamper recovery under various attacks. Additionally, the proposed scheme is not vulnerable to the collage attack, constant-average attack and four-scanning attack.

Keywords: fragile watermarking, self-recovery, block-neighborhood characterization, constant-average attack.

1 Introduction

Digital image authenticity is greatly threatened in that it is not difficult to modify or forge the image content without leaving detectable traces by publicly available image processing software packages. Thus many researchers have proposed to use the watermarking techniques for image verification [1-9]. Compared to traditional image authentication techniques, watermarking-based authentication not only has the capability of indicating where image contents have been tampered with [1-4], but also provides more information on how the image is modified [5]. Watermarking schemes with the ability to recover the corrupted regions of the image are also desirable for protection of the content and the integrity of images.

S. Katzenbeisser and A.-R. Sadeghi (Eds.): IH 2009, LNCS 5806, pp. 132–145, 2009.

Self-recovery fragile watermarking schemes [6-9] have received great attention in recent years. In 1999, Fridrich and Goljan [6] developed a fragile watermarking scheme with self-correcting capabilities. To achieve the self-correction, they employ an information chain scheme by dividing the image into 8×8 blocks, and inserting the binary code of important DCT coefficients of each block into the least significant bits (LSBs) of other distant blocks. Fig. 1 depicts the information chain and the structure of a watermarked block. Here, the code of block X_{i0} is embedded in the block X_{i1}, the code of block X_{i1} is embedded in the block X_{i2}, and the code of block X_{i2} is embedded in the block X_{i3}, and so on. This strategy effectively breaks block-wise independency, and makes the self-recovery watermarking schemes not vulnerable to the counterfeiting attacks [10, 11]. Unfortunately, this chain scheme makes the watermarking algorithm difficult to detect and localize the possible tampering. For example, if X_{i2} is tampered, then the code generated from the content of X_{i2} does not agree with the code inserted in X_{i3}. This may bring about another false discrepancy: the code obtained by the content of X_{i1} is inconsistent with the code embedded in X_{i2}. Clearly, the inconsistent blocks X_{i2} is tampered, whereas the inconsistent block X_{i1} is authentic. This implies that the inconsistent blocks cannot be simply judged as invalid in this self-recovery watermarking scheme. As a result, the tamper detection method of self-recovery watermarking should have capability to effectively distinguish the tampered blocks (X_{i2}) from the genuine blocks (X_{i1}). Here we intend to cope with the above problem, i.e., to distinguish whether the content is replaced or the code embedded in other block is manipulated when the block is inconsistent.

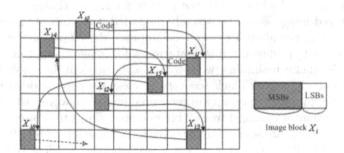

Fig. 1. Information chain and structure of watermarked block

To address this problem, Fridrich and Goljan [6] proposed that the image block (X_{i2}) could be considered as invalid just when there are two inconsistencies in it. One inconsistency is that the content of X_{i2} is not consistent with the code embedded in X_{i3}, and another is the code inserted in X_{i2} does not agree with the content of X_{i1}. Unfortunately, this method fails to detect the tampered blocks whose content is modified, but LSBs are intact (we call it only-content-tampering attack). This is because only one inconsistency occurs, i.e., the content of X_{i2}

is inconsistent with the code embedded in X_{i3}. As a result, Fridrich and Goljan concluded later in [6] that it is impossible to design an automatic procedure that would distinguish whether the LSBs of X_{i3} were manipulated or the MSBs of X_{i2} were replaced when there is one inconsistency in block X_{i2}.

On the other hand, Lin et al. proposed a hierarchical digital watermarking method for tamper detection and recovery [7]. It adopted parity check and intensity-relation check (the 2-bit authentication watermark) to determine the legitimacy of the 2×2 block and four-level hierarchical inspections to increase the tamper detection rate. However, Lin scheme's level-1 inspection cannot resist the collage and VQ attacks because the 2-bit authentication watermarks are block-wise independent [8]. When the protected image is maliciously modified by collage or VQ attacks, although Lin's level-4 inspection detects the malicious attack, it fails to distinguish the genuine blocks from the inconsistent ones (see Fig. 6). Based on the work of [7], Wang and Chen [8] proposed a majority voting based watermarking technique for tamper detection and recovery of color images. In this algorithm, authentication data of each 2×2 block is extended from 2 bits to 16 bits and a majority-voting scheme is employed to determine the authenticity of image blocks. This method, however, may not work well for the 8-bit gray image. On one side, it is not practical to embed 22 (16+6) bits watermark in the 2×2 block. On the other side, it reduces the capacity of watermark embedding of the Lin algorithm because 32 pixels are required to embed the 16-bit authentication. This would decrease the accuracy of tamper localization of the self-recovery system.

Another concern is the quality of reconstructed image. As pointed by Fridrich [6], if large portions of the image are replaced, it is quite likely that both tampered block X_i and the block with the feature for X_i are changed. The quality of the recovered image would be severely degraded if the image blocks were reconstructed using the altered feature. To improve the quality of the recovered image, Lee et al [9] proposed a dual watermark for image tamper detection and recovery. This scheme maintains two copies of watermark of the whole image and provides second chance for block recovery in case one copy is destroyed. Dual watermark can improve the quality of recovered image. However, the watermark embedding payload is enlarged from 2 bit per pixel (bpp) to 3 bpp.

In summary, there are some main drawbacks in these schemes [7-9]. First, the watermark embedding payload is enlarged. For example, to identify the validity of the image block, the authentication data except the recovery data of each image block is required in these schemes. Apparently, increasing the watermark payload alone is not adequate to improve the performance of tamper detection and tamper recovery. Second, these schemes are vulnerable to the constant-average attack proposed by Chang et al [12] in that the watermark data is generated using the average intensity of an image block. In addition, they adopted the linear transform to generate the block-chain $\{\cdots, X_i, X_{i'}, \cdots\}$, where the recovery data of block X_i is embedded into the block $X_{i'}$. Because of the inherent weakness of linear transform, if an attacker obtains one or more watermarked images, it is possible to obtain the block-chain [13], so that would bring the self-recovery watermarking schemes [12, 13] to the security flaw.

To improve the performance of tamper detection and recovery, this paper develops an effective self-recovery digital watermarking scheme without increasing the watermark payload. The proposed method overcomes the drawbacks mentioned above and provides improved performance compared to the existing algorithms. The encrypted watermark of an image block is embedded in its mapping block generated based on a non-linear transform to improve security. In the tamper detection process, instead of independently examining the consistency of the test block, we take into account the block-neighborhood characterization of the test block and its mapping block. Moreover, the block-neighborhood characterization is also used to optimize the performance of tamper detection under different attacks and improve the quality of the recovered image. Experimental results demonstrate that the proposed tamper detection and recovery method performs superiorly under various malicious attacks.

2 Proposed Self-recovery Fragile Watermarking Algorithm

This section describes in detail the proposed self-recovery fragile watermarking algorithm. The proposed scheme inserts the 8-bit encrypted watermark, consisting of 6-bit recovery data and 2-bit key-based data, into another image block and determines the validity of the image block by the 8-bit watermark. Then it incorporates the block-neighborhood characterization for tamper detection and recovery. The proposed algorithm is described through four stages: watermark embedding, watermark extraction, tamper detection, and tamper recovery.

2.1 Block-Based Watermark Embedding

The proposed watermark embedding scheme is illustrated in Fig. 2. Two user keys k_1 and k_2 are adopted to improve the security against the various known malicious attacks such as collage attack, constant-average attack, and four-scanning attack. As depicted in Fig. 2, the embedding process consists of five operations. The details are described as follows.

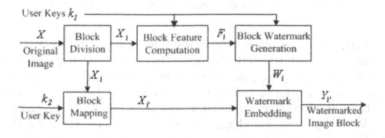

Fig. 2. Watermark embedding process

(1) Block Division. The original image X of size $2m \times 2n$ pixels is partitioned into N ($= m \times n$) non-overlapping blocks X_i of 2×2 pixels, expressed as,

$$X_i = \begin{bmatrix} x_{i0} & x_{i1} \\ x_{i2} & x_{i3} \end{bmatrix}, i = 1, 2, \cdots, N. \tag{1}$$

(2) Block-chain generation. Using the secret key k_2, a pseudorandom sequence $B = (b_1, b_2, \cdots, b_N)$ is firstly produced, and then an ordered index sequence $(a_1, a_2, \cdots, a_N)$ such that $b_{a_1} \leq b_{a_2} \leq \cdots \leq b_{a_N})$ is obtained by sorting out the pseudorandom sequence B. The one-to-one block-chain $(X_i, X_{i'})(i, i' \in [1, N])$ is generated by assigning the index of the block $X_{i'}$ be $i' = a_i$. This allows the proposed algorithm overcomes the linear mapping weakness of Lin's algorithm, and enlarges the key space [4].

(3) Block Feature Computation. The 8-bit feature of image block X_i, denoted as $F_i = \{f_{i0}, f_{i1}, \cdots, f_{i7}\}$, consists of the 6-bit recovery data and 2-bit key-based data. The recovery data is utilized to restore the blocks which have been tampered with, while the key-based data is used to resist the constant-average attack. Fig. 3 illustrates the process of block feature generation. The 6-bit recovery data is obtained by,

$$f_{ij} = mod(\frac{\lfloor ave\_X_i \rfloor}{2^j}, 2), j = 0, 1, \cdots, 5 \tag{2}$$

The symbol $\lfloor x \rfloor$ denotes the largest integer less than or equal to x, mod(a, b) is the modulo operation , and ave_X_i computes the average intensity by truncating the two LSBs of each pixel in block X_i (see Fig. 3).

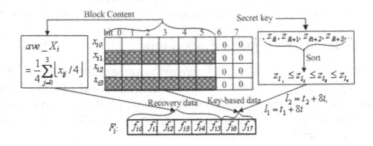

Fig. 3. Block feature generation based on the user key k_1

To resist the constant-average attack, the 2-bit key-based data was produced by combining the secret key with the image block content. For each block X_i, four elements $\{z_{8i}, z_{8i+1}, z_{8i+2}, z_{8i+3}\}$ are extracted from the random sequence $Z = (z_1, z_2, \cdots, z_{8N+7})$ generated by the secret key k_1. Let $8i + t_1$ and $8i + t_2$ represent the indices of the two smallest elements in $\{z_{8i}, z_{8i+1}, z_{8i+2}, z_{8i+3}\}$. For example, in Fig. 3, z_{8i+1} and z_{8i+3} are the two smallest elements. In the ith block, the two pixels x_{i1} and x_{i3} are chosen to produce the 2-bit key-based data f_{i6} and f_{i7}. This process can be expressed as,

$$f_{i6} = \begin{cases} 1 & , \quad 2 \times ave\_X_i > (\lfloor x_{it_1}/4 \rfloor + \lfloor x_{it_2}/4 \rfloor) \\ 0 & , \quad otherwise \end{cases} \tag{3}$$

$$f_{i7} = \begin{cases} 1 & , \quad x_{it_1} > x_{it_2} \\ 0 & , \quad otherwise \end{cases} \tag{4}$$

(4) Block Watermark Generation. This step is to improve the security against the four-scanning attack [12]. The block feature F_i is encrypted using secret key k_1 to generate an 8-bit watermark $W_i = (w_{i0}, w_{i1}, \cdots, w_{i7})$ by the exclusive-or (XOR) operation

$$X_i = B_i \oplus F_i \tag{5}$$

The binary sequence $B_i = (b_{i0}, b_{i1}, \cdots, b_{i7})$ is obtained from $\{z_{8i}, z_{8i+1}, \cdots, z_{8i+7})\}$ extracted from the random sequence Z. That is,

$$b_{ij} = \begin{cases} 1 & , \quad z_{8i+j} > 0.5 \\ 0 & , \quad otherwise \end{cases}, j = 0, 1, \cdots, 7 \tag{6}$$

(5) Watermark Embedding. For each block X_i, its mapping block $X_{i'}$ is obtained based on the block-chain generation algorithm described in Step 2. The watermarked image block $Y_{i'}$ is generated by inserting the 8-bit watermark W_i of the block X_i into the two LSBs of each pixel in the paired block $X_{i'}$,

$$y_{i'j} = 4\lfloor y_{i'j}/4 \rfloor + 2w_{i(2j)} + w_{i(2j+1)}, j = 0, 1, 2, 3 \tag{7}$$

2.2 Watermark Extraction

Watermark extraction can be considered as the inverse process of watermark embed-ding. Let Y^* represents the test image, which can be a distorted watermarked image or unaltered one. The watermark extraction scheme consists of five functional blocks.

(1) Block division. As in the watermark embedding process, the test image Y^* is first divided into non-overlapping 2×2 blocks Y_i^* and the random sequence $Z = \{z_1, z_2, \cdots, z_{8N+7}\}$ is generated based on the secret key k_1.

(2) Block feature computation. For each test block Y_i^*, the 8-bit feature F_i^* is calculated according to step 3 in the embedding process.

(3) Watermark extraction and recovery. The 8-bit watermark $W_i^* = \{w_{ij}^* \mid j = 0, 1, \cdots, 7\}$ inserted in the LSBs of block Y_i^* is extracted by the following formula

$$w_{ij}^* = \begin{cases} mod(y_{i\lfloor j/2 \rfloor}^*, 2) & , \quad j = 1, 3, 5, 7 \\ mod(y_{i\lfloor j/2 \rfloor}^*, 4) & , \quad j = 0, 2, 4, 6 \end{cases} \tag{8}$$

The 8-bit feature $E_{i'}^*$ extracted from the block $Y_{i'}^*$ is reconstructed by

$$E_{i'}^* = W_{i'}^* \oplus B_i \tag{9}$$

where B_i is obtained by (6) from the random sequence Z.

(4) Block mapping. Using the secret key k_2, all paired blocks $(Y_i^*, Y_{i'}^*)$ are obtained by following Step 2 of the embedding process.

(5) Marking Block-consistency. To detect the consistency of each block, we construct the block consistency mark (BCM) $D = \{d_i | i = 1, 2, \cdots, N\}$, where

$$d_i = \begin{cases} 0 & , \quad (f_{ij}^* = e_{i'j}^*), \forall j \in [0, 7] \\ 1 & , \quad otherwise \end{cases} \tag{10}$$

The block Y_i^* is inconsistent if $d_i = 1$; otherwise, it is consistent. On the other hand, a constant-average BCM $D^A = \{d_i^A | i = 1, 2, \cdots, N\}$ is required to resist the constant-average attack,

$$d_i = \begin{cases} 1 & , \quad (\sum_{j=0}^5 |f_{ij} - e_{i'j}| = 0) \ \& \ (\sum_{j=6}^7 |f_{ij} - e_{i'j}|) \neq 0) \\ 0 & , \quad otherwise \end{cases} \tag{11}$$

If the image block Y_i^* is randomly modified, we have the probabilities $P\{d_i = 1\} = 1 - 1/2^8$ and $P\{d_i^A = 1\} = 3/2^8$. The ratio between the number of non-zero pixels in D_A and that in D is

$$R = \frac{\rho_T \times N \times P\{d_i^A = 1\}}{\rho_T \times N \times P\{d_i = 1\}} = \frac{3}{255} \tag{12}$$

where ρ_T is the ratio between the number of the tampered blocks and the number of blocks N in the test image. Thus we reason that the tampered blocks Y_i^* with $d_i^A = 1$ is likely to suffer the constant-average attack if R calculated by (12) is greater than 0.05.

2.3   Tamper Detection: Block-Neighborhood Characterization

This section describes in detail the proposed block-neighborhood based detection method. The notation $\Delta^D = \{\delta_i^D | i = 1, 2, \cdots, N\}$ is used to describe the neighborhood characteristic of the binary image D, where δ_i^D denotes the number of nonzero pixels except itself in a 3×3 neighborhood of the ith pixel in D. In this work, we use a binary sequence $T = \{t_i | i = 1, 2, \cdots, N\}$ called the tamper detection mark (TDM) to represent the location of tampering. If $t_i = 1$, the corresponding block Y_i^* is invalid; otherwise, the block Y_i^* is valid. Procedure of the proposed block-neighborhood characterization tamper detection method is described below.

(1) Initialization. From the BCM D and its block-neighborhood characterization Δ^D, we obtain the initial TDM $T^0 = (t_i^0)$,

$$t_i^0 = \begin{cases} 1 & , \quad if \ (d_i = 1) \ \& \ (\delta_i^D \geq \delta_{i'}^D) \\ 0 & , \quad otherwise \end{cases} \tag{13}$$

It follows from (13) that the inconsistent block is said to be tampered if the block-neighborhood characterization of it is more than or equal to that of its mapping block. Otherwise, the inconsistent block is genuine.

(2)Optimization. The block-neighborhood characterization is used to improve the tamper detection rate under malicious attacks. First, the ratio R between the number of non-zero pixels in D^A and that of non-zero pixels in D is computed. If R is less than or equal to 0.05, every pixel in the constant-average BCM $D^A = \{d_i^A | i = 1, 2, \cdots, N\}$ is assigned a value of zero; if not

$$d_i^A = \begin{cases} 1 & , \quad if \ (\delta_i^{D^A} > 1) \ or \ (d_i^A = 1) \\ 0 & , \quad otherwise \end{cases} \tag{14}$$

where $\delta_i^{D^A}$ denotes the number of nonzero pixels in 8 adjacent pixels of pixel d_i^A in the constant-average BCM D^A. Combining the initial TDM with the constant-average BCM generated by (14) yields the TDM

$$t_i = \begin{cases} 0 & , \quad if \ (t_i^T = 0) \ \& \ (d_i^A = 0) \\ 1 & , \quad otherwise \end{cases} \tag{15}$$

where t_i^T is computed by the following expression,

$$t_i^T = \begin{cases} 0 & , \quad if \ (t_i^0 = 1) \ \& \ (\delta_i^{T^0} < 2) \\ 1 & , \quad if \ (t_i^0 = 0) \ \& \ (\delta_i^{T^0} \geq 5) \\ t_i^0 & , \quad otherwise \end{cases} \tag{16}$$

$\delta_i^{T^0}$ denotes the number of nonzero pixels in 8 adjacent pixels of pixel t_i^0 in the initial TDM T^0 obtained by (13).

2.4 Tamper Recovery

After detection, all the blocks are marked as either valid or invalid. Only invalid blocks need to be reconstructed. The proposed recovery procedure consists of two operations.

(1) Initialization. The recovered image $Y^R = \{Y_i^R | i = 1, 2, \cdots, N\}$ can be initialized by,

$$Y_i^R = \begin{cases} Y_i^* & , \quad if \ t_i = 0 \\ 4 \times ave\_Y_i^* + mod(Y_i^*, 4) & , \quad otherwise \end{cases} \tag{17}$$

Where, $ave\_Y_i^*$ is the reconstructed average intensity by the feature $E_{i'}^*$ extracted from the associated block $Y_{i'}^*$. That is,

$$ave\_Y_i^* = \sum_{j=0}^{5} (2^j \times e_{i'j}^*) \tag{18}$$

(2) Optimization. To mark the tampered blocks whose feature hidden in another block is destroyed, the binary matrix $M = \{m_i | i = 1, 2, \cdots, N\}$ is obtained by the following expression,

$$m_i = \begin{cases} 1 & , \quad if \ (t_i = 1) \ \& \ (t_{i'} = 1) \\ 0 & , \quad otherwise \end{cases} \tag{19}$$

If $m_i = 1$, the recovered block Y_i^R is considered as invalid due to the fact that the feature $E_{i'}^*$ hidden in block $Y_{i'}^*$ is likely to be lost. Therefore, for each block

Y_i^R with $m_i = 1$, each pixel in Y_i^R is revised by the average intensity of valid neighboring blocks of block Y_i^R.

3   Experimental Results

We conducted three experiments to demonstrate the effectiveness of the proposed self-recovery fragile watermarking scheme. Comparison with the method of [7] on the performance of tamper detection and tampered image restoration is also given. The first experiment is for images with ordinary tampering, the second concerning collage attack, the third for the constant-average attack and only-content-tampering attack. We did not compare with the approaches in [8] and [9] because the watermark payload is different, 3 bit per pixel in their schemes.

Two measures were introduced for performance evaluation. They are the probability of false acceptance (PFA) and the probability of false rejection (PFR) defined as

$$\textbf{PAR: } P_{fa} = (1 - N_{td}/N_t) \times 100\% \qquad (20)$$

$$\textbf{PFR: } P_{fr} = N_{vd}/(N - N_t) \times 100\% \qquad (21)$$

where N denotes the number of image blocks in the tested image, N_t the number of actually tampered blocks, N_{td} the number of tampered blocks which are correctly detected, and N_{vd} the number of valid blocks which are falsely detected. The smaller the PFA and PFR are, the better the performance of fragile watermarking techniques.

Self-recovery watermarking schemes enable the detection of tampering or replacement of a watermarked image [6-9]. The distinction mainly lies in the tamper localization accuracy and the quality of recovered images. Below is the performance of the proposed method under common tampering. The Rub image, which is of size 768×1024 and shown in Fig.4(a), is chosen for this purpose. A watermarked Rub image generated by the proposed scheme, as shown in Fig. 4 (b), has the PSNR of 44.15 dB. Fig. 4(c) is the tampered image. There are three alterations: (1) a rat is inserted in the left of watermarked image, (2) a little cup is inserted in the right-bottom of watermarked Rub, and (3) some letters "ITP Southwest Jiaotong University" is written in the top of watermarked Rub. The BCM and TDM of the proposed method are depicted in Figs. 4(d) and 4(e), and the detection result of Lin's scheme is shown in Fig. 4(g), respectively. The initial recovered image (the recovered image before the optimization step) of the proposed method, shown in Fig. 4(g), has the PSNR of 27.79 dB, the recovered image of the proposed method, shown in Fig. 4(h), has PSNR of 41.85 dB and that of Lin scheme, shown in Fig. 4(i), has PSNR of 25.84 dB.

The proposed tamper detection method is effective in determining whether or not the inconsistent blocks of 2×2 pixels are tampered. Both the clustered and randomly distributed white spots in Fig. 4(d) denote the inconsistent blocks. It can be seen from the TDM image of Fig. 4(e) that the inconsistent blocks in the tampered regions are invalid, while those not tampered are valid. Accordingly, the proposed tamper detection method is able to discriminate the authentic blocks from invalid ones when the block is inconsistent. We also find that the PFA and PFR of the proposed scheme are1.13% and 0.05% and those of Lin's scheme are 0.06% and 1.31%, respectively. The PFA of Lin's method is smaller than that of the proposed scheme,but at the expense of localization accuracy(block size of 44 pixels) and the PFR rises to 1.31%. Moreover, it can be seen from Fig.4 that the proposed scheme had a superior quality recovered image. The PSNR value of the recovered image by the proposed scheme is about 14 dB higher than that of the initial recovered image by the proposed scheme and 16 dB higher than that of Lin's scheme. This is mainly due to the fact that the proposed method would reconstruct the invalid blocks whose associated block is tampered using the valid neighboring blocks of it.

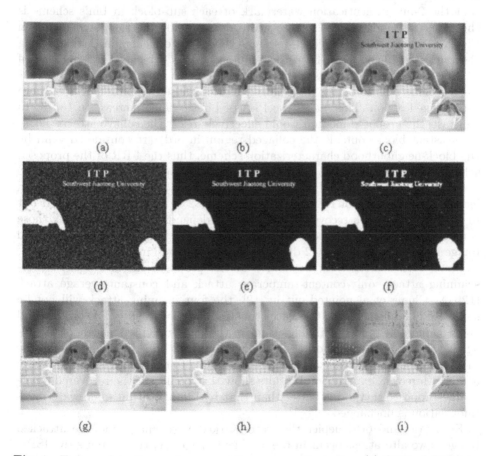

Fig. 4. Tamper detection and recovery by common tampering. (a) Original Rub image, (b) watermarked image, (c) tampered image, (d) and (e) BCM and TDM of the proposed scheme, (f) detected result of Lin's scheme, (g) and (h) initial recovered image and recovered one of the proposed scheme, (i) recovered image of Lin's scheme [7].

The second experiment considers the effect of collage attack [11], which is a variation of the Holliman-Memon counterfeiting attack [10]. In this test, two images, 'Mona Lisa' and 'Napoleon', both of size 372×288, were watermarked using the same key. The watermarked images of Napoleon and Mona Lisa are shown in Fig. 5(a) and Fig. 5(b), respectively. We constructed the collage image, Fig. 5(c), by copying the face of Mona Lisa and pasting it onto the Napoleon image while preserving their relative spatial location within image. The tampering ratio of the counterfeit image is about 17.65%. Figures 5(d), 5(e), and 5(f) display the BCM, TDM, and the recovered image by our scheme, respectively. The detection results by Lin's level-1 and level-4 schemes are shown in Figs. 5(g) and 5(h), respectively, and the recovered image in Fig. 5(i). Since no invalid blocks (white spots) are present in Fig. 5(g), the collage image is deemed genuine by Lin's level-1 scheme. This shows that Lin's level-1 scheme is not capable of withstanding the collage attack. This may be due to the fact that the 2-bit authentication watermark of each sub-block in Lin's scheme is the block-wise independent. Those white dots outside the tampered region in Fig. 5(h) imply that Lin's level-4 scheme may have difficulty in distinguishing the tampered image block from the genuine one, as evidenced by the PFR of 17.39%. And the black dots in the collaged region in Fig. 5(h) indicate that Lin's scheme fails to detect the collaged blocks whose mapping blocks fall into the collaged region. This makes the PFA of Lin's scheme increase to 18.9%. In contrast, the proposed method would effectively resist the collage attack. Those inconsistent blocks outside the collaged region in 5(d) are considered valid by the block-neighborhood characterization scheme, thus the FRR of the proposed scheme is lowered to 0.01%. This block-neighborhood characterization scheme also significantly reduces the number of black spots in the collaged region, which leads to the increase of PFA from 18.1% to 3.82%. Moreover, as pointed out in [8], the quality of a recovered image highly depends on how accurately those tampered blocks be identified. PSNR of the recovered image to the watermarked image is 31.94 dB, which is 12 dB higher than that by Lins scheme.

Finally we demonstrate the ability of the proposed method against four-scanning attack, only-content-tampering attack and constant-average attack [12]. As Chang et al pointed out in [12], the four-scanning attack will not be successfully implemented if the feature of sub-block is encrypted. So our method is not vulnerable to four-scanning attack in that the encrypted feature of the image block is embedded in another block. Further, the 2-bit key-based data and the block-neighborhood optimization strategy are used to resist the constant-average attack. Moreover, experimental results show that quality of the recovered image by the proposed method is better than that by Lin algorithm when watermark information is unchanged.

Figs. 6(a) and 6(b) depict the watermarked Vase image and the attacked image. Two alterations occur in the attacked image: (1) the contents (6 MSBs) of a 192×196 rectangular region in the left side of the watermarked image are replaced by contents of another image, and (2) the rectangular region in the right side of the watermarked image is modified by the constant-average attack,

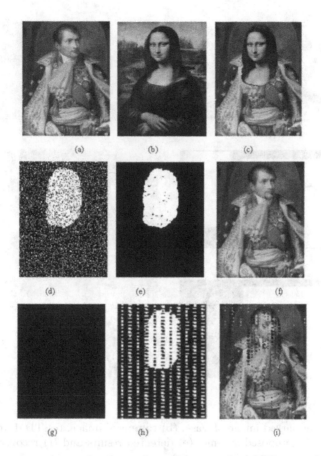

Fig. 5. Tamper detection and recovery by collage attack. (a) Watermarked Napoleon, (b) watermarked Mona Lisa, (c) tampered Napoleon, (d) BCM, (e) TDM, (f) recovered image by the proposed scheme, (g) and (h) detected invalid blocks by Lin's level-1 and level-4 schemes, respectively, (i) recovered image by Lin scheme.

where the size of modification is of 160×96 pixels. Fig. 6(c) and 6(d) are the TDM and the recovered image by the proposed scheme, respectively. Fig. 6(e) and 6(f) are the detected results and recovered image by Lin's scheme. PSNR of the recovered images by the proposed and Lin schemes to the watermarked image are 25.49 dB and 12.85 dB, respectively.

Both the proposed and Lin schemes effectively detect content modifications with high probability, as can be seen from Fig. 6. The PFA for the proposed method is 2.86%, and that for the Lin scheme is 0. The low PFA by Lin scheme, however, does not transform to a high quality image recovery, as shown in Fig. 6(f). This is mainly due to the fact that, by Lins strategy, the invalid block will not be reconstructed if the associated block is not legitimate. In contrast, our method effectively recovers all tampered blocks except some blocks located on the boundary of the tampered region. For the region tampered by the

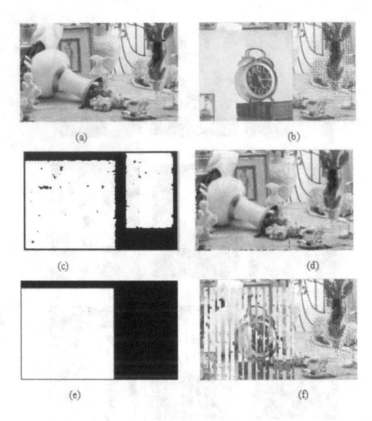

Fig. 6. (a) Watermarked image of Vase, (b) tampered image, (c) TDM and (d) recovered image by the proposed scheme, (e) detected results and (f) recovered image by Lin scheme [7]

constant-average attack, Lins scheme fails to detect the modifications and the attacked portion of image cannot be recovered. This indicates that Lin scheme does not withstand the constant-average attack. On the other hand, the proposed method performs well in tamper detection and image recovery, indicated by the PFA of 0.54% and Fig. 6(d).

4   Conclusion

We have presented a self-recovery fragile watermarking method with superior localization and recovery properties. The block-neighborhood characterization scheme enables an automatic tamper detection procedure that can discern the genuine blocks from the tampered ones when the blocks are inconsistent. The proposed scheme exactly identifies the tampered 2×2 blocks in terms of lower PFA and PFR, even though the test image is maliciously modified by collage attack, constant-average attack and only-content-tampering attack. In addition, the encrypted feature and the non-linear block-mapping sequence make it difficult to obtain the information of the block-mapping sequence. Thus security of the proposed fragile watermarking scheme is enhanced. Future research includes extending this approach to resist mild distortion such as random noise and JPEG compression, and analytic investigation on the tamper detection performance of the watermarking-based authentication techniques.

Acknowledgment

This work was supported in part by the Doctors Innovation Funds of Southwest Jiaotong University (No. 2007), the National Natural Science Foundation of China (Grant No. 60572027), and by the Research Fund for the Doctoral Program of Higher Education (Grant No. 20070613024).

References

1. Wong, P., Memon, N.: Secret and public key image watermarking schemes for image authentication and ownership verification. IEEE Trans. Image process. 10(10), 1593–1601 (2001)
2. Yuan, H., Zhang, X.-P.: Multiscale fragile watermarking based on the Gaussian mixture model. IEEE Trans. Image process. 15(10), 3189–3200 (2006)
3. Zhang, X., Wang, S.: Statistical fragile watermarking capable of locating individual tampered pixels. IEEE Signal Process. Lett. 14(10), 727–731 (2007)
4. He, H.-J., Zhang, J.-S., Tai, H.-M.: Block-chain Based fragial watermarking Scheme with Superior Localization. In: Solanki, K., Sullivan, K., Madhow, U. (eds.) IH 2008. LNCS, vol. 5284, pp. 147–160. Springer, Heidelberg (2008)
5. Kundur, D., Hatzinakos, D.: Digital watermarking for telltale tamper proofing and authentication. Proceedings of IEEE 87(7), 1167–1180 (1999)
6. Fridrich, J., Goljan, M.: Protection of digital images using self embedding. In: Content Security and Data Hiding in Digital Media, NJIT, NJ (May 1999)
7. Lin, P.L., Hsieh, C.K., Huang, P.W.: A hierarchical digital watermarking method for image tamper detection and recovery. Pattern Recognition 38(12), 2519–2529 (2005)
8. Wang, M.S., Chen, W.C.: A majority-voting based watermarking scheme for color image tamper detection and recovery. Computer Standards & Interfaces 29(5), 561–570 (2007)
9. Lee, T.-Y., Lin, S.D.: Dual watermark for image tamper detection and recovery. Pattern Recognition 41, 3497–3506 (2008)
10. Holliman, M., Memon, N.: Counterfeiting attacks on oblivious block-wise independent invisible watermarking schemes. IEEE Trans. Image Processing 9(3), 432–441 (2000)
11. Fridrich, J., Goljan, M., Memon, N.: Cryptanalysis of the Yeung-Mintzer fragile watermarking technique. J. Electronic Imaging 11, 262–274 (2002)
12. Chang, C., Fan, Y.-H., Tai, W.-L.: Four-scanning attack on hierarchical digital watermark-ing method for image tamper detection and recovery. Pattern Recognition 41(2), 654–661 (2008)
13. He, H.J., Zhang, J.S., Wang, H.X.: Synchronous counterfeiting attacks on self-embedding watermarking schemes. Intern. J. Comput. Sci. Network Security 6(1), 251–257 (2006)

Perception-Based Audio Authentication Watermarking in the Time-Frequency Domain

Sascha Zmudzinski and Martin Steinebach

Fraunhofer Institute for Secure Information Technology SIT
Rheinstr. 75, 64295 Darmstadt, Germany

Abstract. Current systems and protocols based on cryptographic methods for integrity and authenticity verification of media data do not distinguish between legitimate signal transformation and malicious tampering that manipulates the content. Furthermore, they usually provide no localization or assessment of the relevance of such manipulations with respect to human perception or semantics. We present an algorithm for a authentication audio watermarking that uses a perception-based robust hash function in combination with robust watermarking to verify the integrity of audio recordings. Experimental results show that the proposed system provides both a high level of distinction between perceptually different audio data and a high robustness against signal transformations that do not change the perceived information.

1 Motivation

Modern computer hardware, software and the Internet provide many ways of producing, recording, post processing, editing trimming and cutting, archiving and distribution of multimedia data. In many scenarios, digital audio data contains important information, for example, telephone calls to call center agencies (phone banking, emergency calls etc.), air traffic communication or recordings preserving the cultural heritage. As the audio data can easily be modified or even manipulated, mechanisms for verifying the *integrity* of the audio content and the *authenticity* of its origin are of special interest.

Most of cryptography-based approaches for authentication like digital signatures include a number of drawbacks regarding the properties of multimedia data:

- Cryptography-based mechanisms by design are fragile to *any* kind of change in the content. But inaudible signal transformations can be tolerated in many scenarios (e.g. file format conversion). Here, only *malicious* manipulations that actually change what a listener *hears* or even *understands* from the meaning of the recording shall be detected.
- In many standard security protocols no localization of such malicious manipulations is provided. They only provide a verification of the *complete* recording or transmission, respectively.

S. Katzenbeisser and A.-R. Sadeghi (Eds.): IH 2009, LNCS 5806, pp. 146–160, 2009.

– Furthermore, the verification information is stored separated from the protected digital media itself: the verification is dependent on a security protocol and an existing infrastructure that provides the verification codes.

A promising approach to accept these challenges is given by authentication watermarking approaches, especially *content-fragile watermarking*. This approach, originally introduced by *Dittmann et al* is derived from content-based audio retrieval methods in combination with digital watermarking [4]. The challenge is to develop a suitable retrieval system that is able to detect audible modifications *and* that can be combined with audio watermarking.

We will introduce a content-fragile watermarking approach based on an extension of an existing audio retrieval method by *Haitsma, Kalker et al.* [10,9]. These retrieval mechanisms are combined with an existing robust audio watermarking algorithm [17]. Experimental results will demonstrate that our authentication watermarking approach features a high distinction between inaudible changes from malicious attacks on the audio data.

2 Introduction

This chapter explains how content-based audio feature retrieval methods can serve for the detection of audible modifications of audio data in an authentication watermarking systems. Therefore, we explain current authentication watermarking systems in general and the involved audio retrieval approaches, namely *audio fingerprinting* and *robust hashing*.

2.1 Content-Based Authentication Watermarking

First audio watermarking approaches for data authentication were given by *fragile watermark* and *semi-fragile watermark* embedding schemes which are, by design, very sensitive to *any* kind of modification of the watermarked data. Here, the watermark can be seen a *digital seal* that is broken at modified parts of the protected audio file.

In the remainder of this paper we will focus on an approach for content-based authentication watermarking. It was originally introduced by *Dittmann et al* [4]. The design relies on the extraction of perceptually relevant audio features. Detection of malicious manipulations is done on the basis of changes of these features. The verification is done in two stages:

1. **Protection Stage.** The audio file is divided in segments and from every audio segment perceptively relevant audio features are extracted. This is done by means of content-based retrieval methods such as audio fingerprinting and robust hashing. The extracted audio features are then embedded as a robust digital watermark into the audio data, see figure 2.

2. Verification Stage. As the original features are provided by a robust watermark they can be retrieved even after the protected file was subject to file format changes. If no or moderate transformation of the content is applied after embedding, the embedded *original* audio features can be retrieved at any later date. They can be used as an authentication code and can be compared with the *current* audio features, see figure 2. In contrast, if major transformations of the content are applied, the watermark can not be detected correctly (if at all) which in effect successfully indicates major integrity infringements.

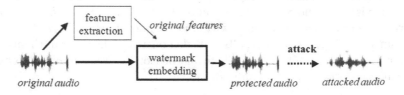

Fig. 1. Protection Stage

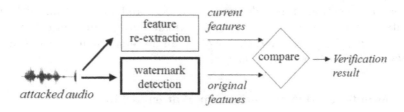

Fig. 2. Verification stage

The challenge of a fingerprint based verification framework is to extract a highly compact representation of the audio data that provides a high distinction between tolerable transformations and malicious manipulations [3]. Both watermarking and feature extraction must provide a similar level of robustness against signal distortions: Additionally, the distortion introduced by watermark embedding must not significantly affect the robust hash in order to avoid false alarms. Finally, the watermarking algorithm must provide a sufficient capacity for embedding the authentication code. Here, the capacity requirements are significantly higher (typically 128+ bits per each protected audio segment of a few seconds) than for transaction watermarking for copy prevention (typically a few dozen bits for the *complete* file).

This content-fragile watermarking concept is also referred to as *mixed watermarking-fingerprinting* [7]. A number of approaches can be found in the literature for general audio data [18,12,19,15,7,8] and for speech data [21,20,23].

2.2 Robust Hash Functions for Authentication

Definition. A common technique for the purpose of data authentication are cryptographic hash functions. A hash function is a mathematical function that maps a variable length input message to an output message digest of fixed length [16].

Cryptographic hash algorithms by design are extremely sensitive to changes in the input data. For audio data this high sensitivity is inappropriate in many scenarios because media data is often transcoded between different file formates either lossless or lossy for the purpose of transmission, broadcast or archiving. For multimedia retrieval applications a number of specially designed audio fingerprinting algorithms have been introduced that are tolerant against inaudible or moderate transformations of audio signals. As such approaches allow to recognize acoustic events that sound similar to each other, it is very likely that they can also detect that pieces of audio have a *dissimilar* sound because they were potentially manipulated. Thus, we will investigate, how audio fingerprinting and robust audio hashing can be used to detect audible modifications of audio data for integrity verification.

Requirements. Under more strict conditions, fingerprinting algorithms are referred to as *robust hash* or *perceptual hash* in the literature. In order for a fingerprint algorithm to serve as a *robust audio hash* it must meet a number of requirements. The most important requirements are [12]:

- Distinction: For the detection of perceptually relevant transformations of the signal we require that the hash values should be different for perceptually different audio signal. This requirement allows the detection malicious tampering of the signal.
- Robustness: The robust hash must provide the invariance for perceptually similar audio data. The hash should be robust against signal transformations that do not affect the perceptual quality of the data.
- Security: The features must survive attacks that are directly aimed at the feature extraction.
- Localization: The design of the system should provide a temporal localization of an attack.

3 Proposed Authentication Watermarking System

In this section we introduce an authentication watermarking system following the content-fragile approach. It is based on a combination of robust watermarking and secure robust audio hashing, which we will explain both in the following sections.

3.1 Watermark Embedding

For embedding the robust audio hash we use a blind spread-spectrum Patchwork watermarking approach [2,22] in the domain of Fourier magnitude coefficients. Its basic implementation was presented by us in an earlier work [17]. Basically, the embedding of a message relies on enforcing statistical signal properties of the Fourier coefficients to sort of "abnormal" values that unmarked cover data does not show. This abnormal behavior can be detected by the *non-informed* watermark detector, i.e. without the cover data, and indicates the presence of the watermark.

The embedding of a watermark message of length M bit is done as follows: The audio signal is divided into audio segments containing L audio frames. Each frame consists of a number of N PCM samples, usually a power of two. Using the fast Fourier transformation (FFT) the spectrum of Fourier magnitude coefficients $e(n, t)$ is calculated, where $n = 1 \ldots N/2$ denotes the band index and $t = 1 \ldots L$.

Then, for every message bit $m_i \in \{0, 1\}$ two subsets A_i and B_i $(i = 1, ..., M)$ containing R coefficients each are selected from the complete set of coefficients based. This selection is done pseudo-randomly depending on a secret watermark key K_1. thus, it defines a "random cloud" of FFT coefficients in the time-frequency domain. We assume that for unmarked cover data the FFT coefficients from different time steps and band indixes are sufficiently independent and identically distributed and that the subsets contain sufficiently many elements. Then, the partial sums

$$S_{A_i} := \frac{1}{R} \sum_{e \in A_i} e(n, t), \qquad S_{B_i} := \frac{1}{R} \sum_{e \in B_i} e(n, t) \qquad i = 1...M \quad .$$

are approximately identically, namely *Gaussian* distributed with identical mean and variance. This is given by the Central Limit Theorem. In practice, for a skillful selection of cover data representation and sizes of the subsets ($R \approx 50$), this assumption is sufficiently true. As a consequence; the random variable

$$S_i = S_{A_i} - S_{B_i}$$

is approximately Gaussian-distributed and shows a mean value close to zero. For embedding a message bit "'1'" the coefficients in A_i are slightly increased while the coefficients in B_i are slightly decreased, and vice versa for an embedded "'0'". The degree of modification of the coefficients is controlled by a psychoacoustic model similar to MPEG audio layer 2 coding to provide maximum robustness and transparency by considering the perceptual properties of the human auditory system. The enforced difference S_i in the partial energies is a robust feature that survives many kinds of signal transformations for multimedia data.

The modified coefficients are then written back to the cover data by replacing the original FFT values. The modified spectrum is then transformed to the time domain and written to the output PCM file.

The mean energy difference S_i can be detected and the correct bit information "one" or zero "zero" can be retrieved as follows: assumed that the correct watermark key is provided to the detector, the same subsets are selected from the marked data and the two partial sums S_{A_i} and S_{B_i} are calculated again and compared to get an estimator of the embedded message bit:

$$m_i = \begin{cases} "1" & \text{if} \quad S_i \geq 0 \\ "0" & \text{if} \quad S_i < 0 \end{cases}$$

The set of all message bits m_i are embedded according to the scheme mentioned above by selecting N pairs of subsets A_i and B_i, each pairwise disjoint.

Each watermark message is preceded by a *synchronization* pattern, that is, a given watermark pattern that is fixed and identical for all watermark messages. The detector first searches for the presence of this sync pattern and then starts the detection of the message bits [17].

3.2 Robust Hash and Message Authentication Code

In this section we propose a message authentication code algorithm for perception-based verification of the integrity of audio data. Our approach is an extension on an audio fingerprinting scheme introduced by *Haitsma et al* [10,9]. This robust feature extraction uses a time-frequency analysis of the Fourier magnitude coefficients of the audio signal. A similar approach for video data based on average block luminance values has been introduced by the same authors [14].

Proposed FFT based time-frequency feature extraction. In the original algorithm [10,9] the audio signal is digitally represented by PCM samples and it is divided into overlapping frames containing N PCM samples where t denotes the time-step of the frame and transferred to the Fourier domain and finally mapped to a logarithmically scaled frequency axis. This especially takes into account that the human perception of frequency and pitch can be represented on a logarithmic frequency scale, i.e. the *Bark* scale.

Then, in the original algorithm, the energy differences of adjacent energy bands n and $n + 1$ at a given time t are compared to those with the same band indices in the next consecutive time-step $t + 1$. It should be noted that the value of each hash bit is dependent on two pairs of energy coefficients in consecutive frames. By design, both spectral properties and temporal properties of the signal are considered. This extracted audio feature provides a high level of robustness against encoding to lossy compression formats,re-sampling, filtering, dynamics compression, noise addition and analog tape recording.

Psychoacoustic Model-based Quantization. Crucial for the distinction performance of fingerprinting algorithms is the sophisticated selection and/or postprocessing of audio features that are relevant with respect to human perception. Therefore, it is advised to incorporate results from the research on human hearing and lossy audio data compression here.

For example, it is well known that the human ear shows different sensitivity to incoming sound depending on the frequency of the sound [5]. Furthermore, the ear shows the effect of instantaneous *frequency masking* and *temporal masking* such that dominant spectral components (*"'maskers"'*) are able to decrease (and even annihilate) the sound sensations in a certain range along the frequency axis and the time axis, as well [25,13] .

In the following, we will incorporate the MPEG Audio Layer 2 psychoacoustic modeling as published in deep detail in the appendix of the mp3 specification [11]. First, we estimate the masking curve for each audio frame. As introduced by us in an earlier publication [24], we introduce to represent those areas in the spectrum that are less audible or even inaudible, i.e. below the masking threshold, using coarse quantization steps. On the other hand, areas that are clearly audible are represented in fine quantization steps (see figure 3 for an example). As a result we obtain the spectrum represented in non-uniformly quantized values, denoted as $e'(n, t)$ in the remainder.

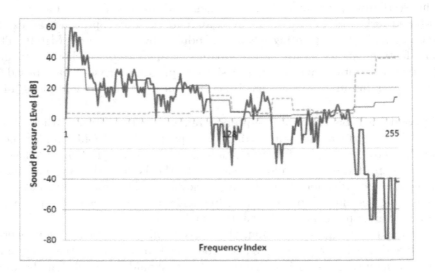

Fig. 3. Non-uniform quantization of FFT coefficients example – thick line: quantized FFT magnitude spectrum; thin line: instantaneous masking threshold; dashed line: quantization step size (range: 3 to 40 dB); magnitude coefficients below masking threshold are represented in coarse quantization steps

Key Dependent Feature Selection. An analysis of the security of the algorithm, i.e. attacks aimed on the robust hash under knowledge of the algorithm was not given by the authors [10,9] as the security in many scenarios is not a relevant requirement for audio retrieval purposes. For integrity protection the security must be provided with respect to the requirements given in section 2.2 in a way that an attacker can not generate a hash collision or succeed in a pre-image attack. Therefore, as pointed out by *Fridrich et al.* the security must be provided by a key dependent selection of features in the feature extraction stage already [6,1]. Thus, we introduce the following extension: In the original approach for calculation of every fingerprint bit only energy coefficients from *consecutive* bands k and $k+1$ and *consecutive* time-steps t and $t+1$ were used. Here, we introduce that each code will now be extracted from an audio segment consisting of L consecutive frames, typically a few hundred (representing a number of seconds playing time). In contrast to the original approach, we introduce to derive the hash bits H' from the sign of the difference of *two* FFT coefficients at *arbitrary* time-steps t_1, t_2 and frequency band indices k_1, k_2 in the time-frequency domain.

$$H'_{K_2} = \begin{cases} 1 & \text{if } e'(k_1, t_1) - e'(k_2, t_2) \geq 0 \\ 0 & \text{if } e'(k_1, t_1) - e'(k_2, t_2) < 0 \end{cases} \tag{1}$$

The selection shall be *pseudo-randomly* dependent on a secret key K_2. Here, the security is introduced as it is obscure to an attacker which bands are selected for the hash bit calculation (and which are not). Because of its key-dependence, the extracted authentication code H'_{K_2} can be regarded as a *robust message authentication code* (denoted as "rMAC" in the remainder).

Coordination of feature extraction with watermark embedding. As pointed out in section 3.1, in a content-fragile watermarking system it is essential that the original audio data distortions caused by embedding the rMAC as a content-fragile watermark do not significantly change the values of the rMAC. Therefore, we will *coordinate* the process of rMAC feature extraction and the watermarking embedding.

As described in section 3.1 the embedding is done by modifying a pseudo-randomly selected set of Fourier magnitude coefficients (on a linear frequency scale). Thus, the rMAC bits will be calculated from the FFT-spectrum on a *linear* scale, too (unlike the original algorithm, where a logarithmic frequency scale was used). This facilitates the separation of rMAC feature extraction and our watermark embedding algorithm.

Then, in order to ensure that the rMAC calculation is not affected by the embedding (an vice versa), only those FFT-magnitude coefficients will be used for rMAC extraction if they had *not* been selected by the watermark key K_1 for watermark embedding. This can only be done if the rMAC extraction is provided with the secret watermark key K_1. Therefore, the extraction algorithm for this new rMAC is not only dependent on the secret rMAC key K_2 but also on the given secret watermarking key K_1.

Normalization of the FFT spectrum. For real-world audio data, for example music or speech recordings, the FFT magnitude coefficients are neither equally distributed nor statistically independent. For example, in most speech recordings, the coefficients related to lower frequencies (e.g. below 1000 Hz) usually have a higher mean energy than coefficients related to higher frequencies. Thus, the key dependent selection of bands for fingerprint extraction raises problems with respect to the security requirements listed in section 2.2.

For example, if such low frequency coefficient is selected by the rMAC key as the first summand in equation (1) to calculate a particular hash bit, that coefficient will dominate the sum and causing the single hash bit to be more likely a "one" than a "zero" *for any kind of data.* Thus, the complete rMAC would not be equally distributed and rMACs from different music segments would not be independent, allowing systematic security attacks on the rMAC.

Therefore, we introduce a *normalization* of the FFT spectrum as follows: We regard all FFT coefficients $e'(n_0, t)$ of a given band index n_0 of all time-steps $t = \{1, ..., L\}$ in an audio segment as a random variable with expectation μ_n and variance σ_n^2. We introduce a normalization given as follows:

$$e''(n, t) := \frac{e(n, t) - m(n)}{s(n)} \qquad (2)$$

where $m(n)$ and $s^2(n)$ denote the empirical mean and variance along the time-axis. As can be seen from the linearity of the variance, the transformed quantities $e''(n, t)$ of a given band index n have mean 0 and variance 1. Finally, calculating the rMAC bits is done on the normalized FFT coefficients.

Similar to the coordination mechanism described in section 3.2 we have to ensure that the normalization, and the rMAC in consequence, remains independent of the watermark embedding. Therefore, we introduce that watermarked coefficients will not contribute to $m(n)$ and $s^2(n)$ by excluding watermarked coefficients here.

Finally, the comparison of the FFT coefficients is done on the normalized FFT coefficients selected as described above:

$$d_k'' := e''(n_1, t_1) - e''(n_2, t_2) \qquad (3)$$

where $n_{1,2,3,4} \in \{1, 2, ..., N\}, t_{1,2,3,4} \in \{1, 2, ...L\}$. In order to provide a sufficient degree of security against brute force attacks, a minimum of 128 rMAC bits will be extracted, i.e. $k = 1...128$.

As we will show later in the experimental results the related modified fingerprint

$$H_{K_2}'' = \begin{cases} 1 & \text{if } d_k'' \geq 0 \\ 0 & \text{if } d_k'' < 0 \end{cases}$$

meets the requirements for a robust hash function listed in section 2.2 with the additional property of key-dependence. The distribution of the extracted audio features d_k'' obtained from a audio test data set can be seen in figure 4.

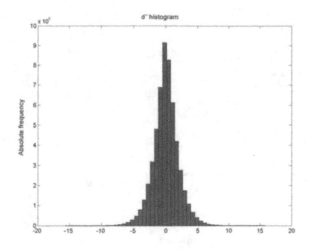

Fig. 4. Histogram of extracted audio feature d''

Protecting the block order. On protection time, the audio file is divided into separate blocks which are protected independently. In order to prevent removal attacks, we additionally embed the index number of the respect block. Therefore, we concatenate the block index as a 10 bit identifier to the rMAC watermark message. This allows to verify the correct *order* of the sections and the detection of removal or duplication of audio sections in the file. An alternative to this approach could be to embed the index number of the following block which defines a *chain* of authentication.

4   Experimental Evaluation

4.1   Test Data and Simulated Audio Attacks

The detection success was tested on a set of speech audio book files and radio plays taken different genre and different production quality (44.1 kHz, 16 bit, mono, playing time approximately 1.5 hours total). The audio files were divided into sections of 5 seconds (approximately 1100 total) and an 128 bit rMAC was extracted from each section. The frequency range we selected was 100 Hz to 10000 Hz. The FFT frame size is 1024 samples which provides a sufficient frequency resolution.

The rMACs were embedded with a robust audio watermark algorithm as explained in the previous chapter. The embedding strength was chosen in such that the modifications of the Fourier coefficients do not exceed the masking threshold by more than 1 dB which is hardly noticeable for an average listener [17].

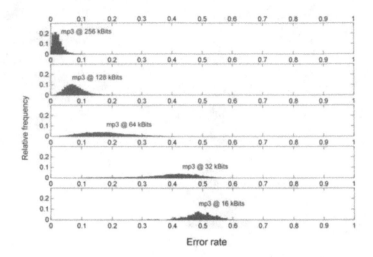

Fig. 5. Histogram of bit error rate for mp3 encoding

First of all, we investigated the distortions introduced by the watermark embedding process itself. This defines the minimum bit error rate (BER) we can expect at the verification stage even for *authentic* content. The average BER here is found to be 0.022. Closer analysis shows, that especially those rMAC bits whose related value of d'' (see eq. 3 and fig. 4 have a small magnitude are more likely to be affected by robustness attacks. This is subject to further research as it affects the overall distinction performance, especially the false alarm rate.

We also investigated the behavior of the rMAC extraction with respect to increasing distortion of the protected audio signal caused by lossy compression. In a training stage the original files were subject to lossy compression by applying an mp3 encoding at bitrates 256, 128, 64, 32 and 16 kBit/s, CBR mono. As can be seen from figures 5 and 6 the authentication watermark shows a good robustness at 256 kbit/s and 128 kbit/s mono. That is, the BER remains low for moderate lossy mp3 compression. In addition, this means also that the key-dependent extraction does not necessarily result in a decreased robustness against mp3 compression compared to the original implementation presented by *Haitsma, Kalker et al.* [10,9].

At low bit rate mp3 coding at 32 kbit/s and 16 kbit/s mono, the BER significantly increases. That is, the authentication watermark successfully indicates the distortion of significant perceivable quality degradation caused by low bit rate encoding.

4.2   Brute Force Attack

To demonstrate the key-dependence of the algorithm we compared the rMAC using different rMAC keys. This simulates the result of a brute force attack trying to authenticate the content without knowledge of the correct rMAC key.

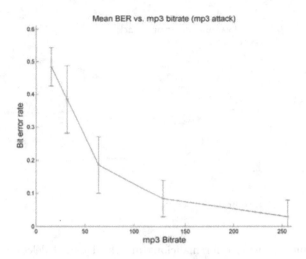

Fig. 6. Average bit error rate for mp3 encoding

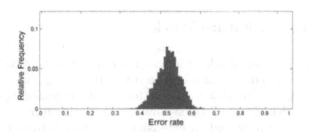

Fig. 7. Error rate for brute force key attack (mean=0.4996, stddev=0.0441)

7 show that compared rMAC are identical only by coincidence (mean BER = 63.95/128 = 49.96%). As required, the distribution of the Hamming distance behaves like it can be expected from uncorrelated binary random vectors. That is, without knowledge of the rMAC key the protected audio can not be verified as authentic.

4.3   Authentication Example

As an example, we attacked one of the audio books chapters by deleting one sentence of the spoken text after approximately 20 seconds play time. The rMAC block size was 3 seconds. As can be seen from figure 8, the Hamming distance increases significantly at the attacked file positions, i.e. in the 11th audio block. That is, the detected rMAC successfully indicate such audible filtering transformation. The retrieved block index information correctly indicates an *offset* of 3 blocks after the attacked section because of the malicious deletion.

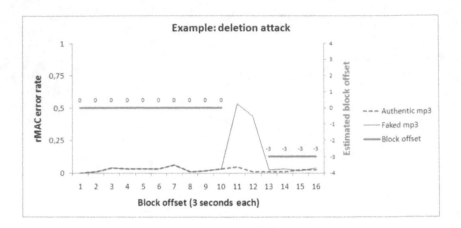

Fig. 8. rMAC hamming distance for malicious attack: detected deletion of 3 audio blocks at time index $t = 11$; dahed line: rMAC error rate for authentic content; thin line: rMAC error rate for forged content; thick line: estimated time index offset

5   Conclusion and Future Work

This paper introduces an approach for a perception-based authentication watermarking for digital audio data. Our aim is to detect tampering that changes the cover audio data perceivably while inaudible modifications remain ignored.

Our approach is based on an audio fingerprinting algorithm by *Haitsma, Kalker et al.* [10,9]. We presented an extension with respect to security of the algorithm. Especially, we included the usage of a secret key thus extending the original fingerprinting algorithm toward a true robust hash and robust message authentication coding (rMAC), respectively. Furthermore, we introduce a coordination strategy to provide a watermarking compliant rMAC extraction and embedding.

We successfully incorporate our rMAC extraction into a robust audio watermarking scheme in order to realize an integrated authentication watermarking system like *content-fragile watermarking* originally introduced by *Dittmann et al.*[4]. Unlike cryptographic hash functions our approach shows a high robustness against signal transformations that do not perceivably change the audio data. It should be noted that the authentication is done based on the human *perception* only. A semantic assessment of the detected attacks on the integrity is not covered in this work.

Experimental results show a good distinction between tampering and non-tampering signal changes. In extension to our previous work, we achieve a significant increase in the capacity of the watermark embedding. This is crucial as it offers to divide the audio content into smaller section (play time of few seconds) which can be protected independently. This improves both the localization and the detection performance even for malicios attacks of small duration.

Because of its robustness, security and distinction performance our proposed algorithm can provde perception-based audio authentication in many scenarios, for example in protecting archives preserving the cultural heritage or other sensitive or delicate audio data. In addition, it can improve the security of fingerprint based filter methods for peer-to-peer networks or broadcast monitoring systems[3]. Apart from audio authentication purposes, our embedding strategy can have an impact on *copyright* watermarking applications, as well.

Acknowledgements

The work described in this paper has been partially funded by the *Center of Advanced Security Research Darmstadt (CASED)* (http://www.cased.de).

References

1. Mao, Y., Swaminathan, A., Wu, M.: Security of feature extraction in image hashing. In: IEEE Conference on Acoustic, Speech and Signal Processing (ICASSP), Philadelphia, PA (March 2005)
2. Bender, W., Gruhl, D., Morimoto, N., Lu, A.: Techniques for data hiding. IBM Systems Journal, MIT Media Lab 35(3,4), 313–336 (1996)
3. Cano, P., Gmez, E., Batlle, E., de Gomes, L., Bonnet, M.: Audio fingerprinting: Concepts and applications. In: 2002 International Conference on Fuzzy Systems Knowledge Discovery (FSKD 2002), Singapore (November 2002)
4. Dittmann, J., Steinmetz, A., Steinmetz, R.: Content-based digital signature for motion pictures authentication and content-fragile watermarking. In: Proceedings of the IEEE International Conference on Multimedia Computing and Systems (ICMCS 1999), Washington, DC, USA, vol. 2, p. 209. IEEE Computer Society, Los Alamitos (1999)
5. Fletcher, H., Munson, W.A.: Loudness, its definition, measurement, and calculation. Journal of the Acoustical Society of America 5, 82–108 (1933)
6. Fridrich, J., Goljan, M.: Robust hash functions for digital watermarking. In: Proc. ITCC 2000, Las Vegas, Nevada, March 27-29, pp. 173–178 (2000)
7. Gomez, E., Cano, P., de Gomes, L., Batlle, E., Bonnet, M.: Mixed watermarking-fingerprinting approach for integrity verification of audio recordings. In: International Telecommunications Symposium ITS 2002, Natal, Brazil (2002)
8. Gulbis, M., Muller, E., Steinebach, M.: Audio integrity protection and falsification estimation by embedding multiple watermarks. In: 2006 International Conference on Intelligent Information Hiding and Multimedia, pp. 469–472. IEEE Computer Society, Los Alamitos (2006)
9. Haitsma, J.A., Oostveen, J.C., Kalker, A.A.C.: A highly robust audio fingerprinting system. In: 2nd International Symposium of Music Information Retrieval (ISMIR 2001), Indiana University, Bloomington, Indiana, USA, October 15-17 (2001), http://ismir2001.ismir.net/proceedings.html (link verified: 2004-05-10)
10. Haitsma, J.A., Oostveen, J.C., Kalker, A.A.C.: Robust audio hashing for content identification. In: Content based multimedia Indexing (CBMI) 2001, Brescia Italy (2001)

11. ISO/IEC 11172-3. Mpeg-1 - coding of moving pictures and associated audio for digital storage media at up to about 1.5 mbit/s – Part 3: Audio, Appendix D: Psychoacoustic Models. ISO/IEC JTC 1/SC (May 1993)

12. Mihçak, M.K., Venkatesan, R.: A perceptual audio hashing algorithm: A tool for robust audio identification and information hiding. In: Moskowitz, I.S. (ed.) IH 2001. LNCS, vol. 2137, p. 51. Springer, Heidelberg (2001)

13. Moore, B.C.J. (ed.): Hearing – Handbook of Perception and Cognition, vol. 1. Academic Press, London (1995)

14. Oostveen, J., Kalker, T., Haitsma, J.: Visual hashing of video: application and techniques. In: Wong, P.W., Delp III, E.P. (eds.) IS&T/SPIE 13th Int. Symposium on Electronic Imaging San Jose, Security and Watermakring of Multimedia Contents, CA, USA, January 2001, vol. 4314. SPIE–The International Society for Optical Engeneering (2001)

15. Radhakrishnan, R., Memon, N.D.: Audio content authentication based on psychoacoustic model. In: Delp, E.J., Wong, P.W. (eds.) Proc. SPIE, Security and Watermarking of Multimedia Contents IV, April 2002, vol. 4675, pp. 110–117 (2002)

16. Schneier, B.W.: Applied Cryptography, ch. 18, 2nd edn. Wiley, Chichester (1996)

17. Steinebach, M.: Digitale Wasserzeichen fuer Audiodaten. PhD thesis, TU Darmstadt, Germany (2003)

18. Steinebach, M., Dittmann, J.: Watermarking-based digital audio data authentication. EURASIP Journal on Applied Signal Processing 10, 1001–1015 (2003)

19. Wang, C.-T., Liao, C.-H., Chen T.-s.: Audio-signal authenticating system based on asymmetric signature schemes. In: 2007 International Conference on Multimedia and Ubiquitous Engineering (MUE 2007), pp. 656–661 (2007)

20. Wu, C.-P., Jay Kuo, C.C.: Speech content authentication integrated with celp speech coders. In: Proceedings of the 2001 IEEE International Conference on Multimedia and Expo, ICME 2001, Tokyo, Japan, August 22-25 (2001)

21. Wu, C.-P., Jay Kuo, C.-C.: Speech content integrity verification integrated with itu g.723.1 speech coding. itcc, 0680 (2001)

22. Yeo, I.-K., Kim, H.J.: Modified patchwork algorithm: A novel audio watermarking scheme. In: Proceedings of the International Conference on Information Technology: Coding and computing (ITTC 2001), April 2–4. IEEE, Las Vegas (2001)

23. Yuan, S., Huss, S.A.: Audio watermarking algorithm for real-time speech integrity and authentication. In: MM&Sec 2004: Proceedings of the 2004 multimedia and security workshop on Multimedia and security, pp. 220–226. ACM Press, New York (2004)

24. Zmudzinski, S., Steinebach, M.: Psycho-acoustic model-based message authentication coding for audio data. In: 10th ACM Workshop on Multimedia and Security (ACM MMSEC 2008), Oxford, UK, September 22-23 (2008) (to appear)

25. Zwicker, E., Fastl, H.: Psychoacustics – Facts and Models. Springer, Berlin (1990)

An Improvement of Short 2-Secure Fingerprint Codes Strongly Avoiding False-Positive*

Koji Nuida

Research Center for Information Security (RCIS), National Institute of Advanced Industrial Science and Technology (AIST)
Akihabara-Daibiru Room 1003, 1-18-13 Sotokanda, Chiyoda-ku,
Tokyo 101-0021, Japan
k.nuida@aist.go.jp

Abstract. A 2-secure fingerprint code proposed by Nuida et al. (IEEE CCNC 2007) has very desirable characteristics that false-positive never occur under Marking Assumption against at most two pirates and that false-positive is very unlikely to occur even in the absence of these assumptions. However, its code length could be further reduced; in fact, another 2-secure code proposed in the same work has significantly shorter code length. In this article, we demonstrate how to mix those two codes to inherit both of their advantages. The resulting 2-secure codes have short lengths, and possess the above characteristics whenever the number of pirates (may exceed two but) is not too large.

1 Introduction

1.1 Backgrounds

Recently, digital content distribution services have been widespread due to the progress of information technology. Digitization of contents has been promoted convenience for many people. However, it does also work better for malicious pirates, increasing the number of illegal content copying/redistribution very rapidly. Technical countermeasures for such illegal activities are strongly desired.

Digital fingerprinting is a possible solution for the above problems. Here we focus on code-based schemes; a content server first encodes each user's ID and then embeds each codeword into a content that will be sent to the user, for the sake of traceability of the pirate from the codeword in a pirated content. However, if two or more pirates collude, then strong attacks (collusion attacks) to the embedded codeword are possible. Thus any fingerprint code should be equipped with an appropriate pirate tracing algorithm that determines a pirate correctly with an overwhelming probability even from an attacked codeword. Such a code that works properly against at most c pirates is called c-secure [2]. Under the conventional Marking Assumption [2] several c-secure codes (e.g., [2,5,6,8,10,11]), including 2-secure ones (e.g., [3,4,9,12]), have been proposed.

---

* This work was supported by 2007 Research Grants of the Science and Technology Foundation of Japan (JSTF).

S. Katzenbeisser and A.-R. Sadeghi (Eds.): IH 2009, LNCS 5806, pp. 161–175, 2009.

Tracing errors of fingerprint codes consist of false-negative (outputting no pirates) and false-positive (outputting an innocent user). In many practical cases the latter is more crucial than the former, therefore an additional desirable requirement for c-secure codes would be *perfect* avoidance of false-positive. This strong property has in fact been achieved by some c-secure codes [3,4,9,12].

On the other hand, security of c-secure codes is usually evaluated under the bound c of the number of pirates and Marking Assumption. However, it is generally hard to estimate the possible size of pirates' coalitions and to realize digital watermarking schemes sufficiently robust to satisfy Marking Assumption. Thus another desirable requirement would be avoidance of false-positive (to some significant extent) *without those two assumptions*. Even this strong property has been achieved by [6,9,10,11]. (Slight relaxation of Marking Assumption was also studied [5,8,11].) However, to our best knowledge *both* of the two properties of strongly avoiding false-positive are simultaneously attained by no c-secure codes, except the 2-secure code recently proposed by Nuida et al. in [9].

In fact, they gave two versions for their 2-secure codes. One of them satisfies the above two requirements, while the other satisfies the first requirement and has significantly shorter code length. However, it has not been clear whether the latter code satisfies the second requirement as well, thus there seems to exist a trade-off between short code lengths and strong avoidance of false-positive among the two codes. The motivation of our work was to resolve the trade-off by showing, if possible, that the latter version also satisfies the second requirement.

1.2 Our Contributions and Organization of the Article

After giving a formulation of fingerprint codes and some definitions in Sect. 2 and summarizing the preceding work [9] in Sects. 3.1–3.3, first in Sect. 3.4 we evaluate false-positive probabilities of the first version of [9] in the absence of Marking Assumption, and observe that the probability cannot be meaningfully bounded. Thus the abovementioned trade-off in [9] does certainly exist. Then in Sect. 4 we propose an improved construction that is a mixture of the original two codes. This intends to inherit both advantages of the two codes. Intuitive ideas of how to mix the two codes and why the idea would work are also exhibited in Sect. 4.1. We evaluate error probabilities and code lengths of our codes in Sect. 5, and give some numerical examples in Sect. 6. These results show that in many practical settings, our codes have both significantly short lengths and the property of strongly avoiding false-positive. Some novel proof techniques and observation for proper choices of security parameters are also presented.

2 Fingerprint Codes

Following the conventional treatment, we define a *fingerprint code* as a pair (Gen, Tr) of a *codeword generation algorithm* Gen and a *tracing algorithm* Tr. The algorithm Gen outputs an $N \times m$ binary matrix W (and some auxiliary element, in general), with each row corresponding to a *user* for the code. Let

w_i denote the codeword of i-th user (i.e., i-th row) u_i. The algorithm Tr takes the matrix W and a word y of length m over an expanded alphabet $\{0, 1, ?\}$ as input, and outputs a set of users. We call each '?' in y an *unreadable bit*.

We suppose that ℓ users $u_{i_1}, \ldots, u_{i_\ell}$ are adversaries, called *pirates*, who create a word y as above (called a *pirated word*) from their codewords $w_{i_1}, \ldots, w_{i_\ell}$ by using an attack algorithm. Let U and C denote the sets of all users and of all pirates, respectively. Users in $U \setminus C$ are called *innocent users*. In this article, superscripts 'P' and 'I' (such as u^P and w^I) indicate "pirate" and "innocent user", respectively. The events $\mathsf{Tr}(W, y) \cap C = \emptyset$ and $\mathsf{Tr}(W, y) \not\subset C$ are called *false-negative* and *false-positive*, respectively, and their union is called a *tracing error* (or an *error* in short). The fingerprint code is *c-secure (with ε-error)* [2] if the tracing error probability is not higher than a sufficiently small value ε under the following two assumptions, called a *standard assumption* in this article:

- The number ℓ of pirates is not larger than c;
- *Marking Assumption* [2]: $y_j = w_{i_1,j}$ whenever the ℓ bits $w_{i_1,j}, \ldots, w_{i_\ell,j}$ of pirates in j-th positions coincide (we call such a position *undetectable*).

In this article, we focus on properties of strongly avoiding false-positive. We say that a fingerprint code is *c-secure PFPA (with ε-error)* if it is c-secure (with ε-error) and the false-positive probability is zero under the standard assumption ("PFPA" stands for "perfectly false-positive-avoiding"). A code is *(c, c')-secure (with $(\varepsilon, \varepsilon')$-error)* if it is c-secure (with ε-error) and the false-positive probability is not higher than a sufficiently small value ε' under the assumption that $\ell \leq c'$, *without Marking Assumption* (i.e., y can be an arbitrary word of length m over $\{0, 1, ?\}$). A code is *(c, c')-secure PFPA (with $(\varepsilon, \varepsilon')$-error)* if it has both of the above two properties. For example, codes in [3,4,12] are 2-secure PFPA, while codes in [6,10,11] are (c, N)-secure. Moreover, 2-secure PFPA codes and $(2, N)$-secure PFPA codes are proposed in [9], as explained in the next section.

3   The Original Schemes

In this section, we summarize the construction of abovementioned two versions of the 2-secure codes in [9]; one is 2-secure PFPA and the other is $(2, N)$-secure PFPA. In Sect. 3.4, we evaluate the false-positive probability of the first code in the setting of $(2, c')$-security. The result sounds negative rather than affirmative.

3.1   Common Characteristics

First, both of the two versions are equipped with the same codeword generation algorithm Gen, which generates each entry $w_{i,j}$ of the matrix W independently and uniformly at random. That is, every W is output with the same probability.

In the tracing algorithms of both versions the following auxiliary algorithm PS is used, called a *parent search*:

Definition 1. *The algorithm* PS, *with the matrix* W *and a binary word* y *as input, outputs every pair* $(u_i, u_{i'})$ *of distinct users who can create the word* y *under Marking Assumption; i.e.,* $y_j = w_{i,j}$ *whenever* $w_{i,j} = w_{i',j}$. *Such a pair* $(u_i, u_{i'})$ *is called a* parent pair *of* y, *and* u_i *and* $u_{i'}$ *are called* parents *of* y.

3.2   The First Tracing Algorithm

First, the tracing algorithm Tr_1 of the first version replaces a pirated word y with a binary word $\widehat{y}$ by replacing each unreadable bit '?' with 0 or 1 independently and uniformly at random. Then Tr_1 performs the parent search PS for W and $\widehat{y}$. Finally, Tr_1 outputs every parent u_i of $\widehat{y}$ who belongs to all the parent pairs. For example, if $(u_1, u_2), (u_2, u_3)$ are the parent pairs then Tr_1 outputs u_2; if (u_1, u_2) is the unique parent pair then Tr_1 outputs both u_1 and u_2; and Tr_1 outputs nobody if $(u_1, u_2), (u_2, u_3), (u_3, u_4)$ are the parent pairs or no parent pairs exist.

Note that under the standard assumption, the two pirates (when $\ell = 2$) or the pirate and any innocent user (when $\ell = 1$) always form a parent pair. By this fact it was shown [9] that the code is 2-secure PFPA with ε-error, where $\varepsilon = (N - 2)(3N - 7)(3/4)^m/2$, if $N \geq 2$. Note that a similar idea had appeared earlier in [1], where only an asymptotic error probability was evaluated.

3.3   The Second Tracing Algorithm

The output of the tracing algorithm Tr_2 of the second version is in fact a subset of the output of Tr_1. For each output user u_i of Tr_1, Tr_2 outputs u_i if and only if, for every parent pair $(u_i, u_{i'})$ of $\widehat{y}$ including u_i we have $d(u_i, \widehat{y}) \leq d(u_{i'}, \widehat{y})$, where d denotes the Hamming distance. Intuitively speaking, Tr_2 is more prudent than Tr_1, and for each parent pair, Tr_2 excludes less suspicious user of the two from candidates of the output. (This description in fact differs from [9] but is equivalent to that.) Now it was shown [9] that the code is $(2, N)$-secure PFPA (descriptions of the values ε and ε' are omitted here due to the intricacy).

Table 1 gives the shortest code lengths of these two versions to attain the specified false-negative probabilities under the standard assumption (with $c = 2$). This table shows a significant trade-off between short code lengths and strong avoidance of false-positive.

3.4   Evaluation of the First Version

In the original work [9], it has not been clarified whether, as well as the second version, the first version of their 2-secure codes are $(2, c')$-secure for some c'. Here we evaluate the false-positive probability of the first version (see Sect. 3.2) in the absence of Marking Assumption.

First, in a slightly affirmative direction we have the following result:

Proposition 1. *Let* ℓ *be the number of pirates. Then, without Marking Assumption, the false-positive probability of* (Gen, Tr_1) *(Sect. 3.2) is not higher than*

$$\left(1 - \frac{1}{N - \ell}\right)^{N - \ell - 1} + (N - \ell - \chi_e(N - \ell))\left(\frac{N - \ell - \chi_o(N - \ell)}{2} * \left(\frac{3}{4}\right)^m\right) , \quad (1)$$

Table 1. Code lengths of 2-secure codes in [9]

N	version	error probability ε					
		10^{-4}	10^{-5}	10^{-6}	10^{-7}	10^{-9}	10^{-11}
10^2	first	66	74	82	90	106	122
	second	84	99	114	128	157	186
10^3	first	82	90	98	106	122	138
	second	99	114	128	143	172	201
10^4	first	98	106	114	122	138	154
	second	114	128	143	157	186	215
10^5	first	114	122	130	138	154	170
	second	128	143	157	172	201	230
10^6	first	130	138	146	154	170	186
	second	143	157	172	186	215	245

where we put $k * x = 1 - (1 - x)^k$ and define

$$\chi_o(k) = \begin{cases} 1 & \text{if } k \text{ is odd,} \\ 0 & \text{if } k \text{ is even,} \end{cases} \quad \chi_e(k) = \begin{cases} 0 & \text{if } k \text{ is odd,} \\ 1 & \text{if } k \text{ is even.} \end{cases}$$

The proof uses the following lemma.

Lemma 1. *Let $x_1, \ldots, x_k$ be i.i.d. random variables, and let $\mathcal{P}$ be a property such that each unordered pair $x_i x_j$ ($i \neq j$) satisfies $\mathcal{P}$ with common probability p. Then $Pr[$ some $x_i x_j$ satisfies $\mathcal{P}] \leq (k - \chi_e(k))(\frac{k - \chi_o(k)}{2} * p)$.*

Proof. First, the set of the $\binom{k}{2}$ unordered pairs $x_i x_j$ ($x_i \neq x_j$) has a partition into $k' = k - \chi_e(k)$ subsets $X_1, \ldots, X_{k'}$ of $(k - \chi_o(k))/2$ mutually disjoint pairs. This is an easy consequence of the well-known fact (e.g., [13]) that the k-vertex complete graph K_k has an edge k'-coloring. Now for each h, the events that $x_i x_j$ satisfies $\mathcal{P}$ are independent for all $x_i x_j \in X_h$, therefore some $x_i x_j \in X_h$ satisfies $\mathcal{P}$ with probability $\frac{k - \chi_o(k)}{2} * p$. This implies the desired bound. $\square$

Proof (Proposition 1). By the definition of Tr_1, false-positive occurs only if **(I)** $(u_1^{\mathrm{I}}, u_2^{\mathrm{I}})$ is a parent pair of $\hat{y}$ for some distinct $u_1^{\mathrm{I}}, u_2^{\mathrm{I}} \in U \setminus C$, or **(II)** there is a unique $u^{\mathrm{I}} \in U \setminus C$ such that **(*)** $(u^{\mathrm{I}}, u^{\mathrm{P}})$ is a parent pair of $\hat{y}$ for some $u^{\mathrm{P}} \in C$. For (I), since the choice of $\hat{y}$ is independent of each innocent user's codeword, for fixed $u_1^{\mathrm{I}} \neq u_2^{\mathrm{I}}$ the probability that $(u_1^{\mathrm{I}}, u_2^{\mathrm{I}})$ is a parent pair is $(3/4)^m$. Thus by Lemma 1, the probability of (I) is bounded by the second term of (1).

On the other hand, for (II), let p denote the probability of (*) for a fixed u^{I}, fixed pirates' codewords and a fixed $\hat{y}$. Note that the events (*) for all u^{I} are independent with each other, therefore the value p is common for every u^{I}. Thus the probability of (II) is $f(p) = (N - \ell)p(1 - p)^{N - \ell - 1}$. Now an elementary analysis shows that $f(p)$ takes the maximum value at $p = 1/(N - \ell)$, and the maximum value is equal to the first term of (1). Hence Proposition 1 holds. $\square$

Now the first term of (1) is a decreasing function of $N - \ell$ and converges to $e^{-1} \approx 0.368$ when $N - \ell \to \infty$. Thus the bound in Proposition 1 is in fact not very effective. Moreover, we can even observe that *this bound is very likely to be almost tight*, as follows. First, choosing a sufficiently long code length m to make the code 2-secure, the probability of the event (I) in the above proof becomes negligibly small, thus we may assume for simplicity that the event (I) does not occur. Now in the absence of Marking Assumption, it is very likely that pirates can freely create the word y so that no parent pairs of two pirates exist and the probability p in the above proof is close to $1/(N - \ell)$. (This is indeed clear in the case of single pirate, i.e., $\ell = 1$.) Under the above assumption, this implies that the false-positive probability is *exactly* $f(p)$ which is close to the first term $f(1/(N - \ell))$ of (1), therefore the bound is almost tight in this situation.

Hence we have observed that the first version $(\mathsf{Gen}, \mathsf{Tr}_1)$ of the above codes is *not* $(2, c')$-secure. From now, we improve the above construction to make the code $(2, c')$-secure for a significantly large c', still with short code lengths.

4   Our Proposal

In Sect. 3 we have seen the significant trade-off between $(2, c')$-security and short code lengths among the two versions of 2-secure codes in [9]. In this section, we propose an improvement of the construction that is a mixture of the two versions (with some further modification to simplify the scheme). This intends to resolve the above trade-off by inheriting both of the advantages of the two versions simultaneously. First in Sect. 4.1 we explain an intuitive idea of how to mix the original two versions for inheriting both advantages, where the observation for $(2, c')$-insecurity given in Sect. 3.4 plays a key role. Then we give the improved construction of our codes in Sect. 4.2. Security evaluations and numerical examples of our codes will be demonstrated in the following sections.

4.1   An Intuitive Idea

To improve the construction, here we recall the argument in Sect. 3.4 that has led $(2, c')$-insecurity of the code $(\mathsf{Gen}, \mathsf{Tr}_1)$. The key observation was that, in the absence of Marking Assumption, pirates can create the pirated word so that there exists a *unique* innocent user u^{I}, with an appropriately high probability, such that $(u^{\mathrm{I}}, u^{\mathrm{P}})$ is a parent pair for some pirate u^{P}. Now if the number ℓ of pirates is not too large, then their codewords are likely to differ from each other to sufficiently large extent, therefore the above pirate u^{P} with $(u^{\mathrm{I}}, u^{\mathrm{P}})$ being a parent pair is also likely to be *unique*.

Summarizing, in most of the false-positive cases for the first version $(\mathsf{Gen}, \mathsf{Tr}_1)$ of the original codes, there exists a *unique* parent pair of the form $(u^{\mathrm{I}}, u^{\mathrm{P}})$ (provided ℓ is not too large). On the other hand, the $(2, N)$-security of the second version $(\mathsf{Gen}, \mathsf{Tr}_2)$ of the original code means that the tracing algorithm Tr_2 can prevent false-positive even in such a dominant case of a unique parent pair. From the observation, we are motivated to mix the original two tracing algorithms in such a way that we use the second version Tr_2 if just one parent pair exists, while we use the first version Tr_1 if two or more parent pairs exist. Note that this modification does not increase false-negative under the standard assumption in comparison with Tr_1, since now existence of just one parent pair means that this pair is either the pair of two pirates (when $\ell = 2$) or a pair of the pirate and an innocent user (when $\ell = 1$), in which case Tr_2 also outputs a pirate correctly. (Note also that further use of Tr_2 in cases where two parent pairs exist may decrease the false-positive probability, but increases the false-negative probability which also leads increase of the code lengths.)

4.2   The Construction

Following the above observation, in this subsection we give the improved construction of the codes. Here we also intend to modify the original construction in such a way that the resulting tracing algorithm does not need the phase of replacing unreadable bits with usual bits, for the sake of simplification and derandomization of the scheme. For the purpose, first we extend the notion of parent pairs in the following manner:

Definition 2. *We define the* extended parent search algorithm $\widehat{\mathsf{PS}}$ *to output, with the matrix W and a pirated word y over $\{0, 1, ?\}$ as input, every pair $(u_i, u_{i'})$ of distinct users such that $y_j \in \{w_{i,j}, w_{i',j}\}$ if $y_j \in \{0, 1\}$ and $w_{i,j} \neq w_{i',j}$ if $y_j = ?$. Such a pair $(u_i, u_{i'})$ is called a* parent pair *of y, and u_i and $u_{i'}$ are called* parents *of y.*

Note that Definition 2 coincides with Definition 1 in the case that y is a binary word. Let $\mathcal{P}_y$ denote the set of the parent pairs of y. Moreover, we also write the Hamming distance $|\{j \mid w_j \neq y_j\}|$ between a binary codeword w and a pirated word y over $\{0, 1, ?\}$ as $d(w, y)$.

Our improved fingerprint code uses the same codeword generation algorithm Gen as the original codes (namely, every matrix W is output uniformly at random). On the other hand, our improved tracing algorithm Tr is defined as follows:

Definition 3. *From the matrix W and a pirated word y as input, the following algorithm* Tr *outputs a (possibly empty) set of suspected users:*

1. *Perform the algorithm $\widehat{\mathsf{PS}}$ to enumerate the parent pairs of y.*
2. *If $\mathcal{P}_y = \emptyset$, then output nobody.*
3. *If $\mathcal{P}_y$ consists of a unique pair (u_1, u_2), then output u_1 when $d(w_1, y) < d(w_2, y)$, output u_2 when $d(w_1, y) > d(w_2, y)$, and output both u_1 and u_2 when $d(w_1, y) = d(w_2, y)$.*
4. *If $\mathcal{P}_y$ consists of two or more pairs, then output every user who belongs to all pairs in $\mathcal{P}_y$.*

As we explained in Sect. 4.1, the algorithm Tr imitates Tr_2 in Case 3 and Tr_1 in Case 4. Note that the argument in Sect. 4.1 is owing to the property that the number ℓ of pirates is not too large, and unfortunately our code is likely not

$(2, N)$-secure (while the second version $(\mathsf{Gen}, \mathsf{Tr}_2)$ of [9] is). However, when c' is not too large our code is in fact $(2, c')$-secure, as shown in the following sections.

One may feel that our tracing algorithm is time-consuming since the algorithm $\widehat{\mathsf{PS}}$ searches all pairs of users. However, a sophisticated implementation of $\widehat{\mathsf{PS}}$ would be able to reduce the running time in comparison to a naive implementation. Such implementation of $\widehat{\mathsf{PS}}$ will be a future research topic.

5   Security Evaluation of Our Codes

In this section, we evaluate the security of our codes proposed in Sect. 4; namely false-negative probability under the standard assumption with $c = 2$ (Sect. 5.1), false-positive probability being zero under the same assumption (Sect. 5.2), and false-positive probability in the absence of that assumption (Sect. 5.3). These show that our codes are $(2, c')$-secure PFPA for any, not too large c'.

5.1   2-Security

We evaluate the false-negative probability under the standard assumption (with $c = 2$). First, if $\ell = 1$, then a pair of the pirate and any innocent user is always a parent pair (owing to Marking Assumption). Thus false-negative occurs only if some pair of innocent users forms a parent pair, and its probability is evaluated by the same argument as Proposition 1 in the following manner:

Theorem 1. *When $\ell = 1$, the false-negative probability under Marking Assumption is not higher than the following value (see Proposition 1 for notations)*

$$(N - 1 - \chi_o(N)) \left(\frac{N - 1 - \chi_e(N)}{2} * \left(\frac{3}{4} \right)^m \right)$$

(note that $\chi_e(N - 1) = \chi_o(N)$ and $\chi_o(N - 1) = \chi_e(N)$).

Note that this value is much smaller than the false-negative probability for $\ell = 2$ (evaluated below) under practical choices of parameters.

From now, we consider the case $\ell = 2$. For pirates u_1^{P} and u_2^{P}, put

$$A(u_1^{\mathrm{P}}, u_2^{\mathrm{P}}) = \{j \mid w_{1,j}^{\mathrm{P}} = w_{2,j}^{\mathrm{P}}\} \ , \quad B_1(u_1^{\mathrm{P}}, u_2^{\mathrm{P}}) = \{j \mid w_{1,j}^{\mathrm{P}} = y_j \neq w_{2,j}^{\mathrm{P}}\} \ ,$$
$$B_2(u_1^{\mathrm{P}}, u_2^{\mathrm{P}}) = \{j \mid w_{1,j}^{\mathrm{P}} \neq y_j = w_{2,j}^{\mathrm{P}}\} \ , \quad B_? = \{j \mid y_j = ?\} \ .$$

Then Marking Assumption implies that the four sets are disjoint and form a partition of the set $\{1, 2, \ldots, m\}$. Moreover, let E_a denote the event that $|A(u_1^{\mathrm{P}}, u_2^{\mathrm{P}})| = a$; $E_{a,b_?}$ the event "E_a and $|B_?| = b_?$"; and $E_{a,b_?,b_1,b_2}$ the event "$E_{a,b_?}$, $|B_1(u_1^{\mathrm{P}}, u_2^{\mathrm{P}})| = b_1$ and $|B_2(u_1^{\mathrm{P}}, u_2^{\mathrm{P}})| = b_2$". Now let u_i^{I} denote i-th innocent user, write the event "$u_i^{\mathrm{I}} u_1^{\mathrm{P}} \in \mathcal{P}_y$ and $u_i^{\mathrm{I}} u_2^{\mathrm{P}} \in \mathcal{P}_y$" as E_i^1, and for $i > i'$ write the event "$u_i^{\mathrm{I}} u_1^{\mathrm{P}}, u_{i'}^{\mathrm{I}} u_2^{\mathrm{P}} \in \mathcal{P}_y$ or $u_i^{\mathrm{I}} u_2^{\mathrm{P}}, u_{i'}^{\mathrm{I}} u_1^{\mathrm{P}} \in \mathcal{P}_y$ or $u_i^{\mathrm{I}} u_{i'}^{\mathrm{I}} \in \mathcal{P}_y$" as $E_{i,i'}^2$ (see Fig. 1). Then, since $u_1^{\mathrm{P}} u_2^{\mathrm{P}} \in \mathcal{P}_y$ always holds by Marking Assumption, the event of false-negative is the union of all E_i^1 and $E_{i,i'}^2$. Now the probabilities of the events are evaluated as follows:

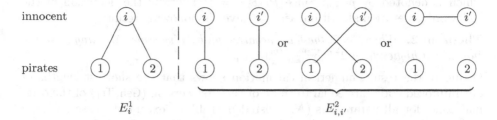

Fig. 1. Definitions of the events E_i^1 and $E_{i,i'}^2$ (where edges are parent pairs)

Lemma 2. *For* $0 \le a \le m$ *and* $0 \le b_? \le m - a$, *let*

$$g_1(a) = \left(\frac{1}{2}\right)^{m-a}\left(1 - \left(\frac{3}{4}\right)^a\right)\left(2 - \left(\frac{1}{2}\right)^{m-a}\right) + \left(\frac{3}{4}\right)^m ,$$

$$g_2(a, b_?) = \left(\frac{1}{2}\right)^{m-a+b_?-1}\left(1 - \left(\frac{3}{4}\right)^a\right) + \left(\frac{2}{3}\right)^{b_?}\left(\frac{3}{4}\right)^m .$$

Then we have

$$Pr\left[E_i^1 \mid E_{a,b_?}\right] = \begin{cases} 2^{a-m} & \text{if } b_? = 0 \\ 0 & \text{if } b_? > 0 \end{cases}, \qquad Pr\left[E_{i,i'}^2 \mid E_{a,b_?}\right] = \begin{cases} g_1(a) & \text{if } b_? = 0 \\ g_2(a, b_?) & \text{if } b_? > 0 \end{cases}.$$

Proof. The claim for E_i^1 is easily derived from the definition of parent pairs. For $E_{i,i'}^2$, let $\overline{E}_1, \overline{E}_2, \overline{E}_3$ denote, respectively, the three sub-events that appear in the definition of $E_{i,i'}^2$ (see Fig. 1). Then we have

$$Pr\left[\overline{E}_1 \text{ or } \overline{E}_2 \text{ or } \overline{E}_3\right] = \sum_{k=1}^{3} Pr\left[\overline{E}_k\right] - \sum_{k<k'} Pr\left[\overline{E}_k, \overline{E}_{k'}\right] + Pr\left[\overline{E}_1, \overline{E}_2, \overline{E}_3\right]$$

where Pr denotes the probability conditioned on $E_{a,b_?}$. Now the claim is derived from the definition of parent pairs by straightforward calculation. $\qquad\square$

Now by Lemma 1, we have

$$Pr\left[\text{some } E_i^1 \mid E_{a,b_?}\right] = (N - 2) * Pr\left[E_i^1 \mid E_{a,b_?}\right] ,$$

$$Pr\left[\text{some } E_{i,i'}^2 \mid E_{a,b_?}\right] \le (N - 2 - \chi_e(N))\left(\frac{N - 2 - \chi_o(N)}{2} * Pr\left[E_{i,i'}^2 \mid E_{a,b_?}\right]\right)$$

for any $a, b_?$, while for fixed a, an elementary analysis shows that the values $Pr\left[E_i^1 \mid E_{a,b_?}\right]$ and $Pr\left[E_{i,i'}^2 \mid E_{a,b_?}\right]$ both take maximum values at $b_? = 0$. Thus to bound the probability we may assume that $b_?$ is always 0, therefore the false-negative probability conditioned on E_a is not higher than the value

$$\min\left\{1, (N-2) * \left(\frac{1}{2}\right)^{m-a} + (N - 2 - \chi_e(N))\left(\frac{N - 2 - \chi_o(N)}{2} * g_1(a)\right)\right\}$$

which is denoted by $p_{\text{FN},a}$. Since $Pr[E_a] = \binom{m}{a}/2^m$ by the definition of the codeword generation algorithm Gen, we have the following result:

Theorem 2. When $\ell = 2$, the false-negative probability under Marking Assumption is not higher than $2^{-m} \sum_{a=0}^{m} \binom{m}{a} p_{\text{FN},a}$.

Owing to the result, numerical calculation shows that the shortest lengths of our improved codes are equal to those of the first version $(\mathsf{Gen}, \mathsf{Tr}_1)$ of the original codes for all parameters (N, ε) listed in Table 1, except the case $(N, \varepsilon) = (10^6, 10^{-4})$ where our code length is 129 (not 130). Thus our code is 2-secure as well as the original codes. Since the effect of our scheme itself is essentially the same as $(\mathsf{Gen}, \mathsf{Tr}_1)$ under the standard assumption, this slight improvement in code lengths would be due to the new ideas (such as Lemma 1) used in our evaluation of false-negative probabilities. Note that our code lengths for parameters considered in Table 1 approximately satisfy the relation

$$m = 16 \log_{10} N + 8 \log_{10}(1/\varepsilon) + 2 \approx 6.9487 \log N + 3.4744 \log(1/\varepsilon) + 2 \ ,$$

where $\log$ and $\log_{10}$ denote the natural and common logarithms, respectively.

5.2 PFPA Property

Regarding false-positive under the standard assumption, note that the pair of the two pirates is always a parent pair when $\ell = 2$, and that a pair of the pirate and any innocent user is also always a parent pair when $\ell = 1$. This means that (except a trivial case $(N, \ell) = (2, 1)$) for each innocent user u^{I} there always exists a parent pair that does not involve u^{I}, therefore false-positive never occur (cf. Sect. 3.2). Hence our codes are 2-secure PFPA.

5.3 $(2, c')$-Security

From now, we evaluate the false-positive probabilities of our codes in the absence of Marking Assumption. Let $u_1^{\text{P}}, \ldots, u_\ell^{\text{P}}$ be the ℓ pirates and $u_1^{\text{I}}, \ldots, u_{N-\ell}^{\text{I}}$ the innocent users. We use the notations in Sect. 5.1, and introduce further notations:

$$\beta = |B_?| \ , \quad \gamma = \max_{1 \leq i \leq \ell}(m - d(w_i^{\text{P}}, y)) \ , \quad \delta = \min_{i \neq i'} d(w_i^{\text{P}}, w_{i'}^{\text{P}}) \ (\text{for } \ell \geq 2).$$

Moreover, fix an index i_0 such that $m - d(w_{i_0}^{\text{P}}, y) = \gamma$. Now for each u_h^{I} and each u_i^{P} define the event $E_{h,i}^3$ by "$u_h^{\text{I}} u_i^{\text{P}} \in \mathcal{P}_y$ and $d(w_h^{\text{I}}, y) \leq d(w_i^{\text{P}}, y)$"; for each u_h^{I} and each $u_i^{\text{P}} \neq u_{i'}^{\text{P}}$ define the event $E_{h,i,i'}^4$ by "$u_h^{\text{I}} u_i^{\text{P}} \in \mathcal{P}_y$ and $u_h^{\text{I}} u_{i'}^{\text{P}} \in \mathcal{P}_y$"; and for each u_h^{I} define the event E_h^5 by "$u_{h'}^{\text{I}} u_{i_0}^{\text{P}} \notin \mathcal{P}_y$ for any $u_{h'}^{\text{I}} \neq u_h^{\text{I}}$". Note that E_h^5 is independent of $E_{h,i}^3$ and $E_{h,i,i'}^4$.

For any fixed y, for each $u_h^{\text{I}} \neq u_{h'}^{\text{I}}$ the probability of $(u_h^{\text{I}}, u_{h'}^{\text{I}})$ being a parent pair is $(3/4)^{m-\beta}(1/2)^\beta \leq (3/4)^m$ by the definition of parent pairs, therefore Lemma 1 implies that the probability that there is a parent pair of two innocent users is not higher than the following value

$$p_{\text{FP},1} = (N - \ell - \chi_e(N - \ell)) \left(\frac{N - \ell - \chi_o(N - \ell)}{2} * \left(\frac{3}{4} \right)^m \right) \ .$$

From now, we evaluate the probability that false-positive occurs and there are no parent pairs of two innocent users. Let $u^I_{h_0}$ be an output innocent user. Then in this case, $E^5_{h_0}$ occurs since there are no parent pairs that do not involve $u^I_{h_0}$. Moreover, by the definition of the tracing algorithm, if just one parent pair containing $u^I_{h_0}$ exists then $E^3_{h_0,i}$ occurs for some i, while if two or more pirate pairs containing $u^I_{h_0}$ exist then $E^4_{h_0,i,i'}$ occurs for some $i \neq i'$ (recall that we are now assuming that there are no parent pairs of two innocent users). Thus, by defining the event E^6_h for each u^I_h as "$E^3_{h,i}$ for some i or $E^4_{h,i,i'}$ for some $i \neq i'$", a necessary condition for $u^I_{h_0}$ being output in this situation is "$E^5_{h_0}$ and $E^6_{h_0}$". Note that for given y and pirates' codewords, $E^5_{h_0}$ and $E^6_{h_0}$ are independent.

For the event $E^3_{h,i}$ we have the following result:

Lemma 3. *In the above situation, given a pirated word y and pirates' codewords, the event $E^3_{h,i}$ occurs with probability not higher than $e^{-\xi m}$, where*

$$\xi = 2\sqrt{9 - 2\log 2} + \log 2 - 6 \approx 0.211736 \ .$$

In the proof, we use the following fact that is a special case of Hoeffding's Inequality [7]:

Lemma 4 (cf. [7]). *Let S be the sum of n independent uniform random variables on $\{0,1\}$. Then for any $t > 0$, we have $Pr[S - n/2 \geq nt] \leq e^{-2nt^2}$.*

Proof (Lemma 3). Put $a = m - d(w^P_i, y)$. Then, given y and w^P_i, straightforward calculation shows that $E^3_{h,i}$ occurs with probability $2^{-m} \sum^a_{k=2a+\beta-m} \binom{a}{k}$, which equals to $2^{a-m} Pr[S - a/2 \geq at]$ where $t = 3/2 - (m - \beta)/a$ and S is as in Lemma 4 with $n = a$. By Lemma 4, this value is bounded by $\rho(a, \beta)$, where $\rho(a, \beta) = 2^{a-m}$ if $t \leq 0$ (namely $a \leq 2(m - \beta)/3$) and $\rho(a, \beta) = 2^{a-m}e^{-2at^2}$ otherwise. This function $\rho(a, \beta)$ for $0 \leq \beta \leq m$ and $0 \leq a \leq m - \beta$ takes the maximum value at $a = 2(m - \beta)/\sqrt{9 - 2\log 2}$ and $\beta = 0$, and the maximum value is equal to $e^{-\xi m}$. Hence Lemma 3 holds.   □

Thus the probability that $E^3_{h,i}$ occurs for some i is not higher than $\ell e^{-\xi m}$.

Secondly, we consider the event $E^4_{h,i,i'}$. Note that such an event is not defined if $\ell = 1$, thus we assume here that $\ell \geq 2$. Moreover, note that this event does not occur if $B_? \not\subset A(u^P_i, u^P_{i'})$, therefore we may assume that $B_? \subset A(u^P_i, u^P_{i'})$ (i.e., $w^P_{i,j} = w^P_{i',j}$ whenever $y_j = ?$). Now we have the following:

Lemma 5. *In the above situation, given pirates' codewords and a pirated word, the event $E^4_{h,i,i'}$ occurs with probability not higher than $(1/2)^{m-\gamma+\delta/2}$.*

Proof. Let a' be the number of j such that $w^P_{i,j} = w^P_{i',j} = y_j$. By the definition of parent pairs, $E^4_{h,i,i'}$ occurs with probability $(1/2)^{m-a'}$. Now we have

$$\gamma \geq \frac{(m - d(w^P_i, y)) + (m - d(w^P_{i'}, y))}{2} = a' + \frac{|B_1(u^P_i, u^P_{i'})| + |B_2(u^P_i, u^P_{i'})|}{2}$$

and the right-hand side is equal to $a' + d(w^P_i, w^P_{i'})/2$ since $B_? \subset A(u^P_i, u^P_{i'})$. This implies that $\gamma \geq a' + \delta/2$, therefore $(1/2)^{m-a'} \leq (1/2)^{m-\gamma+\delta/2}$.   □

Thus the probability that $E^4_{h,i,i'}$ occurs for some $i \neq i'$ is not higher than $\binom{\ell}{2}(1/2)^{m-\gamma+\delta/2}$.

Moreover, for the event E^5_h, the choice of the index i_0 implies that for each $u^I_{h'} \neq u^I_h$, the event $u^I_{h'}u^P_{i_0} \notin \mathcal{P}_y$ occurs with probability $1 - (1/2)^{m-\gamma}$. Since those events are independent with each other, the probability that E^5_h occurs is $(1 - (1/2)^{m-\gamma})^{N-\ell-1}$.

Summarizing, if $\ell \geq 2$, then by putting

$$g_3(\delta_0) = \max_{0 \leq \gamma \leq m} \left[\left(\ell e^{-\xi m} + \binom{\ell}{2}\left(\frac{1}{2}\right)^{m-\gamma+\delta_0/2} \right) \left(1 - \left(\frac{1}{2}\right)^{m-\gamma} \right)^{N-\ell-1} \right]$$

for $0 \leq \delta_0 \leq m$, the probability that false-positive occurs and there are no parent pairs of two innocent users, conditioned on $\delta = \delta_0$, is not higher than

$$g_4(\delta_0) = \min\{1, (N-\ell)g_3(\delta_0)\} .$$

By the definition, g_4 is a non-increasing function and $0 \leq g_4(\delta_0) \leq 1$. On the other hand, since $d(w^P_i, w^P_{i'}) \leq \delta_0$ occurs with probability $2^{-m}\sum_{k=0}^{\delta_0}\binom{m}{k}$ for each $u^P_i \neq u^P_{i'}$, we have $Pr[\delta \leq \delta_0] \leq \min\{1, g_5(\delta_0)\}$ where

$$g_5(\delta_0) = \binom{\ell}{2}2^{-m}\sum_{k=0}^{\delta_0}\binom{m}{k} .$$

These results imply the following:

Lemma 6. *In the above situation, put $\delta_M = \max\{\delta_0 \mid g_5(\delta_0) < 1\}$ (note that $g_5(m) \geq 1$ since $\ell \geq 2$). Then the probability that false-positive occurs and there are no parent pairs of innocent users is not higher than the following value*

$$p_{\mathrm{FP},2} = \binom{\ell}{2}2^{-m}\sum_{\delta_0=0}^{\delta_M}\binom{m}{\delta_0}g_4(\delta_0) + (1 - g_5(\delta_M))g_4(\delta_M + 1) .$$

Proof. Set $g_4(m+1) = 0$. Then this probability is not higher than

$$\sum_{\delta_0=0}^{m} Pr[\delta = \delta_0]\, g_4(\delta_0) = \sum_{\delta_0=0}^{m} (Pr[\delta \leq \delta_0] - Pr[\delta \leq \delta_0 - 1])g_4(\delta_0)$$

$$= \sum_{\delta_0=0}^{m} Pr[\delta \leq \delta_0]\, (g_4(\delta_0) - g_4(\delta_0 + 1)) .$$

Put $\widehat{g_5}(\delta_0) = \min\{1, g_5(\delta_0)\}$. Since $g_4(\delta_0) \geq g_4(\delta_0 + 1)$, the above value is

$$\leq \sum_{\delta_0=0}^{m} \widehat{g_5}(\delta_0)(g_4(\delta_0) - g_4(\delta_0 + 1))$$

$$= \sum_{\delta_0=0}^{m} (\widehat{g_5}(\delta_0) - \widehat{g_5}(\delta_0 - 1))g_4(\delta_0)$$

$$= \sum_{\delta_0=0}^{\delta_M} (g_5(\delta_0) - g_5(\delta_0 - 1))g_4(\delta_0) + (1 - g_5(\delta_M))g_4(\delta_M + 1) = p_{\mathrm{FP},2} \ . \qquad \square$$

On the other hand, for the case $\ell = 1$, a similar but simpler argument shows that the probability that false-positive occurs and there are no parent pairs of innocent users is not higher than $p_{\mathrm{FP},2} = (N - 1)e^{-\xi m}$.

Summarizing, we have obtained the following result:

Theorem 3. *In the absence of Marking Assumption, the false-positive probability of our code is not higher than $p_{\mathrm{FP},1} + p_{\mathrm{FP},2}$ (see above for notations).*

The numerical examples given in the next section show that this theorem indeed provides significant bounds of false-positive probabilities, at least for not too large number ℓ of pirates, in contrast to the case of Proposition 1. Hence our codes are $(2, c')$-secure PFPA for any, not too large c'.

6   On Parameter Choices for Error Probabilities

Finally, this section shows numerical examples for security of our codes. First, we give an observation for proper choices of bounds of false-negative probability and false-positive probability that are used to decide parameters for our codes.

In the security evaluation, we have considered the following two cases:

1. $\ell \leq 2$ and Marking Assumption is satisfied;
2. $\ell \leq c'$, and either $\ell > 2$ or Marking Assumption is not satisfied.

Choose parameters $\varepsilon, \varepsilon'$ such that our code is $(2, c')$-secure with $(\varepsilon, \varepsilon')$-error. Here we assume for simplicity that one of the above two conditions is always satisfied (this would be practically reasonable when we choose sufficiently large c'). Let q be the probability of the second case, therefore the probability of the first case is now $1 - q$. Then, since our code is 2-secure PFPA and it is not expected anymore that some pirate is output by the tracing algorithm in the second case, the resulting bounds of *total* false-negative probability η_{FN} and *total* false-positive probability η_{FP} are given by

$$\eta_{\mathrm{FN}} = (1 - q)\varepsilon + q \ , \quad \eta_{\mathrm{FP}} = q\varepsilon' \ .$$

Thus the ratio of the false-positive among all the cases where the output is non-empty can be determined by

$$\eta_{\mathrm{ratio}} = \frac{\eta_{\mathrm{FP}}}{1 - \eta_{\mathrm{FN}} + \eta_{\mathrm{FP}}} = \frac{q\varepsilon'}{(1 - q)(1 - \varepsilon) + q\varepsilon'}$$

that is an increasing function of $0 < q < 1$, $0 < \varepsilon < 1$ and $0 < \epsilon' < 1$. Note that

$$q = \frac{\eta_{FN} - \varepsilon}{1 - \varepsilon} \text{ and } \varepsilon' = \frac{\eta_{ratio}(1 - \eta_{FN})(1 - \varepsilon)}{(1 - \eta_{ratio})(\eta_{FN} - \varepsilon)} .$$

Now the probability of an output user being innocent is getting higher as the ratio η_{ratio} becomes higher, which diminishes reliability of output itself of the scheme. Thus in practical cases, to decrease η_{ratio} has high priority over decreasing η_{FN}.

We give some numerical examples. In the example, we set $\varepsilon = \eta_{FN}/2$, therefore $q = \eta_{FN}/(2 - \eta_{FN}) = \varepsilon/(1 - \varepsilon)$. Note that $q \leq \eta_{FN}$ holds in any case, and the current choice of q is not too far from the maximal possible value of q. Moreover, set $\eta_{ratio} = \alpha\eta_{FN}$ for a small value α. Then we have

$$\varepsilon' = \frac{2\alpha\varepsilon(1 - 2\varepsilon)(1 - \varepsilon)}{(1 - 2\alpha\varepsilon)(2\varepsilon - \varepsilon)} = \frac{2\alpha(1 - 2\varepsilon)(1 - \varepsilon)}{(1 - 2\alpha\varepsilon)} .$$

We use the parameters ε and N listed in Table 1 and the corresponding code lengths m given in Sect. 5.1 (that are almost the same as "first" rows in Table 1, except $m = 129$ for $(N, \varepsilon) = (10^6, 10^{-4})$). Moreover, we use the parameters $\alpha \in \{10^{-2}, 10^{-3}, 10^{-4}\}$. Then for each choice of parameters the corresponding value of ε' is derived (note that $\varepsilon' \approx 2\alpha$ for such parameters), and some calculation based on Theorem 3 determines the maximum value of c' such that the code is $(2, c')$-secure with $(\varepsilon, \varepsilon')$-error. See Table 2 for the results. This table shows that in these situations, our codes with code lengths determined in Sect. 5.1 are $(2, c')$-secure for some $c' > 2$, and in many cases the maximum values of c' are far from $c = 2$. This means that our codes can strongly avoid false-positive.

Table 2. Maximum values of c' for $(2, c')$-security of our codes

N	α	10^{-4}	10^{-5}	10^{-6}	10^{-7}	10^{-9}	10^{-11}
		false-negative probability ε					
10^2	10^{-2}	14	22	32	47	97	100
	10^{-3}	7	10	14	21	47	97
	10^{-4}	3	5	7	10	22	47
10^3	10^{-2}	32	48	71	105	231	511
	10^{-3}	14	21	32	47	103	227
	10^{-4}	6	10	15	22	47	103
10^4	10^{-2}	71	105	156	231	511	1118
	10^{-3}	32	47	70	103	227	495
	10^{-4}	14	21	32	47	103	224
10^5	10^{-2}	156	231	343	511	1118	2474
	10^{-3}	69	103	153	227	495	1093
	10^{-4}	30	47	70	103	224	490
10^6	10^{-2}	326	511	758	1118	2474	5401
	10^{-3}	144	227	336	495	1093	2386
	10^{-4}	62	102	151	224	490	1070

7 Conclusion

We proposed a 2-secure fingerprint code that is a mixture and an improvement of two codes in [9]. By inheriting the advantages of both codes, our codes have as short lengths as the shorter version of [9], and have characteristics that false-positive never occur under Marking Assumption against at most two pirates and that, whenever the number of pirates is not too large, false-positive is still very unlikely to occur even if more than two pirates exist or Marking Assumption is not satisfied. Thus our code has very desirable properties in practical situations.

Acknowledgments. The author would like to thank Dr. Teddy Furon and the anonymous referees for their invaluable comments.

References

1. Blakley, G.R., Kabatiansky, G.: Random Coding Technique for Digital Fingerprinting Codes. In: Proc. IEEE ISIT 2004, p. 202. IEEE, Los Alamitos (2004)
2. Boneh, D., Shaw, J.: Collusion-Secure Fingerprinting for Digital Data. IEEE Trans. Inform. Th. 44, 1897–1905 (1998)
3. Cotrina-Navau, J., Fernandez, M., Soriano, M.: A Family of Collusion 2-Secure Codes. In: Barni, M., Herrera-Joancomartí, J., Katzenbeisser, S., Pérez-González, F. (eds.) IH 2005. LNCS, vol. 3727, pp. 387–397. Springer, Heidelberg (2005)
4. Fernandez, M., Soriano, M.: Fingerprinting Concatenated Codes with Efficient Identification. In: Chan, A.H., Gligor, V.D. (eds.) ISC 2002. LNCS, vol. 2433, pp. 459–470. Springer, Heidelberg (2002)
5. Guth, H.-J., Pfitzmann, B.: Error- and Collusion-Secure Fingerprinting for Digital Data. In: Pfitzmann, A. (ed.) IH 1999. LNCS, vol. 1768, pp. 134–145. Springer, Heidelberg (2000)
6. Hagiwara, M., Hanaoka, G., Imai, H.: A Short Random Fingerprinting Code against a Small Number of Pirates. In: Fossorier, M.P.C., Imai, H., Lin, S., Poli, A. (eds.) AAECC 2006. LNCS, vol. 3857, pp. 193–202. Springer, Heidelberg (2006)
7. Hoeffding, W.: Probability Inequalities for Sums of Bounded Random Variables. J. Amer. Statist. Assoc. 58, 13–30 (1963)
8. Nuida, K., Fujitsu, S., Hagiwara, M., Kitagawa, T., Watanabe, H., Ogawa, K., Imai, H.: An Improvement of Discrete Tardos Fingerprinting Codes. Des. Codes Cryptogr. 52, 339–362 (2009)
9. Nuida, K., Hagiwara, M., Kitagawa, T., Watanabe, H., Ogawa, K., Fujitsu, S., Imai, H.: A Tracing Algorithm for Short 2-Secure Probabilistic Fingerprinting Codes Strongly Protecting Innocent Users. In: Proc. IEEE CCNC 2007, pp. 1068–1072. IEEE, Los Alamitos (2007)
10. Nuida, K., Hagiwara, M., Watanabe, H., Imai, H.: Optimization of Tardos's Fingerprinting Codes in a Viewpoint of Memory Amount. In: Furon, T., Cayre, F., Doërr, G., Bas, P. (eds.) IH 2007. LNCS, vol. 4567, pp. 279–293. Springer, Heidelberg (2008)
11. Tardos, G.: Optimal Probabilistic Fingerprint Codes. J. ACM 55(2), 1–24 (2008)
12. Tô, V.D., Safavi-Naini, R., Wang, Y.: A 2-Secure Code with Efficient Tracing Algorithm. In: Menezes, A., Sarkar, P. (eds.) INDOCRYPT 2002. LNCS, vol. 2551, pp. 149–162. Springer, Heidelberg (2002)
13. West, D.B.: Introduction to Graph Theory, 2nd edn. Prentice Hall, Englewood Cliffs (2001)

Estimating the Minimal Length of Tardos Code

Teddy Furon[1,*], Luis Pérez-Freire[2], Arnaud Guyader[3], and Frédéric Cérou[3]

[1] Thomson Security Lab, Cesson-Sévigné, France
[2] GRADIANT - Galician R&D Center in Advanced Telecommunications, Vigo, Spain
[3] INRIA, Centre Rennes - Bretagne Atlantique, Rennes, France

Abstract. This paper estimates the minimal length of a binary probabilistic traitor tracing code. We consider the code construction proposed by G. Tardos in 2003, with the symmetric accusation function as improved by B. Skoric *et al.* The length estimation is based on two pillars. First, we consider the Worst Case Attack that a group of c colluders can lead. This attack minimizes the mutual information between the code sequence of a colluder and the pirated sequence. Second, an algorithm pertaining to the field of rare event analysis is presented in order to estimate the probabilities of error: the probability that an innocent user is framed, and the probabilities that all colluders are missed. Therefore, for a given collusion size, we are able to estimate the minimal length of the code satisfying some error probabilities constraints. This estimation is far lower than the known lower bounds.

Keywords: Traitor tracing, Fingerprinting, Tardos code, Rare event.

1 Introduction

This article deals with traitor tracing which is also known as active fingerprinting, content serialization, user forensics or transactional watermarking. The typical application is as follows: A video on demand server distributes personal copies of the same content to n buyers. Some are dishonest users whose goal is to illegally redistribute a pirate copy. The rights holder is interested in identifying these dishonest users. For this purpose, a unique user identifier consisting on a sequence of m symbols is embedded in each video content thanks to a watermarking technique, thus producing n different (although perceptually similar) copies. This allows tracing back which user has illegally redistributed his copy. However, there might be a collusion of c dishonest users, $c > 1$. This collusion mixes their copies in order to forge a pirated content which contains none of the identifiers but a mixture of them.

The traitor tracing code invented by Gabor Tardos in 2003 [1] becomes more and more popular. This code is a probabilistic weak fingerprinting code, where

---

* This work is supported in part by the French national programme "Securité ET INformatique" under project NEBBIANO, ANR-06-SETIN-009.

S. Katzenbeisser and A.-R. Sadeghi (Eds.): IH 2009, LNCS 5806, pp. 176–190, 2009.

the probability of accusing an innocent is not null. The decoding of this code is focused, in the sense that it states whether or not a given user is guilty. Its performances are usually evaluated in terms of the probability ϵ_1 of accusing an innocent and the probability of missing all colluders ϵ_2. Most of the articles dealing with the Tardos code aim at finding a tight lower bound of the length of the code. In his seminal work G. Tardos shows that, in order to guarantee that the probability of accusing an innocent is below ϵ_1, the inequality $m > Kc^2 \log n/\epsilon_1$ with $K = 100$ must be satisfied. Many researchers found the constant $K = 100$ not accurate. Better known approximations are, for instance, $K = 4\pi^2$ [2], $K = 38$ [3]. Other works propose more practical implementations of the Tardos code [4]. The reader will find a pedagogical review of this code in [5].

The goal of this paper is to propose yet another evaluation of the Tardos constant. Whereas the previous articles proposed values based on theoretical bounds, our approach is radically different because it is purely experimental. For a given length of code m, we estimate the probability of accusing an innocent and the probability of missing all colluders. This task is not easy because the probabilities to be estimated are very small. Indeed, a classical Monte-Carlo algorithm would take too long time. The algorithm we propose in Sec. 4 is the result of a collaboration between statistician experts in rare event analysis and watermarkers. It is very generic and much more efficient than a classical Monte Carlo estimator. It estimates the probability P that a set of data $\mathbf{x} \in \mathcal{X}$ with a known pdf $p_{\mathbf{X}}$ has a score $s(\mathbf{x})$, with $s(.) : \mathcal{X} \to \mathbb{R}$ a deterministic score function, bigger than a given threshold τ: $P = \Pr[s(\mathbf{x}) > \tau]$.

This experimental approach has also the advantage to be closer to what really matters in practice. All the aforementioned theoretical bounds are based on the mean of the accusation scores of the colluders. This is needed for mathematical tractability but it provides an upper bound of the probability of false negative in the 'Detect-one' case: if the mean of the accusation scores is below the threshold, then at least one colluder is not accused, hence a false negative. In our experimental setup, we estimate the probability that the maximum (resp. minimum) of the colluders scores is below the threshold. This is the exact definition of a false negative event for the 'Detect-one' strategy (resp. 'Detect-all' strategy) [6].

The second main idea of this paper is the Worst Case Attack. Sec. 2 presents the model supporting a collusion strategy which is compliant with the well known *marking assumption* [7]. Among these collusion strategies, it appears that some of them have a deeper impact on the accusation performances than others. This is quite surprising because the Tardos decoding was previously believed to be invariant against the collusion strategy [5]. The Worst Case Attack (WCA) is thus defined as the collusion strategy minimizing the accusation performances. In order to evaluate these performances in the broadest sense, Sec. 3 relies on the concept of achievable rate of a traitor tracing code introduced in [6] as the criterion to be minimized. The experimental assessment is then based on the WCA in order to estimate the true minimal Tardos constant K.

2   The Setup

2.1   Code Generation

We briefly remind how the Tardos code is designed. The binary code $\mathbf{X}$ is composed of n sequences of m bits. The sequence $\mathbf{X}_j = (X(j,1), \cdots, X(j,m))$ identifying user j is composed of m independent binary symbols, with $\mathrm{Pr}_{X(j,i)}[x(j,i) = 1] = p_i$, $\forall i \in [m]$, with $[m]$ denoting $\{1, \ldots, m\}$. $\{P_i\}_{i \in [m]}$ are independent and identically distributed auxiliary random variables in the range $[0,1]$: $P_i \sim f(p)$. Tardos proposed the following pdf, $f(p) = (\pi\sqrt{p(1-p)})^{-1}$, which is symmetric around $1/2$: $f(p) = f(1-p)$. It means that symbols '1' and '0' play a similar role with probability p or $1-p$. The actual occurrences $\{P_i\}_{i \in [m]}$ of these random variables are drawn once for all at the initialization of the code, and they constitute its secret key.

2.2   Collusion Process

Denote the subset of colluder indices by $\mathcal{C} = \{j_1, \cdots, j_c\}$, and $\mathbf{X}_{\mathcal{C}} = \{\mathbf{X}_{j_1}, \ldots, \mathbf{X}_{j_c}\}$ the restriction of the traitor tracing code to this subset. The collusion attack is the process of taking sequences in $\mathbf{X}_{\mathcal{C}}$ as inputs and yielding the pirated sequence $\mathbf{Y}$ as an output.

Fingerprinting codes have been first studied by the cryptographic community and a key-concept is the *marking assumption* introduced by Boneh and Shaw [7]. It states that, in its narrow-sense version, whatever the strategy of the collusion $\mathcal{C}$, we have $Y(i) \in \{X(j_1,i), \cdots, X(j_c,i)\}$. In words, colluders forge the pirated copy by assembling chunks from their personal copies. It implies that if, at index i, the colluders' symbols are identical, then this symbol value is decoded at the i-th chunk of the pirated copy.

This is what watermarkers have understood from the pioneering cryptographic work. However, this has led to misconceptions. Another important thing is the way cryptographers have modelized a host content: it is a binary string where some symbols can be changed without spoiling the regular use of the content. These locations are used to insert the code sequence symbols. Cryptographers assume that colluders disclose symbols from their identifying sequences comparing their personal copies symbol by symbol. The colluders cannot spot a hidden symbol if it is identical on all copies, hence the marking assumption.

In a multimedia application, the content is divided into chunks. A chunk can be a few second clip of audio or video. Symbol $X(j,i)$ is hidden in the i-th chunk of the content with a watermarking technique. This gives the i-th chunk sent to the j-th user. In this paper, we mostly address collusion processing where the pirated copy is forged by picking chunks from the colluders' personal copies. The marking assumption in the studied problem still holds but for another reason: as the colluders ignore the watermarking secret key, they cannot create chunks of content watermarked with a symbol they do not have. However, contrary to the original cryptographic model, this also implies that the colluders might not know which symbol is embedded in a chunk.

At the end of the paper, we also consider a content post-processing: After mixing their copies, the colluders apply a coarse compression for instance. We assume that this yields decoding errors at the watermarking layer. However, we suppose the colluders do not control or know where the errors appear, and at which rate. Therefore, the collusion consists in two independent processing: mixing of copies followed by a degradation of the watermarking layer.

2.3 Mathematical Model

Our mathematical model of the collusion is essentially based on four main assumptions. The first assumption is the *memoryless* nature of the collusion attack. Since the symbols of the code are independent, it seems relevant that the pirated sequence Y also shares this property. Therefore, the value of $Y(i)$ only depends on $\{X(j_1, i), \cdots, X(j_c, i)\}$.

The second assumption is the *stationarity* of the collusion process. We assume that the collusion strategy is independent of the index i in the sequence. Therefore, we can describe it for any index i, and we will drop indexing for sake of clarity in the sequel.

The third assumption is the *exchangeable* nature of the collusion: the colluders select the value of the symbol Y depending on the values of their symbols, but not on their order. Therefore, the input of the collusion process is indeed the type of their symbols (*i.e.* the empirical probability mass function). In the binary case, this type is fully defined by the following sufficient statistic: the number $\Sigma(i)$ of symbols '1': $\Sigma(i) = \sum_{k=1}^{c} X(j_k, i)$.

The fourth assumption is that the collusion process may be deterministic (for instance, majority vote, minority vote), or *random* (for instance, the symbol pasted in the pirated sequence is decided upon a coin flip).

These four assumptions yield that the collusion attack is fully described by the following parameter: $\boldsymbol{\theta} = \{\theta_0, \ldots, \theta_c\}$, with $\theta_\sigma = \Pr_Y[1|\Sigma = \sigma]$. There is thus an infinity of collusion attacks, but we can already state that they all share the following property: The marking assumption enforces that $\theta_0 = 0$ and $\theta_c = 1$. A collusion attack is thus defined by $c - 1$ real values belonging to the hypercube $[0, 1]^{c-1}$.

At the end of the paper, we consider a content processing on top of the collusion. The model is a Binary Symmetric Channel with error rate ϵ. Since the colluders do not control the value of ϵ, their collusion strategy is independent of this additional degradation. Its impact transforms $\boldsymbol{\theta}$ into $\boldsymbol{\theta}(\epsilon) = (1 - 2\epsilon)\boldsymbol{\theta} + \epsilon$.

3   The Worst Case Attack

3.1   Tardos Decoding

The accusation proposed by G. Tardos belongs to the class of "simple decoders", using the nomenclature introduced by P. Moulin [6]. For any user j, a simple decoder calculates a score depending on the code sequence $\mathbf{x}_j$, the sequence $\mathbf{y}$

decoded from the pirated copy, and the secret of the code $\mathbf{p} = (p_i, \ldots, p_m)$. B. Skoric *et al.* [8] proposed a symmetric version of the original Tardos score:

$$s(\mathbf{x}_j, \mathbf{y}, \mathbf{p}) = \sum_{i \in [m]} \delta_{y(i)}(x(j,i)) \sqrt{\frac{1 - p_{y(i)}}{p_{y(i)}}} - (1 - \delta_{y(i)}(x(j,i))) \sqrt{\frac{p_{y(i)}}{1 - p_{y(i)}}}, \quad (1)$$

with $p_{y(i)} = p_i^{y(i)}(1 - p_i)^{1-y(i)}$, and $\delta_a(b)$ the Kronecker mapping equalling 1 if $a = b$, 0 else. User j is accused if $s(\mathbf{x}_j, \mathbf{y}, \mathbf{p})$ is bigger than a threshold τ. This last parameter sets the trade-off between probabilities ϵ_2 and ϵ_1.

Paper [5] explains what seems to have been the rationale of G. Tardos. The collusion attack $\boldsymbol{\theta}$ is a nuisance parameter because it is not known at the accusation side. Nevertheless, the performances of the code should be guaranteed whatever the value of this nuisance parameter. The decoding proposed by Tardos and improved by Skoric *et al.* has indeed a very strong invariance property: for a given collusion size, the mean and the variance of the scores of the innocent and the colluders do not depend on $\boldsymbol{\theta}$. Therefore, no collusion is worse than another.

Yet, the rationale of [5] is in practice flawed. The typical behavior of the scores boils down to mean and variance if and only if they are Gaussian distributed. Being the sum of statistically independent random variables, the Central Limit Theorem (CLT) states that this is the case only when the code length is infinite which is of course not true in practice. The achievable rate reflects this fact.

3.2   The Achievable Rate

The rate of a traitor tracing code is defined by $R = \log_2(n)/m$. Loosely speaking, the achievable rate is a parameter which tells the maximum code rate that can be achieved yet guaranteeing a reliable accusation process exists [6]. The achievable rate for the simple decoder against a given collusion attack, under the assumptions stated in this paper, is given by [6]:

$$\begin{aligned} R_{simple}(\boldsymbol{\theta}) &= \mathbb{E}_P \left[I(Y; X | P = p) \right] \\ &= \mathbb{E}_P \left[H(Y | P = p) \right] - \mathbb{E}_P \left[H(Y | X, P = p) \right], \\ &= \mathbb{E}_P \left[D_{KL}(p_{Y|X} \cdot p_X \| p_X \cdot p_Y | P) \right], \end{aligned} \quad (2)$$

where $\mathbb{E}_P \, []$ denotes expectation over P, $I(Y; X | P = p)$ is the mutual information between Y and X conditioned on $P = p$, and $H(x) = -x \log_2(x) - (1-x) \log_2(1 - x)$ is the binary entropy function [9]. Notice that the achievable rate depends on the considered collusion attack $\boldsymbol{\theta}$ through the probabilities involved in the computation of the mutual information. The equality (2) provides us with an interesting interpretation. The accusation can be seen as a hypothesis test: $\mathcal{H}_0$ the user is innocent, $\mathcal{H}_1$ the user is guilty. The performances of the test are theoretically limited by the Kullback-Leibler distance, D_{KL}, between the pdf of the observations under both hypotheses. Under $\mathcal{H}_0$, the sequence $\mathbf{Y}$ is created from sequences statistically independent from the user sequence $\mathbf{X}$. Therefore, their joint pdf is indeed the product $p_{\mathbf{X}} \cdot p_{\mathbf{Y}}$. Under $\mathcal{H}_1$, on the contrary, there exists a conditional pdf linking the two sequences. The conditioning over P comes from the fact that the accusation uses this secret parameter as side information. The bits of the sequences being independent, the KL distance of the sequences is the sum of the KL distances of the samples, which is m times the expectation per symbol.

The Stein lemma [9] states that, asymptotically, $\epsilon_1 \to 2^{-mR_{simple}(\boldsymbol{\theta})}$. Consider $n = 2^{mR}$ with R the rate of the code. Then, asymptotically, the probability of falsely accusing any user is bounded by $n\epsilon_1 < 2^{-m(R_{simple}(\boldsymbol{\theta})-R)}$. This bound has a positive error exponent (i.e., an exponential decrease as the code gets longer) if the rate of the code is lower than the achievable rate: $R < R_{simple}(\boldsymbol{\theta})$. Moreover, this should hold for any collusion attack, and thus, for the Worst Case Attack (WCA) defined as follows:

$$\boldsymbol{\theta}^\star = \arg\min_{\boldsymbol{\theta}} R_{simple}(\boldsymbol{\theta}). \tag{3}$$

The WCA is thus defined as the collusion attack $\boldsymbol{\theta}^\star$ minimizing the rate of the code, or equivalently, the asymptotic positive error exponent. To calculate the achievable rate, we need the following expressions of the probabilities induced by $\boldsymbol{\theta}$:

$$\Pr_Y[1|p] = \sum_{k=0}^{c} \theta_k \binom{c}{k} p^k (1-p)^{(c-k)}, \tag{4}$$

$$\Pr_Y[1|X=1,p] = \sum_{k=1}^{c} \theta_k \binom{c-1}{k-1} p^{k-1} (1-p)^{(c-k)}, \tag{5}$$

$$\Pr_Y[1|X=0,p] = \sum_{k=0}^{c-1} \theta_k \binom{c-1}{k} p^k (1-p)^{(c-k-1)}. \tag{6}$$

The achievable rate is then simply:

$$R_{simple}(\boldsymbol{\theta}) = \mathbb{E}_P\left[H(\Pr_Y[1|p])\right]$$
$$- \mathbb{E}_P\left[p \cdot H(\Pr_Y[1|X=1,p]) - (1-p) \cdot H(\Pr_Y[1|X=0,p])\right]. \tag{7}$$

3.3   Identifying the WCA

The expression (7) can be evaluated through numerical integration for a given $\boldsymbol{\theta}$. To identify the WCA, we use a classical optimization algorithm to find the minimum of the achievable rate. This is however only tractable for a small collusion size. Here are the results:

$$c = 2 : \boldsymbol{\theta}^\star = (0, 0.5, 1),$$
$$c = 3 : \boldsymbol{\theta}^\star = (0, 0.652, 0.348, 1),$$
$$c = 4 : \boldsymbol{\theta}^\star = (0, 0.488, 0.5, 0.512, 1),$$
$$c = 5 : \boldsymbol{\theta}^\star = (0, 0.594, 0.000, 1.000, 0.406, 1). \tag{8}$$

The fact that the WCA satisfies the relationship $\theta_k = 1 - \theta_{c-k}$ for any $k \in [c]$ is very surprising. The WCA belongs to the class of collusion named 'sighted colluders', also known as 'multimedia collusion' [5]. This relationship means that the colluders do not need to know which symbol is indeed in the i-th block of content. They just need to compare their blocks of content and to count the similar versions they received: They have $\Sigma(i)$ times the same version, and $c - \Sigma(i)$ the other version. But, they don't know which version indeed conveys the symbol '1' or '0'. This information is not required for launching the WCA. This is mostly due to the symmetry of the distribution $f(p)$ which implies that symbols '0' and '1' play similar roles.

Another surprise is that there is no connection with the 'extremal strategy' defined by Skoric et al [8]. The 'extremal strategy' just focuses on one characteristic of the pdf of the scores (it minimizes the differences between the expectations of the colluder and innocent scores), whereas the WCA minimizes the distance between the two pdf.

4   A Rare Event Analysis

Our algorithm estimating probabilities of rare events is explained in a very general manner, and then its application to traitor tracing is discussed. The goal is to estimate the probability P of the rare event A that a set of data, called hereafter a particle, $\mathbf{x} \in \mathcal{X}$ with a known pdf $p_{\mathbf{X}}$ has a score $s(\mathbf{x})$, with $s(\cdot) : \mathcal{X} \to \mathbb{R}$ a deterministic score function, bigger than a given threshold τ: $\pi = \mathrm{Pr}_{\mathbf{X}}[s(\mathbf{x}) > \tau]$.

4.1   The Key Idea

To factorize a probability into a product of bigger probabilities, we use the following trick: let $A_N = A$ be the rare event, and A_{N-1} a related event such that when A_N occurs, A_{N-1} has also occured. However, when A_{N-1} occurs, it doesn't imply that A_N is true. Hence, A_{N-1} is less rare an event than A_N. This justifies the first equality in the following equation, the second one being just the Bayes rule:

$$\mathrm{Pr}[A_N] = \mathrm{Pr}[A_N, A_{N-1}] = \mathrm{Pr}[A_N|A_{N-1}] \cdot \mathrm{Pr}[A_{N-1}]. \tag{9}$$

Repeating the process, we finally obtain:

$$P = \mathrm{Pr}[A_N] = \mathrm{Pr}[A_N|A_{N-1}]\mathrm{Pr}[A_{N-1}|A_{N-2}] \cdots \mathrm{Pr}[A_2|A_1]\mathrm{Pr}[A_1] \tag{10}$$

provided that $\{A_j\}_{j=1}^{N}$ is a sequence of nested events. Knowing that estimation of a probability is easier when its value is bigger, we have succeeded in decomposing a hard problem into N much easier problems.

This decomposition is very general, but the construction of this sequence of nested events is usually not a simple task. An exception is when the rare event

A_N admits a geometrical interpretation: A_N occurs when $\mathbf{x} \in A_N$. A sequence of nested events translates then in a sequence of subsets $A_N \subset A_N \subset \ldots \subset A_1$. The task is even simpler in traitor tracing problem because an indicator function of these events can be as follows: $\mathbf{x} \in A_j$ if $s(\mathbf{x}) > \tau_j$. Nested events are created for a sequence of increasing thresholds: $\tau_1 < \tau_2 < \cdots < \tau_N = \tau$.

4.2 Generation of Vectors

The first step estimates $\pi_1 = \Pr[A_1]$. In practice, N is large enough so that this probability is not lower than 0.1. Then, a classical Monte Carlo estimator is efficient. We generate l_1 vectors $\mathbf{x}$ distributed as $p_{\mathbf{x}}$, we calculate their score and count the number k_1 of times it is higher than τ_1. This first step leads not only to an estimator $\hat{\pi}_1 = k_1/l_1$, but also to a generator of the event A_1. It is not very efficient because approximately only $\pi_1 l_1$ occurrences of the event A_1 are produced.

4.3 Replication of Particles

The issue of the second step is the estimation of $\pi_2 = \text{Prob}[A_2|A_1]$. We set the threshold τ_2 just above τ_1, so that this probability is large (typically not lower than 0.1). A MC estimator is $\hat{\pi}_2 = k_2/l_2$, where k_2 is the number of particles $\mathbf{x}$ of the set A_1 which also belong to A_2. We need to generate l_2 particles $\mathbf{x}$ distributed according to $p_{\mathbf{x}}$ and in the set A_1. We could apply the first step of the algorithm to generate these particles, but it is not efficient enough as such.

We then resort to a so-called replication process, which almost multiplies by a factor ρ the size of a collection in a particular region of the space. For each particle, we make ρ copies of it, and then we slightly modify the copies in a random manner. This modification process must leave the distribution of the particle invariant: if its inputs are distributed according to $p_{\mathbf{x}}$, its outputs must follow the same distribution. A modified copy is likely to belong to the set if the modification is small. However, we check whether this is really the case, and go back to the original particle if not. The replication process is thus a modification followed by a filter.

Since we have run the first step, we have already k_1 particles in A_1. We choose a replication factor $\rho_1 \approx \hat{\pi}_1^{-1}$ approximately keeping the same number of particles. We calculate the scores of the $\rho_1 k_1$ modified copies. We keep the copies whose score is bigger than τ_1, and replace the others by their original particle. This makes the $l_2 = \rho_1 k_1$ input particles of the MC estimator. These two first steps lead to an estimator of π_2 and a generator of events A_2.

The core of the algorithm is thus the following one. The selection kills the particles whose score is lower than an intermediate threshold τ_i, these are branched on selected particles. The replication proposes randomly modified particles and filters those that are still above the intermediate threshold. Selection and replication steps are iterated to estimate the remaining probabilities $\pi_3, \cdots, \pi_N$. The estimator $\hat{\pi}$ is then simply $\hat{\pi}_1 \ldots \hat{\pi}_N$.

4.4   Adaptive Thresholds

The difficulty is now to give the appropriate values to the thresholds $\{\tau_i\}_1^{N-1}$, and also to the sizes of the sets $\{l_i\}_1^N$. The probabilities to be estimated must not be very weak in order to maintain reasonable set sizes. Moreover, it can be shown that the variance of $\hat{\pi}$ is minimized when the probabilities $\{\hat{\pi}_i\}_i^N$ are equal [10]. We would need the map $\tau = F^{-1}(\pi)$ to set the correct value of the thresholds, which we have not. Otherwise, we would already know the value of $\pi = F(\tau)$.

The idea is to set the thresholds adaptively. The number of particles is kept constant in all the experimental rounds: $l_i = l \, \forall i \in \{1 \cdots N\}$. The threshold τ_i has the value such that $k_i = k$. Thus, k and l are the parameters of the algorithm. The estimated probabilities are all equal to $\pi_i = k/l$, $\forall i \in [N-1]$. It means that the selection sorts the scores in a decreasing order, and adaptively sets τ_i as the value of the k-th higher score. Particles whose score is below this threshold are removed from the stack, and replaced by copies of other particles. The size of the stack is constant and the replication factors $\{\rho_i\}$ are all equal to l/k (k divides l). All the particles in the stack are independently modified. The modification of a particle is accepted only if its new score is still above the threshold.

The last step is reached when $\tau_i > \tau$. Then, we set $N = i$, $\tau_N = \tau$ and k_N is the number of scores above τ, so that, for this last iteration, $\hat{\pi_N} = k_N/l$. At the end, the probability of the event A_N is estimated by:

$$\hat{\pi} = \frac{k_N k^{N-1}}{l^N}. \tag{11}$$

The number of iterations is expected to be as follows:

$$\mathbb{E}\,[N] = \lfloor \log \pi^{-1} / \log l/k \rfloor + 1. \tag{12}$$

The total number of detector trials is lN, which has a logarithmic scale with respect to π^{-1}, whereas a classical MC estimator would need at least π^{-1} trials.

The method is given in pseudo-code in Algorithm 1. Note that the thresholds $\{\tau_i\}$ are stored in memory. This is not useful when estimating π, but this gives a nice byproduct for ROC curves: the map $\pi = f(\tau)$ is estimated through the following points: $\{((k/l)^j, \tau_j)\}_{j=1}^{N-1}$. From [11], the method inherits the asymptotic properties of consistency and normality, with equations:

$$\hat{\pi} \xrightarrow[l \to +\infty]{a.s.} \pi \tag{13}$$

$$\sqrt{l}(\hat{\pi} - \pi) \xrightarrow[l \to +\infty]{\mathcal{L}} \mathcal{N}(0, \sigma^2) \tag{14}$$

with

$$\sigma^2 \gtrsim \pi^2 \left((N-1) \left(\frac{l}{k} - 1 \right) + \frac{l}{k_N} - 1 \right) \tag{15}$$

4.5   Estimation of ϵ_1

We use our algorithm to estimate the probability of accusing an innocent. Particles in this framework are now binary code sequences of length m. The GENERATE subroutine is given by the construction of the code [1] and the SCORE function is given by Eq. (1). One very important fact is that the symbols in a code sequence are statistically independent and distributed according to their own law. The MODIFY subroutine is thus very simple: we randomly select a fraction μ of them (parameter μ sets the modification strength), and re-generate them according to their own law: $\Pr_{X_{j,i}}[1] = p_i$. These non deterministic changes leave the distribution of the code sequence invariant.

We generate c code sequences of length m. The collusion strategy is the WCA. Then, we estimate the map $\tau = F^{-1}(\Pr_X[s(\mathbf{x}, \mathbf{y}, \mathbf{p}) > \tau | \mathbf{y}, \mathbf{p}])$ with our algorithm. Indeed, the target threshold is fixed to a very high value so that the algorithm stops after $N_{\max}$ iterations. The obtained mapping is $N_{\max}$ couples $(\hat{\tau}_j, (k/l)^j)$. However, this holds for a special occurrence of $\mathbf{y}$ and $\mathbf{p}$. Therefore, we need to integrate this conditional probability over $\mathbf{y}$ and $\mathbf{p}$. To do so, we run W times the estimator. At each run, the secret key $\mathbf{p}$ is different, and c code sequences are drawn independently and uniformly to forge a new pirated sequence. The j-th threshold is averaged over the W estimates. We estimate the plot mapping ϵ_1 and the threshold τ, for different couples (c, m).

4.6   Estimation of ϵ_2

The second part of the experiment measures probability ϵ_2 of missing all colluders, i.e. the false negative for the 'Detect-one'. A particle is now a set of c Tardos sequences $\{\mathbf{x}_1, \ldots, \mathbf{x}_c\}$ and sequence $\mathbf{y}$ forged from these c sequences by the WCA. The MODIFY subroutine modifies the c sequences as described above.

The SCORE function is more complicated. From a particle, it calculates the c accusation sums. The score of the particle is then their mean or their maximum. Tardos and his followers based their analysis on the mean of the scores of the colluders because this leads to tractable equations. The rationale is that if the mean is below the threshold, then there is at least one colluder whose score is lower than the threshold. However, the probability that the mean is below the threshold τ is a very rough estimate of the probability of false negative ϵ_2. We choose to follow Tardos' choice of the mean to appreciate the refinement by our experimental investigation compared to the constants found by Tardos and his followers via Chernoff bounds. However, we can also set the score of a particle as the maximum of the c accusation sums in order to really estimate ϵ_2 as the probability that none of the c colluders gets caught.

The rest of the second part works like the first part. We are interested in estimating the mapping $\tau = F^{-1}(\text{Prob}(\max_{i \in [c]} s(\mathbf{x}_i, \mathbf{y}, \mathbf{p}) < \tau))$ (max or mean) using our algorithm. The experiment is run W times, and the intermediate thresholds are averaged for a better precision. Then, we plot in the same

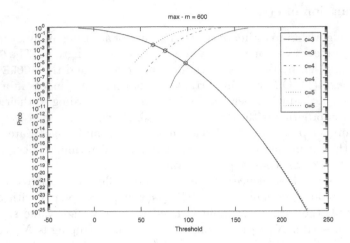

Fig. 1. Mappings of the false positive probability (blue) and false negative probability to the power $4/c$ (red) against the threshold. $m = 600$, $c \in \{3, 4, 5\}$. The score of a particle is the max of the colluders scores. The collusion is the worst as given in (8).

figure (see Fig. 1) the false positive mapping and the false negative mapping, except that for this latter one, the probability is taken to the power $4/c$ to provide a fair comparison to previous evaluations of constant K where ϵ_2 was set to $\epsilon_1^{c/4}$ (original Tardos setup). The intersection of the two mappings at a point $(T_0(m, c), \epsilon_0(m, c))$ implies that it is possible to find a threshold such that $\epsilon_1 = \epsilon_0(m, c)$ and $\epsilon_2 = \epsilon_0(m, c)^{c/4}$. This value indeed reflects the best we can do given m and c. We cannot achieve a lower significance level while preserving the relationship $\epsilon_2 = \epsilon_1^{c/4}$ because no threshold fulfills this constraint at a lower significance level than $\epsilon_0(m, c)$. The only way to get lower significance levels is to increase the code length for a given collusion size.

5   Experimental Evaluation

Several experimentations have been carried out with various code lengths $m \in \{100, 150, 200, 300, 400, 600\}$ and collusion size $c \in \{3, 4, 5\}$ to obtain different values of $\epsilon_0(m, c)$. The final plot draws m against the function $c^2 \log \epsilon_0(m, c)^{-1}$, see Fig. 2.

The most striking fact is that the evaluated lengths are indeed much lower than foreseen by the theoretical bounds in $m > Kc^2 \log \epsilon_1^{-1}$. With the symmetric accusation scoring, $K = 50$ (Tardos) or $K = 2\pi^2$ (Skoric et al.). Here, the experiment clearly shows that $m \approx K_1 c^2 \log \epsilon_1^{-1} + K_0(c)$, with a negative $K_0(c)$ and $K_1 < K$. Yet, this is not a contradiction: previous works claimed that if m is bigger than the lower bound, one could be sure that the requirements on the probabilities of errors were met. We just show that indeed these lower bounds

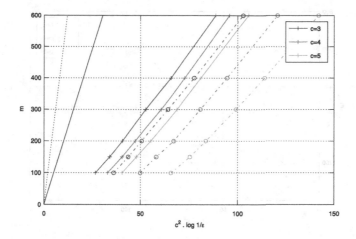

Fig. 2. Code length needed to obtain $\epsilon_2 = \epsilon_1^{c/4}$ for $c = 3$, 4 or 5 colluders (WCA), against function $c^2 \log \epsilon_1^{-1}$. The probability ϵ_2 has been estimated with the mean of the colluders' scores (solid lines) or their maximum (dotted lines). Aforementioned bounds appear in black: Tardos $K = 50$ (dotted line), Skoric *et al.* $K = 2\pi^2$ (solid line).

are over-pessimistic. It is not very clear whether the slope of the plot K_1 is independent of the collusion size. However, if this holds, this is a very very light dependency, and more experiments should be carried out to confirm this fact.

5.1   Maximum and Mean Score

The evaluation of the false negative rate from the mean of the scores or their maximum doesn't change the nature of the plot. Whereas constant K_1 is not really different, the difference on constant K_0 might have a big impact in practice: for $c = 4$ and $m = 600$, the minimum achievable error probability is $\epsilon_1 = \epsilon_2 = 2{,}5 \cdot 10^{-3}$ for the mean score, and $5{,}3 \cdot 10^{-4}$ for the maximum score, or, in the other way around, for a given ϵ_1 and $c = 4$, the code length is more than 200 bits shorter than foreseen by mean-based estimations. Indeed, these are overestimating the power of the colluders. It is much more difficult to forge a pirated copy such that all the accusation scores is below a given τ, than to forge a pirated copy such that the mean of these scores is below τ.

Table 1. Identification of the model $m = K_1 c^2 \log \epsilon_1^{-1} + K_0$

	Majority vote		WCA		WCA $\epsilon = 0.05$		WCA $\epsilon = 0.1$	
	K_1	K_0	K_1	K_0	K_1	K_0	K_1	K_0
$c = 3$	7.2	-180	7.6	-180	9.3	-210	11.6	-245
$c = 4$	7.0	-270	7.1	-265	8.6	-305	10.6	-355
$c = 5$	6.7	-380	6.6	-340	8.0	-405	9.6	-465

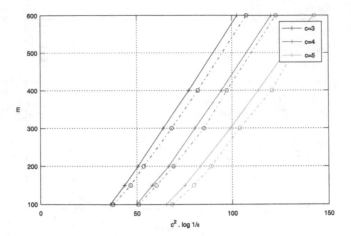

Fig. 3. Code length needed to obtain $\epsilon_2 = \epsilon_1^{c/4}$ for $c = 3$, 4 or 5 colluders. The colluders lead a WCA (solid lines) or a Majority vote (dashed lines).

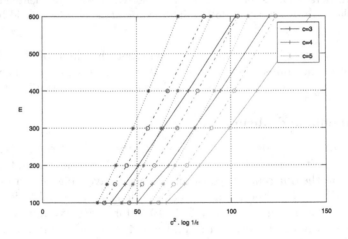

Fig. 4. Code length needed to obtain $\epsilon_2 = \epsilon_1^{c/4}$ for $c = 3$, 4 or 5 colluders. A Binary Symmetric Channel modifies the pirated sequence forged by the WCA, with error rate $\epsilon = 0$ (solid lines), $\epsilon = 0.05$ (dashed lines) and $\epsilon = 0.1$ (dotted lines).

5.2   The Impact of the Worst Collusion Attack

Fig. 3 compares the impact on the code length of the WCA and the Majority attack. Clearly, the WCA increases the length of code for given collusion size and probabilities of errors. A linear predictor shows that the constant K_1 for the WCA is approximately the same as when the collusion attack is a majority vote (cf. Table 1). This supports the commonly accepted fact, as stated in previous articles, that the collusion attack has no impact on the asymptotic

Algorithm 1. Estimation of the probability that $s(\mathbf{x}) > \tau$, when $\mathbf{x} \sim p_{\mathbf{X}}$

Require: subroutines GENERATE, SCORE, HIGHER_SCORE & MODIFY

```
1: for i = 1 to l do
2:     x_i = GENERATE(p_X);  sx_i = SCORE(x_i);
3: end for
4: N = 1;
5: τ_N = HIGHER_SCORE(sx, k);  τ' = τ_N;
6: while τ' < τ and N < N_max do
7:     t = 1;
8:     for i = 1 to l do
9:         if sx_i ≥ τ' then
10:            y_t = x_i;  sy_t = sx_i;  t = t + 1;
11:        end if
12:    end for
13:    for i = 1 to k do
14:        for j = 1 to l/k do
15:            z = MODIFY(y_i);
16:            if SCORE(z) > τ' then
17:                x_{(i-1)l/k+j} = z;  sx_{(i-1)l/k+j} = SCORE(z);
18:            else
19:                x_{(i-1)l/k+j} = y_i;  sx_{(i-1)l/k+j} = sy_i;
20:            end if
21:        end for
22:    end for
23:    N = N + 1;  τ_N = HIGHER_SCORE(sx, k);  τ' = τ_N;
24: end while
25: k' = 0;
26: for i = 1 to l do
27:     if sx_i > τ then
28:         k' = k' + 1;
29:     end if
30: end for
31: return  π̂ = (k'k^{N-1})/(l^N);
```

expression of the code length when the accusation rule (1) is used. Nevertheless, the WCA imposes a bigger offset K_0, making a big difference for not so small error probabilities.

5.3   The Impact of the Binary Symmetric Channel

Fig. 4 shows the impact of the error rate ϵ of the BSC on top of the WCA attack. It is not surprising to note that the code length grows as ϵ increases. Table 1 clearly reveals that the BSC error rate has a dramatic impact on both constants K_1 and K_0. To outline the impact of the BSC, let us consider a channel producing erasures (unreadable bits) with a rate η. At the accusation side, the erasures are not considered, and everything acts as if the code length is reduced by a factor η. Hence, for a given couple (c, ϵ_1), one needs $m\eta$ extra bits, which changes the constants in $K_1(1+\eta)$ and $K_0(1+\eta)$. The impact of the BSC channel is much stronger: an error rate of 5% produces an increase of 20%, an error rate of 10% increases the constant K_1 by 50%. Therefore, it is of utmost importance to resort to a very robust watermarking scheme.

6   Conclusion

The estimation of the code length of a Tardos code requires two skills: to assess what is the worst attack the colluders can lead, and to experimentally assess the probabilities of false positive and false negative for a given collusion size and code length. The worst case attack is defined as the collusion minimizing the achievable rate of the code. This theoretical definition has a very broad scope: whatever the accusation algorithm, we are sure that the colluders cannot lead a stronger attack than this. We propose an estimator of weak probabilities whose scope is far broader than the traitor tracing problem. Our experimental evaluation gives lengths of code which are far smaller than the previously known theoretical lower bounds.

References

1. Tardos, G.: Optimal probabilistic fingerprint codes. In: Proc. of the 35th annual ACM symposium on theory of computing, San Diego, CA, USA, pp. 116–125. ACM, New York (2003)
2. Skoric, B., Vladimirova, T., Celik, M., Talstra, J.: Tardos fingerprinting is better than we thought. IEEE Tran. on IT 54 (2008), arXiv:cs/0607131v1
3. Blayer, O., Tassa, T.: Improved versions of Tardos' fingerprinting scheme. Des. Codes Cryptography 48, 79–103 (2008)
4. Nuida, K., Fujitsu, S., Hagiwara, M., Kitagawa, T., Watanabe, H., Ogawa, K., Imai, H.: An improvement of Tardos's collusion-secure fingerprinting codes with very short lengths. In: Boztaş, S., Lu, H.-F(F.) (eds.) AAECC 2007. LNCS, vol. 4851, pp. 80–89. Springer, Heidelberg (2007)
5. Furon, T., Guyader, A., Cérou, F.: On the design and optimization of Tardos probabilistic fingerprinting codes. In: Solanki, K., Sullivan, K., Madhow, U. (eds.) IH 2008. LNCS, vol. 5284, pp. 341–356. Springer, Heidelberg (2008)
6. Moulin, P.: Universal fingerprinting: capacity and random-coding exponents. IEEE Transactions on Information Theory (2008) (submitted),
http://arxiv.org/abs/0801.3837
7. Boneh, D., Shaw, J.: Collusion-secure fingerprinting for digital data. IEEE Trans. Inform. Theory 44, 1897–1905 (1998)
8. Skoric, B., Katzenbeisser, S., Celik, M.: Symmetric Tardos fingerprinting codes for arbitrary alphabet sizes. Designs, Codes and Cryptography 46, 137–166 (2008)
9. Cover, T.M., Thomas, J.A.: Elements of Information Theory. Wiley series in Telecommunications (1991)
10. Lagnoux, A.: Rare event simulation. PEIS 20, 45–66 (2006)
11. Cérou, F., Furon, T., Guyader, A.: Experimental assessment of the reliability for watermarking and fingerprinting schemes. Accepted to EURASIP Jounal on Information Security (2009)

Roughness-Adaptive 3D Watermarking
of Polygonal Meshes

Kwangtaek Kim[1], Mauro Barni[2], and Hong Z. Tan[1]

[1] Haptic Interface Research Laboratory, Purdue University,
465 Northwestern Avenue, West Lafayette, Indiana 47906 USA
[2] Department of Information Engineering, University of Siena,
via Roma 56, 53100, Siena, Italy

Abstract. We present a general method to improve watermark robustness by exploiting the masking effect of surface roughness on watermark visibility, which, to the best of our knowledge, has not been studied in 3D digital watermarking. Our idea is to adapt watermark strength to local surface roughness based on the knowledge that human eyes are less sensitive to changes on a rougher surface patch than those on a smoother surface. We implemented our idea in a modified version of a well known method proposed by Benedens [3]. As an additional contribution, we modified Benedens's method in two ways to improve its performance. The first improvement led to a blind version of Benedens's method that no longer requires any key that depends on the surface mesh of the cover 3D object. The second improvement concerned the robustness of bit '1' in the watermark. Experimental results showed that our new method permits to improve watermark robustness by 41% to 56% as compared to the original Benedens's method. Further analyses indicated that the average watermark strength by our roughness-adaptive method was larger than that by the original Benedens's method while ensuring watermark imperceptibility. This was the main reason for the improvement in robustness observed in our experiments. We conclude that exploiting the masking property of human vision is a viable way to improve the robustness of 3D watermarks in general, and therefore could be applied to other 3D digital watermarking techniques.

1   Introduction

Over the past few years, 3D display devices and rendering software have become more affordable than before, accelerating the use of 3D meshes in applications such as video games, CAD (computer-aided design), VR (virtual reality) and medical imaging. The rapid growth of 3D contents on the Internet has led to renewed interests in developing 3D watermarking schemes to protect 3D polygonal meshes from illegal reproductions. Compared to 2D digital watermarking, 3D watermarking is more difficult due to the increased complexity associated with 3D objects with arbitrary shapes. In addition, 3D watermarking is more fragile due to the various ways that embedded watermarks can be destroyed

S. Katzenbeisser and A.-R. Sadeghi (Eds.): IH 2009, LNCS 5806, pp. 191–205, 2009.

by simply altering the meshes making up the 3D objects. For this reason, existing 2D watermarking techniques cannot be directly applied to 3D models, necessitating new approaches that are specifically designed for 3D objects. One straight-forward way to embed watermarks into 3D meshes is to modify the locations of vertices making up the 3D surface. The challenge is to design 3D digital watermarks that are *unobtrusive, robust,* and *space efficient* [1]. The *unobtrusive* requirement means that the embedded watermarks must not interfere with the intended use of a model, which may imply imperceptibility. *Robustness* refers to the ability for watermarks to survive various intentional and unintentional attacks to the watermarked 3D model. This is a very challenging requirement as no algorithm has been shown to be perfectly robust. However, constant improvements are being made that result in more robust watermarking schemes as compared to previous methods. The last requirement is about having enough space for watermark embedding. To meet all those requirements is not trivial.

This paper exploits visual masking as a general method for improving the robustness of 3D digital watermarks. Masking refers to our decreased ability to perceive a stimulus (e.g., the watermark) in the presence of other signals (e.g., polygonal mesh). In the context of watermarking, we expect that stronger watermarks can be embedded in a rougher surface area without compromising imperceptibility. Therefore, we present a new method that adaptively matches watermark strength to local surface roughness, as opposed to the traditional method of choosing the maximum imperceptible watermark strength for the entire surface of a 3D object. To test our idea, we applied a roughness-adaptive watermarking technique to Benedens's geometry-based 3D watermarking method [3] and evaluated its robustness against simulated additive-noise attacks. We also improved the original method in two ways, by achieving a blind-version of Benedens's method and by improving the robustness of bit '1' in the watermark.

1.1   Literature Review of 3D Digital Watermarking

As one of the earliest studies of watermarking on polygonal meshes, Ohbuchi et al. [1] proposed several relatively robust techniques utilizing a combination of geometry (vertex, edge, facet) and topology (mesh connectivity) properties. For instance, the ratio of lines, tetrahedral volume ratio and density of mesh were modified as the embedding primitive for watermarking. Building on Ohbuchi et al.'s work [1], Cayre and Macq proposed a high-capacity blind watermarking scheme that was an extension of the TSPS (Triangle Strip Peeling Sequence) method by employing quantization indices (0 or 1) during the reflection of a triangular vertex on the list of triangles to be traversed [8]. Watermarks by either method were not robust against re-meshing and mesh simplification that can perturb mesh-connectivity, but were robust against geometrical attacks such as rotation, translation, or uniform scaling transformation. To address the robustness problem, Benedens [3] proposed a more robust method using the distribution of surface normals of the input mesh. The main idea was to group the surface normals into distinct sets called bins. Each bin was formed in a cone shape defined by a unique Bin Center(BC) normal and a bin radius (φ^R) with the constraint that no overlapping was allowed among the bins. Watermarks were embedded by modifying the mean normals, the mean angle of normals, or the amount of normals inside each bin predefined by the bin radius (φ^R) from the BC. Due to the advantages associated with the use of surface normals instead of mesh connectivity, the Benedens's method is considered one of the most robust 3D watermarking methods based on geometry property.

In an effort to improve Ohbuchi et al.'s method [1] that uses the ratio of lines and volumes, Wagner [2] proposed a new method that used the relative lengths of vectors of each of two connected points on a polygonal mesh to improve the robustness against affine and similarity transformations. Similarly, Benedens and Busch [4] presented an Affine Invariant Embedding (AIE) technique that was applicable to non-manifolds.

In order to improve the imperceptibility of watermarks, Bors [6,7] employed human detection thresholds to choose the regions where the human eyes are less sensitive to changes. The watermarks were embedded into the selected vertices using two different bounding volumes consisting of two planes and ellipsoids. The method was robust against geometrical transformations such as translation, rotation and scaling as well as cropping and additive noise. Most recently, two blind methods, POA (Principal Object Axis) and SPOA (Sectional Principal Object Axis), were presented by Zafeifiou et al. [12]. For watermark embedding, a conversion to spherical coordinates was required during preprocessing, and the r component, the distance from the origin, was modified to insert bi-directional watermarks along a ray from the origin that passes through a point p determined by a neighborhood operator. The neighborhood operator was formed by computing the value of the mean or the median of the r component of neighbors, or by building a parametric surface using the neighborhood as the control points. POA is robust against rotation, translation, and uniform scaling. SPOA is additionally robust against mesh simplification attacks. Since both schemes are based on principal component analysis, watermarks can be easily destroyed by cropping attacks that perturb the principal object axes.

1.2   Our Contributions

Our work makes two contributions. First, we propose an adaptive method to select watermark strength. A psychophysical experiment on visual masking showed that human detection thresholds for additive noise increase monotonically with local surface roughness. The resulting quantitative model is the basis for roughness-adaptive watermarking algorithm that ensures locally maximal watermark strength while guaranteeing its imperceptibility. Second, we introduce a blind version of Benedens's method with improved robustness of the '1' bit.

The remainder of this paper is organized as follows. In Section 2, we introduce Benedens' method and discuss its limitations. The blind version of Benedens's method is presented in Section 3. Section 4 describes the psychophysical experiment and the roughness-adaptive watermarking algorithm. Evaluation results appear in Section 5. Finally, we conclude the paper in Section 6.

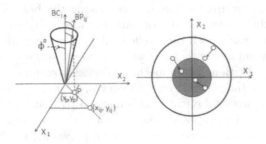

Fig. 1. (left) Transformation of 3D coordinates into 2D coordinates. (right) Embedding a bit '0' by pushing normals into the kernel area. Modified from [3].

2   Benedens's Method and Its Limitations

As mentioned earlier, Benedens's non-blind, geometry-based 3D watermarking method [3] uses the distribution of surface normals on polygonal meshes. The watermark embedding and retrieval procedures of Benedens's methods are briefly described in this section in order to familiarize readers with its basic operations. In Benedens's method, watermarks are embedded by modifying (i) the mean of normals, (ii) the mean angle of normals to a Bin Center (BC) normal, or (iii) the amount of normals in a bin. Our method is based on the third feature because it is most straight-forward to improve blindness and robustness with the amount of normals in a bin. We therefore focus on the third feature in this section. The entire embedding process of Benedens's method is summarized below:

1. Create a unit sphere, and then tessellate the surface of the unit sphere to generate bins defined by a Bin Center (BC) normal and a bin angle (φ^R) (in the following the bin angle will also referred to as bin radius). The same bin radius is used for all the bins. Bins are cone-shaped as illustrated in the left image of Figure 1.

2. Randomly choose a set of bins for embedding the watermark bits and sample surface normals. A surface normal is assigned to a bin if the angle formed between the surface normal (BP) and the Bin Center normal (BC) (Figure 1, left image) is smaller than that formed between the cone's axis (BC) and any line on the surface of the cone that passes through its apex.

3. Compute the ratio of normals (nk_i) inside the bin kernel defined by the kernel angle φ^k for each bin. The 2D projected kernel area is the gray colored inner circle as seen in the right image of Figure 1. The kernel radius (φ^k) is predefined.

4. Transform all the 3D surface normals in each bin into 2D coordinates in the X_1 and X_2 plane (See the left image of Figure 1) and perform the core embedding process as described below.

During the core watermark embedding process, watermark bits are inserted by changing the number of normals inside the kernel area in each bin. For instance, to embed a bit '0', all the normals outside the kernel are moved inside it as depicted in the right image of Figure 1. It means that nk_i (the ratio of normals inside the kernel) becomes 1.0, which is the maximum for any bin. Conversely, a bit '1' is embedded by taking all the normals inside the kernel out of the kernel so that nk_i goes to 0.0, which is the minimum for any bin. In order to search for the new locations of vertices that move the normals to the new directions, an optimization algorithm, the Downhill simplex method, is used to relocate the vertices. Optimization is performed according the two cost functions defined in Eqn. 1, respectively for bit 1 and 0.

$$costs_{f;v \to v'} \begin{cases} cos \left[\dfrac{\pi}{2} \left(\dfrac{cos^{-1}(BP'_{ij}*BC_i)}{\varphi_i^R} \right) \right] & S_i = 1 \\ \dfrac{cos^{-1}(BP'_{ij}*BC_i)}{\varphi_i^R} & S_i = 0 \end{cases} \tag{1}$$

In order to minimize distortions on the surface of the input model, the following constraints are imposed during the watermark embedding process:

- The normal of a face adjacent to a vertex v in the bin is not allowed to change by an angle that is $\geq \alpha$;
- The normal of a face adjacent to a vertex v that is not in the bin is not allowed to change by an angle that is $\geq \beta$;
- No normal is allowed to leave its bin.

For retrieval of the embedded watermarks, the information about bins (bin radius, kernel radius, the ratio of normals in each bin, and the chosen bins used in the embedding process) need to be delivered to the extraction stage. With the watermarked polygonal mesh, repeat the same steps (1 to 6) of the embedding process. Then the ratio of normals nk_i in each bin is compared with the original value of nk_i. If nk_i of the watermarked mesh is larger than the nk_i value of the original model, then the embedded watermark is a bit '0'. Otherwise, it's '1'.

As mentioned earlier, watermarks embedded by Benedens's method are especially robust against mesh-simplification and vertex randomization, because the distribution of surface normals is invariant to these two types of modifications to the polygonal mesh. Benedens's method therefore addressed two major drawbacks of most of the earlier geometry-based watermarking methods.

However, no evaluation against additive noise was conducted in Benedens's paper. Our tests indicated that about one tenth of the embedded bits were destroyed by Gaussian additive noise when its magnitude was set to cause visible, but not annoying, perturbation on the surface of the input mesh. This means that Benedens's method is not robust enough against additive noise. One trivial way to increase the robustness of Benedens's method is simply to increase Bin radius (φ^R) but that will lead to decrease watermark capacity. The other drawback of Benedens's method is its non-blindness because the original nk_is of all bins have to be carried to the extraction stage. This is not acceptable in many practical applications. In the following two sections, we present our approaches to address these major drawbacks.

3   A Blind Version of Benedens's Method

Retrieval of the watermarks embedded by Benedens's method requires the availability of a priori knowledge including bin radius, number of bins, and the original ratio of normals (nk) in the kernel of each bin, to the extractor. This is the secret key needed for retrieval of the watermarks later on. Since the original values of nk depend on the polygonal mesh of the 3D object, Benedens's method is a non-blind watermarking technique. Our work first focused on eliminating the need to carry the original nk values to the extracting stage by using the probability distribution of normals in the kernel area of each bin. The key idea is to choose a kernel radius such that the ratio of surface normals inside the kernel is a fixed value with the assumption that normals are uniformly distributed over the object's surface and hence probabilities correspond to area ratios. Then, the retrieved watermark bit is 0 if the nk value of the watermarked mesh is greater than the fixed ratio at the extractor. Otherwise, it is 1. Therefore, all we have to do is to compute the exact kernel radius φ^k that satisfies the constraint that the ratio of normals inside the kernel area is fixed. A ratio of 0.5 was chosen so that there were equal number of surface normals inside and outside the kernel.

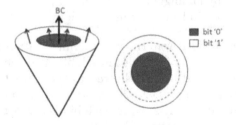

Fig. 2. Two views of a bin with sampled normals. The dark area (inner circle) is the kernel area defined by φ^k, which is used for embedding '0'; the bin excluding the dark area is used for embedding '1'. The dashed circle represents the new zone for embedding '1'.

Given a spherical cap defined by a sphere of radius R and a height H from the top of the spherical cap to the bottom of the base circle, its surface area can be calculated as $A_{spherical\ cap} = 2\pi RH$.

Since $H = R\text{-}Rcos\varphi^R$ for a bin defined by φ^R, the surface area of the bin becomes

$$A_{spherical\ cap\ of\ bin} = 2\pi R^2(1 - cos\varphi^R). \tag{2}$$

The surface area of the kernel defined by φ^k can be calculated similarly as

$$A_{spherical\ cap\ of\ kernel} = 2\pi R^2(1 - cos\varphi^k). \tag{3}$$

We require that

$$\frac{A_{spherical\,cap\,of\,kernel}}{A_{spherical\,cap\,of\,bin}} = 0.5. \tag{4}$$

Therefore the size of the kernel, φ^k, can be computed from Eqns. 2, 3, and 4.

$$\varphi^k = cos^{-1}(1 - \frac{1}{2}(1 - cos\varphi^R)). \tag{5}$$

This way, the original nk values no longer need to be carried to the extraction stage, thus achieving a blind version of Benedens's method.

An additional modification we have made to Benedens's method was to improve the robustness of '1's bits. During the embedding process of the original method, the normals are moved in two opposite directions. When embedding a bit '0', all normals in the bin are moved inside the kernel area (the dark inner circle shown in Figure 2). For better robustness, the normals should be enforced to be as close to the BC line (bin center normal) as possible. When embedding a bit '1', however, the normals are moved towards the border curve and are pushed as closed to the rim of the bin as possible. There are therefore two imaginary embedding zones: one around the BC and the other around the rim of the bin. Ideally, all normals should be placed at either the BC (for bit '0') and one on the rim of the bin (for bit '1'). The problem, however, is that the normals located on the rim of the bin can be easily pushed out of the bin. This is not the case with the normals located at the BC. Therefore, bit 1 is much less robust than bit 0, which is an undesirable feature.

To verify the difference in robustness of bit '0' and bit '1', an experiment with the Bunny model was conducted. We first embedded a sequence of '0' and '1' (20 bits in total), then additive noise following a Gaussian distribution N(0, σ=0.005) was added, and the robustness of bits '0' and '1' were as compared. This experiment was repeated ten times and the results averaged. As expected, the error of the bit '1' (15 %) was higher than that of bit '0' (11 %).

To improve the robustness of bit '1', the ideal embedding zone was moved away from the bin rim, as shown by the dashed circle on the right of Figure 2. The new embedding zone defined by the red dashed circle was defined by a new radius φ^{k1} such that the surface area of the spherical cap is 3/4 of that of the bin. By using Equations 3 to 4, we have:

$$\varphi^{k1} = cos^{-1}(1 - \frac{3}{4}(1 - cos\varphi^R)). \tag{6}$$

With this new embedding zone for bit '1', the error of bit '1' was reduced to 10%. In general, the robustness of bit '0' is expected to be superior to that of bit '1', especially under the condition of strong attacks, because the new embedding zone for bit '1' is still closer to the rim of the bin as compared to the BC which is the embedding zone of bit '0'.

4   Roughness-Adaptive 3D Watermarking

In this section, we present a novel way of adaptively selecting watermark strength that optimizes the conflicting requirements of robustness and imperceptibility. It is well known that stronger watermarks improve robustness while weaker watermarks ensure imperceptibility. The key to optimizing watermark strength is to choose the strongest watermark with the constraint that it remains invisible. The optimization can be performed globally or locally based on certain properties of the polygonal mesh. We propose an adaptive algorithm that selects watermark strengths based on local surface roughness measures. Our algorithm takes advantage of the fact that the human eyes are more sensitive to distortions of smooth surface patches than to those of rough surface patches. The watermark strength is therefore set to the human detection threshold; i.e., the largest watermark that remains invisible, for a given surface roughness. In the remainder of this section, we first describe the psychophysical experiment that estimated the quantitative relation between human watermark detection threshold and local surface roughness. We then present our roughness-adaptive watermarking algorithm.

4.1   Psychophysical Experiment on Human Detection Thresholds

The psychophysical experiment was designed to estimate the relation between visual watermark detection threshold (in terms of watermark strength δ used to restrict the search space in the core embedding process) and roughness of spherical surfaces. Note that the original Beneden's method restricted the search space in the Downhill Simplex optimization method based on the minimum of four parameters including δ. For simplicity and without loss of generality, we used only the δ parameter in our experiments. In the following, δ is expressed as a ratio over the bounding box diameter of the 3D object. Four participants (three males and one female) took part in the experiment. None of the participants reported any visual deficiencies.

Stimuli. The visual display consisted of a spherical surface rendered with 3752 vertices and 7500 faces. The image of the sphere occupied a visual angle of roughly 30 degrees. Six spherical surfaces with different roughness levels were created by introducing varying amount of additive noise to the vertices. The surface roughness level was controlled by the magnitude of the additive noise generated by a Gaussian probability distribution function $N(0,\sigma)$. The direction of the additive noise was randomly chosen between 0 and 360 degrees. Figure 3 shows the six reference stimuli with increasing surface roughness. The left most sphere has a smooth surface with no additive noise. The roughness level of each spherical surface was estimated with a 1-ring roughness measure based on the mutli-scale roughness estimation method proposed by Corsini et al. in [13]. They were 0.000027, 0.000209, 0.001704, 0.003139, 0.010937, and 0.025304, respectively.

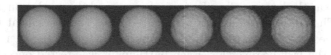

Fig. 3. The six spherical surfaces with increasing roughness used in the present study. The estimated roughness values were 0.000027, 0.000209, 0.001704, 0.003139, 0.010937, and 0.025304, respectively, from left to right. The six spherical surfaces contained the same number of vertices (3752) and faces (7500).

In order to make our experiment as general as possible, we decided not to use any particular watermarking technique. Instead, we measured the visibility of a general noise-like visual stimulus on a surface with controlled roughness.

Additive noise was used to randomly alter chosen vertices of the sphere in the direction of surface normal, as specified below.

$$\overrightarrow{v}_{new}(i) = \overrightarrow{v}(i) + \delta * \overrightarrow{n}(i)$$

where $\overrightarrow{v}_{new}(i)$ is the modified coordinate vector of the i-th vertex $\overrightarrow{v}(i)$, δ denotes stimulus intensity that varied according to the participant's responses, and $\overrightarrow{n}(i)$ is the surface normal vector[1]. In our experiment, the amount of modified vertices was fixed to 3% so that images of spheres with embedded noise could be rendered in a reasonable amount of time from trial to trial.

Procedures. A two-interval forced choice (2IFC) one-up three-down adaptive procedure [15] was used to measure the (watermark) detection thresholds as a function of surface roughness. The threshold so obtained corresponded to the 79.4 percentile point on the psychometric function. On each trial, the participant looked at two spherical surfaces, a reference surface (no embedded noise) and a target surface (reference plus noise), presented on the left and right sides of the monitor. The location of the surface with embedded noise was randomly chosen to be on the left or right of the monitor on each trial. The participant's task was to indicate which spherical surface contained noise. According to the one-up three-down adaptive rule, the stimulus intensity (δ) was increased after a single incorrect response and decreased after three successive correct responses. Otherwise, the value of δ remained the same on the next trial. The initial δ value was chosen to be large enough so that the stimulus was clearly perceptible to the participant. The value of δ then decreased or increased by a fixed step size (0.0004), depending on the participant's responses. After the initial three reversals (a reversal occurred when the value of δ decreased after one more increase, or vice versa), the value of δ changed by a smaller step size (0.0002). The initial larger change in δ was necessary for faster convergence of the δ

---

[1] Though in the experiments the stimulus has a form that does not directly correspond to the watermark distortion, we used the same symbol δ, since the results of the experiments will be used to set the watermark strength.

values, whereas the later smaller change in δ improved the resolution of threshold estimates. The adaptive series was terminated after 12 reversals at the smaller step size. The detection threshold was computed by taking the average of the δ values from the last 12 reversals. Each participant was tested once per surface roughness, resulting in a total of six adaptive series per participant and a total of 24 series for all participants.

Results. The average detection thresholds for the four participants are shown in Figure 4. The thresholds follow a monotonically increasing trend that is well modeled by the following power function,

$$\delta = 0.0291 * S^{0.3907}, \tag{7}$$

where δ is the detection threshold, and S denotes surface roughness.[2]

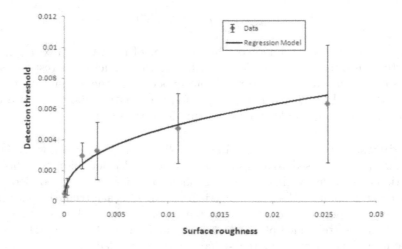

Fig. 4. Human watermark detection threshold data and a power regression model (solid line). See texts for details.

4.2   Selection of Adaptive Watermark Strengths

The results of the psychophysical experiment indicated that a stronger watermark can be hidden into a bumpier surface area with higher roughness. Specifically, the human detection threshold for watermarks is related to the local surface roughness as shown in Eqn.7. So our goal was to use an adaptive watermark strength determined by the local roughness of a surface instead of the constant watermark strength used in Benedens's method. Specifically, we first

---

[2] The r^2 value, which indicates how well a regression model approximates real data points, was 0.9851, where $r^2{=}1.0$ means a perfect fit.

estimated the roughness per vertex, and then chose the maximum imperceptible watermark strength as

$$
\begin{cases}
\delta & = 0.0291 * S^{0.3907} - constant, \ \ if \ S \geq 0.000027 \\
\delta & = 0.0004, \ \ otherwise
\end{cases}
\tag{8}
$$

where the *constant* (0.00004) was used to uniformly reduce the watermark strength so that the embedded watermark strength was not detectable. When the surface roughness is less than 0.000027 which corresponds to the smooth spherical surface, the watermark strength was fixed to 0.0004.

To estimate the local surface roughness around the vertex to be modified for embedding watermarks, we estimated the roughness of all adjacent faces around the vertex using the 1-ring roughness estimation method described in Corsini et al. [13]. Then the value of δ was determined by Eqn. 8 during the watermark embedding process. Note that watermark strength is directly related to δ, since δ defines the radius of the spherical region wherein the new watermarked vertex location is looked for, during the Downhill simplex optimization in Benedens's method. The resulting distance between the old vertex and the new optimized vertex becomes the watermark strength which is linearly proportional to δ. In the present study, bin radius φ^R was fixed at 11 degrees as a compromise between robustness and capacity.

The key steps in our roughness-adaptive watermarking algorithm can be summarized as follows: (1) Measure the local surface roughness per vertex by Corsini et al.'s method [13]; (2) Compute the maximum δ from Eqn. 8; (3) Apply the chosen δ value to in the watermark embedding process; and (4) Repeat steps 1 to 3 for all the vertices to be watermarked.

5 Evaluations

The experiments that we carried out were aimed at evaluating the improvements brought by the modifications we made to the original Benedens's watermarking scheme, with particular reference to roughness-based watermark strength adaptation. We focused our assessment by comparing the watermark strengths between the original and the watermarked models. Note that by increasing

Table 1. A comparison of error to additive-noise attacks. Shown under the two methods are the averages and standard deviations over 10 tests. See texts for details.

Model	Benedens' method		Our method		Improved (%)
-	Error (%)	Std. Dev.	Error (%)	Std. Dev.	-
M1	11	4.95	9.5	4.38	13.6
M2	9	5.68	7	6.32	22.2
M3	8	3.5	7.5	6.77	6.25

Table 2. Key parameters of the 3D models used in the evaluation experiments

Model	# of vertices	# of faces	Avg. roughness	Std. Dev.
Bunny (M1)	5050	9999	1.888E-07	1.754E-07
Happy Buddha (M2)	4952	9932	7.519E-07	4.476E-07
Dragon (M3)	3512	6999	1.3302E-06	8.842E-07

the magnitude of the watermarks in order to improve robustness, the water-marked model will necessarily have higher MSE (mean-square error), under the same condition of watermark invisiability. To simulate random attacks, we used additive Gaussian noise to alter vertex locations. Note that Bene-dens did not evaluate his original method against additive noise, so the data reported in this section provide additional information on the robustness of Benedens's method. Specifically, we compared the performance of the origi-nal Benedens's method with the performance obtained after our proposed im-provements. To do so, we implemented the original Benedens's method and our improvements with Visual C++ with CGAL and OpenGL libraries on a Windows machine with a 2GHz CPU processor. Three 3D models, "Bunny", "Happy Buddha" and "Dragon" were used for the evaluation experiments. The key characteristics of the three models are summarized in Table 2. In what fol-lows, we present two experiments. The first experiment was an evaluation of the proposed improvement to bit '1' robustness. The second experiment mea-sured the additional improvements due to the roughness-adaptive watermarking algorithm.

5.1   Improvements to Bit '1' Robustness

The purpose of the first experiment was to evaluate the improvement to ro-bustness when the new embedding zone (φ^{k1}=9.53 degrees, φ^R = 11degrees) computed by Eqn. 6 for '1' bit was introduced. Watermark strength (δ value) was set to a constant value during the embedding process; e.g., 0.0064 for M1 (see Table 3) . In order to evaluate robustness, a 20-bit watermark was em-bedded. Then attacks simulated with additive noises generated by a Gaussian distribution with zero mean and standard deviation σ=0.0005 was applied to the watermarked model. Error was calculated as the percentage of bits that failed to be retrieved. The error was computed for both the original Benedens's method and our robust bit '1' method. For each test condition the experiment was repeated ten times and the results were averaged. As shown in Table 1, our method which improved bit '1' robustness outperformed the original Benedens's method for all three models tested. The average improvement, calculated as the ratio of reduction in error over the error for Benedens's method, was about 14 %.

5.2   Additional Improvements Due to Roughness-Adaptive Watermarking

In the second experiment, we implemented both the improvement to bit '1' robustness and roughness-based strength adaptation. Attacks were simulated by additive noises generated with a Gaussian distribution ($N(0, \sigma=0.0005)$). The performance of our blind and improved method and Benedens's original method were compared in terms of their robustness against additive noises for a 20-bit watermark. For the experiment on the original Benedens's method, the parameters were set as follows: $\varphi^R = 11$ degrees, $\varphi^k = 9.53$ calculated by Eqn. 5 and $\delta=0.0064$, 0.007, and 0.0059 for M1, M2, and M3, respectively (i.e., constant watermark strength). The constant δ values were chosen by finding the maximum values ensuring invisibility. For the experiment on our method, the same φ^R and φ^k values were used, but adaptive δ values were selected based on the estimated local surface roughness. The experiment with each method was repeated ten times. The resulting images for three models are shown in Figure 5.

Table 3. A comparison of errors to additive-noise attacks for Beneden's method and our new method. See texts for details.

Model	Benedens' method			Our method			Improved (%)
-	Error (%)	Std. Dev.	δ	Error (%)	Std. Dev.	δ	-
M1	11	4.95	0.0064	6.5	3.37	0.00753	40.9
M2	9	5.68	0.007	5	3.33	0.0129	44.4
M3	8	3.5	0.0059	3.5	4.12	0.0116	56.3

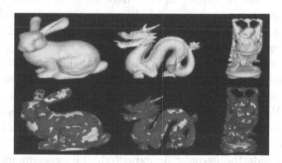

Fig. 5. Resulting watermarked models. Original models (upper row), and the watermarked models (lower row) indicating the modified triangles (red colored triangles). Bunny, Dragon, and Happy Buddha models from the left.

Table 3 shows the results with the original Benedens's method using a constant δ and our new method utilizing adaptive δ values. It is clear that watermarks embedded by our adaptive δ method is more robust against additive-noise attacks for all three models (M1, M2, and M3). The robustness improvement rate achieved by our method was 56.3% with the Dragon model, 44.4% with the Happy Buddha model, and 40.9% with the Bunny model. The largest improvement observed with the Dragon model was to be expected because the standard deviation of the estimated surface roughness for the Dragon model was the largest among the three models tested (see Table 2). It was also found that the average δ size was larger with our method than with the constant used in Benedens's method, more so with the Dragon model than with the Bunny model (see Table 3). Therefore, the model with the largest variation in surface roughness (the Dragon model) benefited most with our method.

6   Concluding Remarks

Developing robust 3D digital watermarking techniques is an ongoing challenging research topic in the field of information hiding. In this paper, we have presented a general way to improve watermark robustness by exploiting visual masking. Our method is based on measured human sensitivity to additive noise as a function of surface roughness of input meshes. Similar approaches have been previously adopted by Bors et al. [6,7] and by Kanai et al. [14]. Bors et al. embedded watermarks into a region where the human eyes are less sensitive to changes. Kanai et al. embedded watermarks by modulating the high frequency signals in an input model where changes are imperceptible to human vision. While both Bors et al. and Kanai et al. focused mainly on watermark imperceptibility, we aimed to improve watermark robustness while maintaining imperceptibility. In addition, these researches used a constant watermark strength in surface areas where humans are less sensitive to watermarks, and they did not embed watermarks in surface areas where humans can detect watermarks more easily. In comparison, our method allows varying watermark strengths per vertex to maximize robustness while maintaining imperceptibility. The watermark strengths were adapted based on local surface roughness, thereby utilizing the whole object surface for watermark embedding. The evaluation experiments of the new scheme with Benedens's method confirmed that the overall watermark robustness was improved greatly by employing roughness-adaptive watermark strengths. We achieved further improvement to robustness by introducing a more robust embedding zone for bit '1', and we introduced a blind version of Benedens's method by choosing kernel radii that resulted in a constant ratio of surface normals inside the kernels. As expected, the experiments demonstrated that the roughness-adaptive watermarking technique brings more benefits for data models with a larger standard deviation of roughness. We showed that, on average, stronger watermarks can be embedded with roughness-adaptive watermark strengths than could be achieved with a constant watermark strength as used by most watermarking methods.

Our approach suggests promising new directions for improving the performance of 3D digital watermarking schemes. In the future, we will test our scheme with other existing geometry-based techniques to verify its generalizability and to compare the results (e.g., improvements in robustness and MSE).

Acknowledgments

The first author (KK) was partially supported by the US National Science Foundation under Grant no. 0836664. The second author (MB) was partially supported by the Italian Ministry of Research and Education under FIRB project no. RBIN04AC9W.

References

1. Ohbuchi, R., Masuda, H., Aono, M.: Watermarking Three-Dimensional Polygonal Models. In: Proceedings of the ACM International Multimedia Conference and Exhibition, pp. 261–272 (1997)
2. Wagner, M.G.: Robust Watermarking of Polygonal Meshes. In: Proceedings of Geometric Modeling and Processing, pp. 201–208 (2000)
3. Benedens, O.: Geometry-Based Watermarking of 3D models. IEEE Computer Graphics and Applications 19(1), 46–55 (1999)
4. Benedens, O., Busch, C.: Towards Blind Detection of Robust Watermarks in Polygonal Models. Computer Graphics Forum 19(3), 199–208 (2000)
5. Yeo, B., Yeung, M.M.: Watermarking 3D Objects for Verification. IEEE Computer Graphics and Applications 19(1), 36–45 (1999)
6. Bors, A.G.: Blind Watermarking of 3D Shapes using localized constraints. In: Proceedings of 3D Data Processing, Visualization and Transmission 2004, 3DPVT, pp. 242–249 (2004)
7. Bors, A.G.: Watermarking Mesh-Based Representations of 3-D Objects Using Local Moments. IEEE Transactions on Image processing 15(3), 687–701 (2006)
8. Cayre, F., Macq, B.: Data Hiding on 3-D Triangle Meshes. IEEE Transactions on Signal Processing 51(4), 939–949 (2003)
9. Cayre, F., Rondao-Alface, P., Schmitt, F., Macq, B., Maitre, H.: Application of spectral decomposition to compression and watermarking of 3D triangle mesh geometry. Signal Processing 18(4), 309–319 (2003)
10. Ohbuchi, R., Takahashi, S., Miyazawa, T., Mukaiyama, A.: Watermarking 3D Polygonal Meshes in the Mesh Spectral Domain. In: Proceedings of Graphics interface, pp. 9–17 (2001)
11. Lin, H.-Y., Liao, H.-Y., Lu, C.-S., Lin, J.-C.: Fragile watermarking for authenticating 3-D polygonal meshes. IEEE Trans. Multimedia 7(6), 997–1006 (2005)
12. Zafeiriou, S., Tefas, A., Pitas, I.: Blind Robust Watermarking Schemes for Copyright Protection of 3D Mesh Objects. IEEE Trans. Visualization and Computer Graphics 11(5), 596–607 (2005)
13. Corsini, M., Gelasca, E.D., Ebrahimi, T., Barni, M.: Watermarked 3D Mesh Quality Assessment. IEEE Transactions on Multimedia (2007)
14. Kanai, S., Date, H., Kishinami, T.: Digital Watermarking for 3D Polygons Using Multiresolution Wavelet Decomposition. In: Proceeding of IFIP WG, pp. 296–307 (1998)
15. Levitt, H.: Transformed Up-Down Methods in Psychoacoustics. The Journal of the Acoustical Society of America 49, 467–477 (1971)

Hardware-Based Public-Key Cryptography with Public Physically Unclonable Functions

Nathan Beckmann[1] and Miodrag Potkonjak[2]

[1] Massachusetts Institute of Technology
beckmann@csail.mit.edu
[2] University of California, Los Angeles
miodrag@cs.ucla.edu

Abstract. A physically unclonable function (PUF) is a multiple-input, multiple-output, large entropy physical system that is unreproducible due to its structural complexity. A public physically unclonable function (PPUF) is a PUF that is created so that its simulation is feasible but requires very large time even when ample computational resources are available. Using PPUFs, we have developed conceptually new secret key exchange and public key protocols that are resilient against physical and side channel attacks and do not employ unproven mathematical conjectures. Judicious use of PPUF hardware sharing, parallelism, and provably correct partial simulation enables 10^{16} advantage of communicating parties over an attacker, requiring over 500 of years of computation even if the attacker uses all global computation resources.

Keywords: PPUF, security, cryptography, public key cryptography.

1 Introduction

Motivation. Cryptography is a scientific and engineering field that develops and analyzes techniques for protecting privacy of stored or communicated information. Currently, it is mainly realized using secret key (a.k.a. symmetric key, shared key, private key, and one key) and public key techniques. The emergence and rapid proliferation of mobile, sensing, health, financial, e-commerce and other pervasive applications has elevated the system importance of sound, practical cryptographic protocols.

Cryptographic techniques, and in particular public key protocols, have been the basis for numerous security applications, ranging from secure email, secure remote access (e.g. passwords and smart cards), remote gambling, and digital signatures to privacy protection, digital rights management, watermarking, and fingerprinting. However, there are two major drawbacks of classical cryptographic techniques that are widely documented in security literature. The first is that the current state-of-the-art cryptographic techniques are based on extremely likely but nevertheless unproven mathematical assumptions. The second is that even if there are no algorithmic weaknesses in public key cryptographical protocols, often they can be easily broken due to software vulnerabilities, physical attacks, or side channels.

Our primary goal in this paper is to present a new type of cryptography that uses a generalized form of physically unclonable functions (PUFs), an approach that resolves

S. Katzenbeisser and A.-R. Sadeghi (Eds.): IH 2009, LNCS 5806, pp. 206–220, 2009.

the two main conceptual and practical limitations of classical public cryptography. The first disadvantage, the use of non-proven mathematical conjectures, is replaced with technological, physical, and chemical laws that prevent manufacturing of fully identical physical systems at gate and transistor levels of silicon technology or other nano-scale systems. The second, more important vulnerability, susceptibility to physical and side channel attacks, is completely eliminated. In addition, PPUF-based security is in many applications much faster and requires significantly less energy. For example, in remote authentication, the new scheme requires only one control cycle to generate the correct answer.

The new cryptographical approach is based on the novel notion of a public physically unclonable function (PPUF). A PUF is a physically system that is intractably complex to replicate. Modern and future silicon technology-based integrated circuits may serve as PUFs due to their intrinsic manufacturing variability. PUFs have been manufactured and their use for secret key-based security applications has been demonstrated. Recently, it has been shown that many types of PUFs can be easily reversed engineered. While these approaches jeopardize some secret key applications of PUFs, they also create starting points for the creation of public key-based protocols that employ unclonable hardware.

PPUFs form a class of PUFs that can be reversed engineered, but once their structure is completely characterized, one still requires very large time to compute the PPUF outputs for a given input. We use PPUF characteristics as a public key. We focus on PPUFs realized as a small circuit. It is relatively easy to envision how PPUF with the ratio of simulation vs. execution times of κ, gives the computational advantage of κ to each of the communicating parties (see below). What is remarkable is that this advantage can not only be used for remote exchange of secret information, but can be further significantly amplified using parallel computations and directly used for creation of a number of security protocols. We believe that PPUF-based cryptography will provide an impetus for the creation of conceptually new security approaches that are not just much faster and use much less energy, but are also resilient against physical attacks and side channels.

The paper is organized as follows. In §2, we discuss the related work in crytography and circuits necessary for description of PPUFs. In §3, we discuss some preliminary results that our work is based on. In §4, we present and analyze a PPUF architecture. In §5, we present a secret key exchange protocol using PPUFs. And §6 concludes the paper.

A Simple Example. We now demonstrate the operation of a PPUF and how it can be used in a secret key exchange protocol. Figure 1 shows a simple PPUF consisting of 6 XOR gates arranged in three rows. The delay through each gate is also shown in Table 1. Due to manufacturing variability, the delays are unequal for each gate and each input (see §3).

We assume that "01" is initially on the input and the circuit has reached a steady state (output "00" on gates E, F). Then, at time $t = 0$, the input becomes "10". At $t = 0.88$, the "0" reaches the output of gate B, which becomes 0. At $t = 1.12$, the "1" reaches the output of gate B, and its output becomes 1. Similarly, at $t = 0.93$ and $t = 1.01$, gate A transitions to 0 and then 1.

Table 1. Gate delays from given input to output (in ps)

	Input 1	Input 2		Input 1	Input 2
E	.86	.95	F	1.24	.96
C	1.11	.90	D	.78	.71
A	.93	1.01	B	1.12	.88

Table 2. Output transitions

E	$\{2.54, 2.64, 2.66, 2.74, 2.78, 2.88, 2.9, 2.98\}$	F	$\{2.55, 2.67, 2.75, 2.79, 3.02, 3.26, 3.28, 3.36\}$
C	$\{1.78, 2.02, 2.04, 2.12\}$	D	$\{1.59, 1.71, 1.79, 1.83\}$
A	$\{.93, 1.01\}$	B	$\{.88, 1.12\}$

Fig. 1. A simple PPUF

This pattern repeats through each row of the PPUF. On row 2, gate C transitions each time a new input arrives. Looking at Table 1, this occurs at transitions of gate A plus 1.11 ps and transitions of gate B plus .90 ps. All in all, gate C transitions at times $t \in \{2.04, 2.12, 2.02, 1.78\}$. Similarly, gate D's output transitions whenever gates A or B transition, plus the delay through gate D. Gate D transitions at times $t \in \{1.71, 1.79, 1.83, 1.59\}$. It should be clear that on row 3, gates E and F will each transition 8 times, when either C or D transition (plus the delay through the gate). This gives rise to an exponential number of transitions on the number of rows (§4.2). See Table 2.

We now show how to exchange a secret key between two parties, Alice and Bob. Suppose Alice owns the above PPUF. The gate-level characterization of the circuit (given by Table 1) is effectively the public key, enabling accurate simulation of the PPUF. Bob begins by choosing two numbers to input into the circuit — suppose he chooses $x_0 = 01$ and $x_1 = 10$. Bob also chooses a time, say $t = 2.7$ ps. Bob then simulates the PPUF starting at steady state on input x_0 with input x_1 arriving at time 0, attempting to determine the output after 2.7 ps. To do so, he computes all 16 output transitions as we have done, concluding that the output reads $y = 10$ at 2.7 ps.

Bob then sends x_0, t, and y to Alice. It is now Alice's job to find x_1. To do so, she iterates over all possible inputs and checks the output of the PPUF for each, clocking the output at $t = 2.7$ ps. In this case, $x_1 = 10$ is the only input that produces output y after 2.7 ps (see Table 3). In a sense, the PPUF is the private key, enabling Alice to quickly find x_1 — the PPUF runs in a matter of picoseconds, so searching the entire input space takes little time.

An attacker, on the other hand, gets the worst of both worlds: he must simulate every possible input until x_1 is found. He is at a disadvantage over Alice of simulating the PPUF instead of running it (see §4). He is at a disadvantage to Bob of simulating several values instead of a single one (see §5). Expanding on these two advantages, we are able to achieve insurmountable advantage over an attacker.

2 Related Work

Cryptography. Since the mid seventies when the first paper on public key cryptography [9] and the first practical realization [30] were published, cryptography has developed into a large field with a wide variety of elegant results. A number of excellent books are available [24] that emphasize both the theoretical [12] and practical [32] aspects. Numerous public key cryptography protocols have been developed for ciphers, hash functions, message digests, message authentication codes, asymmetric public key secure communication and storage, public key infrastructure, digital signatures, authentication, zero knowledge proofs, secret sharing, digital money, secure watermarking, remote gambling, and many other applications. More recently, quantum cryptography has been attracting a great deal of interest.

Table 3. Output at 2.7ps

Input	Output
00	01
01	00
10	10
11	11

Side Channel Attacks. However, quantum cryptography is still a pending technology, and there are several serious problems with traditional mathematical cryptography. While there is relatively little chance that its unproven foundations will be compromised, and although conceptually new algorithmic and statistical attacks are rare and often fixable [5], there is a wide consensus that a great variety of often inexpensive and fast physical and side channel attacks are surprisingly effective [17,34].

Unclonable artifacts and PUFs. Unique and unclonable artifacts were first proposed in early eighties [3]. More recently, several actual implementations have been demonstrated and analyzed [6]. Lofstrom et al. proposed use of silicon manufacturing variability (MV) as a source of unique integrated circuits [20]. Koushanfar et al. proposed used of unique integrated circuits as security and digital right management mechanisms [19]. Papu et al. introduced powerful notion of physical one-way functions [28]. Devadas and his research group realized that silicon MV is a very practical technology for creation and use of such physically unclonable functions (PUFs) and demonstrated and analyzed their properties [11]. The joint efforts of Rice and UCLA system security groups demonstrated a number of techniques for exposing vulnerabilities of a wide classes of initial silicon PUFs [22], and introduced several secure PUF architectures [21].

Timing Precision. There are a large number of techniques for the creation and measurement of rapidly changing signals: (i) interval stretching followed by digital counting, (ii) time-to-amplitude conversion combined with A/D conversion, and three purely digital methods, (iii) the Vernier method with two oscillators, (iv) time-to-digital conversion using a tapped delay line, and (v) the Vernier method using two differential delay lines [16]. Although progress has been steady, it is difficult to achieve time resolution significantly better than 1 picosecond using standard on-chip technology and techniques. However, with the use of lasers and materials that change their properties under the impact of changing light, methods exist for measurements in femtosecond and attosecond range [13,2]. Currently, the most accurate clocks measure time intervals in a range of 10 attoseconds.

3 Preliminaries

In this section, we briefly summarize the sources of manufacturing variability (MV), MV modeling, and its impact on delay, dynamic, and leakage power of a gate, issues and techniques used for gate-level characterization, and introduce our approaches for addressing time variability of these characteristics due to operational and environmental impact.

Manufacturing Variability. As the feature size of silicon integrated circuits keeps shrinking, any given gate from a single design has unique characteristics on each physical implementation of the design [4]. Essentially, a number of unavoidable physical and chemical phenomena, such as silicon lattice imperfections, uneven distribution of dopants, imperfect mask alignment, and non-uniform chemical mechanical polishing, result in gates with sharply different characteristics [31]. Already in 45 nanometer technologies, it is common that the delay of the same gate in different ICs differs by 1/3 from the nominal value and that leakage power differs by factor of 20. Note that while in 1 micron technology, each transistor had a million dopants, in 45 nanometers, the number is only a few hundred [31]. Therefore, even small variations have pronounced impact. In future technologies, this situation is bound to become even more significant. In addition, if the goal is to intentionally create high and unreproducable manufacturing variability, variable exposition to strong light can further enhance MV by at least two orders of magnitude [26].

Gate-level Characterization. Gate-level characterization is a process of characterizing each gate of an IC in terms of its physical properties such as gate width, gate length, and thickness of oxide or its manifestation properties such as delay, leakage power, and switching power. An important observation is that if the physical properties are known, it is straightforward to calculate the manifestation properties and vice versa [23]. There are two main and orthogonal approaches for gate characterization. The first focuses on direct measurement of physical parameters using sophisticated microscopes [10]. The second one measures global delays between flip-flops or static or dynamic power for different input vectors and uses various techniques for solving systems of equations under various assumptions to find individual gate characteristics [33,18,1].

The advantage of the first approach is that one can directly measure all gates on each IC regardless of design structure. However, the approach is very expensive and slow and requires wafer-level inspection, which has significant potential for damage. On the other hand, the second approach is fast, inexpensive, and can be applied on packaged ICs, but sometimes a fraction of gates can not be characterized.

While these efforts address gate-level characterization of an arbitrary IC, Dabiri et al. [8] have developed a specialized architecture that enables complete and accurate characterization of all gates even in presence of significant error measurements. Their technique combines statistical modeling and convex programming for very accurate gate-level characterization. Our architecture design is even better suited to this technique than their requirements, so it is assumed this technique is used for characterization.

Stability. Increases in temperature may significantly increase the delay of pertinent gates. Supply voltage has even greater impact, quadratic on switching power and linear on delay [23]. The surrounding environment and operational conditions may significantly alter the nominal manifestation parameters of each gate, sometimes even in different ways for different gates.

In order to preserve the correctness of our hardware-based cryptography approach, we use three approaches, two synthetic and one operational. First, we place all gates as close as possible and supply them by the same part of the power/ground networks so that the differential impact of manufacturing variability is minimized. Second, we place several delay paths that consist only of inverters and multiplexers that can be rapidly characterized interleaved with the PPUF circuitry. Our cryptographic procedure is invoked only when no or consistent delay changes are detected on these delay paths.

4   Public Physically Unclonable Functions (PPUFs)

We begin with a description of a PPUF and its operation. Later sections demonstrate the cost of simulation in the general case, how to ensure correct operation under a variety of conditions, and technological trends related to PPUFs.

4.1   Description

As defined earlier, a PPUF is a physical system that is unclonable due to its structural complexity, yet whose simulation is feasible, although requiring large time to do so. We describe how to create a simple circuit meeting these criteria.

A PPUF is a rectangular array of gates of size $w \times h$ (Figure 2). Inputs are fed into the bottom row, and outputs are read from the top row. Each intermediate row feeds the next, with each gate having b inputs from the previous row.

Due to manufacturing variability, the delay through each gate will vary by a significant percentage from its neighbors. Furthermore, because of the transistor-level construction of gates, the delay through any given gate for each of its inputs will differ. Thus, as demonstrated in §1, there will be many transitions on the output before the circuit reaches steady state.

In order to operate a PPUF, we need three values: x_0, the previous input; x_1, the input; and t, the output time. We assume that the circuit has reached steady state with input x_0 before x_1 arrives. x_1 is input to the circuit, and we clock the circuit at precisely time t to read the output. This is the final output of the PPUF.

This circuit is a physically unclonable function (PUF) because its output is heavily dependent on manufacturing variability in the delay of its gates. This is inherently unfeasible to replicate with the same manufacturing technology. This circuit is public, however, because given the delay of each gates it can be simulated. As we'll see in the next section, this requires exponential time in the height of the circuit.

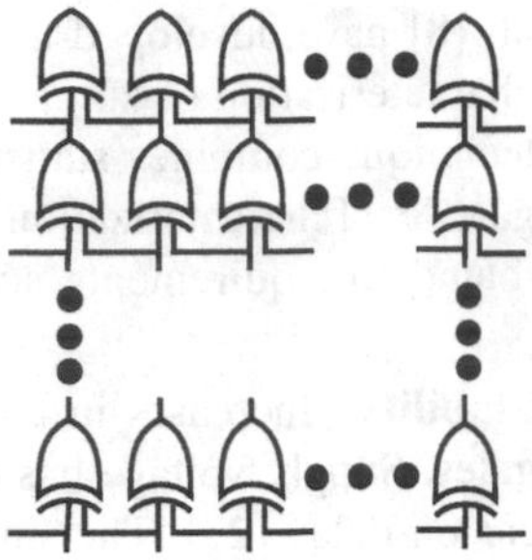

Fig. 2. A canonical PPUF circuit

4.2 Simulation Analysis

We now analyze the simulation cost of a PPUF. We first do a simple analysis assuming all gates are XORs. Then we present a serious flaw with using XOR/XNOR gates and how to negotiate that issue.

Cost Analysis Using XOR. Consider the simulation of the PPUF on input x_1. We must first calculate the state of the circuit when x_0 arrives. Because the circuit has reached steady state, this computation is trivial to perform by going through every row of the PPUF, starting at the input, and computing its output based on the output of the previous level. This can be done in linear time on the number of gates. But because the output of the PPUF is measured before the circuit reaches steady state, simulation is no longer so simple.

We proceed using dynamic programming to compute the timings of transitions for every gate at each level. Because the gates are XORs, a transition on the input will correspond to a transition on the output. We calculate the output level-by-level, as before, except now we must track much more information. We must record every transition that occurs at each level, because the timing that ultimately appears at time t could originate from any of large number of timings from intermediate gates. (There are exponentially many paths from an intermediate gate to an output gate, each with unique delay.)

We therefore measure the simulation cost of a PPUF as the number of transitions on the output and intermediate gates. We assume that x_1 and x_0 are independently selected — that is, the probability of transition between any bit of x_1 and x_0 is $\frac{1}{2}$. Let N_i be the number of transitions at row i in the PPUF. Let n_i be the number of transitions for a *single* gate at level i.

$$N_i = wn_i \tag{1}$$

$$n_i = bn_{i-1} \tag{2}$$

Since the delay from each input of a *single* gate to the output is unique and inputs are random, $\mathbb{E}(n_0) = \frac{1}{2}$. Finally, the expected number of transitions at level i is,

$$\mathbb{E}(N_i) = \frac{1}{2}wb^i \tag{3}$$

The simulation cost of the entire PPUF is measured at level h, $\mathbb{E}(N_h) = \frac{wb^h}{2}$. The simulation cost is exponential in the height of the PPUF. This model agrees extremely well with simulation under the above assumptions.

Table 4. "Good" 3-input gates

Input	A	B	C	D
000	0	0	1	1
001	0	1	0	1
010	1	1	0	0
011	0	0	0	1
100	1	1	0	0
101	0	0	1	0
110	1	1	1	1
111	1	0	1	0

(a) Truth tables

Value	A	B	C	D
B_1	0.5	0.5	1.0	1.0
B_2	0.5	0.5	0.5	0.5
B_3	0.5	1.0	0.5	0.5
B	1.5	2.0	2.0	2.0

(b) Transition rates

Problems with XOR. Until now, we have made a dangerous assumption: gates toggle their output whenever there is a transition on their input. This assumption is valid for XOR and XNOR, but it allows for more efficient simulation of the PPUF, ruining our exponential advantage.

The idea is that if the output toggles at every input transition, then we can easily compute the output transitions for any input based on the transitions generated by each bit of the input. These can in turn be precomputed and sorted, giving logarithmic search time per input. This reduces the simulation time to linear on the size of the circuit.

Let T_i be the set of output transition timings that occur when only input i toggles. This is well-defined because although the output may vary, the timing of transitions will be the same regardless of the previous state of the circuit. Let $a = a_1...a_w$ be an input to the PPUF. (Assume that previously the input was 0, so $a_i = 1$ if and only if the ith input toggles). Then the set of output timings generated by a is $T_a = \cup_{i:a_i=1} T_i$.

We can now use T_a to compute the output at any time after a arrives. First, we compute the output before a arrives in linear time. Then, to compute the output at time t after a arrives, we must know the number of output transitions occurring before t in T_a. This can be computed by summing the number from each T_i. Assuming that each T_i has been precomputed and sorted, this takes $O(\log(b^h)) = O(h \log(b))$. There are w inputs, giving overall simulation cost of $O(wh \log(b))$.

Fortunately, this approach is easily foiled. We can break the key assumption by using a more complicated truth table than XOR. We design the gate so that it has equal numbers of 0's and 1's on the output — this keeps the probability of each $\frac{1}{2}$ for each output, uniformly dividing the PPUF's output through the number space[1]. However, the only 2-input gates that have this property are XOR, XNOR, and functions of a single input, so we must move to at least 3-input gates.

There are many 3-input gates that meet our needs of (i) having equal numbers of 0's and 1's on the output, (ii) depending on all inputs, and (iii) having "complex" output behavior (not toggling on every input transition). Table 4a gives some examples.

---

[1] This isn't completely true, because gates share inputs and therefore aren't independent. Simulation indicates that before the circuit reaches steady state, it is still approximately correct.

Revised Cost Analysis. We must reassess the cost analysis if we use gates that do not always toggle on an input transition. Previously, in Eq. (2) we multiplied n_{i-1} by b because we assumed each input transition produced an output transition. We must replace this with the *expected number of output transitions per input transition* for the gate.

Define B_i as the expected number of output transitions when input i is toggled, and C_i the number of possible transitions if input i is toggled. Clearly, $B_i = \frac{C_i}{2^b}$.[2] For XOR and XNOR, $C_i = 2^b$ and $B_i = 1$ for all i. Now define B as the expected number of output transitions per input transition, $B = \sum_{i=1}^{b} B_i$. Eq. (2) and (3) become (assuming homogenous gates),

$$\mathbb{E}(n_i) = Bn_{i-1} \tag{4}$$

$$\mathbb{E}(N_i) = \frac{1}{2}wB^i \tag{5}$$

Our advantage remains exponential, although slightly diminished. Table 4b gives values of B_i and B for gates in Table 4a. We wrote a simulator for PPUFs of several gate types, and results agreed with the growth rates calculated for each type of gate.

4.3   Limiting Simulation Cost

This section describes a small modification to the PPUF that allows for much less expensive simulation for the simulating party in the secret key exchange protocol (§5).

As indicated in the example (§1), it will be useful to find ways to limit the cost of simulation, so long as doing so does not proportionally reduce the simulation time for an attacker. One such method is to compute a single output gate of the PPUF instead of the complete output. This requires computing a large fraction of the previous rows, but since simulation cost increases exponentially with the height of the circuit, we still save the majority of simulation cost.

This gives us a single bit as the output of the PPUF. This isn't sufficient for our purposes, because we need to be able use the output of the PPUF to distinguish between many different inputs. In order to increase the size of the output, we can simply include the output of several previous rows feeding the final output (Figure 3). These will be mapped through a hash function so that their inclusion does not provide third parties any additional information or enable them to short-circuit the simulation.

Optimistically, we are computing one of w outputs, so we should expect $\frac{1}{w}$ reduced simulation cost. But this ignores the cost of simulating the previous rows, which reduces the savings. Summing over the previous rows, it can be shown that the reduction is roughly $\frac{2}{w}$.

---

[2] Because we have equal numbers of 0's and 1's from each gate and the PPUF's input is assumed to be random, we can assume that the input to each gate will also be random. So for each possible input transition, we can average over all possible inputs.

4.4   Fault Tolerance

A major practical concern in the operation of PPUFs is the timing of the output. With exponential growth in the number of output transitions and the extremely fast operation of circuitry, the mean time between output transitions is tremendously small. Section 2 discussed the state of the art in measurement accuracy. This section presents a few algorithmic techniques to mitigate the problem.

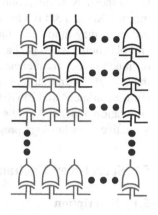

Fig. 3. Inputs "feeding" a PPUF output

There are a number of strategies to increase our ability to clock the output at the proper time. The circuit can be clocked multiple times (both simultaneously and in separate computations), with each measurement "voting" on the final value of the output. This reduces the impact of changing conditions, such as temperature.

More significantly, note that the simulating party is at a distinct advantage. Because the output timings are somewhat randomly distributed, there will be intervals that are much larger than the mean interval time. The simulating party can choose a time that has an unusually long stable interval.

Finally, note that the maturation of developing technologies (§2 and [13,7,2,14,25]) could eliminate this problem as a practical consideration entirely. With accuracy in the attosecond range, combined with the techniques already mentioned, the simulation cost of a PPUF could be raised as high as practically desirable.

4.5   Technological Trends

Any security techniques must be evaluated against technological trends. Although any strategy for predicting the future is inherently risky, it appears that essentially all technological trends favor hardware-based cryptography and security techniques. First of all, rapid progress in high-speed imaging technologies and micro/nano sensing will make side channel attacks even more effective and widespread. Also, the proliferation of horizontal integrated circuit business models where design tools, design, manufacturing, testing, and integration are done by different untrusted companies will increase the danger of hardware Trojan horses and hidden channels. Finally, application trends favor mobile systems where their physical security will be significantly lower.

We believe that six technology trends will have major impact on PPUFs and our new cryptography and security approach: higher levels of VLSI integration, smaller feature sizes, increasingly difficult cooling, new interconnect and input/output technologies, and more economically viable and accurate time measurement technologies.

Higher integration levels have two main ramifications: larger PPUFs and faster simulation. The main consequence is a rapidly increasing execution-simulation gap due to increased PPUF parallelism. Finer feature sizes have three qualitatively novel ramifications: the transistor will not be additionally faster, switching power will begin to increase slowly, and leakage power will become dominant [35]. The net consequence is that thermal management will become more difficult and will effectively reduce simulation speed. New interconnect technologies such as nanowires, photonic crystals, plasmonics, RF, and 3D ICs have potential to increase I/O and data transfer rates by several orders of magnitude and, therefore, favor simulation. However, photonic crystals [29] and plasmonic wires [27] are even more sensitive to manufacturing variability, operate on much higher frequencies, are more complex to simulate, and will greatly increase the execution-simulation gap. In summary, new technologies will keep increasing the simulation speed and PPUF realized in today's technologies will be more susceptible to simulation attacks. At the same time, PPUF-based techniques will become even more attractive as technology progresses.

5   Secret Key Exchange with PPUFs

5.1   Description

We enable two parties, A and B, to exchange a secret key. We assume that A is in possession of a PPUF. B is the "simulating party" who uses the public description of A's PPUF to simulate its output for some input.

The basic idea of the protocol is simple: We consider a range of numbers of size n. B selects some number, x, from this range and simulates the PPUF on this input. B sends the output, y, to A. A then searches through all n numbers until x is found. The full protocol has a few twists to make it work correctly with PPUFs as they are described above and to get a few other useful properties.

Before describing the detailed protocol, we go over a few fundamentals. One way this protocol could be attacked is to precompute the output of the PPUF for every possible input. This is easy to prevent by choosing the secret key, x, to be a fairly long number, say 1024 bits. This would require 2^{1024} bits of storage, which is completely infeasible[3].

Another concern is that we use the output of the PPUF to distinguish between different x, but there might be collisions, leading to false matches and incorrect results. This is addressed in the same fashion by using a long enough output so that the probability of a collision is negligible[4]. Both technique come at very little hardware cost in the PPUF.

The protocol is as follows:

1. B simulates values.
   (a) B randomly selects x_0 from $0...2^w$, where w is input width of the PPUF.
   (b) B selects $x_1...x_m$ from $x_0...x_0 + n$, where n is computed as in §5.2.
   (c) B applies a hashing function, f, to compute $z_1 = f(x_1)...z_m = f(x_m)$.
   (d) B simulates $z_1...z_m$ on A's PPUF, starting with x_0 as the initial input, and timing at $t_1...t_m$. This produces outputs $y_1...y_m$.
2. B sends x_0, m, n, $y_1...y_m$, and $t_1...t_m$ to A.
3. A finds $x_1...x_m$.

---

[3] Actually, it requires much more. One would need to store the PPUF output for all inputs of the form (x_0, x_1, t).

[4] The output of each bit of the PPUF is 0 or 1 with equal probability, as described earlier (§4). Therefore the output is distributed uniformly through the output space, and increasing the length of the output exponentially drops the chance of collisions.

(a) A iterates over each $x \in (x_0, x_0 + n)$.
(b) A computes $z = f(x)$.
(c) A runs the PPUF with x_0 as the steady-state input, z as the input, and clocking at each $t_1...t_m$.
(d) If the output at time t_i equals y_i, then store x as x_i.
(e) Halt when all $x_1...x_m$ are found.
4. A and B concatenate $z_1...z_m$ to form the secret key.

The two new elements of the protocol are the multiple values, m, and the hashing function, f. We use multiple values in order to reduce the variance in the protocol. When a single value is sent, then the search time for A or any attacker has large variance. This is undesirable if we are trying to achieve a specific level of security or allocate a set amount of work for A. By sending more values, we increase the expected fraction of the number space that must be searched and, more importantly, significantly reduce the variance.

We also apply a hashing function, f, to each value before sending it to the PPUF. This is because using partial simulation (§4.3), the PPUF's output doesn't depend on all of its inputs. By selecting from a range $x_0...x_0 + n$, we will have many bits that are shared between numbers. Therefore, the output of the PPUF might no longer be unique, greatly increasing the odds of collisions on the output. By applying a hashing function, we ensure that the bits of the input will be different for each x_i and therefore the output of the PPUF will be unique (with extraordinarily high probability). There are many ways of achieving the same effect — for example, defining $x_i = f^i(x_0)$, or having the output of x_{i-1} be the steady-state input for x_i.

5.2   Analysis

The advantage of this protocol comes because an attacker does not know which values have been selected, nor does he have A's PPUF to enable fast searching. He therefore must search the $x_0...x_0 + n$ values, simulating each, to find each x_i. Even with fairly small m, he will have to search the majority of the n numbers. So his disadvantage over B is roughly n, and his disadvantage over A is roughly κ, the cost of simulation.

More specifically, let W_A be the expected work for the owner of the PPUF. Here, work is normalized to the cost of computing the output of the PPUF. Similarly, W_B is the expected work for the simulating party, and W_O is the expected work for an observer (attacker). If $W_A \neq W_B$, then the effective computational advantage over an attacker is the minimum of either advantage. This imposes the constraint $W_A = W_B$.

The owner of the PPUF's work is dominated by the search for $x_1...x_m$. So W_A is simply the amount of numbers that must be searched to find all x_i. Using simple probability, $W_A = \frac{m}{m+1}n$. Similarly, the simulating party's work is dominated by simulation and $W_B = m\kappa$. This yields,

$$n = (m+1)\kappa \tag{6}$$

The work for an attacker is the same expected number of computations, except each is a simulation of the PPUF.

$$W_O = \frac{mn}{m+1} \cdot \kappa = \frac{W_A{}^2}{m} \tag{7}$$

The attacker performs quadratically more computation than either communicating party.

Including partial simulation (§4.3), W_B is reduced by a factor of $\sim \frac{2}{w}$. This changes the results to,[5]

$$n = \frac{2}{w}\kappa(m+1) \tag{8}$$

$$W_O = \frac{mn}{m+1}\kappa = \frac{w}{2}\frac{W_A^2}{m} \tag{9}$$

Finally, note that the network requirements of this protocol are minimal. We send $2m+1$ values of length w and two fairly small integers. Because m is fairly small, network requirements are no more than 1 kB.

5.3   Practical Performance

This section gives numbers to the equations above and shows the advantage that can be practically gained. Pessimistically assuming that the PPUF operates in the cycle time of a general purpose processor, simulation takes κ cycles. Due to inherent parallelism in the simulation and the availability of multicores, the simulating party should have roughly 10 GHz, or 10^{10} cycles per second of computational power.

If $m = 3$ numbers are simulated and the simulating party takes 10^3 seconds (fifteen minutes) to simulate, then this gives the simulating party roughly $3 \cdot 10^{12}$ cycles of simulation per number. Assuming a PPUF with $w \approx 10^4$ (much less than could be achieved with modern silicon manufacturing technology), the simulation cost is $\kappa \approx 1.7 \cdot 10^{16}$ cycles[6]. The owner of the PPUF should search $n \approx 10^{13}$ numbers, which is obvious since $W_A = W_B$, and the simulating party spends $10^{10} \cdot 10^3 = 10^{13}$ cycles. The attacker must perform $W_O = 1.7 \cdot 10^{29}$ cycles of simulation on average to find the secret key.

Studies indicate that there are no more than one billion computers in the world [15]. The vast majority of these computers are incapable of 10 GHz of computation, but for argument we will assume that each is as powerful as the simulating party's. Then the computational throughput of an attacker has an upper bound of 10^{19} cycles per second. An attacker would take $1.7 \cdot 10^{10}$ seconds, or 528 years to break this protocol.

Throughout this example we have been extremely generous to the attacker. In reality, the security of the scheme is several orders of magnitude better than claimed.

6   Conclusion

We have developed a new approach for exchange of secret keys and public key cryptography. We use the novel notion of a public physical unclonable function and its

---

[5] Since $m \ll n$, the majority of simulations performed by an attacker are unsuccessful and he must simulate all outputs, increasing the cost by a factor of two. This also accounts for the reduction in W_B.

[6] Note that this does not exactly correspond to $N_h = \kappa$ (see Eq (3)), as there are constant factors that require much more than one cycle to process a single transition in the PPUF.

implementation via integrated circuits implementation where easily measured delays of PPUF gates serve as public key. The approach is intrinsicly resilient against physical and side channel attacks due to physical laws and technological constraints that prevent PPUF cloning.

References

1. Alkabani, Y., Massey, T., Koushanfar, F., Potkonjak, M.: Input vector control for post-silicon leakage current minimization in the presence of manufacturing variability. In: Design Automation Conference, pp. 606–609 (2008)
2. Baltuska, A., Udem, T., Uiberacker, M., Hentschel, M., Goulielmakis, E., Gohle, C., Holzwarth, R., Yakovlev, V., Scrinzi, A., Hansch, T., Krausz, F.: Attosecond control of electronic processes by intense light fields. Nature 421, 611–615 (2003)
3. Bauder, D.: An anti-counterfeiting concept for currency systems. Technical report, Sandia National Labs, Albuquerque, NM (1983)
4. Bernstein, K., Frank, D., Gattiker, A., Haensch, W., Ji, B., Nassif, S.R., Nowak, E., Pearson, D., Rohrer, N.: High-performance cmos variability in the 65-nm regime and beyond. IBM Journal of Research and Development 50(4/5), 433–449 (2006)
5. Biham, E., Shamir, A.: Differential cryptanalysis of des-like cryptosystems. Journal of Cryptology 4(1), 3–72 (1991)
6. Chen, Y., Mihcak, M., Kirovski, D.: Certifying authenticity via fiber-infused paper. ACM SIGecom Exchanges 5(3), 29–37 (2005)
7. Corkum, P., Krausz, F.: Attosecond science. Nature Physics 3(6), 381–387 (2007)
8. Dabiri, F., Potkonjak, M.: Hardware aging-based software metering. In: The Design, Automation, and Test in Europe (2009)
9. Diffie, W., Hellman, M.: New directions in cryptography. IEEE Transactions on Information Theory IT-22, 644–654 (1976)
10. Friedberg, P., Cao, Y., Cain, J., Wang, R., Rabaey, J., Spanos, C.: Modeling within-die spatial correlation effects for process-design co-optimization. In: Proceedings of the 6th International Symposium on Quality of Electronic Design, pp. 516–521 (2005)
11. Gassend, B., Clarke, D., van Dijk, M., Devadas, S.: Silicon physical random functions. In: Proceedings of the 9th ACM conference on Computer and communications security, pp. 148–160 (2002)
12. Goldreich, O.: Foundations of Cryptography, vol. 1. Cambridge University Press, Cambridge (2001)
13. Goulielmakis, E., Yakovlev, V., Cavalieri, A., Uiberacker, V.P.M., Apolonski, A., Kienberger, R., Kleineberg, U., Krausz, F.: Attosecond control and measurement: Lightwave electronics. Science 317, 769–775 (2007)
14. Gustafsson, E., Ruchon, T., Swoboda, M., Remetter, T., Pourtal, E., Lpez-Martens, R., Balcou, P., L'Huillier, A.: Broadband attosecond pulse shaping. Physical Review A 76(1) (2007)
15. In 2008 the number of personal computers will reach billion (2008), http://www.science.portal.org/in/71 (accessed on February 15, 2009)
16. Kalisz, J.: Review of methods for time interval measurements with picosecond resolution. Metrologia 41(1), 17–32 (2004)
17. Kocher, P.C.: Timing attacks on implementations of diffie-hellman, rsa, dss, and other systems. In: Koblitz, N. (ed.) CRYPTO 1996. LNCS, vol. 1109, pp. 104–113. Springer, Heidelberg (1996)
18. Koushanfar, F., Boufounos, P., Shamsi, D.: Post-silicon timing characterization by compressed sensing. In: IEEE/ACM International Conference on Computer-Aided Design, pp. 185–189 (2008)

19. Koushanfar, F., Qu, G., Potkonjak, M.: Intellectual property metering. In: Moskowitz, I.S. (ed.) IH 2001. LNCS, vol. 2137, pp. 87–102. Springer, Heidelberg (2001)
20. Lofstrom, K., Daasch, W.R., Taylor, D.: Ic identification circuit using device mismatch. In: IEEE International Solid-State Circuits Conference, pp. 372–373 (2000)
21. Majzoobi, M., Koushanfar, F., Potkonjak, M.: Lightweight secure puf. In: IEEE/ACM International Conference on Computer Aided Design (2008)
22. Majzoobi, M., Koushanfar, F., Potkonjak, M.: Testing techniques for hardware security. In: IEEE International Test Conference (2008)
23. Martin, S., Flautner, K., Mudge, T., Blaauw, D.: Combined dynamic voltage scaling and adaptive body biasing for lower power microprocessors under dynamic workloads. In: IEEE/ACM international conference on Computer-aided design, November 10-14, pp. 721–725 (2002)
24. Menezes, A., van Oorschot, P., Vanstone, S.: Handbook of Applied Cryptography. CRC Press, Boca Raton (1996)
25. Mysyrowicz1, A., Couairon, A., Keller, U.: Self-compression of optical laser pulses by filamentation. New J. Phys. 10, 1–14 (2008)
26. Neureuther, A.: Personal Communication (November 2007)
27. Ozbay, E.: Plasmonics: Merging photonics and electronics at nanoscale dimensions. Science 311, 189–193 (2006)
28. Pappu, R., Recht, B., Taylor, J., Gershenfeld, N.: Physical one-way functions. Science 297(5589), 2026–2030 (2002)
29. Photonic Crystals: Molding the Flow of Light, 2nd edn. Princeton University Press, Princeton (2008)
30. Rivest, R., Shamir, A., Adleman, L.: A method for obtaining digital signatures and public-key cryptosystems. Communications of the ACM 21(2), 120–126 (1978)
31. Roy, S., Asenov, A.: Where do the dopants go? Science 309(5733), 388–390 (2005)
32. Schneier, B.: Applied Cryptography: Protocols, Algorithms, and Source Code in C. John Wiley, Chichester (1996)
33. Shamsi, D., Boufounos, P., Koushanfar, F.: Noninvasive leakage power tomography of integrated circuits by compressive sensing. In: International symposium on Low power electronics and design, pp. 341–346 (2008)
34. Skorobogatov, S.P., Anderson, R.J.: Optical fault induction attacks. In: Kaliski Jr., B.S., Koç, Ç.K., Paar, C. (eds.) CHES 2002. LNCS, vol. 2523, pp. 2–12. Springer, Heidelberg (2003)
35. Thompson, S., Packan, P., Bohr, M.: Mos scaling: Transistor challenges for the 21st century. Intel Technology Journal, Q3, 1–19 (1998)

SVD-Based Ghost Circuitry Detection

Michael Nelson[1], Ani Nahapetian[1], Farinaz Koushanfar[2], and Miodrag Potkonjak[1]

[1] Computer Science Department, UCLA, Los Angeles, CA 90095, USA
{ani,miodrag}@cs.ucla.edu
[2] Computer Science Department, Electrical and Computer Engineering Department,
Rice University, Houston, 77005 TX
farinaz@cs.rice.edu

Abstract. Ghost circuitry (GC) insertion is the malicious addition of hardware in the specification and/or implementation of an IC by an attacker intending to change circuit functionality. There are numerous GC insertion sources, including untrusted foundries, synthesis tools and libraries, testing and verification tools, and configuration scripts. Moreover, GC attacks can greatly compromise the security and privacy of hardware users, either directly or through interaction with pertinent systems, application software, or with data. GC detection is a particularly difficult task in modern and pending deep submicron technologies due to intrinsic manufacturing variability. Here, we provide algebraic and statistical approaches for the detection of ghost circuitry. A singular value decomposition (SVD)-based technique for gate characteristic recovery is applied to solve a system of equations created using fast and non-destructive measurements of leakage power and/or delay. This is then combined with statistical constraint manipulation techniques to detect embedded ghost circuitry. The effectiveness of the approach is demonstrated on the ISCAS 85 benchmarks.

Keywords: Hardware Trojan horses, gate characterization, singular value decomposition, manufacturing variability.

1 Introduction

Ghost circuitry (GC) insertion is an intentional hardware alteration of the design specification and IC implementation. The alterations only affect the circuit's functionality in a few specific circumstances and are hidden otherwise. GC is more difficult to detect than design bugs or manufacturing faults, since it is intentionally implanted to be unperceivable by the current debugging and testing methodologies and tools. The vast number of possibilities for inserting GC further complicates detection.

In a GC insertion attack, the adversary adds one or more gates such that the functionality of the design is altered. The gates can be added so that no timing path between primary inputs and flip-flops (FFs) and primary outputs and FFs is altered. However, leakage power is always altered. Even if the attacker gates the added circuitry, the gating requires an additional gate.

Our goal here is to detect the insertion of GC, specifically added gates, in the face of low controllability and observability of gates. However, the GC detection approach

S. Katzenbeisser and A.-R. Sadeghi (Eds.): IH 2009, LNCS 5806, pp. 221–234, 2009.

is generic enough that it can easily be retargeted to other circuit components, such as interconnect by considering more comprehensive timing and/or power models. The main technical obstacle to GC detection is manufacturing variability, which can have a significant impact on gate timing and power characteristics across ICs.

The basis for our approach is gate-level characterization using a set of non-destructive timing and/or power measurements. The measurements are treated as a set of linear equations and are processed using singular value decomposition (SVD) to fingerprint the circuit. The detection of additional ghost circuitry is carried out by imposing additional constraints on the linear equations in such a way that the results indicate whether circuitry was added. Essentially, we ask if the characterization of gates is significantly more consistent under the assumption of added circuitry.

Gate-level characterization (GLC) has emerged as a premier synthesis, analysis, watermarking, cryptography, and security task in current and even more pending deep submicron silicon technologies subject to manufacturing variability. Two major GLC ramifications are widely addressed post-silicon customization where the pertinent integrated circuit (IC) is differently operated as a function of its gate-level characteristics and design under uncertainty where the design is synthesized in such a way that the consequent impact of manufacturing variability is considered and compensated. Hardware and in particular gate-level and physical design watermarking is greatly impacted in at least two ways: through potential negative impact on the performance overhead and sharply increased detection difficulty. Recently, it has been shown that GLC can be used for hardware-based secret and public-key cryptography that eliminates physical and side channel attacks. Finally, manufacturing variability greatly complicates the defense against hardware security attacks such as gate resizing and addition of GC. In gate resizing, the attacker changes the size of one or more gates in such a way that under general or specific circumstances (e.g. a specific input vectors) the energy consumption is excessive or timing correctness is violated.

While all of the itemized tasks are of paramount importance, our primary goal is detection of gate resizing and GC hardware attacks. The emphasis is on GLC that directly solves gate resizing attack by calculating their power, timing, and other characteristics. GLC, augmented with statistical techniques, is also basis for GC detection.

In the remainder of the paper, we present some background on manufacturing variability, gate-level characterization, and ghost circuitry detection. Then we present our SVD-based approach for carrying out gate-level characterization and the related simulation results. Finally, we present the ghost circuitry detection approaches utilizing the gate-level characterization obtained from our procedure, which incorporates SVD and some post-processing of the results.

2 Related Work

Manufacturing variability is the result of intense CMOS technology scaling, which results in a high degree of variability across ICs from the same design and even from the same wafer, with regards to gate sizing, power consumption, and timing characteristics. A new generation of security techniques based on manufacturing variability (MV) has been developed [8][9][12].

Gate level characterization in the face of manufacturing variability has been examined before in other settings and with other techniques, but some important extensions and differences exist in our work. [18] and [19] use compressed sensing to determine gate level characteristics: power and timing, respectively. However, they make a simplifying assumption necessary for employing their technique; specifically that manufacturing variability is correlated across adjacent gates. In practice, the implantation of dopants is done individually which results in weak local correlation. Our techniques make no assumptions about the correlation of manufacturing variability across gates, and thus our approach is more robust and realistic. [17] uses convex programming to determine gate level characteristics. Its applicability is limited to butterfly networks, where a path exists from each input to each output. [15] and [16] utilize a linear programming approach, whereas, our work uses singular value decomposition (SVD), post-processing of results, and most importantly utilization of gate characterization for GC detection.

Manufacturing variability aware gate-level characterization can be used to optimize manufacturing yield, carry out remote enabling and disabling of ICs [25], determine higher quality IC for appropriate distribution [8], in addition to its applicability to ghost circuitry detection.

Kuhn [23] presents ghost circuitry detection strategies that utilize mask comparison. In our attack model we assume that the embedding of the ghost circuitry is carried with the aim of obfuscating the embedding as manufacturing variability. Additionally, we do not assume that we have access to the masks, as the foundry may be a source of the GC insertion.

3 Preliminaries

3.1 Manufacturing Variability Model

Manufacturing variations are due to the intense industrial CMOS feature scaling. With scaling of feature sizes, the physical limits of the devices are reached and uncertainty in the device size increases [5]. Variations in transistor feature sizes and thus, in gate characteristics, e.g., delay or power, are inevitable. In present and pending technologies, the variation is large compared to the device dimensions. As a result, VLSI circuits exhibit a high variability in both delay and power consumption. In this work, manufacturing variation in gates is modeled as a multiplicative scaling factor.

3.2 Measurement Model

To carry out the ghost circuitry detection using gate level characterization, a limited number of nondestructive measurements are taken. After manufacturing, the original design is available, and it is possible to provide input vectors to the input pins of the manufactured chip and obtain the respective outputs from the output pins. Additionally, it is possible to measure the IC's leakage power consumption. To measure the individual path delays, an input vector is provided to the IC, and then a single input bit is flipped. With knowledge of the IC design, the delay incurred between the input vector application and the output vector change can be used to calculate the delay value of the path.

We assume that it is possible to have measurement error in every single measurement taken, i.e. every single application of an input vector and measurement of it power and delay characteristics at the output. This error, however, has shown to be small on the order of 1% as cited in selected previous literature [24][26]. We model this value in our linear equations and have examined a uniform model for the measurement error in our work.

Generally, the model may be affected by aging and temperature. However, as these circuits are tested shortly after fabrication, aging is not a factor. Temperature is a factor, but normalization with repeated measurements can handle this. Additionally, control of environmental factors such as room temperature and working from cold boot can eliminate the variation that may be witnessed in the circuit behavior due to temperature variation across measurements. The measurements are made in a control environment after fabrication, so it is very easy to eliminate factors such as humidity, dust, presence of electromagnetic radiation, etc.

3.3 Threat Model

Since semiconductor manufacturing demands a large capital investment, the role of contract foundries has dramatically grown, increasing exposure to theft of masks, attacks by insertion of malicious circuitry, and unauthorized excess fabrication [1]. The development of hardware security techniques is difficult due to reasons that include limited controllability and observability (50,000+ gates for each I/O pin in modern designs) [7], large size and complexity (the newest Intel processor has 2.06B transistors), variety of components (e.g., clock, clock distribution interconnect, and finite state machine), unavoidable design bugs, possibility of attacks by non-physically connected circuitry (e.g., using crosstalk and substrate noise), many potential attack sources (e.g. hardware IP providers, CAD tools, and foundries), potentially sophisticated and well-funded attackers (foundries and foreign governments), and manufacturing variability that makes each IC coming from the same design unique [5][11].

In this paper, we assume the attackers can embedded ghost circuitry, even as little as a single gate. This insertion can occur at various stages of the IC manufacturing process, including through CAD tools, through the use of outside IP, and at the foundry during the fabrication process. The attacker can carry out many different types of hardware attacks, including gate resizing, removing gates, and allowing crosstalk. However, in this paper, we consider ghost circuitry attacks that obtain information from the IC, implying that at least one gate is inserted.

4   Singular Value Decomposition for Gate-Level Characterization

4.1 Problem Formulation

Manufacturing variation in power and delay behavior of gates is modeled by associating each gate with a scaling factor, α, which multiplies both delay and leakage current. Measurements of total leakage power and path delay for various circuit inputs gives rise to linear equations with the scaling factors as the unknowns. Each set of measurements produces a linear system $Ga = m+e$ where

- a is the vector of scaling factors, also referred to as the α-values, and related to gate size
- $m+e$ is a vector of measured values
- m would be the measured value if there is no measurement error
- e is the measurement error associated with each measured value
- G is derived from the expected power and/or delay characteristics of the gates.

For N_g number of gates in the circuit and N_m number of measurements, G is $N_m \times N_g$, a is $N_g \times 1$, and m is $N_m \times 1$.

More abstractly, one can imagine the circuit's gate characteristics split into two components represented by G and a. G represents the characteristics of gate classes, i.e. 2-input NANDs power and delay characteristics for a given input vector, and it is inherent the circuit design. This information is readily available and in our experiments we have used the values provided by [21] for delay and [20] for leakage power.

The vector a, which is a vector of α-values for all the gates in the circuit, represents the unknowns in the equation. In other words, a is the fingerprint for the circuit just as the α-value is the fingerprint for the individual gate. Due to manufacturing variability, gate sizes are not exactly matched to the design specifications. The size of each gate in the circuit of each fabricated IC can have a variety of values. All circuits accordingly will have a large variety of sizes for most or all of their gates, and hence the extremely large combinations of possibility for a results in a unique fingerprint for each circuit.

Splitting each manufactured circuit into an invariant and into a variant component results in, G, which is universal across all circuits of the same design for the same set of input vectors, and a, which represents the unique characteristics of the fabricated circuit.

A large set of measurements are taken for the total circuit. As we can only access the input and output pins of the circuit, all the measurements made, represented by $m+e$, are made from a global circuit or path level and not at the individual gate level. Obviously, if we were able to measure these values at the gate level, we would easily be able to solve for each gate's α-value.

We do consider error in the formulation, as measurement error is possible when measuring total leakage power for the circuit and total delay along a path of the circuit from input to output pin. This is represented by e, which is the error that may be introduced in the measurement for each input vector or pair of input vectors.

A singular value decomposition $G = U\Sigma V^T$ is used in the following way. G^+, the pseudo-inverse of G, gives a least-squares solution to the system, a', an approximation of the scaling factors given the possibility of measurement errors being introduced. The procedure for fingerprinting circuits, i.e. determining the α-values as accurately as possible is the following: (1) Choose a set of circuit inputs. (2) Compute G and G^+. (3) Perform measurements on a circuit to produce $m+e$. (4) Compute the fingerprint $a' = G^+(m+e)$.

In this formulation, a' represents the fingerprint that we deciphered from the SVD. It does not necessarily match a, due to the measurement error and also due to gate correlations that hinder gate-level characterization.

In the next subsections, we provide not only the power and delay models, but also a complete example that we solve to demonstrate more clearly procedure followed to accomplish gate-level characterization.

4.2 Power Model

The total leakage power consumed by a circuit is the sum of the leakage power of its gates [20]. For a particular circuit input i and a measurement ML_i of total leakage power with input i, we have the equation, $\sum_g GL_{gi} \cdot \alpha_g = ML_i$ where GL_{gi} is the expected leakage current for gate g when the global input is i. Each equation contributes a row to G and an entry to m in the overall system, $Ga = m+e$.

Table 2 shows a matrix G computed from the example circuit in Figure 1, using input-dependent leakage values from Yuan and Qu [20], shown in Table 1.

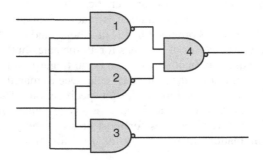

Fig. 1. Example circuit with NAND gates used to demonstrate SVD-based GLC

Table 1. Input-dependent leakage current for a 2-input NAND gate

00	37.84 nA
01	95.17nA
10	100.3 nA
11	454.5 nA

Table 2. Power matrix for example circuit given in Figure 1

Input	Gate 1	Gate 2	Gate 3	Gate 4
000	37.84	37.84	37.84	454.5
001	100.3	37.84	37.84	454.5
010	95.17	100.3	100.3	454.5
011	454.5	100.3	100.3	95.17
100	37.84	95.17	95.17	454.5
101	100.3	95.17	95.17	454.5
110	95.17	454.5	454.5	100.3
111	454.5	454.5	454.5	37.84

4.3 Delay Model

Total delay along paths through the circuit is measured by changing one input to the circuit and waiting for the change to propagate to the outputs. For a pair of circuit inputs i and j, the "before" and "after" inputs, zero or more output measurements will be made. For any measurement MD_p whose output is connected to the changed input by a unique path p, we have the equation

$$\sum_g GD_{gij} \cdot P_{gp} \cdot \alpha_g = MD_p$$

where GD_{gij} is the expected gate delay for gate g when the global input transitions from i to j, and P_{gp} is an indicator function (0 or 1) that tells whether gate g is on path p. Each equation contributes a row to G and an entry to $m+e$ in the overall system, Ga = m+e. Some output measurements will not have unique paths, and in this case, we do not know which path had the shortest delay, even though we do have a lower bound on the delay for these paths.

One can compute the matrix G for the example circuit in Figure 2.1, using delay values from Ercegovac, et. al. [21], shown in Table 3. There do exist newer models for delay characteristics of gates. Our model is independent of these values. In fact, the work can be easily be extended for new and changing model of gate characteristics in terms of delay, leakage power, or other gate characteristics.

Table 3. Delay for a 2-input NAND gate where L is the fanout

$0 \rightarrow 1$	0.05+0.038L ns
$1 \rightarrow 0$	0.08+0.027L ns

4.4 Computing α-Values

The equations generated from leakage and/or delay measurements are combined into the system, $Ga = m+e$. Again recall that N_g is the number of gates in the circuit, and N_m is the number of measurements. A singular value decomposition of G has the form $U\Sigma V^T$, where V is $Ng \times Ng$ and orthogonal, U is $N_m \times N_m$ and orthogonal, and Σ is $Nm \times Ng$ and diagonal; the entries on its diagonal are the singular values. The rank of G is equal to the number of nonzero singular values; by convention, we assume that the nonzero singular values are in the leftmost columns of Σ.

The pseudoinverse of G is $G^+ = V \Sigma^+ U^T$, where Σ^+ is derived from Σ by replacing each nonzero singular value σ with its inverse $1/\sigma$. Performing the multiplication $G^+(m+e)$ gives our fingerprint a', the vector in the column space of G for which the norm of $Ga' - (m+e)$ is minimized. The fingerprint vector a' has the following properties: (1) If G has rank N_g, then a' is an approximation of a. (2) If G has rank < N_g, then a' is an approximation of the portion of a which is not annihilated by G.

Table 4 shows an example a for the circuit in Figure 1. The measurement vector m computed from this a and the power matrix in Table 1 and the resulting fingerprint vector a'. Because this matrix is not full rank, some α-values are inaccurate, even though we did not add any measurement error.

As shown in Figure 1, gates 2 and 3 are both 2-input NANDs and they both have the same input vector in all possible measurements, as they both have by design the same input vectors. As a result, it is not possible to separately characterize gates 2 and 3 since their G matrix entries will be same for all inputs vectors. The best that is achievable is to characterize the sum of their α-values, which in this case is 2.050, and it has been properly characterized. This demonstrates how even without measurement error it is possible to not properly fingerprint a circuit in some cases.

Table 4. α-value fingerprint obtained for example circuit

a	m	a'
1.015	537.4	1.015
1.103	600.7	1.025
0.9473	723.6	1.025
0.9271	755.0	0.9271
	654.9	
	718.2	
	1121	
	1428	

The task of determining the inputs vectors applied for which measurements are taken is not as straightforward as it seems. First, due to the prohibitive size of the input vector domain, an exhaustive search can only applied to the smallest of circuits. Secondly, certain input vectors will maximize the solution quality, while others may be redundant or even obfuscate the true value. For large circuits, a set of input vectors must be chosen that maximizes the rank of G. We have used the following heuristics in our work in this paper. (1) Start with an empty G (2) Choose a random input vector and compute its matrix row 3) If the row is independent of the existing rows of G, add it to G (increasing G's rank) (4) Repeat from step (2).

Since we do not know the maximum possible rank in advance, this process must be repeated until some arbitrary stopping condition is met, such as some number of failed choices in a row. For numerical robustness, N_m should be larger than $rank(G)$, and more random inputs can be added afterward to accomplish this.

5 Gate-Level Characterization (GLC)

Simulations were performed on the ISCAS 85 benchmark circuits [19]. Though the benchmarks are combinatorial circuits, the approach can be extended to sequential circuits simply by scanning the flip-flops as we are doing with the outputs and inputs. Custom software was written in C++ to construct input sets and compute G.

Table 5 shows the number of solvable α-values for each input set. Not all values can be recovered due to gate correlations. Additionally, some sets of α-values can be thought of as a single unit; those for which the sum of the set is solvable, but none of the differences between members are.

Table 6 illustrates the average accuracy of SVD-based GLC results, for five ISCAS85 benchmarks and different measurement modalities. We vary the average percentage of the measurement error for leakage power, timing, and both power and

Table 5. Number of scaling factors for gates recoverable using SVD (Table entries marked n/a were not computed due to their prohibitive size)

Circuits	# of Gates	Power	Delay	Both
c432	160	80	139	153
c499	202	154	136	202
c880	383	113	164	383
c1355	546	18	116	408
c1908	880	26	354	559
c2670	1193	138	287	594
c3540	1669	101	202	N/A
c5315	2307	429	1057	N/A

Table 6. SVD-based GLC for leakage power, delay, and both power and delay, for five ISCAS85 different benchmarks

Accuracy of Recovered Scaling Factor Values (α-Values)				
Measure Err	0.1%	0.5%	1%	10%
c432 Power	0.059	0.295	0.584	5.90
c432 Delay	0.035	0.175	0.351	3.48
c432 Both	0.011	0.054	0.107	1.07
c499 Power	0.372	1.84	3.69	0.362
c499 Delay	0.012	0.060	0.121	1.19
c499 Both	0.009	0.043	0.085	0.852
c880 Power	1.78	8.76	0.179	0.018
c880 Delay	0.016	0.078	0.156	1.57
c880 Both	0.069	0.350	0.689	6.95
c1355 Power	1.24	6.32	0.126	0.013
c1355 Delay	0.056	0.281	0.554	5.56
c1355 Both	0.049	0.244	0.483	4.83
c1908 Power	0.865	4.20	8.72	0.867
c1908 Delay	0.136	0.679	1.34	0.135
c1908 Both	2.78	0.141	0.282	0.028

timing. The results indicate that the quality of GLC is better than the measurement error, implying a successful characterization of the α-values of benchmark circuit gates.

The experiments presented in Table 6 were improved dramatically by averaging the results over several runs. Table 7 shows our results after averaging 100 and 1000 runs, for three different measurement errors. The table's values demonstrate that with post-processing the results can be improved in terms of reducing the average GLC error. In some cases, the post-processing has an effect as large as a factor of 12 and in some cases it drives the error down to 0.

In Figure 2, we represent the result of varying the gate-size range. The graph demonstrates the accuracy with which we are able to characterize the gates, in terms of the average percentage of difference between the original value and the recovered gate size values. The x-axis represents the range of possible gate size values chosen randomly from the uniform range. This graph demonstrates that this variation does not affect the gate-level characterization. The small level of variation is due to the randomly chosen input vector values that actually have an impact on the gate-level characterization accuracy. The graph demonstrates that the level of manufacturing variability does not help or hurt our approach. Rather, the attacker requires the presence of manufacturing variability to help hide its ghost circuitry.

Table 7. GLC accuracy given post-processing of data by averaging of runs

Accuracy of Recovered Scaling Factor Values (c432, c499)			
	# of Averaged Runs		
Measurement Error	**1**	**100**	**1000**
.01%	(%)	(%)	(%)
Power	0.006, 0.037	0.001, 0.004	0.0002, 0.001
Delay	0.003, 0.001	0, 0	0, 0
Both	0.001, 0.001	0, 0	0, 0
.1%	(%)	(%)	(%)
Power	0.059, 0.371	0.006, 0.037	0.002, 0.013
Delay	0.035, 0.012	0.003, 0.001	0.001, 0
Both	0.011, 0.009	0.001, 0.001	0, 0
1%	(%)	(%)	(%)
Power	0.584, 3.69	0.059, 0.374	0.019, 0.016
Delay	0.351, 0.121	0.033, 0.012	0.011, 0.004
Both	0.107, 0.085	0.010, 0.009	0.003, 0.003

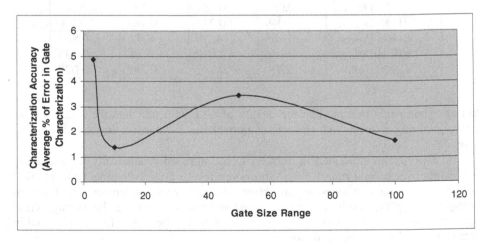

Fig. 2. For the c499 benchmark with 700 measurements the gate-level characterization accuracy for three different ranges of gates sizes, namely 0-3, 0-10, 0-50, and 0-100

6 Ghost Circuitry Detection

Our goal in this section is to address the detection of ghost circuitry using statistical techniques given the results of gate-level characterization. First, consider that there will be a possible shift in the scaling factors of the gates calculated by GLC when there is ghost circuitry present. The reason for this is that the contribution of the delay and the leakage power of the ghost circuitry will be attributed to the other gates in the circuit or the other gates along the paths where the GC is.

We analyze whether a systematic shift of all the scaling factors occurs when a group of ICs are analyzed. If ghost circuitry has been embedded, there is at least one gate that is not included in the linear equations for gate level characterization, and we can expect that a majority of gates will have scaling factors higher than the nominal factors as a result. In particular to conclude that ghost circuitry is present, we check whether the average α-values for all gates are above the average for other circuits and if it does not follow a Gaussian distribution that has been reported for the different silicon processes.

More formally, consider that we will try to solve for a assuming that we have $Ga = m+e$, but with ghost circuitry present we actually have $Ga = m+e+m_g$, where m_g is the vector representing the delay and/or the power contribution of the ghost circuitry. If ghost circuitry is present then α-value(s) of the ghost gate(s) will have an impact on the measurements obtained for the circuit in the case of power and for the applicable paths in the case of delay. However, the matrix G will not represent this ghost gate's contribution. Also, there will be no α-value accounted for in a. This will result in an increase in the average value calculated for the α-values of the other gates. The impact of the ghost circuit's power and delay will be distributed across one or more legitimate gates. As a result, if a shift is noted in the α-values, across different ICs of the same design or even as compared with the expected α-values, then we can use this as a predictor for determining the presence of ghost circuitry.

This technique places two significant assumptions: 1) The use of semiconductor processes does not induce unintentional bias, and 2) the measurement instruments do not have a positive systematic bias. The second assumption can also be eliminated if we add an additional factor to our linear equations notably a nonnegative variable to represent that bias. The advantage of this technique is that it is fast. On the other hand, it may not be applicable in all situations. An important challenge is finding a small number of gates in large circuits. As shown in the experiments below in the small benchmarks it is possible to notice the effects of adding a single ghost circuit, as SVD solution increases the α-value of other gates to compensate for the ghost circuit's delay and power side effects.

Table 8 presents the results of implementing this technique on the c17 and c432 benchmark of the ISCAS 85 benchmark suite. A single NAND gate was inserted randomly into certain circuits and nondestructive delay measurement were examined. The average α-values were compared between the two sets of circuits. As demonstrated there is a systematic positive measurement error, which is a strong indicator that ghost circuitry has been added.

Table 8. The average normalized α-value without the presence of ghost circuitry and the average normalized α-value with the presence of embedded ghost circuitry, along with the average increase in the α-values

Measurement Error	Average α-value without GC (c17, c432)	Average α-value with GC (c17, c432)	Average increase in α-value (c17, c432)
0%	2, 2.610	2.21, 2.629	10.5%, 0.72%
3%	1.94, 3.049	2.16, 3.057	11.3%, 0.262%
6%	1.88, 3.062	1.91, 3.181	1.6%, 3.89%

Table 9. The false positive and false negative rates of GC detection for 1000 different circuits, for two different types of thresholds for the c432 benchmark for 1% error rate with 200 constraints

	False Positive Rate	False Negative Rate
Threshold Set at Mean	25.1%	5.05%
Threshold Set at greater than a Known Non-GC Circuit Average Value	20.3%	5.95%

Table 9 presents the results for 1000 different circuits, 500 of which have a single NAND gate added near gate 25 in the center of the circuit. This would qualify as a very difficult case of GC detection. Given this scenario, if the threshold for determining if a ghost gate is present is set as whether the average of the α-values is greater than the mean of the α-values of the non-GC circuits, then there is only a 5.05% false negative rate. That means that about 95% of the ICs are properly characterized as having ghost circuitry. As expected, 25% of the time this results in a false positive rate. For this benchmark, with no measurement error and 200 constraints both the false positive rate and the false negative rate go to zero.

On the other hand if we use an average of a single non-GC circuit's α-values to set the threshold value, then the false negative rates increases to 5.95%, while the false negative rates decreases to 20.3%. Setting the threshold value is an important parameter in this analysis. We propose a minimization of the sum of the false positive and false negative rate for a learning set of ICs to determine the best threshold value.

In another GC detection technique, we manipulate constraints and the objective function in the nonlinear program, by adding an extra variable to the right side of each constraint. If the gates can be characterized in a more accurate and consistent manner with this addition, there is a strong indication of the presence of ghost circuitry.

To defeat this approach, the attacker would need to add gates such that they were always correlated with another gate. An automated search across the netlist could determine the best location for adding the gate(s). Another difficult attack to detect is if the attacker optimizes circuit design to use the saved delay and power characteristics to hide the ghost circuitry. In general, the attacker will need to carry out an optimization to determine the location to hide the ghost circuit to attempt to avoid diction by our techniques. Simple or random GC insertion will be detected.

7 Conclusion

We have developed a system of techniques for ghost circuitry detection. The techniques apply a system of non-destructive delay and/or power measurements followed by singular value decomposition for gate-level characterization. Once the GLC is completed, statistical data analysis is carried out to determine whether ghost circuitry has been added or not.

References

[1] Defense Science Board (DSB) study on high performance microchip supply (2006), http://www.acq.osd.mil/dsb/reports/2005-02-hpmsreportfinal.pdf

[2] Agrawal, D., Baktir, S., Karakoyunlu, D., Rohatgi, P., Sunar, B.: Trojan detection using ic fingerprinting. In: IEEE Symposium on Security and Privacy (SP), pp. 296–310 (2007)

[3] Anderson, R., Bond, M., Clulow, J., Skorobogato, S.: Cryptographic processors-a survey. Proceedings of the IEEE 94(2), 357–369 (2006)

[4] Anderson, R.J.: Security Engineering: A guide to building dependable distributed systems. John Wiley and Sons, Chichester (2001)

[5] Bernstein, K., Frank, D.J., Gattiker, A.E., Haensch, W., Ji, B.L., Nassif, S.R., Nowak, E.J., Pearson, D.J., Rohrer, N.J.: High-performance CMOS variability in the 65-nm regime and beyond. IBM Journal of Research and Development 50(4/5), 433–450 (2006)

[6] Hwang, D., Schaumont, P., Tiri, K., Verbauwhede, I.: Securing embedded systems. IEEE Security & Privacy 4(2), 40–49 (2006)

[7] Jha, N.K., Gupta, S.: Testing of Digital Systems. Cambridge University Press, Cambridge (2003)

[8] Koushanfar, F., Potkonjak, M.: CAD-based security, cryptography, and digital rights management. In: Design Automation Conference, DAC (2007)

[9] Lofstrom, K., Daasch, W.R., Taylor, D.: IC identification circuits using device mismatch. In: International Solid State Circuits Conference (ISSCC), pp. 372–373 (2000)

[10] Menezes, A., van Oorschot, P., Vanstone, S.: Handbook of Applied Cryptography. CRC Press, Boca Raton (1997)

[11] Srivastava, A., Sylvester, D., Blaauw, D.: Statistical Analysis and Optimization for VLSI: Timing and Power. Series on Integrated Circuits and Systems. Springer, Heidelberg (2005)

[12] Su, Y., Holleman, J., Otis, B.: A 1.6J/bit stable chip ID generating circuit using process variations. In: International Solid State Circuits Conference, ISSCC (2007) (to appear)

[13] Suh, G., Devadas, S.: Physical unclonable functions for device authentication and secret key generation. In: Design Automation Conference (DAC), pp. 9–14 (2007)

[14] Yablonovitch, E.: Can nano-photonic silicon circuits become an intra-chip interconnect technology? In: IEEE/ACM International Conference on Computer-Aided Design (ICCAD), p. 309 (2007)

[15] Alkabani, Y., Koushanfar, F., Kiyavash, N., Potkonjak, M.: Trusted integrated circuits: A nondestructive hidden characteristics extraction approach. In: Solanki, K., Sullivan, K., Madhow, U. (eds.) IH 2008. LNCS, vol. 5284, pp. 102–117. Springer, Heidelberg (2008)

[16] Alkabani, Y., Massey, T., Koushanfar, F., Potkonjak, M.: Input vector control for post-silicon leakage current minimization in the presence of manufacturing variability. In: Design Automation Conference (DAC), pp. 606–609 (2008)

[17] Dabiri, F., Potkonjak, M.: Hardware aging-based software metering. In: Design, Automation, and Test in Europe, DATE (2009)

[18] Koushanfar, F., Boufounos, P., Shamsi, D.: Post-silicon timing characterization by compressed sensing. In: IEEE/ACM International Conference on Computer-Aided Design (ICCAD), pp. 185–189 (2008)

[19] Shamsi, D., Boufounos, P., Koushanfar, F.: Noninvasive leakage power tomography of integrated circuits by compressive sensing. In: International Symposium on Low power electronics and design (ISLPED), pp. 341–346 (2008)

[20] Yuan, L., Qu, G.: A combined gate replacement and input vector control approach for leakage current reduction. IEEE Trans. Very Large Scale Integr. Syst. 14(2), 173–182 (2006)

[21] Ercegovac, M.D., Lang, T., Moreno, J.H.: Introduction to Digital Systems (1999)

[22] Kocher, P., Jaffe, J., Jum, B.: Differential Power Analysis. In: International Cryptology Conference on Advances in Cryptology (1999)

[23] Kuhn, M.: Trojan hardware – some strategies and defenses. Slides from the Schloss Dagstuhl (2008),
http://www.cl.cam.ac.uk/~mgk25/dagstuhl08-hwtrojan.pdf

[24] Rajsuman, R.: Iddq testing for CMOS VLSI. Proceedings of the IEEE 88(4), 544–568 (2000)

[25] Alkabani, Y., Koushanfar, F., Potkonjak, M.: Remote Activation of ICs for Piracy Prevention and Digital Right Management. In: IEEE/ACM International Conference on Computer Aided Design, ICCAD (2007)

Microphone Classification Using Fourier Coefficients

Robert Buchholz, Christian Kraetzer, and Jana Dittmann

Otto-von-Guericke University of Magdeburg, Department of Computer Science,
PO Box 4120, 39016 Magdeburg, Germany
{robert.buchholz,christian.kraetzer,
jana.dittmann}@iti.cs.uni-magdeburg.de

Abstract. Media forensics tries to determine the originating device of a signal. We apply this paradigm to microphone forensics, determining the microphone model used to record a given audio sample. Our approach is to extract a Fourier coefficient histogram of near-silence segments of the recording as the feature vector and to use machine learning techniques for the classification. Our test goals are to determine whether attempting microphone forensics is indeed a sensible approach and which one of the six different classification techniques tested is the most suitable one for that task. The experimental results, achieved using two different FFT window sizes (256 and 2048 frequency coefficients) and nine different thresholds for near-silence detection, show a high accuracy of up to 93.5% correct classifications for the case of 2048 frequency coefficients in a test set of seven microphones classified with linear logistic regression models. This positive tendency motivates further experiments with larger test sets and further studies for microphone identification.

Keywords: media forensics, FFT based microphone classification.

1 Motivation

Being able to determine the microphone type used to create a given recording has numerous applications. Long-term archiving systems such as the one introduced in the SHAMAN project on long-term preservation [3] store metadata along with the archived media. Determining the microphone model or identifying the microphone used would be a useful additional media security related metadata attribute to retrieve recordings by.

In criminology and forensics, determining the microphone type and model of a given alleged accidental or surveillance recording of a committed crime can help determining the authenticity of that record. Furthermore, microphone forensics can be used in the analysis of video statements of dubious origin to determine whether the audio recording could actually have been made by the microphone seen in the video or whether the audio has been tempered with or even completely replaced. Also, other media forensic approaches like gunshot characterization/classification [12] require knowledge about the source characteristics, which could be established with the introduced microphone classification approach.

S. Katzenbeisser and A.-R. Sadeghi (Eds.): IH 2009, LNCS 5806, pp. 235–246, 2009.

Finally, determining the microphone model of arbitrary recordings can help determine the actual ownership of that recording in the case of multiple claims of ownership, and can thus be a valuable passive mechanism like perceptual hashing in solving copyright disputes.

The goal of this work is to investigate whether it is possible to identify the microphone model used in making a certain audio recording by using only Fourier coefficients. Its goal is not comprehensively cover the topic, but merely to give an indication on whether such a classification is indeed possible. Thus, the practical results presented may not be generalizable.

Our contribution is to test the feature extraction based only on frequency domain features of near-silence segments of a recording (using two different FFT window sizes (256 and 2048 frequency coefficients) and nine different thresholds for near-silence detection) and to classify the seven microphones using six different classifiers not yet applied to this problem. In this process, two research questions are going to be answered: First, is it possible to classify microphones using Fourier coefficient based features, thereby reducing the complexity of the approach presented in [1]? Second, which classification approach out of a variety (logistic regression, support vector machines, decision trees and nearest neighbor) is the most suitable one for that task? Additionally, first indications for possible dimensionality reduction using principal component analysis (PCA) are given and inter-microphone differences in classification accuracy are mentioned.

The remaining paper is structured as follows: Section 2 presents related work to place this paper in the larger field of study. Section 3 introduces our general testing procedure, while Section 4 details the test setup for the audio recordings and Section 5 details the feature extraction and classification steps. The test results are then shown in Section 6 and are compared with earlier results. The paper is concluded with a summary and an outlook on future work in Section 7.

2 Related Work

The idea of identifying recording devices based on the records produced is not a new one and has been attempted before with various device classes. A recent example for the great variety is the work from Filler et al. [6] as well as Dirik et al. [7] on investigating and evaluating the feasibility of identifying a camera used to take a given picture. Forensics for flatbed scanners is introduced in [8] and Khanna et al. summarize identification techniques for scanner and printing device in [9]. Aside from device identification, other approaches also look into the determination of the used device model, such as done in for cameras models in [10] or performed for handwriting devices in [11]. However, to our knowledge no other research group has yet explored the feasibility of microphone classification.

Our first idea based on syntactical and semantic feature extraction, analysis and classification for audio recordings was introduced in [13] and described a first theoretical concept of a so-called verifier-tuple for audio-forensics. Our first practical results were presented by Kraetzer et al. [1] and were based on a segmental feature extractor normally used in steganalysis (AAST; computing seven statistical measures and 56 cepstral coefficients). The experiments were conducted on a rather small test setup containing only four microphones for which the audio samples were recorded simultaneously – an unlikely setup for practical applications that limits the generalizability of the results. These experiments also used only two basic classifiers (Naïve Bayes, k-means clustering). The results demonstrated a classification accuracy that was clearly above random guessing, but was still by far too low to be of practical relevance. Another approach using Fourier coefficients as features was examined in our laboratory with an internal study [5] with an extended test set containing seven different microphones. The used minimum distance classifier proved to be inadequate for the classification of high-dimensional feature vectors, but these first results were a motivation to conduct further research on the evaluation of Fourier features with advanced classification techniques. The results are presented and discussed in this paper.

3 Concept

Our approach is to investigate the ability of feature extraction based on a Fourier coefficient histogram to accurately classify microphones with the help of model based classification techniques.

Since Fourier coefficients are usually characteristic for the sounds recorded and not for the device recording it, we detect segments of the audio file that contain mostly noise, and apply the feature extractor only to these segments. The corresponding Fourier coefficients for all those segments are summed up to yield a Fourier coefficient histogram that is then used as the global feature vector.

The actual classification is then conducted using the WEKA machine learning software suite [2]. The microphone classification task is repeated with different classification algorithms and parameterizations for the feature extractor (non-overlapping FFT windows with 256 and 2048 coefficients (therefore requiring 512 and 4096 audio samples per window), and nine different near-silence amplitude thresholds between zero and one for the detection of segments containing noise). With the data on the resulting classification accuracies, the following research questions can be answered:

– Is it possible at all to determine a microphone model based on Fourier coefficient characteristics of a recording using that microphone?
– Which classifier is the most accurate one for our microphone classification setup?

In addition, we give preliminary results on whether a feature space reduction might be possible and investigate inter-microphone differences in classification accuracy.

4 Physical Test Setup

For the experiments, we focus on microphone model classification as opposed to microphone identification. Thus, we do not use microphones of the same type.

The recordings are all made using the same computer and loudspeaker for playback of predefined reference signals. They are recorded for each microphone separately, so that they may be influenced by different types of environmental noise to differing degrees. While this will likely degrade classification accuracy, it was done on purpose in order for the classification results to be more generalizable to situations were synchronous recording of samples is not possible.

There are at least two major factors that may influence the recordings besides the actual microphones that are supposed to be classified: The loudspeaker used to play back a sound file in order for the microphone to record the sample again and the microphone used to create the sound file in the first place. We assume that the effect of the loudspeaker is negligible, because the dynamic range of the high quality loudspeaker used by far exceeds that of all tested microphones. The issue is graver for the microphones used to create the sound files, but varies depending on the type of sound file (see Table 1).

Table 1. The eight source sound files used for the experiments (syntactical features: 44.1kHz sampling rate, mono, 16 bit PCM coding, average duration 30s)

File Name	Content
Metallica-Fuel.wav	Music, Metal
U2-BeautifulDay.wav	Music, Pop
Scooter-HowMuchIsTheFish.wav	Music, Techno
mls.wav	MLS Noise
sine440.wav	440Hz sine tone
white.wav	White Noise
silence.wav	Digital silence
vioo10_2_nor.wav	SQAM, instrumental

Some of our sound samples are purely synthetic (e.g. the noises and the sine sound) and thus were not influenced by any microphone. The others are short audio clips of popular music. For these files, our rationale is that the influence of the microphones is negligible for multiple reasons. First, they are usually recorded with expensive, high quality microphones whose dynamic range exceeds that of our tested microphones. And second, the final piece of music is usually the result of mixing sounds from different sources (e.g. voices and instruments) and applying various audio filters. This processing chain should affect the final song sufficiently in order for the effects of individual microphones to be no longer measurable.

We tested seven different microphones (see Table 2). None are of the same model, but some are different models from the same manufacturer. The microphones are based on three of the major microphone transducer technologies.

Table 2. The seven microphones used in our experiments

Microphone	Transducer technology
Shure SM 58	Dynamic microphone
T.Bone MB 45	Dynamic microphone
AKG CK 93	Condenser microphone
AKG CK 98	Condenser microphone
PUX 70TX-M1	Piezoelectric microphone
Terratec Headset Master	Dynamic microphone
T.Bone SC 600	Condenser microphone

All samples were played back and recorded by each microphone in each of twelve different rooms with different characteristics (stairways, small office rooms, big office rooms, a lecture hall, etc.) to ensure that the classification is independent from the recording environment.

Thus, the complete set of audio samples consists of 672 individual audio files, recorded with seven microphones in twelve rooms based on eight source audio files. Each file is about 30 seconds long, recorded as an uncompressed PCM stream with 16 bit quantization at 44.1kHz sampling rate and a single audio channel (mono). To allow amplitude-based operations to work equally well on all audio samples, the recordings are normalized using SoX [4] prior to feature extraction.

5 Feature Extraction and Classification

Our basic idea is to classify for each recorded file f the microphones based on the FFT coefficients of the noise portion of the audio recordings. Thus, the following feature extraction steps are performed for each threshold t tested ($t \in \{0.01, 0.025, 0.05, 0.1, 0.2, 0.225, 0.25, 0.5, 1\}$ for n=256 and $t \in \{0.01, 0.025, 0.05, 0.1, 0.25, 0.35, 0.4, 0.5, 1\}$ for n=2048; cf. Figure 1):

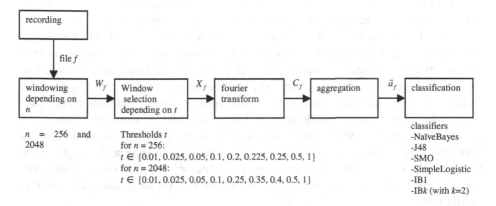

Fig. 1. The classification pipeline

The feature extractor first divides each audio file f of the set of recorded files F into equally-sized non-overlapping windows W_f with size $2n$ samples ($W_f = \{w_1(f), w_2(f), ..., w_m(f)\}$; m=sizeof(f)/($2n$)). Two different values for n are used in the evaluations performed here: n=256 and n=2048. For each file f, only those windows $w_i(f)$ ($1 \leq i \leq m$) are selected for further processing where the maximum amplitude in the window does not exceed a variable near-silence threshold t and thus can be assumed to contain no content but background noise. For each n nine different t are evaluated here.

All s selected windows for f form the set X_f ($X_f \subseteq W_f$, $X_f = \{x_1(f), x_2(f), ..., x_s(f)\}$). These s selected windows are transformed to the frequency domain using a FFT and the amplitude portion of the complex-valued Fourier coefficients is computed. The resulting vector of n Fourier coefficients (harmonics) for each selected window is identified as $\vec{c}_{f,j} = (FC_1, \ FC_2, \ ..., \ FC_n)_{f,j}$ with $1 \leq j \leq s$. Thus, for each file f, a set C_f of s coefficient vectors $\vec{c}_{f,j}$ of dimension n is computed. To create a constant length feature vector $\vec{a}_f$ for each f the amplitudes representing the same harmonic in each element in C_f are summed up, yielding an amplitude histogram vector $\vec{a}_f$ of size n. To compensate for different audio sample lengths and differences in volume that are not necessarily characteristics of the microphone the feature vector is normalized as a last step so that its maximum amplitude value is one.

Parameter Considerations. The test setup allows for two parameters to be chosen with some constraints: the FFT window size ($2n$ and has to be a power of two) and the amplitude threshold t (between 0 and 1) that decides whether a given sample window contains mostly background noise and thus is suitable to characterize the microphone. Both need to be considered carefully because their values represent trade-offs:

If t is chosen too low, too few windows will be considered suitable for further analysis. This leads the amplitude histogram to be based on fewer samples and thus will increase the influence of randomness on the histogram. In extreme cases, a low threshold may even lead to all sample windows being rejected and thus to an invalid feature vector. On the other hand, a high t will allow windows containing a large portion of the content (and not only the noise) to be considered. Thus, the influence of the characteristic noise will reduced, significantly narrowing the attribute differences between different microphones. For the experiments, various thresholds ranging from 0.01 to 1 are tested, with special focus on those thresholds for which the feature extraction failed for few to no recordings, but which are still small enough to contain mostly noise.

For the FFT coefficients, a similar trade-off exists: If the FFT window size is set rather low, then the number n of extracted features may be too low to distinguish different microphones due to the reduced frequency resolution. If the window size is set too high, the chances of the window to contain at least a single amplitude that exceeds the allowed threshold and thus being rejected increases, having the same negative effects as a high threshold. Additionally, since the feature vector size n increases linearly with the window size, the computation time and memory required to perform the classification task increases accordingly. To analyze the effect of the window size on the classification accuracy, we run all tests with $n = 256$ and $n = 2048$ samples. For $n = 2048$, some classifications already take multiple hours, while others terminate the used data mining environment WEKA by exceeding the maximum Java VM memory size for 32 bit Windows systems (about 2GB).

Classification Tests. For the actual classification tasks, we use the WEKA machine learning tool. The aggregated vectors $\vec{a}_f$ for the different sample files in F are aggregated in a single CSV file to be fed into WEKA. From WEKA's broad range of classification algorithms, we selected the following ones:

- Naïve Bayes
- SMO (a multi-class SVM construct)
- Simple Logistic (regression models)
- J48 (decision tree)
- IB1 (1-nearest neighbor)
- IBk (2-nearest neighbor)

All classifiers are used with their default parameters. The only exception is IBk where the parameter k needs to be set to two to facilitate a 2-nearest neighbor classification. The classifiers work on the following basic principles:

Naïve Bayes is the simplest application of Bayesian probability theory. The SMO algorithm is a way of efficiently solving support vector machines. WEKA's SMO implementation also allows the construction of multi-class classifiers from the two class classifiers intrinsic to support vector machines. Simple Logistic builds linear logistic regression models using LogitBoost. J48 is WEKA's version of a C4.5 decision tree. The IB1 and IBk classifiers, finally, are simple nearest neighbor and k-nearest neighbor algorithms, respectively. All classifiers are applied to the extracted feature vectors created with $n = 256$ and $n = 2048$ samples and various threshold values.

Since only a single set of audio samples is available, all classification tests are performed by splitting this test set. As the splitting strategy we chose 10-fold stratified cross-validation. With this strategy, the sample set is divided into ten subsets of equal size that all contain about the same number of samples from each microphone class (thus the term "stratified"). Each subset is used as the test set in turn, while the remaining nine subsets are combined and used as the training set. This test setup usually gives the most generalizable classification results even for small sample sets. Thus, each of the 10-fold stratified cross-validation tests consists of ten individual classification tasks.

6   Experiments and Results

The classification results for $n = 2048$ are given in Table 3 and are visualized in Figure 2, while the results for the evaluations using 256 frequency coefficients are given in Table 4 and Figure 3. The second column gives percentage of recordings for which the amplitude of at least one window does not exceed the threshold and hence features can be extracted.

The first fact to be observed is that the number of samples for which not a single window falls within the amplitude threshold and which thus can only be classified by guessing is quite high even if the threshold used is set as high as 0.1 of the maximum amplitude – a value at which the audio signal definitely still contains a high portion of audible audio signal in addition to the noise. For all classifiers, the classification accuracy dropped sharply when further reducing the threshold. This result was to be expected since with decreasing threshold, the number of audio samples without any acceptable windows at all increases sharply and thus the classification for more and more samples is based on guessing alone.

Table 3. Classification accuracy for $n = 2048$ (best result for each classifier is highlighted)

Threshold t	Percentage of $w_i(f)$	Naive Bayes	SMO	Simple Logistic	J48	IB1	2-Nearest Neighbor (IBk)
0.01	47.5%	36.3%	54.8%	54.9%	45.5%	53.3%	51.8%
0.025	67.6%	42.9%	66.5%	69.0%	50.6%	67.3%	64.9%
0.05	78.6%	45.7%	76.3%	77.4%	60.4%	74.6%	71.1%
0.1	86.8%	44.6%	79.6%	81.0%	61.5%	79.9%	74.7%
0.25	97.3%	46.9%	88.2%	88.2%	68.6%	82.7%	80.2%
0.35	99.7%	35.7%	90.6%	93.5%	71.6%	88.4%	85.4%
0.40	100.0%	36.5%	88.1%	92.1%	74.0%	88.7%	85.7%
0.5	100.0%	32.3%	83.2%	87.2%	76.8%	88.2%	85.4%
1	100.0%	32.3%	83.2%	87.2%	76.8%	88.2%	85.4%

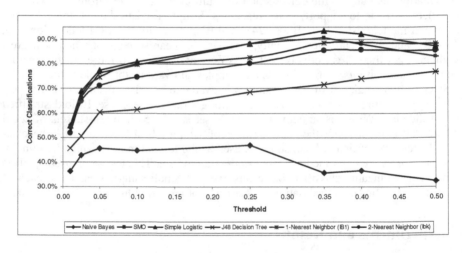

Fig. 2. Graph of the classification accuracy for varying threshold values for $n = 2048$. Results for the threshold of one are omitted since these are identical to those of the threshold of 0.5.

For most classifiers, the optimal classification results are obtained with a threshold that is very close to the lowest threshold at which features for all recordings in the test can be extracted (i.e. each recording has at last a single window that lies completely below the threshold). This, too, is reasonable. For a lower threshold, an increasing number of samples can only be classified by guessing. And for higher thresholds, the amount of signal in the FFT results increases and the amount of noise decreases. Since our classification is based on analyzing the noise spectrum, this leads to lower classification accuracy as well. However, the decline in accuracy even with a threshold of one (i.e. every single sample window in considered) is by far smaller than that of low thresholds.

Table 4. Classification accuracy for $n = 256$ (best result for each classifier is highlighted)

Threshold t	Percentage of $w_i(f)$	Naive Bayes	SMO	Simple Logistic	J48	IB1	2-Nearest Neighbor (IBk)
0.01	64.6%	39.1%	52.6%	65.4%	49.3%	60.6%	56.8%
0.025	80.8%	43.3%	63.6%	76.0%	59.1%	74.9%	71.8%
0.05	87.5%	40.2%	63.7%	77.4%	61.0%	74.9%	71.3%
0.1	95.2%	39.4%	72.3%	83.2%	61.9%	75.3%	72.2%
0.2	99.6%	40.5%	74.1%	87.5%	71.7%	83.5%	78.1%
0.225	99.7%	39.3%	74.4%	88.7%	68.2%	83.0%	77.8%
0.25	100.0%	37.6%	74.7%	90.6%	73.4%	87.1%	82.4%
0.5	100.0%	33.0%	70.2%	84.2%	74.4%	86.8%	83.8%
1	100.0%	33.0%	70.2%	84.2%	74.4%	86.8%	83.8%

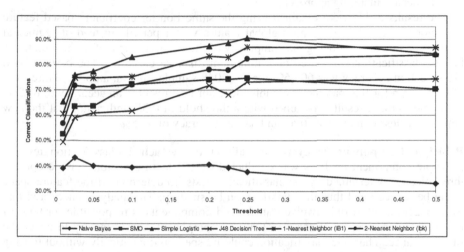

Fig. 3. Graph of the classification accuracy for varying threshold values for $n = 256$. Results for the threshold of one are omitted since these are identical to those of the threshold of 0.5.

The classification results for the two window sizes do not differ much. The Naïve Bayes classifier yields better results when using smaller windows and thus fewer attributes. For all other classifiers, the results are usually better for the bigger window size, owing to the fact that a bigger number of attributes allows for the samples to differ in more ways.

The overall best classification results are obtained with the Simple Logistic classifier, with about 93.5% ($n = 2048$) and 90.6% ($n = 256$). However, for very high thresholds that allow a louder audio signal (as opposed to noise) to be part of the extracted features, the IB1 classifier performs better than the Simple Logistic one.

It should be noted that the computation time of the Simple Logistic classifier by far exceeds that of every other classifier. On the test machine (Core2Duo 3 GHz, 4GB RAM), Simple Logistic usually took about 90 minute for a complete 10-fold cross-validation, while the other classifiers only take between a few seconds (Naïve Bayes) and ten minutes.

One notable odd behavior is the fact that for very small thresholds, the percentage of *correctly classified* samples exceeds the percentage of samples with valid windows, i.e. samples that *can be classified*. This is due to the behavior of the classifiers to in essence guess the class for samples without valid attributes. Since this guess is likely to be correct with a probability of one seventh for seven microphones, the mentioned behavior can indeed occur.

Comparison with Earlier Approaches. In [1], a set of 63 segmental features was used. These were based on statistical measures (e.g. entropy, variance, LSB ratio, LSB flip ratio) as well as mel-cepstral features. Their classification results are significantly less accurate than ours, even though they use a test setup based on only four microphones. Their classification accuracy is 69.5% for Naïve Bayes and 36.5% using a k-means clustering approach.

The results in [5] were obtained using the same Fourier coefficient based feature extractor as we did (generating a global feature vector per file instead of segmental features and thereby reducing the complexity of the computational classification task), but its classification was based on a minimum distance classifier. The best reported classification accuracy was 60.26% for $n = 2048$ samples and an amplitude threshold of 0.25. Even for that parameter combination, our best result is an accuracy of 88.2%, while our optimal result is obtained with a threshold of 0.35 (indicating that the new approach is less context sensitive) and has an accuracy of 93.5%.

Principle Component Analysis. In addition to the actual classification tests, a principle component analysis was conducted on the feature vectors for the optimal thresholds (as determined by the classification tests) to determine if the feature space could be reduced and thus the classification be sped up. The analysis uncovered that for $n = 256$, a set of only twelve transformed components is responsible for 95% of the sample variance, while for $n = 2048$, 23 components are necessary to cover the same variance. Thus, the classification could be sped up dramatically without loosing much of the classification accuracy.

Inter-Microphone Differences. To analyze the differences in microphone classification accuracy between the individual microphones the detailed classification results for the test case with the most accurate results (Simple Logistic, $n=2048$, threshold $t=0.35$) are shown in a confusion matrix in Table 5.

The results are rather unspectacular. The number of correct classifications varies only slightly, between 89.6% and 96.9% and may not be the result of microphone characteristics, but rather be attributed to differences in recording conditions or to randomness inherent to experiments with a small test set size. The quite similar microphones from the same manufacturer (AKG CK93 and CK98) even get mixed up less often as is the case with other microphone combinations. The only anomaly is the frequent misclassification of the T.Bone SC 600 as the Terratec Headset Master. This may be attributed to these two microphones sharing the same transducer technology, because otherwise, their purpose and price differ considerably.

Table 5. The confusion matrix for the test case Simple Logistic, n=2048, t=0.35

Terratec Headset Master	PUX 70 TX-M1	Shure SM 58	T.Bone MB 45	AKG CK 93	AKG CK 98	T.Bone SC 600	classified as
90.60%	1.00%	0.00%	0.00%	0.00%	0.00%	8.40%	Terratec Headset M.
1.00%	**95.00%**	1.00%	1.00%	1.00%	1.00%	0.00%	PUX 70TX-M1
3.10%	0.00%	**89.60%**	5.30%	1.00%	0.00%	1.00%	Shure SM 58
0.00%	0.00%	1.00%	**97.00%**	1.00%	0.00%	1.00%	T.Bone MB 45
1.00%	0.00%	1.00%	2.20%	**93.80%**	1.00%	1.00%	AKG CK 93
0.00%	0.00%	0.00%	0.00%	1.00%	**94.80%**	4.20%	AKG CK 98
2.10%	0.00%	2.10%	0.00%	1.00%	1.00%	**93.80%**	T.Bone SC 600

7 Summary and Future Work

This work showed that it is indeed feasible to determine the microphone model based on an audio recording conducted with that microphone. The classification accuracy can be as high as 93% when the Simple Logistic classifier is used and the features are extracted with 2048 frequency components (4096 samples) per window and the lowest possible threshold that still allows the extraction of features for all samples of the sample set.

Thus, when accuracy is paramount, the Simple Logistic classifier should be used. When computation time is relevant and many attributes and training samples are present, the simple nearest neighbor classifier represents a good tradeoff between speed and accuracy.

As detailed in the introduction, these results do by no means represent a definite answer in finding the optimal technique for microphone classification. They do, however, demonstrate the feasibility of such an endeavor. The research conducted for this project also led to ideas for future improvements:

In some cases, the audio signal recorded by the microphone is a common one and an original version of it could be obtained. In these cases, it could be feasible to subtract the original signal from the recorded one. This may lead to a result that contains only the distortions and noise introduced by the microphone and may lead to a much more relevant feature extraction.

For our feature extractor, we decided to use non-overlapping FFT windows to prevent redundancy in the data. However, it might be useful to have the FFT windows overlap to some degree, as with more sample windows, the effect of randomness on the frequency histogram can be reduced. This is especially true if a high number of windows is being rejected by the thresholding decision.

Another set of experiments should be conducted to answer the question on whether our classification approach can also be used for microphone identification, i.e. to differentiate even between different microphones of the same model.

Furthermore, additional features could be used to increase the discriminatory power of the feature vector. Some of these were already mentioned in [1] and [5], but were not yet used in combination. These features include – among others – the microphone's characteristic response to a true impulse signal and the dynamic range of the microphone as analyzed be recording a sinus sweep.

Finally, classifier fusion and boosting may be valuable tools to increase the classification accuracy without having to introduce additional features.

Acknowledgments

We would like to thank two of our students, Antonina Terzieva and Vasil Vasilev who conducted some preliminary experiments leading to this paper and Marcel Dohnal for the work he put into the feature extractor. The work in this paper is supported in part by the European Commission through the FP7 ICT Programme under Contract FP7-ICT-216736 SHAMAN. The information in this document is provided as is, and no guarantee or warranty is given or implied that the information is fit for any particular purpose. The user thereof uses the information at its sole risk and liability.

References

1. Kraetzer, C., Oermann, A., Dittmann, J., Lang, A.: Digital Audio Forensics: A First Practical Evaluation on Microphone and Environment Classification. In: 9th Workshop on Multimedia & Security, pp. 63–74. ACM, New York (2007)
2. Witten, I.H., Frank, E.: Data Mining: Practical Machine Learning Tools and Techniques, 2nd edn. Morgan Kaufmann, San Francisco (2005)
3. SHAMAN - Sustaining Heritage Access through Multivalent ArchiviNg, http://shaman-ip.eu
4. SoX – Sound Exchange, http://sox.sourceforge.net
5. Donahl, M.: Forensische Analyse von Audiosignalen zur Mikrofonerkennung, Masters Thesis, Dept. of Computer Science, Otto-von-Guericke University Magdeburg, Germany (2008)
6. Filler, T., Fridrich, J., Goljan, M.: Using Sensor Pattern Noise for Camera Model Identification. In: Proc. ICIP 2008, San Diego, pp. 1296–1299 (2008)
7. Dirik, A.E., Sencar, H.T., Memon, N.: Digital Single Lens Reflex Camera Identification From Traces of Sensor Dust. IEEE Transactions on Information Forensics and Security 3, 539–552 (2008)
8. Gloe, T., Franz, E., Winkler, A.: Forensics for flatbed scanners. In: Proceedings of the SPIE International Conference on Security, Steganography, and Watermarking of Multimedia Contents, San Jose (2007)
9. Khanna, N., Mikkilineni, A.K., Chiu, G.T., Allebach, J.P., Delp, E.J.: Survey of Scanner and Printer Forensics at Purdue University. In: Srihari, S.N., Franke, K. (eds.) IWCF 2008. LNCS, vol. 5158, pp. 22–34. Springer, Heidelberg (2008)
10. Bayram, S., Sencar, H.T., Memon, N.: Classification of Digital Camera-Models Based on Demosaicing Artifacts. Digital Investigation 5(1-2), 49–59 (2008)
11. Oermann, A., Vielhauer, C., Dittmann, J.: Sensometrics: Identifying Pen Digitizers by Statistical Multimedia Signal Processing. In: SPIE Multimedia on Mobile Devices 2007, San Jose (2007)
12. Maher, R.C.: Acoustical Characterization of Gunshots. In: SAFE 2007, Washington D.C., USA, April 11-13 (2007)
13. Oermann, A., Lang, A., Dittmann, J.: Verifier-tuple for audio-forensic to determine speaker environment. In: Proc. MM & Sec 2005, New York, pp. 57–62 (2005)

Detect Digital Image Splicing
with Visual Cues

Zhenhua Qu[1], Guoping Qiu[2], and Jiwu Huang[1]

[1] School of Information Science and Technology, Sun Yat-Sen University, China
[2] School of Computer Science, University of Nottingham, NG 8, 1BB, UK
qzhua3@gmail.com, qiu@cs.nott.ac.uk, isshjw@mail.sysu.edu.cn

Abstract. Image splicing detection has been considered as one of the most challenging problems in passive image authentication. In this paper, we propose an automatic detection framework to identify a spliced image. Distinguishing from existing methods, the proposed system is based on a human visual system (HVS) model in which visual saliency and fixation are used to guide the feature extraction mechanism. An interesting and important insight of this work is that there is a high correlation between the splicing borders and the first few fixation points predicted by a visual attention model using edge sharpness as visual cues. We exploit this idea to develope a digital image splicing detection system with high performance. We present experimental results which show that the proposed system outperforms the prior arts. An additional advantage offered by the proposed system is that it provides a convenient way of localizing the splicing boundaries.

1 Introduction

Image splicing or photomontage is one of the most common image manipulation techniques to create forgery images. As shown in Fig. 1, by copying a spliced portion from the source image into a target image, one can create a composite scenery to cheat others. Helped by current state-of-the-art image editing software, even non-professional users can perform splicing without much difficulty. Although experienced experts can still identify not highly sophisticated forgeries, it is still a challenging issue to tackle this complicated problem by machines in a fully automated way.

Fig. 1. The process of image splicing forgery

S. Katzenbeisser and A.-R. Sadeghi (Eds.): IH 2009, LNCS 5806, pp. 247–261, 2009.

Existing methods for detecting splicing images can be roughly classified into two categories: boundary based methods and region based methods. The boundary based methods detect the abnormal transient at the splicing boundaries, e.g., a sharp transition. Farid [1] used high order spectral(HOS) analysis to detect the high order correlation introduced by splicing in the harmonics of speech signals and later the idea was extended to image by Ng et al. [2]. By using the Hilbert-Huang transform(HHT) which empirically decomposes a signal into local harmonics and estimates the instantaneous frequency, Fu et al.[3] improved the accuracy from 72%[2] to 80%. Some researchers used the Wavelet analysis to characterizing the short-time transients in signals. Both the Lipsiz regularity [4] and phase congruency approach [5] can define a normalized measure of local sharpness/smoothness from the wavelet coefficients. Some methods further dealt with post-smoothing utilizing the camera response function (CRF)[6,7], or abnormality of local hue [8]. The region based methods generally rely on a generative model of the image and utilize the inconsistent system parameters estimated from the spliced and the original regions to identify the forgery. For images acquired with digital cameras, these generative models try to model lighting[9], optical lens characteristic[10], sensor pattern noise[11], and post-processing algorithm, such as color filter array interpolation[12,13]. For JPEG images, recompression artifacts are also useful features[14]. In this work, we focus on a boundary based method and assume, as in[2,3], that no further processing, e.g., blur or compression, has been applied to conceal the splicing boundary.

If there are sharp changes between a spliced region and its surrounding areas, such changes may be exploited to detect possible splicing. In many cases, humans can detect such changes and identify splicing effortlessly. However, to develop automatic algorithms to do the same task remains to be extremely difficult. Part of the difficulties comes from the fact that a natural image will consist of complicated edges of arbitrary magnitudes, orientations and curvatures. It is therefore hard to design an edge detector which can robustly distinguish the changes caused by the forgery splicing and the changes that are integral parts of the image signal.

For many years, researchers have been interested in trying to copy biological vision systems, simply because they are so good. The fact that humans can spot splicing in an image with relative ease implies that there must be some underlying mechanisms. Even though exactly how such mechanisms work still remains largely unknown, much research has been done to understand the human visual system (HVS)[15,16,17].

In this work, we exploit some results from research in HVS, especially those in the areas of visual saliency and visual fixation prediction [16,18], to develop a machine algorithms for splicing forgery detection. We present a novel three-level hierarchical system which provides a general framework for detecting splicing forgery. An innovative feature of the new systems is that it employs a visual fixation prediction algorithm to guide feature selection. Based on a very important discovery that there is a high correlation between the splicing boundaries and the first few visual fixation points predicted by a visual fixation prediction algorithm, we select the visual features from the first few fixation points (empirically about 5) to build a classifier to detect splicing. We introduce a normalized edge sharpness measure which is adaptive to variation in edge direction and curvature to provide a robust representation of edges.The experimental results show that the new scheme significantly outperforms existing methods on a public benchmark database. We will also show that an additional advantage of the new method over existing techniques is that it provides a convenient way to locate the splicing boundaries.

The rest of the paper is organized as follows: Section 2 introduces the three-level hierarchical detecting system. Section 3 describes the saliency guided feature extraction process. Section 4 and 5 deal with the feature fusion and localization problem respectively. Experimental results and conclusion are presented in Section 6 and 7.

2   The Proposed Image Splicing Detection System

As illustrated in Fig. 2, the proposed system use a detection window(DW) to scan across locations. At each location, the DW is divide into nine sub-blocks. To spotlight the "unusual" locations in a sub-block, a visual search is performed by regulating a bottom-up *Visual Attention Model*(VAM) with task-relevant top-down information. The bottom-up VAM used here is the Itti-Koch model[16]. It takes an image as input and construct a *Saliency Map* (SM) from low level feature pyramids, such as intensity, edge direction. The visual salient locations, or more formally called as fixations, are identified as the local maximums of the SM. In order to use the edge sharpness cues as top-down regulations to the VAM, , we extract two maps from each sub-block, the *Normalized Sharpness Map* (NSM) and the *Sharpness Conspicuous Map* (SCM). The NSM defines "*what*" is a splicing boundary by scoring the edge sharpness with a normalized value. The SCM is created by modulating the NSM with edge gradient. It implies "*where*" both the edge sharpness and edge gradient are large should be most conspicuous to an inspector and attract more attentions. The SCM is then inspected by the VAM to identify fixations which are the "unusual" spots within the SCM . Discriminative feature vectors are extracted from the most salient k fixations of the NSM to train a hierarchical classifier.

The hierarchical classifier is constituted by three types of meta classifier C_{low}, C_{mid}, C_{high}. C_{low} accept a single feature vector as input and outputs a probability p_{low}. The k p_{low}s from the same sub-block are send as a feature vector to C_{mid}. Analogously, the C_{mid} outputs a p_{mid} for a sub-block. Nine p_{mid}s of the DW are sent to a C_{high} for a final judgment.

3   Feature Extraction

In this section, we discuss how to gather discriminative features to identify if an image is spliced or not.

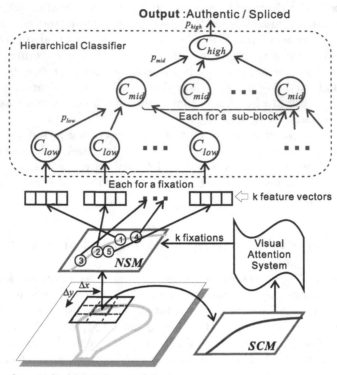

Fig. 2. Proposed system architecture

3.1   Edge Sharpness Measure

The key of detecting splicing forgery is to figure out the sharp splicing edges. The methods mentioned in Section 1 are not specified in analyzing splicing edges and thus have some limitations in practice. The HOS[2] and HHT[3] based detection methods are not good at analyzing small image patches due to the large sample size they often required. Wavelet or linear filtering based methods are limited by their finite filtering directions. When their filtering direction mismatches the splicing boundary which may have arbitrary directions, the filter's response will not correctly reflect the edge's property and thus increases the ambiguity of the spliced and the "natural" boundaries.

To derive a more specific solution which only accounts for the edge sharpness and adaptable to the variations of edge directions, we propose a non-linear filtering approach here based on Order Statistic Filter (OSF). An OSF can be denoted as $OSF(X, n, h \times w)$, where the input X is a 2-D signal and its output is the n'th largest element within a local $h \times w$ window. For example, $OSF(X, 5, 3 \times 3)$ performs a 2-D median filtering.

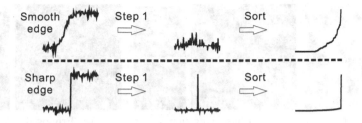

Fig. 3. The changes of sorted output values of sharp edges of step one are steeper than that of smooth edges

Described by Algorithm 1, our method involves three steps: In the first step, the horizontal/vertical abrupt changes are detected as impulse signals with a median filter. Then the output values of step one are sorted as shown in Fig. 3. We can see the sharp step edge has a much steeper peak than a smooth "natural" edge. This steepness provides us a mean to calculate a normalized measure of edge sharpness. Consequently, the Eq.(2) in step two and Eq.(3) in step three suppress those peak values with small local steepness which mostly correspond to the relatively smoother "natural" edges while the steep impulses which correspond to a step edge will be enhanced to be more noticeable. Figure 4 shows the effectiveness of our method.

Algorithm 1. Computing the normalized sharpness map (NSM)

Input: Image $I(x, y)$

1) For each color channel $I^c, c \in \{R, G, B\}$ of I, detect abrupt change with order filtering in horizontal and vertical direction. Only the horizontal direction is demonstrated.
- Horizontal denoise: $I_h^c = OSF(I^c, 2, 1 \times 3)$.
- Horizontal derivation: $D_h^c = \frac{\partial I^c}{\partial x}$.
- Calculate the absolute difference:
$$E_h^c = abs\left[D_h^c - OSF\left(D_h^c, 3, 1 \times 5\right)\right] \tag{1}$$

2) Combine all color channels $E_h = \sum_c E_h^c$ and the horizontal normalized sharpness is obtained by
$$\bar{E}_h = \frac{E_h}{E_h + OSF(E_h, 2, 1 \times 5) + \varepsilon} \tag{2}$$
The division here is entry-wise for matrix. $\bar{E}_v$ can be obtained similarly.

3) Combine horizontal and vertical directions $\bar{E} = \max(\bar{E}_h, \bar{E}_v)$ and obtain a final normalized sharpness map with
$$NSM = \frac{\bar{E}}{\bar{E} + OSF(\bar{E}, 10, 5 \times 5) + \varepsilon} \tag{3}$$

Output: A normalized sharpness map (NSM).

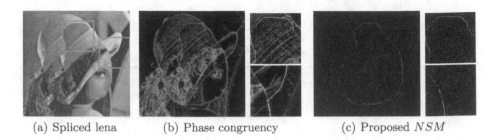

(a) Spliced lena   (b) Phase congruency   (c) Proposed NSM

Fig. 4. Edge sharpness of a spliced Lena image given by phase congrency and the proposed NSM. Two regions with different contrast are magnified.

3.2   Visual Saliency Guided Feature Extraction

In the NSM, some edges are more suspicious than others because their sharpness or edge directions are quite abnormal when compared to their surroundings. To identify these locations, we use a VAM proposed by Itti et al [16] which can highlight the most "unusual" spots within an image. We use a publicly available implementation, the Saliency Toolbox [16], and introduce two alterations to the original model.

Sharpness Based Saliency. To utilize edge sharpness as a task-relevant information to guide the visual search, a *Sharpness Conspicuous Map*(SCM) rather than the original color image is used as the input of the *SaliencyToolbox*[16]. For more details about how task-relevant information will influence the attention model, please refer to [19]. The SCM is created by modulating the NSM with the edge's gradient magnitude, as follow

$$SCM = NSM \cdot \sum_{c} \nabla I^c \tag{4}$$

where $\nabla I^c = \sqrt{(\partial I^c/\partial x)^2 + (\partial I^c/\partial y)^2}$. The matrix multiplication here is also entry-wise. In practice, it suppresses the low level feature of specific edges. It means that those edges with high sharpness and also large gradient magnitude are more likely to be a splicing boundary.

With the SCM, the SaliencyToolbox generates an *Saliency Map*(SM) and the fixations are sequentially extracted as the SM's k largest local maximums, as illustrated in Fig. 5. For a spliced image block, most of the fixations will locate on the sharp splicing boundary. While for authentic image blocks, they may fall onto some "natural" sharp edges. The feature vectors extracted from a local patch at these locations will be used to classify the spliced and authentic images.

Localized Saliency. The VAM is applied to fixed-size local image blocks rather than the whole image here. To evaluate the influences of blocksize on the visual

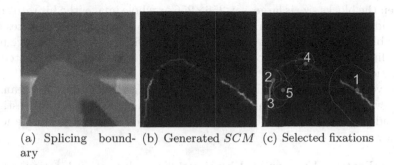

(a) Splicing bound-   (b) Generated SCM (c) Selected fixations
ary

Fig. 5. Fixations extraction process. (b) is the SCM obtained from (a). The red dots in (c) label the location of fixations and the number indicates their order sorted by saliency. The yellow contour line indicates a prohibit region surrounding a fixation which prevent new fixations falling into the same region.

search process, we conduct four tests on spliced images of different size: $64 \times 64, 128 \times 128, 256 \times 256$ and whole image. The whole spliced image is selected from the Columbia image splicing detection dataset described in Sec. 6.1. The fixed-size spliced image blocks are cropped from them. In each tests, 180 spliced images are used to extract the first 10 fixations from their SCMs. The resulted fixations of each test are grouped according to their rank, say $k \in [1, 10]$, as a group $\mathcal{G}_k$. The efficiency of the visual searching process relies on the fixation correctly located on the splicing edges. It is quantitatively measured by the *Hit Rate* of $\mathcal{G}_k$ which indicates the co-occurrence of kth fixation with a splicing edge.

$$HR_k = M_k/N_k \qquad (5)$$

where N_k is the number of fixations in $\mathcal{G}_k$, M_k is number of fixations which correctly "hit" a splicing edge in $\mathcal{G}_k$. Fig. 6 summarizes the variation of HR_k with fixation rank k and blocksize.

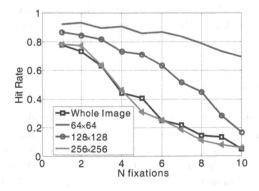

Fig. 6. Relation between the spliced image size and the hit rate of the kth fixation

When the blocks size is large, say 256×256 or whole image, the hit rate curve is lower and also declines steeper than those smaller blocksize. This indicates that a smaller blocksize will result in a higher fixation splicing-boundary co-occurrence probability, meaning that more discriminative features can be extracted from the fixations[1].

However, the blocksize cannot be too small, e.g., below 64x64, because the system will become inefficient with too many tiny blocks to be investigated. We decide to use 128x128 blocksize as a traded off between performance and efficiency.

Extract Feature Vectors at Fixations. At each fixation location, we draw a small local patch (11×11) centered at the fixation from the NSM. The histogram of this patch is extracted as a feature vector. It depicts the distribution of sharpness scores in that small local area. Since we extract k fixations for a sub-block and nine sub-blocks within a DW, there are $9 \cdot k$ feature vectors for representing a single DW.

4   Hierarchical Classifier for Feature Fusion

To classify a DW with its $9 \cdot k$ feature vectors, we design a hierarchical classifier [20] with a tree architecture as illustrated in Fig. 2. The top level classifier C_{high} has nine C_{mid} descendants each in charge of classifying a sub-block. Every C_{mid} has k C_{low} descendants each in charge of classifying a feature vector extracted at a fixation within the sub-block. The high level final decision is obtained by fusing the outputs of lower levels.

The use of this classifier structure has two benefits. Firstly the three meta classifiers are of low dimensional input which makes it easier to collect enough training samples to train the whole classifier. Secondly, by considering multiple sub-blocks together, the high level classifier C_{high} can make use of some of the structural information of neighboring sub-blocks to provide a context for making the decision.

we use LIBSVM [21] to implement support vector machines (SVMs) with a radial basis function(RBF) kernel as the meta classifiers. Each of them outputs a probability ranged in $[0, 1]$ rather than just a binary decision to its predecessor. Detailed training setups are presented in Section 6.2.

5   Localization

Different from an edge detector, the aim of this splicing detection system is not to find out the whole splicing boundary. We just label some of the most suspicious edges patches to indicate splicing. This is especially useful when further region based analysis or human inspection are needed. With the above hierarchical structure, localizing the splicing boundary is straight forward. For each

---

[1] Further analysis will be given in Section 6.3.

DW classified as spliced, we start a width-first-search from the root of tree. According to the output probability p_{mid}, p_{low} estimated for the C_{mid} and C_{low}, the sub-blocks and fixations which are classified as spliced are marked up. In the experimental results shown in Fig. 8, we give a concrete implementation by combining a more delicate sub-block search within each DW. It only labels the most suspicious DW of an image. The sub-blocks and fixations within this DW are treated with the same principle. These indications can be further utilized to extract an integral segment of splicing edge but not implemented this work.

6   Experimental Results

6.1   Image Database

We test our proposed algorithm on the Columbia image splicing detection dataset [7] including 180 authentic(auth) and 183 spliced (splc) TIFF images of different indoor/outdoor scenes. The spliced images are created using Photoshop software with no concealment. The database also provides an edgemask for each image. For a splc image, it labels the splicing boundary. For an auth image, it marks some most signification edges obtained from a segmentation algorithm.

6.2   Training

We split the database into two halves, and use one half for training (90 auth/90 splc) and the other for testing. The three meta classifier are trained with image patches drawn from the training set. According to the hierarchical structure, a low level meta classifier must be trained before its higher level predecessor. The feature extraction methods for each meta classifier is listed as follows:

The C_{low} is trained to classify 11×11 patches. By using the edgemasks, we randomly draw some 11x11 patches that locate on "natural"/splicing edges. A 10 dimensional local histogram obtained from the NSM of a patch is used as feature vector for C_{low}, as mentioned in Section 3.1.

The C_{mid} is trained to classify 128×128 sub-blocks. The 128×128 training and testing image are similarly selected using the edgemasks. For each sub-block, the first k fixations are extracted from its SCM using the SaliencyToolbox[16]. Then one 11×11 patch is drawn at each of these fixation locations and turned into a feature vector with the feature extraction procedure for patches. The trained C_{low} will turn the k feature vectors into k p_{low}s for training the C_{mid}.

The C_{high} is trained to handle 384×384 DWs. The selection strategy of image blocks is the same as C_{mid} except that the edge length contained in the inner ring of a DW, say $[33 : 352, 33 : 352]$, should includes at least 128 pixels. We divide the DW into nine 128×128 sub-blocks. After turning them into nine p_{mid} with the feature extraction procedure for sub-blocks and a trained C_{mid}, we packed the nine p_{mid}s up as a feature vector for training C_{high}.

At first, all the patches are randomly selected as the *Basic Set*. Then we adopt a bootstrapping strategy which intensionally adds some near-spliced auth samples into the basic training set and re-train the classifiers. Table 1 summarizes the detailed training setups.

Table 1. Training setups for meta classifiers. k is the number of fixations extracted in a 128×128 sub-block.

	C_{low}	C_{mid}	C_{high}
Image size	11×11	128×128	384×384
Feature dimension	10	k	9
Basic set (auth/splc)	1800/1800	1800/1800	540/540
Bootstrap set (auth)	NA	794	105

6.3 Classification Performance

Determining the Fixation Number k. There are two major parameters influence the classification performance of our system: the blocksize determined in Section 3.2 and the fixation number k extracted from each sub-block. We determine the rank of k by increasing k until the classification accuracy of C_{mid} stops growing. As shown in Fig. 7 , C_{mid}'s accuracy stop climbing after the first 5-6 fixations have been selected. Another curve is the classification accuracy when only the fixations ranked k of each block are used to train C_{mid}. Its steep declining from 6 evidents that the lower ranking fixations(7-10) are unreliable features for classification not only because they are not so salient in the sense of sharpness but also for their low co-occurrence with splicing boundaries as shown in Fig. 6. Thus they provide little extra performance gain when the first few fixations are already . An important insight given by this experiment is that the first few fixations contain the most discriminative information for detecting splicing boundaries. Consequently, we experimentally determine the number of selected fixation as $k = 5$.

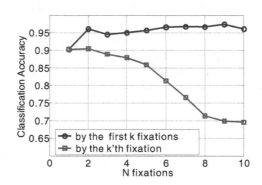

Fig. 7. Relation of fixation number and classification accuracy

Performance of Meta Classifiers. Table 2 shows the performance of the meta classifiers. The $C_{low}, C_{mid}, C_{high}$ are trained and tested with the Basic set. Their accuracy shows that the feature extracted for each meta classifier is discriminative and induce reasonably good results. Note that performance of C_{high} also represents the overall performance of hierarchical classifier C_{hie}. For detecting splicing forgery, we should not just concern about classification accuracy but also the false positive rate. Because a splicing detection system shall take the whole images as a fake even if only a small part of it is classifier as spliced when the DW scanning across it. A high false positive rate classifier will hardly had any practical use. So we re-trained C_{mid} and C_{high} by adding a bootstrap set into the training set of Basic set as mentioned above and keep the testing set unchanged. This can further bring down the detection false positive rate to about 1.11%.

For a comparison with non-saliency based feature extraction methods, we also implemented the detection method proposed by Chen et. al[5] with wavelet and phase congruency based features. Since the original method was only for classifying 128 × 128 grayscale image blocks, we extend it to color image by putting the feature vectors obtained from each color channel together. And they did not provide a scheme to integrate higher level information to handle large size image, the performance is only compared in sub-block level and without bootstrap(C_{mid} without re-training). As shown in Table 2, the accuracy and true positive rate of the proposed method is higher and the false positive rate is lower than the reference method.

Table 2. Performance of meta classifiers. The performance of C_{mid} is compared to Chen's method in [5] as indicated by bold font.

	C_{low}	C_{mid}	C_{mid} re-trained	C_{high}	C_{high} re-trained	Reference method
Accuracy(%)	95.22	**96.33**	92.83	94.07	91.30	**89.39**
True positive rate(%)	93.67	**95.22**	86.78	92.22	83.7	**90.44**
False positive rate(%)	3.22	**2.56**	1.11	4.07	1.11	**11.67**

6.4   Splicing Detection and Localization

In detecting splicing forgeries in a whole image, the detector need to be scanned across locations. This is done by shifting the detecting window by $(\Delta x, \Delta y) = (64, 64)$. The step size will affect the detection accuracy and speed.

Fig. 8 shows the detection results of the system. With a total of 180 testing images, the 90 splc image are all correctly classified and only 7 auth image misclassified as splc. As shown in subfigure (j-l), the errors are mostly caused by the straight edges of tiny gaps, iron fences and window frames in a distance and with a high contrast.

The average hit rate of the fixations marked with yellow is about 84.6%. As shown in subfigure (a-f), most of the fixations fall onto a visually conspicuous segment of a splicing edge which suggests that the localization performance of the proposed system is reasonably good and is to some extent consistent with human's visual perception.

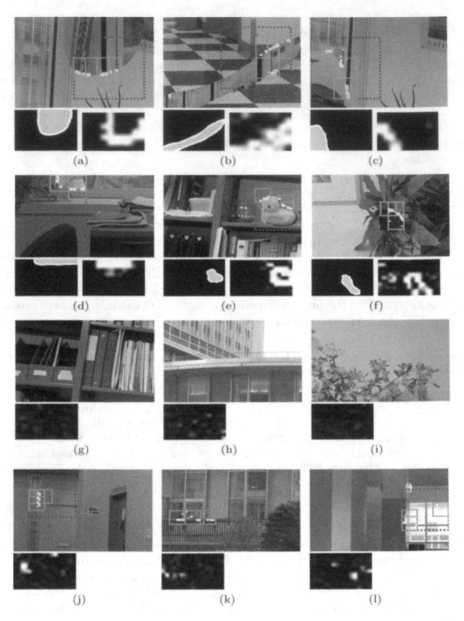

Fig. 8. Real Image Test. (a-f) and (g-i) are the results of spliced and authentic image respectively. (j-l) gives some examples of mis-classified images. For each image, a block-wisely evaluated p_{mid} map generated by the C_{mid} is given in the lower left of each subfigure. And for spliced images, the ground truth edgemask is given on the lower right conner. The red dash-line rectangle marks a DW with the largest p_{high} over the other DWs in the same image. The three green solid-line rectangles marks three sub-blocks with the three largest p_{mid}s in the DW. The tiny yellow dots mark the fixations within the sub-blocks and encode the p_{low} with its size.

6.5 Subjective Test

A natural question one may raise would be if the proposed HVS based splicing detection system is comparable to a human. We give some preliminary subjective testing results conducted on three male and three female testers to show how well can human performs on the same task. We randomly select 360(180 auth/180 splc) edge patches from the C_{mid}'s training and testing set[2]. Each of the 128 × 128-pixel image blocks is displayed on the center of a monitor without rescaling. None of the testers have ever seen them before. The testers are required to make judgments as fast as they can by clicking buttons. We also record the time they take to judge every block.

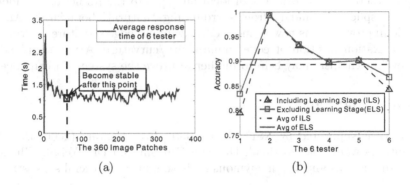

(a)   (b)

Fig. 9. Subjective testing results. (a) shows the average response time of six testers. The dash line indicates an observed learning stage in which the response time keeps on decreasing. (b) shows the individual and average accuracy of the six testers.

It is observed from Fig. 9(a) that there is a learning stage(about 60 images) before a tester gets familiar to use the system and their judgment time becomes stable (about 1 second per block) after that stage. From Fig. 9(b), we can see that the average performance of a human is about 90% which is lower than the proposed system. Only one of six testers outperforms our system with an accuracy of 99.43% (learning stage excluded). Due to a small number of testers, these observations remain to be further investigated.

7 Discussions and Conclusions

In this work, we described a fully automatic system for detecting digital image splicing forgeries based on the sharp splicing boundaries. The novelty of the proposed system includes the introduction of an OSF based edge sharpness

---

[2] The subjective test is confined to small block size to avoid the influence of image content information.

measure, a visual saliency guided feature extraction mechanism and also a hierarchical classifier into the solution of splicing detection problem. We show that a reliable hierarchical classifier can be trained with the discriminative features extracted from the first few fixations predicted with a visual attention model with edge sharpness as visual cues. The hierarchical classifier also provides a convenient way for localizing splicing boundaries. Experimental results based on a publicly available image database show that the proposed system achieves reasonably good performance and outperforms previous techniques reported in the literature.

A limitation of the proposed system is that the edge sharpness cues currently used will fail when concealing measures, such as blur, is applied. This may be improved by incorporating new blur-resistant feature as visual cues, such as CRF based method[7] or abnormality of local hue[8], into the framework to identify a blurred splicing boundary from surrounding "natural" boundaries. Another possible improvement is how to more effectively use edge structure information, such as fixation position or edge connectivity/curvature. A more sophisticate high level mechanism may help to further improve the system performance.

Acknowledgment

This work is supported by NSFC (60633030), 973 Program (2006CB303104). The authors would like to thank Dr. Yun-Qin Shi and Dr. Wei-Shi Zheng for helpful discussions and the anonymous reviewers for their useful suggestions.

References

1. Farid, H.: Detecting digital forgeries using bispectral analysis. Technical Report AIM-1657, AI Lab, MIT (1999)
2. Ng, T.T., Chang, S.F., Sun, Q.B.: Blind detection of photomontage using higher order statistics. In: ISCAS, vol. 5, pp. V688–V691 (2004)
3. Fu, D.D., Shi, Y.Q., Su, W.: Detection of image splicing based on hilbert-huang transform and moments of characteristic functions with wavelet decomposition. In: Shi, Y.Q., Jeon, B. (eds.) IWDW 2006. LNCS, vol. 4283, pp. 177–187. Springer, Heidelberg (2006)
4. Sutcu, Y., Coskun, B., Sencar, H.T., Memon, N.: Tamper detection based on regularity of wavelet transform coefficients. In: Proc. of IEEE ICIP 2007, vol. 1-7, pp. 397–400 (2007)
5. Chen, W., Shi, Y.Q., Su, W.: Image splicing detection using 2-d phase congruency and statistical moments of characteristic function. In: Proc. of SPIE Security, Steganography, and Watermarking of Multimedia Contents IX, vol. 6505 (2007), 65050R
6. Lin, Z.C., Wang, R.R., Tang, X.O., Shum, H.Y.: Detecting doctored images using camera response normality and consistency. In: Proc. of IEEE CVPR 2005, vol. 1, pp. 1087–1092 (2005)
7. Hsu, Y.F., Chang, S.F.: Image splicing detection using camera response function consistency and automatic segmentation. In: Proc. of IEEE ICME 2007, pp. 28–31 (2007)

8. Wang, B., Sun, L.L., Kong, X.W., You, X.G.: Image forensics technology using abnormity of local hue for blur detection. Acta Electronica Sinica 34, 2451–2454 (2006)
9. Johnson, M.K., Farid, H.: Exposing digital forgeries in complex lighting environments. IEEE Trans. IFS 2(3), 450–461 (2007)
10. Johnson, M.K., Farid, H.: Exposing digital forgeries through chromatic aberration. In: ACM MM and Sec 2006, vol. 2006, pp. 48–55 (2006)
11. Chen, M., Fridrich, J., Lukáš, J., Goljan, M.: Imaging sensor noise as digital X-ray for revealing forgeries. In: Furon, T., Cayre, F., Doërr, G., Bas, P. (eds.) IH 2007. LNCS, vol. 4567, pp. 342–358. Springer, Heidelberg (2008)
12. Popescu, A.C., Farid, H.: Exposing digital forgeries in color filter array interpolated images. IEEE Trans. SP 53(10 II), 3948–3959 (2005)
13. Swaminathan, A., Wu, M., Liu, K.J.R.: Optimization of input pattern for semi non-intrusive component forensics of digital cameras. In: IEEE ICASSP, vol. 2, p. 8 (2007)
14. He, J.F., Lin, Z.C., Wang, L.F., Tang, X.O.: Detecting doctored jpeg images via dct coefficient analysis. In: Leonardis, A., Bischof, H., Pinz, A. (eds.) ECCV 2006. LNCS, vol. 3953, pp. 423–435. Springer, Heidelberg (2006)
15. Serre, T., Wolf, L., Bileschi, S., Riesenhuber, M., Poggio, T.: Robust object recognition with cortex-like mechanisms. IEEE TPAMI 29(3), 411–426 (2007)
16. Itti, L., Koch, C., Niebur, E.: A model of saliency-based visual attention for rapid scene analysis. IEEE Trans. PAMI 20(11), 1254–1259 (1998)
17. Rybak, I.A., Gusakova, V.I., Golovan, A.V., Podladchikova, L.N., Shevtsova, N.A.: A model of attention-guided visual perception and recognition. Vision Research 38(15-16), 2387–2400 (1998)
18. Hou, X.D., Zhang, L.Q.: Saliency detection: A spectral residual approach. In: Proc. of IEEE CVPR 2007, pp. 1–8 (2007)
19. Navalpakkam, V., Itti, L.: Modeling the influence of task on attention. Vision Research 45(2), 205–231 (2005)
20. Heisele, B., Serre, T., Pontil, M., Poggio, T.: Component-based face detection. In: IEEE CVPR 2001, vol. 1, pp. I657–I662 (2001)
21. Chang, C.C., Lin, C.J.: LIBSVM:a library for support vector machines (2001), http://www.csie.ntu.edu.tw/~cjlin/libsvm

Feature-Based Camera Model Identification Works in Practice
Results of a Comprehensive Evaluation Study

Thomas Gloe, Karsten Borowka, and Antje Winkler

Technische Universität Dresden
Institute of Systems Architecture
01062 Dresden, Germany
{Thomas.Gloe,Antje.Winkler}@tu-dresden.de

Abstract. Feature-based camera model identification plays an important role in the toolbox for image source identification. It enables the forensic investigator to discover the probable source model employed to acquire an image under investigation. However, little is known about the performance on large sets of cameras that include multiple devices of the same model. Following the process of a forensic investigation, this paper tackles important questions for the application of feature-based camera model identification in real world scenarios. More than 9,000 images were acquired under controlled conditions using 44 digital cameras of 12 different models. This forms the basis for an in-depth analysis of a) intra-camera model similarity, b) the number of required devices and images for training the identification method, and c) the influence of camera settings. All experiments in this paper suggest: feature-based camera model identification works in practice and provides reliable results even if only one device for each camera model under investigation is available to the forensic investigator.

1 Introduction

Progress in digital imaging technologies over the past decade enable the acquisition and processing of images in high quality. Consequently, digital images are employed in various settings, ranging from simple snap-shots to professional pictures. Revealing information about the image acquisition device, digital images can form valuable pieces of evidence in forensic investigations to link persons with access to devices of the employed model or with access to the employed device itself.

To identify the source of an image, several approaches have been proposed. They can be broadly separated into four subclasses with increasing granularity: The first class of methods enables a separation between natural and computer generated images [1,2]. Methods to identify the class of the employed image acquisition devices [3], e.g. digital camera, flatbed scanner or camcorder, form the second class. The third class consists of methods to identify the employed device

S. Katzenbeisser and A.-R. Sadeghi (Eds.): IH 2009, LNCS 5806, pp. 262–276, 2009.

model [4,5,6,7,8] and, finally, the fourth class of methods enables to identify the employed source device itself [9,10,11,12,13,14].

This paper belongs to the third class and focuses on feature-based camera model identification, an approach to identify the employed camera model by analysing different model-dependent characteristics. It is based on an approach that has been originally proposed by Kharrazi, Sencar and Memon [4] for digital camera model identification, and has further been investigated by Çeliktutan, Avcibas and Sankur for low resolution cell-phone cameras [6,15]. Using small sets of digital cameras or cell-phone cameras, reliable results for both camera and cell-phone model identification were reported. However, little is known about the real world performance of feature-based camera model identification within forensic investigations, where the number of cameras and models is much larger. In particular, it remains unclear if the features actually capture model-specific characteristics (as claimed in the literature), or rather device-specific components. Recent results by Filler, Fridrich and Goljan [8] strengthened the conjecture that in fact device-specific PRNU might influence the features and thus drive the classification success in Kharrizi et al.'s seminal publication [4].

This study employs a set of 12 digital camera models with altogether 44 digital cameras to analyse the performance of feature-based camera model identification in a realistic forensic investigation scenario. Generally, the features used for camera model identification should be chosen in a way that the intra-camera model similarity is high, i.e., the feature values of devices of the same model are similar. In contrast, the inter-camera model similarity between different camera models should be small.

With respect to the limited resources and limited budget of forensic investigators, this paper contains valuable information regarding the intra-camera model similarity as well as the number of required images and devices for training the identification method by analysing a large camera set. Another important aspect for camera model identification is the influence of typical camera settings, namely, focal length and flash, as well as the influence of scene content. This aspect is investigated by using images acquired with different camera settings.

The remainder of the paper is organised as follows: Section 2 introduces and extends the scheme for camera model identification. Section 3 discusses the employed test setup as well as properties of the acquired images. Section 4 presents and discusses the results for feature-based camera model identification using a large set of camera models and, finally, the paper concludes with a discussion in Section 5.

2   Camera Model Identification

Motivated by differences in the internal image acquisition pipeline of digital camera models, Kharrazi, Sencar and Memon proposed a set of 34 features in order to identify the camera model [4]. They argued that the features were stable for all devices of one model and, therefore, would capture characteristics inherent in each image acquired with the same camera model. The analysed characteristics can be classified into three main groups: colour features describing the colour reproduction of a camera model, wavelet statistics quantifying sensor noise and image quality metrics measuring sharpness (quality of scene reproduction by the optical system) and noise. Figure 1 illustrates the basis of the three groups in the simplified model of a digital camera.

To create visually pleasing images, the manufacturers specifically fine-tune the used components and algorithms for each digital camera model. Details on this fine-tuning are usually considered as trade secrets. Colour features try to characterise the employed camera model-dependent combination of colour filter array and colour interpolation algorithm as well as the algorithms used in the internal signal-processing pipeline including, for example, its white-point correction.

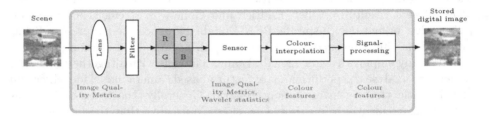

Fig. 1. Simplified image acquisition pipeline of a digital camera model and the main feature groups coarsely capturing characteristics of camera components

Considering the original feature set, Kharrazi et al. propose to use only average values of the three colour channels without analysing their relationships. However, it is important to include the dependencies between the average values of the colour channels. Therefore, 6 additional features characterising white point correction are included. Namely, the factors for white point correction and the difference between the original version and the white-point corrected version of an image measured by the normalised L_1- and L_2-norm are included in the extended set of colour features (see App. A).

Furthermore, we follow Farid and Lyu [16] and Çeliktutan et al. [15] in extending the original set of wavelet statistics by using the empirical standard deviation and skewness of the 3 wavelet sub-bands of the greyscale version of an image. Altogether, the extended feature set consists of 46 different features.

Practical investigations in this paper were done by both using the original feature set proposed by Kharrazi et al. and the extended feature set. Depending on the experiment, the overall success rates could be improved slightly by up to 3 percentage points. For brevity, only the increased performance using the extended feature set is reported here.

To determine the employed source camera model of an image under investigation, a machine-learning algorithm – for example a support vector machine (SVM) [17] – is trained with features of images of each digital camera model under investigation. Afterwards the trained machine-learning algorithm is ready to determine the corresponding camera model of an image under investigation by finding the closest match of feature values.

3 Practical Test Setup

To study the performance of feature-based camera model identification in a real world scenario, we use a subset of the 'Dresden' image database for benchmarking digital image forensics [18]. Table 1 summarises the 12 selected digital camera models[1], the number of corresponding devices and images, and basic camera specifications. The database includes both, typical consumer digital camera models and digital SLR semi-professional cameras.

Table 1. List of digital cameras in this study, including basic camera specifications. Note, in case of the Nikon D200 digital camera, two SLR-camera bodies were used with interchanging 2 different lenses for each acquired scene.

Camera Model	No. Devices	Resolution [Pixel]	Sensor Size [inch]	Focal Length [mm]	No. of Images (flash off/on)
Canon Ixus 55	1	2592×1944	1/2.5"	5.8−17.4	302 (235/67)
Canon Ixus 70	3	3072×2304	1/2.5"	5.8−17.4	581 (459/122)
Casio EX-Z150	5	3264×2448	1/2.5"	4.65−18.6	941 (761/180)
Kodak M1063	5	3664×2748	1/2.33"	5.7−17.1	1077 (746/331)
Nikon Coolpix S710	5	4352×3264	1/1.72"	6.0−21.6	931 (758/173)
Nikon D200 Lens A/B	2	3872×2592	23.6×15.8 mm	17−55/ 18−135	875 (793/82)
Nikon D70/D70s	2/2	3008×2000	23.7×15.6 mm	18−200	767 (689/78)
Olympus μ1050SW	5	3648×2736	1/2.33"	6.7−20.1	1050 (702/348)
Praktica DCZ 5.9	5	2560×1920	1/2.5"	5.4−16.2	1024 (749/275)
Rollei RCP-7325XS	3	3072×2304	1/2.5"	5.8−17.4	597 (444/153)
Samsung L74wide	3	3072×2304	1/2.5"	4.7−16.7	690 (544/146)
Samsung NV15	3	3648×2736	1/1.8"	7.3−21.9	652 (542/110)
Σ	44				9487 (7422/2065)

The employed image database includes 12 camera models with 1 up to 5 available devices for each model. This is substantial more in comparison to existing work, where feature-based camera model identification was tested using a small set of digital cameras (5 camera models) [4] or a small set of cell-phone cameras with low resolution (13 cell-phone models with altogether 16 devices) [15]. Another difference to existing work is the variation of camera settings.

The image database was created using different scenes of natural and urban environments as well as indoor and outdoor environments. To investigate the influence of image content on feature-based camera model identification, a tripod was used to acquire the same scene with each digital camera. The images were acquired using full automatic or, when available, program mode. All images were

---

[1] Due to the availability of only one single device of camera model Canon Ixus 55, it was not included in all experiments.

stored in the compressed JPEG image file format using the maximum available quality setting and the maximum available resolution. Furthermore, each scene was photographed with each digital camera using 3 different settings of focal length. The flash mode was set to automatic mode and in case of flash release, an additional image was taken with flash turned off. A more detailed description of the 'Dresden' image database has been submitted to another venue [18].

To evaluate the quality of the image database, the number of saturated image pixels was calculated in a greyscale version of each image. Image pixels are counted as saturated if either their value is ≤ 5 or ≥ 250. In brief, 97% of all images contain less than 25% saturated image regions and 89% of all images contain less than 10% saturated image pixels.

All investigations in this paper make use of the support vector machine developed by Chang and Lin with a radial based kernel function [17].

4   Experiments

4.1   Intra- and Inter-Camera Model Similarity

The ability to separate between different camera models and not between different devices is important for all camera model identification schemes. Therefore, the features used for camera model identification should be chosen in a way that the intra-camera model similarity is high, i.e., the feature values of cameras of the same model are similar. In contrast, the inter-camera model similarity between different camera models should be minimised.

To investigate intra-camera model similarity, the feature-based camera model identification scheme is applied in order to identify the employed device (and not the employed camera model – contrary to its original purpose). The intra-camera model similarity is investigated for each camera model independently by training a support vector machine for each device of one model.

Additionally, the similarity between devices of the same series is exemplarily investigated on the basis of the Canon Ixus 55 and the Canon Ixus 70 cameras, which are equipped with similar optics and equally sized sensors but provide different sensor resolutions. Generally it is expected that devices of the same series are difficult to separate.

The support vector machine is trained with 60% of the images of each device for training and the remaining images are used for testing. The test is repeated 250 times for each camera model, and within each run, the images are randomly assigned to either the training or test set.

Table 2 summarises the results for image source identification in case of devices of the series Canon Ixus. This test illustrates two important aspects: First, images acquired with devices of the same series are correctly assigned to the corresponding camera model with an negligible false identification rate, and, second, images acquired with devices of the same model are assigned diffusely within the corresponding set.

Table 2. Intra-camera similarity in case of the camera model series Canon Ixus (overall correct device identification 79.67%)

	Identified as			
Device	Ixus 55	Ixus 70 A	Ixus 70 B	Ixus 70 C
Ixus 55	**99.99**	-	0.01	-
Ixus 70 A	-	**74.50**	11.92	13.57
Ixus 70 B	0.06	16.49	**68.03**	15.43
Ixus 70 C	0.08	18.77	16.42	**64.72**

Reconsidering the aspect of diffuse assignment of images within the corresponding set of devices of the same model, the results summarised in Tab. 3 support this observation for camera model Casio EX-Z150 and illustrate another interesting effect: Device B of the Casio EX-Z150 model represents a centroid in the feature space of all devices of this model. Consequently, the probability of assigning images to device B is higher than for all other devices of the Casio EX-Z150. In contrast to the results for Canon Ixus 70, the images are assigned more diffusely, which indicates a better intra-camera model similarity.

Table 3. Intra-camera similarity in case of camera model Casio EX-Z150 (overall correct device identification 18.64%)

	Identified as				
Device	Casio A	Casio B	Casio C	Casio D	Casio E
Casio A	13.96	**39.54**	22.69	13.98	9.83
Casio B	17.55	**34.46**	24.06	12.94	10.99
Casio C	14.77	**37.64**	22.23	14.10	11.26
Casio D	15.23	**36.23**	23.03	12.57	12.94
Casio E	13.44	**37.22**	22.41	17.15	9.78

Within the employed image database, the results for the Nikon D200 represent an anomaly. In contrast to the results for all other camera models, Tab. 4 illustrates that correct device identification is possible with a correct identification rate of 98.41% using the feature-based camera model identification scheme. This result is unexpected, especially due to the fact that both devices acquired images of each scene by interchanging the employed lenses. Possibly, the intra-camera model deviation within this class of semi-professional SLR cameras is larger than in case of typical consumer cameras, which leads to the clear separability. Future research has to include more devices of the same semi-professional SLR camera model to further investigate this aspect.

To visualise intra-camera model similarity as well as inter-camera dissimilarity of all employed devices, the 10 most influential features for separating all devices are selected using principal component analysis and the calculated centroids are mapped to a 2D-plot depicted in Fig. 2. The calculated plot supports the

Table 4. Intra-camera similarity in case of camera model Nikon D200 SLR (overall correct device identification 98.41%)

	Identified as	
Device	Nikon D200 A	Nikon D200 B
Nikon D200 A	**98.73**	1.27
Nikon D200 B	1.97	**98.03**

discussed aspects of intra-camera model similarity and clearly visualises inter-camera model dissimilarity as a basis for differentiating between camera models. For example, the calculated centroids of the 5 Casio EX-Z150 cameras are very close to each other. This is similar for all other camera models except the Nikon D200 SLR. Moreover, the deviation between centroids of the Samsung NV15 devices is larger than for other camera models.

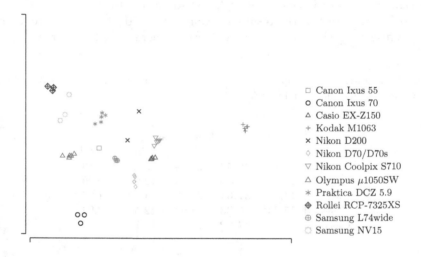

Fig. 2. Calculated 10 most influential features to characterise each device plotted to 2D using multidimensional scaling. Each symbol of one camera model corresponds to the centroid of one device. The centroids of devices of the same model are close to each other whereas the centroids of other models are farther apart.

Figure 2 visualises only the centroid of each device of one model in a 2D mapping of the feature subspace. To illustrate the separability between images of different camera models, Fig. 3 depicts a 2D plot of the calculated features of all images in the database for the camera model Canon Ixus 70 and the camera model Nikon Coolpix S710 using multidimensional scaling. As expected, it is possible to clearly separate between both camera models but not between different devices of one model. Thus, the features are appropriate for camera model identification.

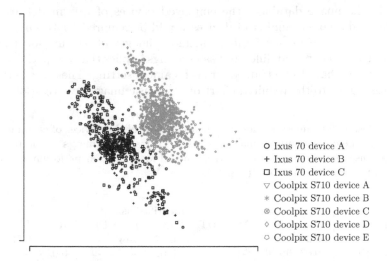

Fig. 3. 2D plot of the two most distinctive principal components of the calculated features of all images acquired with the model Canon Ixus 70 (black) and of all images acquired with the model Nikon Coolpix S710 (green). Inter-camera model variation is larger than intra-camera model variation, hence, a clear separation between images acquired with the Ixus 70 and the S710 is possible. Different symbols of the same colour indicate the device of each model, hence, a separation between devices of the same model is not possible.

4.2 Naive Test of Feature-Based Camera Model Identification

A first naive test of feature-based camera model identification on the image database investigates the reliability of the method. Therefore, we select for each model 60% of the devices and used all corresponding images for training. The images of the remaining devices are used for testing the identification algorithm. In case of the Nikon D200 SLR camera model, one device is assigned for training and the other device is assigned for testing the performance of the identification method.

This approach simulates a typical forensic investigation scenario, where several camera models in question are purchased and used for training the identification scheme and the images under investigation correspond to the test set. To measure the influence of the number of selected devices for the training and the test set, the naive test scenario is repeated 15 times while the assignment of each device either to the training or to the test set is iterated over all possible combinations.

Table 5 summarises the results for correct camera model identification. In all cases, the majority of test images is correctly assigned to the correct camera model. The achieved results are convincing and promise a correct camera model identification for more than 98% of all images of all camera models with exception of the Nikon D200. The results for the Nikon D200 are similar to the investigations of the intra-camera model similarity. Compared to other camera models in the image database, the employed devices of this model are more dissimilar and a larger number of devices would be required for training.

The fact that the image database includes images of varying focal length, different environments and different flash settings implies that no special support vector machines have to be trained for each camera setting. These are very good news with regard to the required effort of a forensic image investigation.

Table 5. Results for camera model identification: 60% of the devices of each model are selected and the corresponding images are used for training. Images of the remaining devices are used for testing (overall correct model identification performance 97.79%, worst result 96.5% and best result 98.7%).

Camera model	I	E	M	DT	DS	μ	DC	R	L	N
					Identified as					
Ixus 70 (I)	**99.28**	-	-	-	0.07	0.14	-	-	0.52	-
EX-Z150 (E)	0.02	**99.95**	-	-	0.02	-	-	0.02	-	-
M1063 (M)	-	-	**99.97**	-	-	-	-	-	-	0.03
D200 (DT)	1.89	1.65	1.00	**88.31**	-	5.51	-	0.55	0.03	1.06
D70/D70s (DS)	0.58	0.31	0.14	0.10	**97.94**	0.02	0.12	-	0.71	0.07
μ1050SW (μ)	0.46	0.32	-	0.24	-	**98.48**	0.03	0.02	0.03	0.43
DCZ 5.9 (DC)	-	-	-	-	0.62	-	**99.36**	0.02	-	-
RCP-7325XS (R)	-	-	-	-	-	-	-	**100.00**	-	-
L74Wide (L)	0.14	-	-	-	0.03	-	-	-	**99.83**	-
NV15 (N)	0.03	-	0.61	0.03	0.03	0.37	-	-	-	**98.93**

However, the applied naive test includes two weak points: First, images in the image database for each device were acquired using the same scene, which is very unlikely for a forensic investigation, and, second, the size of the images is different for each model, which might 'leak' information about the employed camera model.

4.3   Critical Test of Feature-Based Camera Model Identification

To form a more critical test of feature-based camera model identification, the influence of the number of devices and images available for training is investigated. In contrast to the naive test, images with similar scene content are either included in the training or in the test set of images. Furthermore the overall number of images used for training and testing is fixed to 175 per device, which equals to the minimum number of available images for each device.

Similar to the naive test, the influence of the selected devices is measured by repeating the tests 15 times. The assignment of a device to the training and test set is iterated over all possible variations. The tests are repeated with 10% (17 images), 20% (35 images), 30% (52 images), 40 % (70 images), 50% (87 images), 60% (105 images), 70% (122 images), 80% (140 images) and 90% (157 images) of the fixed set of 175 images per device for training and the remaining images with dissimilar scene content for testing.

Depending on the available number of devices for each camera model, the number of employed devices is varied between 1 up to 4 devices for training. Camera models with less than 5 devices are used with the maximum available number of cameras for training, whereas always one device is include in the test set only. This scenario seems to be similar to a real forensic investigation, where it might be impossible to purchase the same number of devices for each model.

Table 6 and 7 exemplarily summarise the results for varying the number of images employed for training the machine-learning algorithm. The correct camera model identification performance clearly increases with the number of employed images for training from 74.7% in case of 10% of all images up to 95.65% in case of 90% of all images. The reliable performance in case of using 90% of all images of one device for training is only slightly increased by using more than one device for training the machine-learning algorithm: 96.64% for ≤ 2 devices for training, 97.30% for ≤ 3 devices for training and 96.79% for ≤ 4 devices for training.

Observe that the number of camera models employed for training the support vector machine is negligible compared to the number of required images to train the classification algorithm reliable. Furthermore, the results are similar to the naive test indicating that the feature set is quite invariant to scene content. So during a forensic investigation of digital images, it is not necessary to acquire images with the same scene content like the images under investigation and it also seems unnecessary to purchase more than one device for each model.

To tackle the second weak point of the naive test – the possible influence of image size on the feature-based camera model identification scheme – all images are cropped to the same size in the frequency domain without applying re-compression. Thus, no new JPEG-compression artefacts distort the test results. The smallest image size in the image database (2560×1920, Praktica DCZ 5.9) is used to crop the images to constant size.

The previous test of this subsection is repeated with the cropped images. Table 8 exemplarily summarises the results for camera model identification using 90% of all cropped images of one device for each camera model for training and the remaining cropped images for testing. Compared to the corresponding test in this subsection that used images in their original size, the overall correct camera model identification performance considerably decreases from 95.65% to 89.66% for the cropped images. Apparently, there is an influence of image size on feature-based camera model identification. A closer look at the results indicates that the performance decrease is different for the camera models and most evident for the camera models Nikon D200, Nikon D70/D70s and Samsung NV15. In practice, this effect might be negligible for images available in their original size. However, in all cases where it is difficult to validate the originality of the image size, it is important to know this effect for correct result interpretation.

Figure 4 summarises the overall results for correct camera model identification varying the number of images and the number of devices used for testing. This visualisation clearly depicts the performance increase depending on the number of employed images for training and the performance decrease between original sized and cropped images. Additionally, the number of devices used for training

Table 6. Results for camera model identification using 10% of the images of 1 device of each model for training and 90% of the images of the remaining devices for testing (overall correct model identification performance 74.70%, worst result 72.42% and best result 79.75%)

Camera model	I	E	M	DT	DS	S	μ	DC	R	L	N
					Identified as						
Ixus 70 (I)	**66.60**	1.53	-	1.34	3.95	-	7.18	0.70	0.25	15.16	3.29
EX-Z150 (E)	1.83	**84.51**	0.32	6.05	3.21	-	0.32	1.91	-	1.86	-
M1063 (M)	-	6.01	**90.63**	1.48	0.25	1.62	-	-	-	-	-
D200 (DT)	6.43	8.62	8.45	**60.40**	0.08	2.46	3.65	2.78	1.21	2.31	3.95
D70/D70s (DS)	6.79	7.52	0.17	1.23	**56.23**	-	0.20	16.52	0.13	11.21	-
S710 (S)	-	0.65	0.12	-	0.01	**96.57**	0.88	-	-	-	1.77
μ1050SW (μ)	9.69	3.29	-	0.96	0.34	-	**54.34**	0.29	0.89	3.73	26.48
DCZ 5.9 (DC)	0.38	1.33	-	0.20	7.42	-	0.73	**86.59**	0.50	2.52	0.33
RCP-7325XS (R)	2.10	0.06	-	0.06	0.79	-	6.14	3.97	**85.43**	0.34	1.10
L74wide (L)	16.56	20.51	-	0.45	3.97	-	2.99	3.57	0.42	**51.52**	-
NV15 (N)	4.54	1.15	-	5.03	0.13	1.30	22.99	4.01	1.49	0.04	**59.32**

Table 7. Results for camera model identification using 90% of the images of 1 device of each model for training and 10% of the images of the remaining devices for testing (overall correct model identification performance 95.65%, worst result 93.40% and best result 97.33%)

Camera model	I	E	M	DT	DS	S	μ	DC	R	L	N
					Identified as						
Ixus 70 (I)	**100.00**	-	-	-	-	-	-	-	-	-	-
EX-Z150 (E)	-	**99.50**	-	0.49	-	-	-	-	-	-	-
M1063 (M)	-	0.39	**97.74**	1.86	-	-	-	-	-	-	-
D200 (DT)	0.39	0.20	0.78	**96.86**	-	-	0.78	-	-	-	0.98
D70/D70s (DS)	2.88	2.09	1.57	0.52	**79.47**	-	-	0.52	-	12.68	0.26
S710 (S)	-	-	-	-	-	**100.00**	-	-	-	-	-
μ1050SW (μ)	1.57	-	-	0.59	-	-	**89.11**	-	-	-	8.73
DCZ 5.9 (DC)	-	-	-	-	1.96	-	-	**98.3**	-	-	-
RCP-7325XS (R)	-	-	-	-	-	-	-	-	**100.00**	-	-
L74wide (L)	0.20	0.98	-	-	0.20	-	-	-	-	**98.62**	-
NV15 (N)	0.59	-	-	0.98	-	-	3.73	-	-	-	**94.70**

the machine-learning algorithm increases the correct identification performance only slightly.

In case of the cropped images an anomaly occurs in the overall performance results. The overall results for camera model identification decrease with the number of employed devices, which is absolutely unexpected. This effect can be traced back to the influence of the Nikon D200 digital SLR camera only. Increasing the number of devices employed for training the machine-learning algorithm obviously complicates the correct separation of the camera model Nikon D200 from other devices. The reason is probably the observed intra-camera model dissimilarity, which emphasises the need for a larger number of devices of this model in the image database.

Table 8. Results for camera model identification using 90% of the cropped images of 1 device of each model for training and 10% of the cropped images of the remaining devices for testing (overall correct model identification performance 89.66%, worst result 85.74% and best result 93.23%)

Camera model	I	E	M	DT	DS	S	μ	DC	R	L	N
					Identified as						
Ixus 70 (I)	**97.64**	-	-	-	-	-	1.37	0.20	-	-	0.78
EX-Z150 (E)	0.49	**93.72**	-	0.29	0.20	1.76	-	0.20	-	3.33	-
M1063 (M)	-	0.49	**98.13**	0.29	1.08	-	-	-	-	-	-
D200 (DT)	8.04	0.78	-	28.43	**40.00**	1.37	-	8.63	-	12.16	0.59
D70/D70s (DS)	1.70	1.70	2.22	10.85	**75.81**	1.70	-	-	-	3.66	2.35
S710 (S)	-	0.20	-	-	-	**99.60**	0.20	-	-	-	-
μ1050SW (μ)	0.10	-	-	-	1.57	-	**94.11**	1.08	-	0.20	2.94
DCZ 5.9 (DC)	-	-	-	0.29	0.10	0.10	0.10	**98.23**	-	-	1.18
RCP-7325XS (R)	-	-	-	0.20	-	-	-	1.57	**98.23**	-	-
L74wide (L)	1.37	0.59	-	0.20	2.55	-	0.20	0.78	-	**94.31**	-
NV15 (N)	8.43	-	-	0.20	-	0.20	2.55	8.24	0.20	0.78	**79.41**

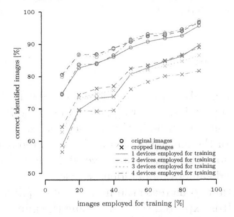

Fig. 4. Overall results for correct camera model identification in relation to maximum number of employed devices and in relation to the employed number of images for training. The remaining images are used for testing the method. Note, the number of images is fixed to 175 images, which equals the smallest number of images available for each camera model.

Figure 5 depicts overall performance results exemplarily for the Casio EX-Z150 camera model and for the Samsung NV15 camera model. Depending on the camera model, the influence of the number of images employed for training and the influence of cropping varies. In case of the Casio EX-Z150, the number of required images to obtain identification results $\geq$ 90% is considerably lower than in case of the Samsung NV15 camera model. This conforms with the calculated intra-camera model similarity of both camera models, which is higher for the Casio EX-Z150 and obviously results in a lower number of required images for training.

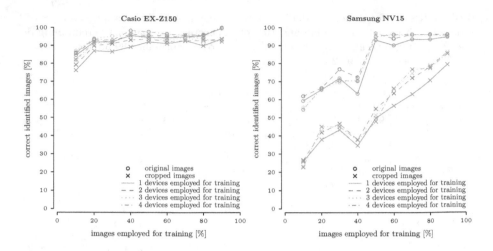

Fig. 5. Selected results for correct camera model identification of Casio EX-Z150 and Samsung NV 15 in relation to maximum number of employed devices / number of employed images for training and number of employed images for testing the identification scheme

5   Concluding Remarks

The reported results in this paper document that feature-based camera model identification works in practice. Generally, it enables reliable identification results and therefore is a valuable method in the toolbox for image source identification. The very good news for the limited budget and the limited resources of all forensic investigators is: it is not necessary to buy several devices of one model in order to train the feature-based camera model identification scheme accurately. In fact it is much more important to increase the number of acquired images for training each camera model. It is expected that increasing the number of acquired images in the critical test to a similar level of the naive test increases the results for correct camera model identification. Furthermore, it seems unnecessary to acquire images of scenes with similar content for training the machine-learning algorithm. In fact the dependence between scene content and calculated features appears negligible. Note that the fraction of saturated image pixels was constantly low for all images used for training the machine learning algorithm. It is also important to mention that it is not necessary to train the feature-based camera model identification scheme for each camera setting separately. In fact reliable results are obtained in case of mixed image sets covering different camera settings.

   The semi-professional digital SLR camera Nikon D200 turned out to behave anomalous in the employed image database. The intra-camera model similarity of this camera model is very high, thus enabling reliable source camera identification using the feature-based camera model identification scheme. More devices are needed in the training set to tell whether this anomaly is due to a malfunction of one of our test cameras or a more systematic phenomenon. This aspect will be further investigated in future work using more devices of this camera model and other SLR cameras.

Acknowledgements

The authors would like to thank Rainer Böhme for fruitful discussions and all sponsors for borrowing their camera equipment. Namely, the staff members of the faculty of computer science, the staff members of the AVMZ (TU Dresden), and the following companies for their generous support (in alphabetical order): AgfaPhoto & Plawa, Casio, FujiFilm, Kodak, Nikon, Olympus, Pentax, Praktica, Ricoh, Rollei, Samsung and Sony. Special thanks go to our colleagues and friends supporting the creation of the underlying image database during some of the probably coldest days of the year.

References

1. Lyu, S., Farid, H.: How realistic is photorealistic? IEEE Transactions on Signal Processing 53(2), 845–850 (2005)
2. Dehnie, S., Sencar, H.T., Memon, N.: Digital image forensics for identifying computer generated and digital camera images. In: Proceedings of the 2006 IEEE International Conference on Image Processing (ICIP 2006), pp. 2313–2316 (2006)
3. Khanna, N., Mikkikineni, A.K., Chiu, G.T.C., Allebach, J.P., Delp, E.J.: Forensic classification of imaging sensor types. In: Delp, E.J., Wong, P.W. (eds.) Proceedings of SPIE: Security and Watermarking of Multimedia Content IX, vol. 6505 (2007), 65050U
4. Kharrazi, M., Sencar, H.T., Memon, N.: Blind source camera identification. In: Proceedings of the 2004 IEEE International Conference on Image Processing (ICIP 2004), pp. 709–712 (2004)
5. Bayram, S., Sencar, H.T., Memon, N.: Improvements on source camera-model identification based on CFA. In: Proceedings of the WG 11.9 International Conference on Digital Forensics (2006)
6. Çeliktutan, O., Avcibas, İ., Sankur, B.: Blind identification of cellular phone cameras. In: Delp, E.J., Wong, P.W. (eds.) Proceedings of SPIE: Security and Watermarking of Multimedia Content IX, vol. 6505 (2007), 65051H
7. Swaminathan, A., Wu, M., Liu, K.J.R.: Nonintrusive component forensics of visual sensors using output images. IEEE Transactions on Information Forensics and Security 2(1), 91–106 (2007)
8. Filler, T., Fridrich, J., Goljan, M.: Using sensor pattern noise for camera model identification. In: Proceedings of the 2008 IEEE International Conference on Image Processing (ICIP 2008), pp. 1296–1299 (2008)
9. Lukáš, J., Fridrich, J., Goljan, M.: Determining digital image origin using sensor imperfections. In: Said, A., Apostolopoulus, J.G. (eds.) Proceedings of SPIE: Image and Video Communications and Processing, vol. 5685, pp. 249–260 (2005)
10. Chen, M., Fridrich, J., Goljan, M.: Digital imaging sensor identification (further study). In: Delp, E.J., Wong, P.W. (eds.) Proceedings of SPIE: Security and Watermarking of Multimedia Content IX, vol. 6505 (2007), 65050P

11. Gloe, T., Franz, E., Winkler, A.: Forensics for flatbed scanners. In: Delp, E.J., Wong, P.W. (eds.) Proceedings of SPIE: Security, Steganography, and Watermarking of Multimedia Contents IX, vol. 6505 (2007), 65051I
12. Gou, H., Swaminathan, A., Wu, M.: Robust scanner identification based on noise features. In: Delp, E.J., Wong, P.W. (eds.) Proceedings of SPIE: Security and Watermarking of Multimedia Content IX, vol. 6505 (2007), 65050S
13. Khanna, N., Mikkikineni, A.K., Chiu, G.T.C., Allebach, J.P., Delp, E.J.: Scanner identification using sensor pattern noise. In: Delp, E.J., Wong, P.W. (eds.) Proceedings of SPIE: Security and Watermarking of Multimedia Content IX, vol. 6505 (2007), 65051K
14. Goljan, M., Fridrich, J., Filler, T.: Large scale test of sensor fingerprint camera identification. In: Delp, E.J., Dittmann, J., Memon, N., Wong, P.W. (eds.) Proceedings of SPIE: Media Forensics and Security XI, vol. 7254, 7254-18 (2009)
15. Çeliktutan, O., Sankur, B., Avcibas, İ.: Blind identification of source cell-phone model. IEEE Transactions on Information Forensics and Security 3(3), 553–566 (2008)
16. Farid, H., Lyu, S.: Higher-order wavelet statistics and their application to digital forensics. In: IEEE Workshop on Statistical Analysis in Computer Vision (in conjunction with CVPR) (2003)
17. Chang, C.C., Lin, C.J.: LIBSVM: A library for support vector machines (2001), http://www.csie.ntu.edu.tw/~cjlin/libsvm
18. Gloe, T., Böhme, R.: The 'Dresden' image database for benchmarking digital image forensics. Submitted to the 25th Symposium on Applied Computing, ACM SAC 2010 (2010)
19. Adams, J., Parulski, K., Spaulding, K.: Color processing in digital cameras. IEEE Micro. 18(6), 20–30 (1998)

A   Additional Colour Features

To get natural-looking images, white-point correction is a very important step in the signal-processing pipeline of a digital camera. The simplest model for white-point correction is based on the grey world assumption [19], where the average of each colour channel is assumed to be equal, or generally speaking a grey value. To apply white-point correction using the grey world assumption, the following equations are applied to the red and blue colour channel:

$$\hat{\mathbf{i}}_r = \frac{\mathrm{avg}(\mathbf{i}_g)}{\mathrm{avg}(\mathbf{i}_r)} \cdot \mathbf{i}_r \qquad \hat{\mathbf{i}}_b = \frac{\mathrm{avg}(\mathbf{i}_g)}{\mathrm{avg}(\mathbf{i}_b)} \cdot \mathbf{i}_b, \qquad (1)$$

where $\mathrm{avg}(\mathbf{i}_{\mathcal{C}})$ denotes the average of all intensity values in colour channel $\mathcal{C}$ and $\hat{\mathbf{i}}_{\mathcal{C}}$ indicates the white-point corrected version of colour channel $\mathcal{C}$.

The proposed additional colour features are calculated as follows:

$$F_1 = \frac{1}{3}(|\mathrm{avg}(\mathbf{i}_r) - \mathrm{avg}(\mathbf{i}_g)| + |\mathrm{avg}(\mathbf{i}_r) - \mathrm{avg}(\mathbf{i}_b)| + |\mathrm{avg}(\mathbf{i}_g) - \mathrm{avg}(\mathbf{i}_b)|) \qquad (2)$$

$$F_2 = \frac{\mathrm{avg}(\mathbf{i}_g)}{\mathrm{avg}(\mathbf{i}_r)} \quad F_3 = \frac{\mathrm{avg}(\mathbf{i}_g)}{\mathrm{avg}(\mathbf{i}_b)} \qquad (3)$$

$$F_4 = \frac{1}{3} \sum_{\mathcal{C} \in \{r,g,b\}} ||\mathbf{i}_{\mathcal{C}} - \hat{\mathbf{i}}_{\mathcal{C}}||_{\bar{1}} \qquad (4)$$

$$F_5 = ||\mathbf{i}_r - \hat{\mathbf{i}}_r||_{\bar{2}} \quad F_6 = ||\mathbf{i}_b - \hat{\mathbf{i}}_b||_{\bar{2}} \qquad (5)$$

Author Index